Canada Revisited 6
Concept Map

● Chapters 1, 2, 3, 4, 5

● Chapters 6, 7, 8, 9, 10

● Chapters 11, 12

Social Studies Concepts

Environmental Interaction

Balance

Technology

Cultural Contact

Exploration

Section

I   II   III

Section Structure

Section Story
Chapter Visual Overview
Chapter Focus
Chapter Preview/Prediction
Chapter Content
Chapter Review

Assessment
Summarizing the Chapter
Understanding Concepts
Developing Research Skills
Developing Communication Skills
Applying Concepts
Challenge Plus

Canada Revisited 6

Aboriginal Peoples and European Explorers

Phyllis A. Arnold

with

Betty Gibbs

ARNOLD
PUBLISHING LTD.

For more information contact
Nelson
1120 Birchmount Road
Scarborough, Ontario
M1K 5G4

Or you can visit our Internet site at
http://www.nelson.com

Authors

Phyllis A. Arnold with Betty Gibbs

Canadian Cataloguing in Publication Data

Arnold, Phyllis A.
    Canada revisited 6

Includes index.
ISBN 0-919913-65-2

1. Canada—History—to 1663 (New France)—Juvenile literature. 2. Indians of North America—Canada—History—Juvenile literature.
I. Gibbs, Betty. II. Title. III: Title: Canada revisited six.
FC172.M285 1999a   971.01'1   C99-910814-X
F1008.2.A76 1999

Arnold Publishing Project Team

Editor-in-Chief: Karen Iversen
Project Manager: Betty Gibbs
Project Co-ordinators: Judi McIntyre, Christina Barabash
Educational Editors: Phyllis A. Arnold, Lynn Soetaert
Editors: Betty Gibbs, Christina Barabash
Design: Linda Tremblay, Marcey Andrews
Production: Marcey Andrews, Judy Bauer, Colette Howie,
        Zenna Shuttleworth, Anna Singkhone, Leslie
        Stewart, Tracy Suter, Linda Tremblay
Cover Design: Marcey Andrews

Assisted by

Illustration: Don Hight, Claudette MacLean, Nokomis
Maps: Johnson Cartographics Inc., Wendy Johnson
Photography: Roth and Ramberg Photography

Manufacturers

Trans Global, Transcontinental

Printed and bound in Canada
3 4 5 6 7   05   04 03

Cast of Characters

Kishana Armstrong
Zachary Auger
Brad Cardinal
Christine Daniels
Michael Hopkins
Norman Quinney
Joan Simpson
Samantha Simpson
Joseph Thia Son
Leisha Tremblay
Alex van Elst

Support Materials

Canada Revisited 6 Integrated Unit
ISBN 0-919913-56-3

Canadian Historical Images ClipArt CD-ROM,
Macintosh, ISBN 0-919913-41-5
Windows, ISBN 0-919913-71-7

Cover Photographs

Front: tl © NATIONAL MARITIME MUSEUM, London; tr Photo: Tourism Newfoundland and Labrador; br c Ted Curtin for Plimoth Plantation, Box 1620, Plymouth, MA 02362; bl Gary Andrashko for Plimoth Plantation, Box 1620, Plymouth, MA 02362

Back: tc Photo: Parks Canada/Shane Kelly/1996; tr c Ted Curtin for Plimoth Plantation, Box 1620, Plymouth, MA 02362; br © Fred Cattroll; bl Courtesy Betty Peters,© Betty Peters; ml Courtesy NASA

Acknowledgements

Thank you to Bernie Rubinstein for encouraging me to write this textbook, to Jack MacFadden and Jeff McNairn for their continued support and ideas, and to Vern Douglas for his patience in teaching me about the ways of Canada's Aboriginal peoples.

I especially appreciated working with Betty Gibbs and Linda Tremblay, who shared my vision and transformed it into meaningful educational material.

It was a pleasure to be surrounded by such a creative team: Karen Iversen, Judi McIntyre, Marcey Andrews, Judy Bauer, Leslie Stewart, Christina Barabash, Zenna Shuttleworth, and Colette Howie. Thank you all for your dedication and support.

And to Arnie, who helped keep my life on track over the many months of writing, and now will inservice and market the book, my very special thanks.

Phyllis A. Arnold

Working on this textbook at a much earlier stage than usual and having creative input into it has been a rich learning experience for me. Thank you, Phyllis, for this opportunity.

Thanks also to the many people who coped with my telephone questions and were generous with their knowledge, especially Isobel Ball, John Smith, Jeff McNairn, and Nokomis. Wendy Johnson and Claudette MacLean provided skills, professionalism, and willingness to be called to make changes at any hour.

However, my greatest appreciation goes to my co-workers on the **Canada Revisited 6** team: Linda, Judy, Christina, Judi, Zenna, Marcey, Leslie, and Karen.

Betty Gibbs

Validators

FIRST NATIONS CONTENT VALIDATORS
Isobel L. Ball
Assistant Director
Wilfrid Laurier University
Archaeology Department
Waterloo, Ontario
Grade 5 Teacher
Simcoe County District School Board
James Keating Elementary School
Penetanguishene, Ontario

Brenda G. Davis
Teacher/Program
Consultant/Principal (retired)
Six Nations Education District
Department of Indian and Northern Affairs
Ohsweken, Ontario

L. James Dempsey
Member of Blood Tribe
Professor
University of Alberta
School of Native Studies
Edmonton, Alberta

Laura Horton
Director—Post Secondary Education
Rainy Lake Ojibway Education Authority
Fort Frances, Ontario

Sheila Staats
Researcher
Working World New Media
Six Nations of the Grand River Territory
Brantford, Ontario

HISTORICAL VALIDATORS
Jeffrey L. McNairn
Postdoctoral Fellow
Department of History
York University
Toronto, Ontario

Dr. Barry Gough
Professor of History
History Department
Wilfrid Laurier University
Waterloo, Ontario

EDUCATIONAL VALIDATORS
Jack MacFadden
Teacher/Researcher
W. H. Day Elementary School
Bradford, Ontario

Carleen Van Dam
Teacher
St. Agnes Elementary School
Waterloo, Ontario

Patricia Waters
Curriculum Consultant (retired)
Program Services, Waterloo Catholic District School Board
Waterloo, Ontario

Bias Reviewer
John Smith
Principal
Green Glade Senior Public
Mississauga, Ontario

Special Thanks
Keith Lickers
Curriculum and Assessment Policy Branch
Ontario Ministry of Education
Toronto, Ontario

National Archives of Canada
Ottawa, Ontario

Rogers Communications, Inc.
(Confederation Life Gallery of Canadian History)
Toronto, Ontario

For artifacts and props:
Judy Bauer, Dr. Sheri Dalton, Darren Hanson, Paula Horstemeier, Edmonton Public Schools—Maintenance North Electrical.

We acknowledge the financial support of the Government of Canada through the Book Publishing Industry Development Program for our publishing activities.

Canada

Table of Contents

To the Student

Revisiting Canada's Past

These students and Mrs. Maziuk are featured in Section stories and on various activity pages. You are invited to join them as they learn about Canada's past.

Focus of the Text

By looking at history we can often examine the roots of events and issues of today. People and events that affected the history of Canada appear throughout this text. People in history faced situa-tions that relate to present-day concerns. Ideas and methods used in our past can help us prevent some problems from happening today.

Canada Revisited 6 presents the history of Aboriginal peoples and European explorers. Information is given in the order in which events happened, whenever possible.

Understanding history can help you think about and resolve the issues of today.

Learning How to Learn

Canada Revisited 6 focuses on the way you learn. Activities for "revisiting" Canadian history are provided in the textbook. The activities will help you understand historical changes. Making predictions, then reading further to check your prediction and add to your knowledge, will help you learn.

As you increase your knowledge of Canada's past, you will be building thinking and learning skills. You will "revisit" Canada's history through photo essays, works of art, stories, and excerpts from historical documents. Role-plays and exercises in problem solving, critical thinking, and decision-making will draw you into historical situations. This will help you understand them.

A variety of activities are provided to suit your interests and learning style. Challenge yourself by selecting a range of different activities. Challenge Plus, problem solving, research projects, and Review activities help you apply your skills and knowledge of Canadian history to other topics.

Understanding the way you learn can help you become more confident, involved, and respon-sible for your own learning.

The pages that follow provide more detail about the features of this text and how you can best use them to understand and experience Canada's past.

Have fun and enjoy revisiting Canada's past!

About the Text

Canada Revisited 6 encourages you to relive history. This will make it more meaningful and enjoyable and you will learn more.

Visual Cues

The design of this textbook will help you locate, understand, organize, and remember information.

Graphics present information visually. Read the maps, illustrations, charts, and graphs for information. See pages 22 and 121 for examples.

Titles in each chapter are coded by size and colour so you can tell when a new idea begins. As the title size decreases, the idea is explained in more detail. There are four main heading sizes:

Level I headings are used to show the main ideas of the chapter. See the heading "Environmental Interaction" on page 34 for an example. Level I headings are listed in the Table of Contents under each Chapter title.

Level II headings are usually the subtopics of the main ideas. See the headings "Shaping Culture" and "Types of Regions" on page 34.

Level III headings show the subtopics of Level II headings. See the heading "Landform Regions" on page 34.

Level IV headings show the subtopics of Level III headings. See the headings "Land-forms," "Climate," and "Vegetation" on page 45 for examples.

Features

Stories have a coloured border and a row of dots along the top of the page. Fictional narratives are based on actual facts and events but portray the lives of fictional people. See page 61 for an example. Stories from the oral tradition of First Nations are marked by a blue sticky-note that says History, Primary Source. See page 10 and page 12.

Focus On sections appear on a tabbed divider page with a tan background colour. They offer more detailed information about places and events. See page 57 for an example.

Eyewitness Accounts are written in a smaller size of type in shorter lines. Quotations use the actual words of people who were present at the time of the events described. They can help you understand times in the past. See page 167 for an example.

Vocabulary words or expressions in **bold** print are explained at the bottom of that page. They also appear in the Glossary at the end of the textbook (pages 266–270). Check for unfamiliar words in the Glossary.

Footnotes are marked by asterisks (*). They signal that something on the page is explained in more detail at the bottom of the page. See page 5 for an example.

Canada Revisited sections highlight historic or archaeological sites, people, and events. See page 96 for an example.

Each of the **Case Studies** describes the way of life of a particular Aboriginal group. Case studies are detailed examples that help you understand ideas.

Timelines are a visual way of showing a series of events in chronological order. (Chronological means the order in which something happened.) See pages 116, 117, and 196 for examples.

Numbered Dots are used to relate different kinds of information to each other: text and pictures (see pages 236 and 237), and text and map locations (see pages 19 and 20).

The **Inside Back Cover** provides maps to which you may wish to refer regularly and a chart that explains the climate symbols used in case studies.

The **Inside Front Cover** is a concept map. It summarizes the organization of the book and the icons used in it. (Icons are described on page viii.)

Predicting

Section Stories relate to students' lives and introduce the Section theme. See page 4 for an example.

Questions to Talk About relate each Section story to the main ideas to be covered in that section. See page 5 for an example.

Overviews at the beginning of each chapter show the main ideas of the chapter. See page 6 for an example.

The Chapter **Focus** points out which of the Social Studies concepts described on pages viii and 3 will be emphasized. See page 7 for an example.

A **Preview/Prediction** activity helps you make predictions about the main ideas to be covered in that chapter. See pages 7 and 119 for examples.

Activities

Problem Solving activities ask you to become involved in an historic event by solving a problem. They have a heading like the example below.

An Exercise in Problem Solving

Decision-making activities require you to make a choice related to an historical event. These have a heading like the example below.

An Exercise in Decision-Making

Critical Thinking activities ask you to think about various points of view. Critical Thinking activities look like the example below.

An Exercise in Critical Thinking

Special Projects allow you to share what you have learned with others, like parents and classmates. See pages 114 and 115 for an example.

Research Projects ask you to find and present materials related to history. See page 37 for an example.

Role-play activities ask you to place yourself in the situation of one of the individuals you are studying about. See pages 150 and 151 for an example.

For Your Notebook questions ask you to understand and work with information you have read.

Exploring Further questions ask you to extend your learning beyond the information in the chapter.

A **Review** section is found at the end of each chapter. This includes a chance to check the predictions you made at the beginning of the chapter. Review activities will help you understand concepts, and develop research and communication skills. Reading, writing, listening and speaking, viewing and representing activities are given. You can also apply and extend what you have learned in Applying Concepts and Challenge Plus activities. See pages 158 and 192 for examples.

Icons

Social Studies Concept Icons that show which concepts are the focus of the chapter appear in colour. The five Social Studies concepts used in *Canada Revisited 6* follow. Wherever an icon appears—at the beginning of a paragraph, or in an exercise—the concept is a focus of that section.

Environmental Interaction
The environment influences people and people interact with and change the environment.

Balance
The relationship between humans and nature needs to remain in balance. Balance refers to having respect for all life. Also, the balance between body, mind, and spirit keeps us healthy.

Technology
Technology is used to change raw materials into something needed. Technology includes new skills, ideas, and tools. Technology is developed to make life easier or more comfortable.

Cultural Contact
When groups of people come into contact they interact. They may exchange or trade ideas and technology. Conflicts may arise when different groups wish to change or control each other.

Exploration
When individuals or cultures seek lands new to them or new routes to lands they know, they explore. Exploration may be for profit, adventure, control of territory, or curiosity.

Learning How to Learn Icons appear with exercises and Review questions. Some examples are shown below. A complete list appears inside the front cover of the text.

Look in the Appendix (pages 256–265) for icons that match those shown by some activities. The Appendix provides ideas and information you can use for doing the activities.

 The **Research Model Icon** reminds you to look on pages x and xi to find information about completing a research project.

The **Ongoing Project Icon** signals continuing projects. The Section I project is introduced on page 5 and the Section II project on page 114.

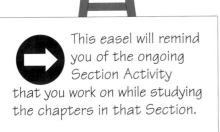

This easel will remind you of the ongoing Section Activity that you work on while studying the chapters in that Section.

Learning Skills

Understanding how you learn can help you become more confident, involved, and responsible for your own learning.

The **Learning How to Learn Appendix** is on pages 256–265. When working on exercises and Review Activities, the Learning How to Learn icons direct you to the Appendix for learning ideas.

Learning How to Learn
Thinking as an Historian

Thinking as a(n) . . . Historian, Archaeologist, Geographer Notes provide tools for studying

cultures of the past and the environments where they developed. These features are designed as a yellow note pad. See pages 7, 8, and 34 for examples.

Sticky-notes appear on some pages to draw your attention to tools used by Historians, Archaeologists, or Geographers. See pages 12, 14, and 38 for examples.

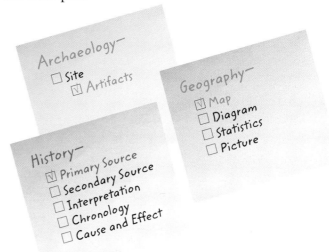

 This icon suggests using the internet to do further research.

***Canada Revisited 6* Homepage**
Arnold Publishing invites you to visit our web site at http://www.arnold.ca/ on the internet. For additional information, select Learning How to Learn (SKIMM™).

Concept Map

A Concept Map to *Canada Revisited 6* is included inside the front cover. It is a visual summary of the organization and features of the book. The coloured rings show the three Sections of the book. Chapters found within each Section are also identified. For example, Section III (light rose ring) contains Chapters 11 and 12. The Section Structure box on the right page lists regular features of each Section and Chapter. Icons on the far bottom right are cues to information about the five social studies concepts. The icons on the left page are cues to learning strategies used in the book (see Appendix pages 256–265).

A Research Model

Research means using an organized procedure to locate useful information on a topic. In various activities in *Canada Revisited 6* you are asked to do research and solve problems or make decisions about issues. The research model shown below is provided to help you. You may modify the model or design your own research model to suit your needs.

This model divides research into three parts: Gathering Information, Examining and Organizing Information, and Communicating the Information.

Gathering Information

 1. Understanding what you are to do

 2. Planning the project

 3. Locating the information

 4. Recording the information

Examining and Organizing Information

 5. Examining the information

 6. Organizing the information

Communicating the Information

 7. Preparing the presentation

8. Sharing the presentation

9. Assessing what you've done

Gathering Information

1. **Understanding what you are to do**
   Focus on the topic you are researching.
   - Read your topic several times and think about what you are being asked to do.
   - Examine the topic by asking what, why, which, where, when, who, and how.
   - Rewrite the topic in your own words or explain the topic to another student.

2. **Planning the project**
   Make a list of what you need to know and do before you start solving the problem.
   - Develop questions to guide your research:
     –What type of information is needed?
     –What key terms do you have to define?
     –What are possible sources of information?
   - Decide on the steps to follow to locate your information.
   - Think about the **criteria** you will use to assess your project. Decide how best to meet the requirements. See Appendix page 263 for self-assessment ideas.
   - Decide on an action plan to outline how you are going to do your research. (See page 115 for a sample action plan.)
   - Set target dates for stages of completion.
   - Remember your plan of action must be flexible. Review it often and revise it if it isn't working.
   - Think about how you will present your research project later on.

Criteria—standards by which something is judged or categorized

X

3. **Locating the information**
Use a variety of information sources:

–almanacs
–charts and graphic organizers
–cartoons
–CD-ROMS
–data bases
–diaries and journals
–dictionaries
–encyclopedias
–fiction and non-fiction material
–government records
–graphs (circle, bar, line)
–reconstructed historical sites
–internet
–interviews and surveys
–legal documents

–maps
–monuments
–museum displays and artifacts
–newspapers and magazines
–photographs
–posters and banners
–radio and television programs
–re-enactments
–reference books
–scrapbooks
–scripts and transcripts
–songs
–speeches
–statistics
–textbooks
–videos and films

* Do surveys.
* Interview a variety of people about your topic.
* Contact experts.
* Skim read; use the table of contents, the index, the glossary.
* Keep a record of reference materials you use by following this format: author's last name, first name, book title, place of publication, date of publication (e.g., Marcotte, Nancy Sellars, ***Ordinary People in Canada's Past***, Second Edition, Edmonton, AB, Arnold Publishing Ltd., 1997).

4. **Recording the information**
Record only information related to your project.
* Use one of the following or a combination:
 –make graphic organizers and notes (see Appendix pages 257, 258, and 261)
 –draw pictures, maps, and create graphs
 –make diagrams and charts
* Record definitions that relate to your topic.
* Write the information in your own words.

Examining and Organizing Information

5. **Examining the Information**

6. **Organizing the Information**
Examining information and organizing information are difficult to separate. These steps are often done at the same time.
* Go through all the information you have collected. Organize it into groups of similar types using graphic organizers such as charts, webs, diagrams, and maps. (See Appendix pages 257–258 and 261.)
* Decide if you need to do more research.
* Decide on an answer or a conclusion to end your project.

Communicating the Information

7. **Preparing the presentation***
* Ask yourself if you really have done what you were assigned to do.
* Decide how you wish to communicate your research findings to others. Choose a presentation idea from the Appendix on page 262.
* Prepare your presentation.

8. **Sharing the presentation**
* Practise sharing your presentation.
* Show it to a friend before you share it with others.

9. **Assessing what you've done**
* Judge your project based on the criteria you determined when planning it. See Appendix page 263 for Self-assessment ideas.
* Record in your History Journal what you would do differently next time. Record what you would do the same.

---

*Presentation, as used in this book, refers to communicating information in visual, oral, or written forms.

Canadian History
Overview

"Mrs. Maziuk, I don't think you will get very far in that ship!" said Dani. She smiled at her teacher, who was carrying a wooden ship model.

"We may get farther than you think," said Mrs. Maziuk. She set the ship down beside a **replica** of a canoe and a space shuttle puzzle.

"Are we going to study transportation this year?" asked Dale, Dani's twin brother.

"That's certainly a part of what we will study," the teacher answered. "Who can make a **prediction** about what we will study this year, based on these models? I will type your predictions into the computer. We will check them later to see how accurate your predictions were."

"Trade?"

"How about travel through the ages . . . ?"

"I thought we were doing Canadian History in Grades 6, 7, and 8 . . . so it must be early history," said Nicole. "It must be the **Aboriginal** people and early exploration. But what's the space shuttle for?"

The students talked among themselves. Then Niels had an idea. "I bet that's exploration too, space exploration. Maybe we will look at the present day and maybe the future."

"These are all good predictions. Let me project the

Replica—an exact copy
Prediction—a statement about what is expected to happen in the future
Aboriginal—the first people to live in a region

course outline I have made," said Mrs. Maziuk. She called up a file on her laptop computer and displayed it on the classroom screen.

"Great, the Vikings!" exclaimed Niels. "Did I ever tell you my **ancestors** were Vikings?" he asked.

said Mrs. Maziuk. "Some of my ancestors were Aboriginal as well. And Nicole's were French and Mark's English. These groups were all important in the exploration of Canada."

File Edit Object Type Filter View Window Help

Section I Aboriginal Peoples	**Section II** European Explorers	**Section III** Today and Tomorrow
• The First People	• Early Exploration (the Vikings)	• Aboriginal People Today
• Environmental Interaction	• An Age of Exploration	• Exploration Today
• The Wendat	• Exploring and Claiming Lands	
• The Woodland Cree	• Exploring and Colonizing Lands	
• The Anishinabe	• Quebec Colony and the Fur Trade	

Dale smiled at him. "Just every year so far," he said. "And Dani's and my ancestors were Aboriginal. It will be interesting to see how history compares with the stories our families have told us."

"I'm very glad to have you in this class for that reason,"

Ancestor—a person from whom one is descended

Icons

Mrs. Maziuk showed the students five icons on the screen. "These icons are used in the textbook *Canada Revisited 6*. They will help you organize your study of history. They mark five important concepts in social studies.

"First you will learn about how the **environment** influenced how the First People lived. The first two icons relate to that: Environmental Interaction and Balance. The third icon will bring your attention to information about Technology. The fourth refers to Cultural Contact. The fifth icon refers to Exploration.

"The descriptions of the icons contain words you may not understand yet. However, you will learn much more about them in the weeks ahead! I want you to set up your history binders right away. If you draw

---

Environment—all of the natural parts in our surroundings—landforms, water, air, vegetation, and animal life

and label the icons in your notes and then colour them, you will remember them more easily," she concluded.

 Environmental Interaction—The environment influences people ➡ and people interact with and change the environment ⬅.

 Balance—The relationship between humans and nature needs to remain in balance. Balance refers to having respect for all life. Also, the balance between body, mind, and spirit keeps us healthy.

 Technology— Technology is used to change raw materials into something needed. Technology includes new skills, ideas, and tools. It is developed to make life easier or more comfortable.

 Cultural Contact— When groups of people come into contact they interact. They may exchange or trade ideas and technology. Conflicts may arise when different groups wish to change or control each other.

Exploration— When individuals or cultures seek lands that are new to them or new routes to lands they know, they explore. Exploration may be for profit, adventure, control of territory, or curiosity.

Notebook Organization

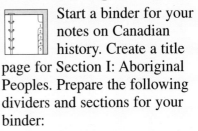 Start a binder for your notes on Canadian history. Create a title page for Section I: Aboriginal Peoples. Prepare the following dividers and sections for your binder:

a) a section for your notes, activities, maps, and illustrations called Activities, with a chapter title page for each chapter
b) a section called WordBook for vocabulary
c) a section for your thoughts, ideas, and feelings on history called History Journal
d) a section called Learning How to Learn for information about how to learn and think

"I have to work for a while tomorrow morning, Dani," my father said. "We've run into a small problem with the CD-ROM we're developing. This means we can't go out to practise with your new digital camera until after lunch. Why don't you come to work with me? I think you'll find the morning quite interesting. I could use your advice."

Dad owns a company that creates multimedia products. They are producing three CD-ROMS about Canada's Aboriginal peoples—First Nations, Inuit, and Metis. He often tests material from projects on my twin brother Dale and me. We try out the CD-ROMs to see if they are interesting and work well. He says we're the computer generation.

Section I

The First Nations

Saturday morning when I came down an **Elder** was drinking coffee with Dad. Dad nodded for me to join them. "This is Grandmother Yvonne," said Dad.* "She is Elder-in-Residence at the University." I nodded politely and sat down to listen. They were talking about the origins of the First People in North America.

"Aboriginal history and beliefs tell that Aboriginal people were placed on North America by the Creator," said the Elder.

I wondered about that. Our teacher told us about the theory of the First People coming from Asia. It says they crossed a land bridge called Beringia and then moved down into North America. She showed us a map of the northern part of North America covered by huge sheets of ice. The ocean shoreline was also different than today.

Dad took a package of tobacco from his shirt pocket. I knew he didn't smoke so I wondered what he was doing. He placed the package on the table before Grandmother Yvonne. "Dani,

---

Elder—an older person who is considered by the Aboriginal community to be wise and is greatly respected

*Grandmother is a term of respect. Children and younger people may refer to members of the senior generation as Grandmother and Grandfather whether they are related or not.

Grandmother Yvonne has a great amount of knowledge of our ancestors. When I give her this tobacco I am asking her for some information about the old ways. This is one of the **traditions** of **First Nations** people."

Then Dad said to the Elder, "Our multimedia team is working on a project. We would like your help as a cultural advisor on how our people lived long ago. We will be taking some photos and shooting video to use in a CD-ROM."

Dad put his hand on the pouch of tobacco and slid it across the table to the Elder. "We want to show three things. First, we would show how Aboriginal cultures developed many different ways of life. Then, our project will show how their ways of life related to their environment and the natural resources available to them. Finally, we will look at how conservation and living in harmony

with nature were part of their ways of life."

Neither Dad nor Grandmother Yvonne spoke for a long time. I found the silence a little uncomfortable. Finally the Elder took the tobacco pouch and put it in her handbag. This meant she was agreeing to help Dad and his production team. She said she would come into Dad's studio next week.

I hoped my father would let Dale and me spend more time on the project. This could be a real opportunity to learn about our ancestors' way of life.

Questions to Talk About

Discuss the following questions by referring to the story you have just read.

1. What are the two ideas that describe how the First People came to North America?
2. Predict ways the environment may have influenced Aboriginal ways of life.
3. Predict ways Aboriginal people might have lived in balance with nature.
4. Predict what contributions Aboriginal people made to the development of Canada.

Note: Keep your predictions from the above questions in mind as you read the five chapters in this section.

Traditions—customs, beliefs, and stories handed down from older people to younger people for a long time
First Nation—a group that identifies itself as having been a nation living in Canada at the time Europeans came; a nation is a group of people with a shared language, territory, way of life, and government
*The Wendat have been called the Huron in history books, but this name was given to them by Europeans. They called themselves Wendat.

Section 1 Presentation Activity

  At the end of Section 1 (in approximately 3 months) you will be asked to make a presentation to the class. It will show the relationship between the environment and the culture of the Wendat* or the Woodland Cree people before Europeans came to Canada. (You will receive further instructions about this project as you proceed through Chapters 1–5.) This easel will remind you of this project.

5

Chapter 1
The First People

O v e r v i e w

Use this Overview to predict the events of this chapter.

❶ Origins
According to the First Nations

For many centuries, the Elders have passed on stories of how the First People in North America were created by the Creator, and placed here. The people have always lived here. All peoples have Creation stories.

According to Some Scientists

Approximately 32 000 to 36 000 years ago, ice-age hunting peoples, following herds of animals, travelled from Siberia across the Beringia land bridge into North America.

Beringia
Ice
Ice
North America

❸ Culture

Culture is a group's shared way of life. It includes the group's knowledge, beliefs, and learned behaviours. Culture describes the ways a group meets its needs.

❷ Who Are the First Nations?

Aboriginal people were living all over what is now Canada before any Europeans arrived. Although related in some ways, nations were different from each other. Two ways groups can be described are by the language they spoke and their way of life (how they met their basic needs).

❹ Culture of the Siksika

The culture of the Siksika was based on following herds of buffalo across the broad plains.

Chapter 1 Focus

This chapter focuses on Canada's First People. It looks at their origins and defines who the groups are. A model for studying culture is provided. Physical, psychological, and group needs are explained. The way of life of one First Nation (the Siksika) provides an example.

This book uses five concepts to organize the ideas of Canada's early history. The concepts of environmental interaction and balance are the focus of Chapter 1.

Environmental Interaction   Balance   Technology   Cultural Contact   Exploration

Vocabulary

origin	pre-Contact
oral tradition	culture
traditional	physical needs
migration	psychological needs
Beringia	group (social) needs
theory	economic
adapt	social
language families	political

Chapter Preview/Prediction

1. In pairs or small groups, use the overview on page 6 to predict the four major topics of this chapter.
2. a) Locate each of the four major topic areas in Chapter 1. What colour are these titles? (See page vii for information on title sizes.)
   b) Locate the sub-headings under the main topic. Sub-headings are coloured green. The second level of sub-heading in this chapter is black.
   c) What is the difference between major headings and sub-headings?
3. Make a web showing the headings and two levels of sub-headings in this chapter. As you study this chapter, add information to this web.

Learning How to Learn
Thinking as an Historian

History is the study of the past. Historical thinking requires you to understand history, not just memorize facts. One way to do this is by critical thinking. This means examining several points of view about an event.

Anything that gives you information about a topic is a source. Studying a variety of historical sources helps you understand history.

There are two types of sources: primary and secondary.

- Primary Sources are written, visual, or audio accounts by someone who lived at the time of the event. It is evidence from that time in history.
- Secondary Sources are created after the time they happened. Often, secondary sources use primary sources for reference and research. This textbook is a secondary source. It contains some primary sources in it. They are "eyewitness accounts."

Information may be communicated in written, illustrated, or spoken form. Examples of written sources are books, maps, diaries, pictures.

In the Oral Tradition, information is passed down from one group of people to another through storytelling, songs, poems, or other oral teachings. Storytellers use different aids to remember. You will learn about wampum belts, one type of aid, in Chapter 3.

His Story...Her Story

"You will need to do some critical thinking in this class today," said Mrs. Maziuk. "I'm going to ask Nicole and Niels to share their feelings about the new computers. Listen carefully to each one's point of view."

"I think it's great that the school will have more computers," said Nicole. "Our old computers weren't fast enough to run some of the new software. We will be able to do more research on the internet. Maybe we will get to create a web page for the class. We could share some of our work with other classes, or even other schools!"

"But computers and software cost a lot of money!" argued Niels. "The school needs so many other things. We need new sports equipment. Most of our soccer balls are worn out and there is a hole in one of the nets. When other schools come here, their players tease us about it. It's embarrassing!"

"All right," said Mrs. Maziuk. "This is an example of how to do critical thinking. We have heard Nicole's and Niels's opinions. Now let's look at each side separately."

She took a marker and turned to the whiteboard. "Let me diagram this so we can talk about points of view. We'll see how this will help us to think critically about issues that have more than one side to them."

Learning How to Learn
Critical Thinking

 Each of us has our own point of view (viewpoint). This affects how we look at situations and issues. An issue is a problem or question for debate. Issues may not have definite answers. Critical thinking involves

- examining ideas or issues in order to make a judgement about them
- looking at ideas and issues from different points of view
- questioning information that is presented
- recognizing fact and opinion

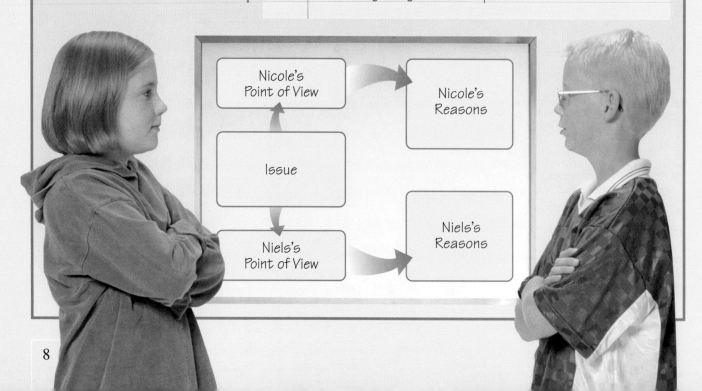

8

Origins

Who are the First People? How did the First People come to be in the Americas? Many **theories** have been suggested to explain this mystery. Two theories follow on pages 9–17.

According to the First Nations

Humans are all curious and wish to understand what is unknown. It is part of the way we think. All peoples try to explain the way things are in the world. Many ask the question "how did life on earth begin?"

Almost all groups, in their old, respected stories, tell of how their people came to be on the earth. All First Nations have such stories. The **traditional** belief of these peoples is that they have always been in North America. They believe the people were made and placed here on the land by the Creator.

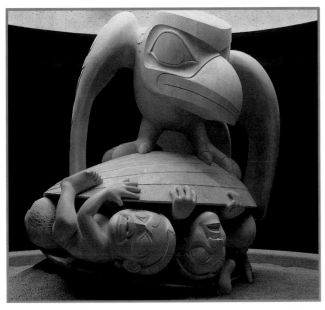

Bill Reid's sculpture, *Raven and the First Men*, is carved in yellow cedar. It illustrates a scene from a Haida Creation story. In the story, Raven finds the first men in a clam shell.

Theory—an idea about something; a possible explanation
Traditional—believing in the old ways; the old customs and traditions
Migrating—moving from one place to another in search of food or because of changing seasons

An Exercise in Critical Thinking

Part I

There are different ideas about the origins of the First People. Many First Nations people believe that the First People were placed in North America by the Creator. All First Nations people have similar stories. Elders pass their people's history from one generation to another through stories.

Many scientists believe that Asian people followed **migrating** animals from Asia to North America. Scientists call the land bridge they crossed Beringia. When glaciers formed in the last million years, ocean levels dropped between 65 and 140 metres. Large masses of land were exposed. Siberia and the North American continent were joined. Ice covered much of North America except for a central ice-free corridor. The scientists' theory is that the people followed that route. (See map page 14.)

Your Task

Read pages 10–17. Use this information and resources from the library to decide how you think the First People came to the Americas.

History—
☑ Primary Source
☐ Secondary Source
☐ Interpretation
☐ Chronology
☐ Cause and Effect

The Creation of Turtle Island

–story and illustration
by Ojibway author and artist Nokomis

The Anishinabe (Ojibway) people lived in an area that extended from what is now the western edge of Quebec; south to Ontario, Michigan, Wisconsin, and Minnesota; west into Manitoba and even parts of Saskatchewan; and north to about the 51st parallel. Creation stories may vary slightly depending on influences from other cultures nearby, but this is the story common to many of the Ojibway living north of the Great Lakes in Ontario, Manitoba, and Quebec.

Before the universe existed there was nothing. But within the emptiness there existed the idea that all things were possible. The greatest possibility was that all that we know and all that we don't know could come to be.

It would take a great Being to envision everything that could be created and everything that could happen and everything that could be felt in the heart. The Ojibway call this Being Kitchi-Manitou—the Great Mystery. Words can't describe Kitchi-Manitou, just as it is difficult to use words to explain the verb "to be."

Kitchi-Manitou had a vision. He saw in his mind all the suns and the moons that we know and all the ones that we don't know. He saw creatures that fly and swim and walk and wriggle. He perceived their feelings and needs and envisioned how those needs could be provided. And then from nothing other than by seeing, hearing, touching, tasting, smelling, sensing, and knowing what was possible, he brought the universe, our world, the other Manitous (Spirits), the vegetation, and all creatures into existence.

At first he was satisfied but in time realized that it was also possible to create Beings like himself that could have dreams and visions. Geezhigo-Quae, a Manitou we might call Sky Woman, agreed to bear children in this image, and she made a home on the moon.

The Water Manitous were very upset. No one had asked them if they wanted such powerful Beings in the world. To fight back, they used their powers to cause a great flood all over the Earth. Because of the water, Sky Woman had nowhere to raise her children.

Geezhigo-Quae, the Sky Woman, called to the animals that could swim but breathed air. These animals weren't under the control of the Water Manitous. The animals invited her to sit on the giant turtle's back and discuss what to do next. She asked that they dive deep and bring her some of the original soil that Kitchi-Manitou had made. The beavers and martens and loons and others tried without success. At the end of the day the little muskrat finally took a deep breath and dived down and down. He didn't return. It wasn't until the next day that Sky Woman pulled his body from the water and found clutched in his paw the soil from Kitchi-Manitou's world. To thank the little muskrat she breathed life back into him, and that is why we still have muskrats today.

Then she took the soil and breathed into it. Her breath gave the soil the ability to provide nourishment, shelter, teachings, and dreams to the beings that would live upon it. She rubbed the soil on the turtle's back. As she did so, the soil grew into the land Muzzu-kummick-quae (the Earth Mother) as Kitchi-Manitou had first imagined it. That land is known as Turtle Island.

Sky Woman gave birth, and her children and her children's children became known as the Anishinauback, the Good Beings. As time went on and the people spread across the land they sometimes were known as the Ojibway or Chippewa, the Ottawa, Pottawatomi, and Mississauga.

History—
☑ Primary Source
☐ Secondary Source
☐ Interpretation
☐ Chronology
☐ Cause and Effect

Anishinabe Creation Story

–story by Wisconsin Ojibway author Edward Benton-Banai; illustration by artist Don Hight. Excerpt from Edward Benton-Banai, *The Mishomis Book: The Voice of the Ojibway.* Hayward, Wisconsin: Indian Country Communications, Inc. © July 1988, Red School House. Reprinted with permission by Indian Country Communications, Inc.

I would like to tell you an account of how man was created on this Earth. This teaching was handed down by word of mouth from generation to generation by my ancestors. Sometimes the details of teachings like this were recorded on scrolls made from Wee´-gwas (birchbark). I am fortunate to be the keeper of several of these scrolls. They will help me remember some of the details of what I give to you.

When Ah-ki´ (the Earth) was young, it was said that the Earth had a family. Nee-ba-gee´-sis (the Moon) is called Grandmother, and Gee´-sis (the Sun) is called Grandfather. The Creator of this family is called Gi´-tchie Man-i-to´ (Great Mystery or Creator).

The Earth is said to be a woman. In this way it is understood that woman preceded man on the Earth. She is called Mother Earth because from her come all living things. Water is her life

blood. It flows through her, nourishes her, and purifies her.

On the surface of the Earth, all is given Four Sacred Directions—North, South, East, and West. Each of these directions contributes a vital part to the wholeness of the Earth. Each has physical powers as well as spiritual powers, as do all things.

When she was young, the Earth was filled with beauty.

The Creator sent his singers in the form of birds to the Earth to carry the seeds of life to all of the Four Directions. In this way life was spread across the Earth. On the Earth the Creator placed the swimming creatures of the water. He gave life to all the plant and insect world. He placed the crawling things and the four-leggeds on the land. All of these parts of life lived in harmony with each other.

Gitchie Manito then took four parts of Mother Earth and blew into them using a Sacred Shell. From the union of the Four Sacred Elements and his breath, man was created.

It is said the Gitchie Manito then lowered man to the Earth. Thus, man was the last form of life to be placed on the Earth.

From this Original Man came the A-nish-i-na´-be people.

In the Ojibway language if you break down the word Anishinabe, this is what it means: ANI—from whence, NISHINA—lowered, ABE— the male of the species.

This man was created in the image of Gitchie Manito. He was natural man. He was part of Mother Earth. He lived in brotherhood with all that was around him.

All tribes came from this Original Man. The Ojibway are a tribe because of the way they speak. We believe that we are nee-kon´-nis-ug´ (brothers) with all tribes; we are separated only by our tongue or language.

<table>
</table>

Learning How to Learn
Thinking as an Archaeologist

Archaeologists study the lives of people from ancient times. They look at **evidence** of the people's lives. This includes sites and artifacts. An archaeological site is a place where remains of human activity have been found. For example, the remains of an ancient village is a site. An artifact is an object or other evidence of human life, for example a spearhead.

According to Some Scientists

The stories told by Nokomis and Edward Benton-Banai on pages 10–13 tell about the origins of the Anishinabe (Ojibway).* The following passage looks at the origin of the First People from the point of view of a scientist.

Beringia

People are believed to have travelled east and west across a land bridge between Siberia and Alaska more than 20 000 years ago. Some scientists think they came more than 35 000 years ago. This land bridge is known as Beringia. It appeared only during the Ice Ages, when the water in the ocean was lower than it is today. Many generations of people are thought to have used this land route. Today the waters of the Bering Strait flow over Beringia.

The Beringia theory says that people who crossed from Asia were the first people to come to North, Central, and South America. Scientists believe these people later spread across the continents. They became the ancestors of the Aboriginal peoples. They believe the migrations happened over thousands of years.

Evidence—information used to prove something
*Ojibway has many different spellings, including Ojibwa, Ojibwe, and Chippewa. Many Ojibway prefer to call themselves Anishinabe. This is the name used in their ancient Creation stories to refer to their First People.

Ancient stone weapons such as arrowheads have been discovered along this route. They show that people have lived and hunted there for a very long time. Scientists have tried to understand from this evidence exactly when people first went there.

Ice Age and Beringia

SIBERIA

BERINGIA

Ice cover
Old coastline
Present coastline

0   500 km

NORTH AMERICA

ICE-FREE CORRIDOR

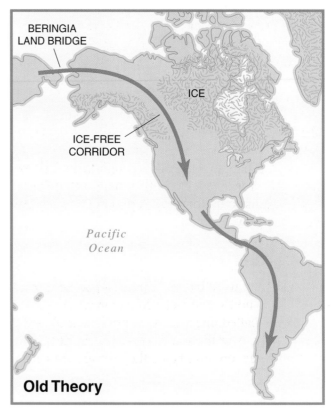

Old Theory

BERINGIA LAND BRIDGE

ICE

ICE-FREE CORRIDOR

Pacific Ocean

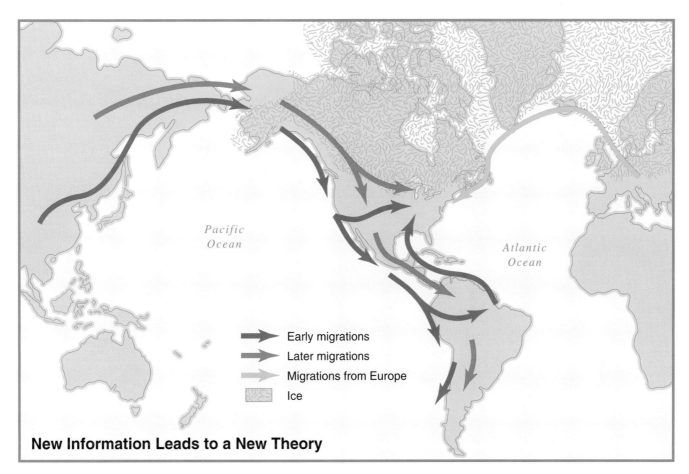

New Information Leads to a New Theory

Legend:
- Early migrations
- Later migrations
- Migrations from Europe
- Ice

New Information

New evidence often causes scientists to change old theories. New evidence suggests that people arrived in the Americas much earlier. See the blue arrows on the map above. Earlier peoples may have moved across the Northern Pacific in small boats. They eventually made their way to the coast of the Americas. From there they moved inland. The orange arrows show migration down the interior. There was a passage free of ice there. Evidence shows this route was used later.

Another new theory is that people from Europe travelled across the ice sheets in the north polar regions. This route to North America is shown by the gold arrow.

Migrations

Once they were in the Americas, people moved south, east, north, and west. Movements of large groups are called migrations. Migrations took place very slowly, over thousands of years. As people moved to new environments they developed new ways of life. They **adapted** to the climate, animals, and plant life of the area. For example, people lived differently in hot, wet forests than in cold, dry regions or among high mountains.

An Exercise in Critical Thinking

Part 2

Complete the critical thinking activity you started on page 9. The Critical Thinking steps on pages 8 and 258 will help you with this activity. Present your findings in paragraph form.

Adapt—change to suit different living conditions

Tlachi

—story by Peigan archaeologist, educator, and author Eldon Yellowhorn; illustration by artist Betty Dieleman

This story supports the scientists' theory. It is about people who hunted caribou and giant bison. They took the skins of mammoths to build their homes and they chipped their knives from stone.

Twilight colours lit the shrubland to the northeast where the sun would soon rise. The clouds reflected the orange rays shining from behind the horizon. The air was chilly and Tlachi could see her breath. The sun had not set long before it rose to begin another day.

The long day of summer was over and now the season had started when the days grew shorter. Too soon it would be the long night of winter. The thought of no sun made Tlachi shiver and she said, "I wish the sun would always stay in the sky."

Kamalin walked over and sat beside her younger sister. "When I was your age I wished for that too. Now I know even the sun has to sleep sometime."

Tlachi rested against Kamalin, who wrapped them both in a caribou hide. "If the sun didn't sleep we would never have to leave this place. I will get lonesome for you when you go with your husband's family," Tlachi said.

"I will miss you too, but they are my family now," Kamalin said and hugged Tlachi closer. They said nothing more and Tlachi felt some tears fill her eyes.

Kamalin hummed a tune to comfort her sister, but there were tears in her eyes also.

Kamalin remembered her sister as a baby. It was twelve summers ago that Tlachi was born. Their mother was very weak afterwards and Kamalin helped care for her new sister. Even when she was just seven summers old she had enjoyed pretending to be Tlachi's mother.

"We should go to the water and join the others. They have already taken down the camp and Father said they would pack everything into the boat soon," Kamalin finally said. They got up and shook the grass off the caribou hide. As they walked Kamalin put her arm around Tlachi's shoulders and said, "I am going to live with my husband in those blue mountains to the north. When I see you next summer I will tell you if they really are made of ice."

"I heard the salmon don't swim that far and the people eat only caribou meat," Tlachi said.

"Yes, my husband says it is very different from where we grew up. He wants to spend a winter there because he has never seen whales," Kamalin said.

"It seems that wherever we travel, every year we move closer to where the sun rises."

When the two sisters arrived, there were already four boats in the water. Each family had a boat. Tlachi's mother had sewn eight caribou hides together to make theirs. Her father and older brothers had put spruce gum along the seams. Then they smeared the hides with grease so they wouldn't get wet. Tlachi helped by cutting the willow branches to make the boat's frame.

Tlachi's people had walked when they travelled to the meeting place last spring. They had made ten camps as they pulled their toboggans along the trails. On their journey home in the fall, the ice would not yet hide the river again. They would make only four camps and they would not have to carry anything.

The boat of Tlachi's family could carry six people, but only five would travel home in it. Kamalin would go with her new husband's family.

The boat was in the water. Tlachi's mother got in first. They handed her the food and some tanned hides. Tlachi got in and helped her mother with the tent. They folded it into a seat and sat down. Her father got in as her brothers slowly pushed the boat into deeper water. He held the steering pole as they climbed in. The boat began to move as Tlachi waved a tearful farewell to Kamalin.

17

Who Are the First Nations?

One of the qualities that human beings share is the need to feel part of a group. Two ways of belonging to a group are to have the same language and to share a way of life.

Language Families

There are more than 500 groups of people that can be called First Nations. They belong to 12 language families. The languages within each family are different but related. The map below shows language groups before the year 1450.

Most First Nations people of modern-day Ontario belong to one of two language families, the Iroquoian and the Algonquian. The majority of the pages in Section I of this textbook focus on three groups:
- the Wendat (Huron) in Chapter 3 are an Iroquoian-speaking people
- the Woodland Cree in Chapter 4 and the Anishinabe (Ojibway)* in Chapter 5 are two groups of Algonquian-speaking peoples.

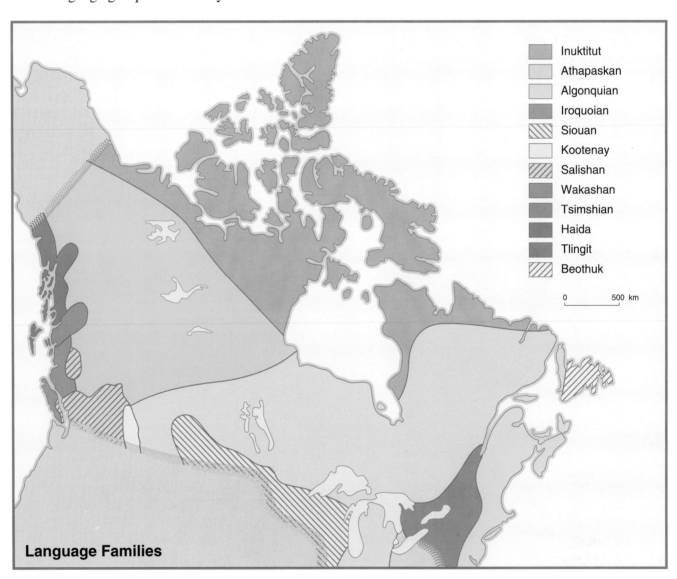

Inuktitut
Athapaskan
Algonquian
Iroquoian
Siouan
Kootenay
Salishan
Wakashan
Tsimshian
Haida
Tlingit
Beothuk

0   500 km

Language Families

---

*In your research, you will often find a group of people referred to by different names. This textbook attempts to call First Nations by the names that they prefer to call themselves.

The Anishinabe have been referred to by the name Ojibway or Ojibwa for hundreds of years. Many people still use it, but others prefer the name Anishinabe.

Traditional Ways of Life

A group's way of life is based on how the people meet their basic needs. Ways of life that have been the same for a long time are called traditional.

Basic needs must be met to survive. They include food, shelter, and clothing. Aboriginal groups used many different means of meeting their basic needs. Most groups hunted, fished, and gathered plants and useful materials from nature. Some groups also farmed. The map below shows regions where people had different traditional ways of life.

The environment in which a group lived for a long time had an effect on the way of life they developed. For example, the traditional lifestyle of the people of the far north is based on hunting. The environment has long, cold winters, few plant resources, and herds of animals that migrate in

search of a food supply. Groups living in the far north developed a migratory, hunting lifestyle.

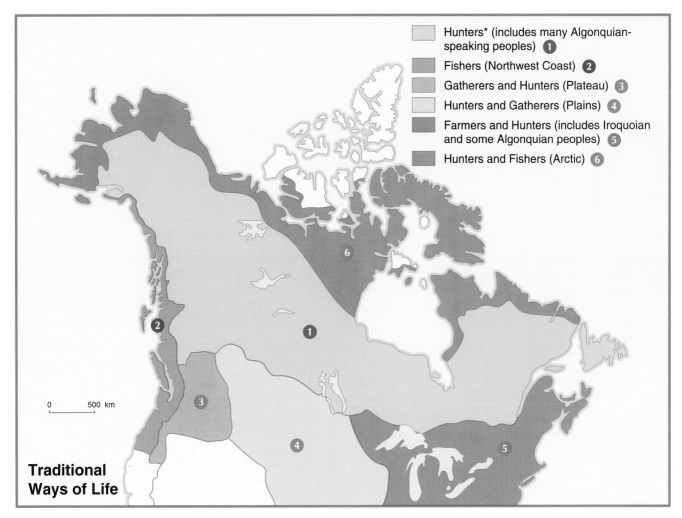

Legend:
Hunters* (includes many Algonquian-speaking peoples) **1**
Fishers (Northwest Coast) **2**
Gatherers and Hunters (Plateau) **3**
Hunters and Gatherers (Plains) **4**
Farmers and Hunters (includes Iroquoian and some Algonquian peoples) **5**
Hunters and Fishers (Arctic) **6**

0   500 km

Traditional Ways of Life

*Note that these categories refer to the primary way of getting food. All Aboriginal peoples used many sources and methods of getting food.

Refer to the numbers on the map on page 19 to determine where these people lived.

❶ Hunters

The people of the northern forests of what is now Canada developed a way of life based primarily on hunting. The region is composed of rock, rivers, lakes, and **coniferous** forests. The soil is thin and not good for farming. The winters are long and cold. Summers are short. Large and small **game** animals, freshwater fish, and birds provided food, clothing, shelter, and tools. The people lived in families or small groups most of the year. They met in larger groups for seasonal activities such as duck hunting.

Coniferous—trees with cones and needles; most species are evergreen
Game—animals and birds hunted for food

❷ Fishers

The fishing people of the Northwest Coast lived in villages. Their environment included mountains, ocean, and **rainforest**. The ocean provided plentiful food. Ocean and river fish, sea mammals, shellfish, birds, deer, and other kinds of game were found in the Northwest Coast. Berries and plants for food and medicines were plentiful. Huge cedar trees were used for building large plank houses. Cedar was also used to build sea-going canoes. Canoes were used for travel and **trade** along the coast.

Rainforest—huge trees and many types of plant life, year-round rainfall, and a mild climate
Trade—exchanging goods for money or other goods

❸ Gatherers and Hunters

The people who lived in the interior of what is now British Columbia met most of their needs through gathering resources from the environment. They also hunted. Summers in the interior are hot and dry in valleys but cooler on the mountain slopes. There is often heavy snow in winter. The valleys have many rivers and small streams. The people got their food from many sources. There were freshwater fish (especially salmon), game animals, birds, nuts, and berries. They dug roots of plants such as wild onion and the blue-flowered camas lily for food.

❹ Hunters and Gatherers

The people who lived on the Plains hunted game for meat. Herds of buffalo* provided most of their needs. The people used every part of the buffalo. The environment was mainly open grassland, with trees and shrubs growing near water sources. Winters on the Plains are cold and summers hot, with clouds of biting insects. The people of the Plains lived a migratory life. They followed the buffalo herds. They also gathered resources, such as berries and plants for medicines.

❺ Farmers and Hunters

The people of the Eastern Woodlands developed a way of life based mainly on farming and hunting. Their main crops were corn, beans, and squash. The peoples of the Woodlands hunted, fished, and gathered plants. The forest environment contained good soils for growing crops. The people built canoes from wood and bark. The many rivers were used as travel and trade routes. Having a farming way of life meant that many people lived in **semi-permanent** villages.

❻ Hunters and Fishers

The peoples of the Arctic lived in a **tundra** environment. Winters were very long and cold and summers short. The tundra vegetation produced little plant food. There were no trees for building. The caribou ranged over huge areas to find pastures. Caribou, musk-oxen, ocean mammals, and fish provided food, clothing, and shelter.

---

*Buffalo is the common name for the North American bison.

Semi-permanent—lasting a long time but not forever

Tundra—the treeless cold desert; vegetation is low to the ground and not plentiful, mainly lichens, mosses, and small plants

Culture

People live together in groups. They learn from one another and develop ways of doing things that are shared by all. This common set of learned behaviours is the group's culture. Culture includes knowledge, beliefs, attitudes, **customs**, traditions, laws, and roles.

The culture of a group is passed from one generation to another. Younger people learn the culture from parents and elders.

A group's culture is all the ways they commonly meet their needs. This includes physical, psychological, and group needs.

Culture has economic, social, and political parts.

- The economic part of culture deals mainly with meeting physical needs. These include the basic needs for food, shelter, and clothing.
- The social part of culture deals mainly with psychological needs. It includes the needs for a sense of belonging, family, friendship, communication, and spiritual meaning.
- The political part of culture deals with group needs. These include the need for direction, a sense of order, security, leadership, and laws.

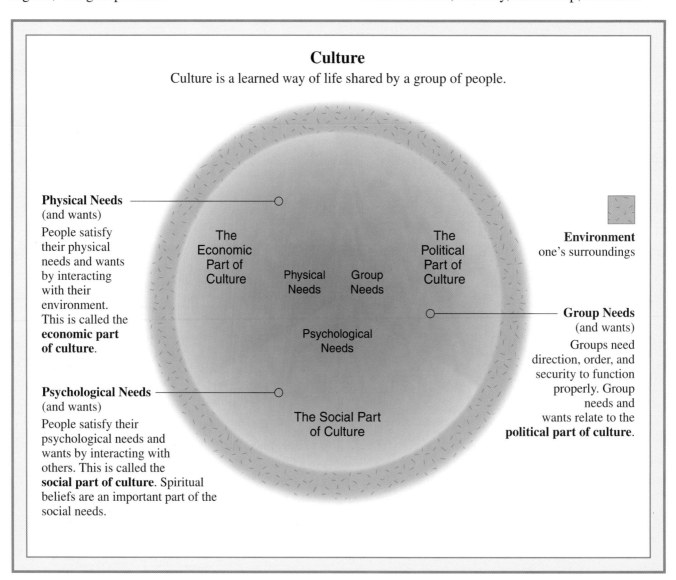

Culture

Culture is a learned way of life shared by a group of people.

Physical Needs (and wants)

People satisfy their physical needs and wants by interacting with their environment. This is called the **economic part of culture**.

The Economic Part of Culture

Physical Needs

Group Needs

Psychological Needs

The Political Part of Culture

Environment one's surroundings

Group Needs (and wants)

Groups need direction, order, and security to function properly. Group needs and wants relate to the **political part of culture**.

Psychological Needs (and wants)

People satisfy their psychological needs and wants by interacting with others. This is called the **social part of culture**. Spiritual beliefs are an important part of the social needs.

The Social Part of Culture

Custom—the usual way of doing things

The diagram on the previous page is just one way to describe the parts of culture. Showing them in a diagram helps us to understand them.

The diagram also shows the environment surrounding the culture. In all First Nations cultures, the environment influenced the ways people lived. The changing seasons provided the rhythm by which they lived.

Many people consider spiritual beliefs to be part of everything. This includes all parts of culture as well as all parts of the environment. This is an important belief in traditional First Nations cultures.

Needs

Needs are what humans require in order to survive as individuals and groups.

Needs may be divided into physical needs, psychological needs, and group (social) needs. People must satisfy these needs to be healthy.

Physical Needs

A physical need must be met to stay alive. When people have a physical need that is not met they feel discomfort or pain. Physical needs include food and water, clothing, shelter, and physical activity. These needs are met through the economic part of culture. Examples of physical needs are shown in the illustration below.

Illustrations on pages 23, 24, and 25 are by the Ojibway artist Nokomis. They show scenes from the culture of the Siksika. In the painting above, a woman uses a tool to cut meat, which she is drying on a rack. Another woman scrapes a hide and a child watches to learn the skill. The man is resting after the hunt.

Psychological Needs

Psychological needs are related to the mind. They have to do with feelings, thoughts, relationships, beliefs, and values.

When people's psychological needs are not met, they may feel lonely, anxious, bored, or afraid. The need for families, support, comfort, love, acceptance, and personal security, are psychological needs. So are traditions, communication, rest, leisure, challenges, and a sense of accomplishment from work. A sense of **identity** is a psychological need. Identity is who you think you are. This is partly based on a sense of belonging.

Beliefs and values are psychological needs. Beliefs relate to what we consider to be true. For many people, this includes the belief in a Creator. Our values are our opinions about what we believe is good or right. Psychological needs are shown in the illustration below.

Sweetgrass had many traditional **ceremonial** uses. A sweetgrass braid (shown above) has three strands, which can **symbolize** the spirit, mind, and body. Burning it is a way of bringing health and balance to all the parts of one's life.

After the buffalo hunt, the men take part in a ceremony of thanks. They burn sweetgrass as they pray and meditate. The women and children in the background have a separate ceremony.

Identity—sense of who you are; sense of self, often based on belonging to a group
Ceremonial—formal activity showing respect
Symbolize—stand for; a symbol is something that can be used to show something else

Group Needs

Human beings live in groups. For a group to be successful and continue to exist, group needs must be met. These include the need for group laws and security, leaders, and organization. People meet their group needs by forming organizations and governments. When group needs are not met, there may be confusion and disorder.

In some cultures, the needs and wants of individual people are more important. Many laws protect individuals. In other cultures, the group is more important. Members are expected to put the needs of the group first. Their individual needs or wants are not as important.

Most traditional First Nations cultures believe the group is more important than the individual. Examples of group needs are shown below.

Case Studies

The **case study** that follows on pages 26–28 briefly examines the culture of the Siksika. In Chapter 2 there is a brief study of the Haida. Chapter 3 presents a case study of the Wendat (Huron), an Iroquoian-speaking group in **pre-Contact** times. Chapter 4 presents the Woodland Cree and Chapter 5 the Anishinabe. Both are Algonquian-speaking peoples.

The leader and the rest of the group are meeting to discuss something of concern to all. In the background, a man keeps watch for danger.

Case study—a detailed example that shows how a theory applies to a real-life situation

Pre-Contact—people as they lived before meeting any Europeans or using their technology

Culture of the Siksika

For Your Notebook

 Pages 26–28 provide some information on the Siksika as they lived before Europeans came.* Use this information to make a large web on their culture. Add to the titles shown above, using different colours for main headings and details. You may want to work with a partner. See Appendix page 261 for an example of a web.

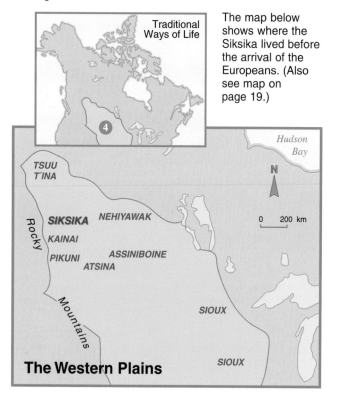

Traditional Ways of Life

The map below shows where the Siksika lived before the arrival of the Europeans. (Also see map on page 19.)

*The information on the Siksika has been written in the past tense. However, many Aboriginal people today continue to follow the beliefs and values described in this textbook.

Note: Locations of peoples shown on both maps above varied over the centuries. There was a great deal of movement of people onto the Plains.

The Environment

 The grassland environment of the Plains had a great influence on how the Siksika lived. Grasslands are the natural home of herds of grazing animals. Buffalo and antelope were an important source of food for the Siksika. The Siksika were excellent hunters and used every part of the animals they killed. They travelled great distances following the buffalo. Their homes and possessions had to be easy to move from place to place. The people were careful to not change the environment so it would continue to supply their needs. They took care with natural vegetation, the homes of the animals, and the lakes and rivers.

Meeting Physical Needs

Hunters had to know the **natural resources** in the area and how to use them for their daily needs. They needed to understand the environment in which they lived and the habits of the animals they hunted.

During the winter the people lived in sheltered river valleys or the foothills of the Rocky Mountains. They lived in small family groups. When spring came they moved out onto the prairie. They were joined there by other family groups.

In summer, the Siksika came together in large groups for the buffalo hunt. They needed to **co-operate** to hunt such large animals. Some groups chased the buffalo over cliffs. Other groups chased them into pounds. These were areas enclosed with bushes. The hunters killed the captured buffalo with bows and arrows or spears. The Siksika were careful to treat the buffalo with respect and to waste no parts of them.

After the buffalo were killed and skinned, the women dried the meat. Most of the dried meat was ground into a powder. It was mixed with melted fat and berries to make pemmican.

Natural resources—materials found in the environment that are useful to people
Co-operate—work together as a group

Every Part of the Buffalo Was Used

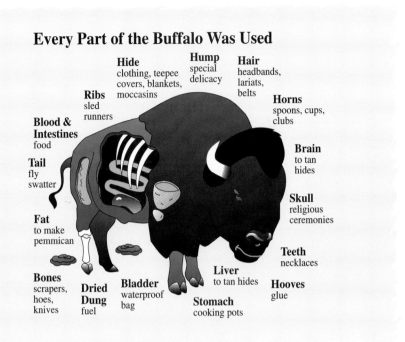

Hide
clothing, teepee covers, blankets, moccasins

Hump
special delicacy

Hair
headbands, lariats, belts

Ribs
sled runners

Horns
spoons, cups, clubs

Blood & Intestines
food

Brain
to tan hides

Tail
fly swatter

Skull
religious ceremonies

Fat
to make pemmican

Teeth
necklaces

Bones
scrapers, hoes, knives

Dried Dung
fuel

Bladder
waterproof bag

Liver
to tan hides

Stomach
cooking pots

Hooves
glue

The Siksika depended on resources from nature, primarily the buffalo, to survive. Buffalo were plentiful in pre-Contact times.

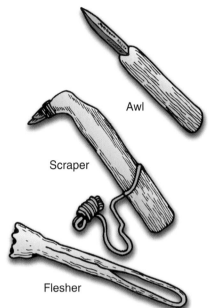

Awl

Scraper

Flesher

The women used tools made of stone or bone to clean hides and make clothing.

Because the buffalo herds moved from place to place, the people moved often too. Thus, shelters had to be portable. Teepees were made from deer or buffalo hides over a frame of poles. These wooden poles were obtained in the foothills where "lodgepole" pines were plentiful. Teepees were taken down when the Siksika moved to a new area. The people took the poles and hides with them.

The Siksika wore clothing made of animal (deer or buffalo) skins. Clothing was sewn with thread made from **sinew**. Warm robes and mittens for winter were made from buffalo hides.

The Siksika used resources that they found in the environment to make tools and other products. Materials like stone, bone, wood, and hide were used. The knowledge and skills for making tools were passed from one generation to the next.

The Siksika had few personal belongings. In summer, they travelled on foot or crossed rivers in bull boats. These were round wooden frames covered with buffalo hides. A **travois** pulled by dogs was used to carry some burdens.*

This woman is pounding berries to add to pemmican.

Sinew—tough, strong fibres that connect muscle to bone
Travois—a wheel-less cart pulled by dogs or horses
*Before Spanish explorers brought horses to North America in the mid-1500s, the dog was the only animal raised by humans for their use. Horses had once existed in the Americas but became extinct about a thousand years before Europeans came to the continent.

Meeting Psychological Needs

The Siksika knew they were just one of the parts of nature. They believed all living things were interconnected. They practised conservation. Only those animals that were needed were killed. The people lived on the land mainly as they found it. They were careful not to upset the balance of nature. They showed respect for all living things.

The Siksika honoured the Creator or Great Spirit. They believed that everything on earth was **sacred** and should be respected. One of the Great Spirit's gifts was sweetgrass. (See the photograph on page 24.)

The Siksika believed strongly in the importance of sharing. Survival depended on co-operation. Everyone was expected to make a contribution, from the elderly to children. Females and males had specific **roles** and jobs to do. Girls and boys learned the knowledge and skills they needed to know from their parents and other adults.

The main roles of young men were as hunters and warriors. They trained from boyhood to acquire the skills and a high level of physical fitness. These were needed both to hunt large game and for defence.

The Siksika did not believe in private ownership of land. They believed the land had been made by the Great Spirit for all to use.

The circle was sacred. Objects such as the teepee, the shield, and the sacred drum showed the circle was an important symbol. The circle was also used to show the cycle of life. Children were an important part of this cycle. They spent a lot of time with their grandparents and the Elders. They learned the culture from them.

The Elders were highly respected for their knowledge of the history and customs of the group. They gave advice. As teachers, they made sure that all members understood the laws and customs. Some Elders led ceremonies. They gave spiritual guidance to their people.

The Siksika did not live in permanent villages. However, small groups of families travelled and lived together. These small bands often joined with other groups for seasonal activities like berry-picking.

Meeting Group Needs

The Siksika followed a consensus model of decision-making. In consensus, no action is taken until all people involved agree with it.

Chiefs did not rule their band, but rather spoke for them at gatherings. At annual gatherings, chiefs made decisions on behalf of the entire Nation about trade or war.

It was important to the Siksika that resources were shared by all so that no one went hungry. Group decisions were respected by everyone.

Sacred—holy; having high spiritual value and given great respect
Role—a part played in life

Review

You will notice some icons on the review pages. These are your cue to refer to the Learning How to Learn Appendix on pages 256–265 or to the Research Model on pages x and xi. These will give strategies on how to do the activities. See the inside front cover for how to access the Arnold Publishing homepage for more information.

Assessment

1. Complete a self-assessment for one assignment from this chapter. See page 263 in the Appendix for ideas.

2.

Section I Presentation Activity

 On page 5 you began preparing for a presentation on the relationship between the environment and the culture of the Wendat (Huron) or the Woodland Cree peoples of Canada.* If you are working with a partner on this project, meet to carry out Steps 1 and 2 (page 262 of the Appendix). Apply the information in this chapter to Steps 3, 4, and 5.

Summarizing the Chapter

3. a) In the Preview Activity on page 7, you started a web of the four major titles in this chapter and two levels of sub-headings. Check that you have at least two details under each sub-heading on your web. Share your work with the class.

   b) Take turns with a partner to **paraphrase** the information under each major title on the Overview on page 6.

---

*See maps on page 53 for the location of the Wendat (Huron) and page 85 for the location of the Woodland Cree.
Paraphrase—to express the meaning of a piece of writing in different words

Understanding Concepts

4. On page 3 you were asked to set up an organization system for your history course. Please refer to this now. Check the organization of your activities for this chapter:
   - chapter title page, notes, activities, maps, illustrations in the Activities section
   - definitions in the WordBook section
   - History Journal and Learning How to Learn writings in the appropriate sections

5. Use one of the strategies for recording vocabulary shown on page 263 of the Appendix to record the following new vocabulary. Put them in the WordBook section of your History binder.

theory	traditional
origins	First Nations

6. Create two concept posters, one on each of the origin theories in this chapter. Concept posters are explained on page 256 of the Appendix.

Developing Communication Skills

Reading and Representing

7. Read Nokomis's Creation story on page 10, or find a copy of Basil Johnston's Creation story in your library. Compare one of these stories with the one on pages 12 and 13.

8. In the library read at least one other Aboriginal Creation story by an Aboriginal author or storyteller. Select something from this that you find interesting and make a picture of it.

Applying Concepts

9. The evidence reported in this textbook was current as of 1999. It will, no doubt, change over the years ahead. If you find new information about the origins of the First Peoples, bring it to school to share and discuss with your classmates. It can be either from a traditional First Nations point of view or from a scientific point of view.

29

Chapter 2
Environmental Interaction

❶ Environmental Interaction

Landforms, climate, and vegetation affected how First Nations cultures developed. The environment influenced the people and the people interacted with and changed the environment.

All of the needs of First Nations people were met from the environment in which they lived. Food, clothing, shelter, and the tools they used came from natural resources.

Balance and harmony were very important. All living things were respected. Interconnections between humans and nature were sacred.

❷ Environment of the Haida

Plentiful resources and travel by water were the bases of the way of life of the peoples of the Northwest Coast.

Chapter 2 Focus

Aboriginal cultures were not all the same.* They were often as different as countries are today. Aboriginal cultures were affected by the environment and the natural resources available. This chapter will look at Canada's environmental regions. Different landforms and climates create different ecosystems. Ecosystems provide plant and animal resources that support different ways of life. Chapter 2 will look at the Haida. The Northwest Coast, where they lived, has both water and land ecosystems.

The focus in this chapter is on the concepts of environmental interaction and balance.

Coastal Ecosystem
An ecosystem is a community of living **organisms**, each one depending in some way on the others. The coastal ecosystem supports a rich variety of life based in the sea, on the shore, and in the zone between, which is exposed when the tide goes out. Many of the sea creatures feed on tiny organisms in the water. They in turn provide food for birds and whales. A coastal ecosystem is especially **vulnerable** to human damage, such as pollution and oil spills.

| Environmental Interaction | Balance | Technology | Cultural Contact | Exploration |

Vocabulary

ecosystem
interconnected
interaction
landforms
climate
precipitation

vegetation
habitat
resources
 (raw materials)
technology
interdependent

Chapter Preview/Prediction

Work with a partner on the following activities:
1. Discuss what you think environmental interaction and balance mean.

2. Examine the visual above right and read the caption. What does ecosystem mean?

3. a) Look at the visuals on page 30 and the titles in this chapter to get an idea of what you will be studying next.
   b) Work with a partner. Look through the chapter and make a web of the chapter's headings and sub-headings.
   c) Look through the chapter's visuals. Record two questions to which you hope to learn the answers by the end of Chapter 2.

*Aboriginal people include Canada's First Nations, Inuit, and Metis people.
Organism—a living body
Vulnerable—sensitive; easily hurt or damaged

Section I Project

Section I Presentation Activity

Use information from this chapter to add to the presentation activity you started on page 5 of Section I.
Do either Question 1 or Question 2.
1. What is the relationship between the environment and the culture of the Wendat in the time before Europeans came to Canada? (Locate the Wendat on the map on page 53.)
2. What is the relationship between the environment and the culture of the Woodland Cree in the time before Europeans came to Canada? (Locate the Woodland Cree on the map on page 85.)

Interactions

• • • • • • • • • • • • • • •

As Dani walked into the classroom she saw a group of students standing in a circle passing a ball of yarn. Yarn crisscrossed the circle every which way. The students held a huge web of interconnected yarn.

"Come join us," encouraged Mrs. Maziuk. "We're demonstrating how the people of the First Nations lived in harmony with nature. They disturbed the ecosystems in which they lived very little.

"We represent a forest ecosystem. Each of us is an animal, a water source, the air, or the soil. We are all interconnected. If anything goes wrong in one part of the circle, we will all be affected."

"Yeah, like this," joked Niels. He pretended to drop his piece of the yarn. Then he caught it again as the web started to tangle.

Mrs. Maziuk continued. "A country such as Canada has many ecosystems. There are

both water and land ecosystems in all regions. Over the next week you will be studying some ecosystems that influenced how Aboriginal peoples lived. I've posted photos of some of these on the bulletin board. Untangle yourselves from the string now. Then I'll give you some questions about environmental interaction."

She took the yarn and the group crowded around the bulletin board. They examined each of the photographs, and discussed the questions Mrs. Maziuk gave them.

Examples of
Canadian Ecosystems

1. the Arctic
2. the coniferous forests of the Subarctic
3. the Northwest Coast
4. the Plains
5. the deciduous forests of Central and Eastern Canada
6. the ocean coast of Atlantic Canada

For Your Notebook

1. What does the ball of yarn in the narrative on the previous page represent?
2. a) What could "go wrong" in the circle?
   b) How would everyone be affected?
   c) How does the ball of yarn demonstrate how the First People lived in harmony with nature?

3. Use a spider definition format (see page 263) to define ecosystem.

4. With a partner describe each ecosystem shown above.

5. a) Record examples to show how plants and animals adapted to the modern-day shoreline ecosystem shown on page 31.

   b) What if . . .
   - the level of the ocean in this ecosystem dropped?
   - sunlight was limited to one hour each day in this ecosystem?
   - a densely populated city was added to this ecosystem?

Environmental Interaction

Environment refers to our surroundings. It includes all the natural parts of a place. Landforms, water, air, and plants and animals are part of environment.

Shaping Culture

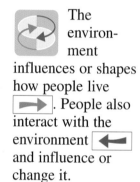 The environment influences or shapes how people live ➡. People also interact with the environment ⬅ and influence or change it.

The environment influenced how the cultures of the First Nations developed. The environment provided nearly everything to meet their needs.

Aboriginal peoples respected and lived in harmony with nature.

Types of Regions

Landform Regions

Landform regions are places with similar features. Mountains, plateaus, hills, and plains are landforms. Mountains are high and rugged. Plateaus are high but fairly level. They are found between or on the edge of large mountain ranges. Hills are lower and less rugged forms of mountains. Plains are found at lower levels. They are usually flat to rolling, and often contain some hills. Valleys are formed by streams and rivers that cut through higher land.

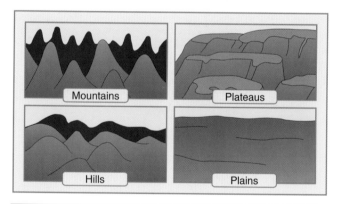

Statistics—information in number form, often displayed in charts and graphs

Climatic Regions

Climatic regions are places with similar weather and seasons. Temperatures, precipitation, and seasonal changes are similar. Rainfall and sunshine affect what plants grow in a climatic region. (See chart inside the back cover for information about climate.)

Precipitation can fall in the form of rain, hail, sleet, or snow. Areas near large bodies of water receive more precipitation than areas farther inland.

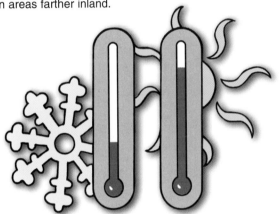

The farther north or the higher up a mountain you go the colder the temperature is. Farther north, summers are shorter and winters longer. Regions with large bodies of water have more moderate climates.

Winds often increase the effects of climate. They may make a region drier or colder, or bring rains to a region.

Vegetation Regions

Vegetation regions are places with similar types of plants. Vegetation is affected by climate.

Tundra vegetation grows in Arctic deserts. This includes mosses, lichens, and low-growing plants and shrubs. The Arctic growing season is very short. Northern areas have permanently frozen ground.

Coniferous trees have needles and cones. Coniferous forests grow where winters are long, but the ground is not frozen all year long. They can grow in shallow soils where rock is close to the surface.

The Northwest Coastal rainforest is mainly coniferous. Rainforests need year-round rainfall and mild climates. Very large trees and many kinds of plants grow in rainforests.

Deciduous trees shed their leaves in the winter. Deciduous forests grow where there is plenty of rainfall, a long warm summer, and four seasons. Mixed forests contain both coniferous and deciduous trees.

Grassland areas with lower rainfall are called prairies. Where there is more rainfall, the grasses are taller and some trees grow.

Mountains contain coniferous forests below the treeline and tundra conditions above the treeline. Mountain valleys may contain grasslands.

Learning How to Learn

Problem Solving

 Problem solving involves considering possible solutions in order to choose the "best" solution to a problem. Often when we are asked to solve a problem such as a math problem, there is one correct answer. Problems related to history often have more than one answer.

There are many ways to solve problems. You will be introduced to some of these ways in this textbook. Use the model on this page to solve the problem on the next page. Make a large chart similar to the one on the bottom right of the next page to record your information.

1 Define the **problem**
What is it you are to find out?

2 Come up with a **hypothesis** to guide your research. (A hypothesis is a rough guess about the solution based on what you know.)

3 Do **research** to locate data (information) about the problem. Gather and examine all relevant **data**.

4 Record information that relates to your hypothesis.

5 **Evaluate** the information by thinking how it relates to the hypothesis. If your hypothesis makes sense, given the facts, proceed to Step 7. If your research data disagree with your hypothesis, do Step 6.

6 Form a new hypothesis if facts disagree with the original hypothesis. You may repeat steps 2, 3, 4, and 5 until your hypothesis makes sense to you and **solves** the problem.

7 Write up your **conclusion**. Share your conclusion.

8 **Thinking About Thinking** What have you learned? How can you apply what you learned?

An Exercise in Problem Solving

Part 1 This exercise involves a study of the Haida. Locate these people on the map on page 45.

It is suggested that you work in pairs or triads for this activity. Follow the Problem Solving steps on the previous page. Complete one chart per group.

Step 1: Record the problem on the chart you've made. **❶**

What part did the environment of the Northwest Coast play in shaping the culture of the Haida?

Read **Step 2** of the problem solving model on the previous page. Think of an hypothesis to guide your research. Record it on your chart. **❷**

In **Step 3** you carry out research. Divide the questions on the right between your group members. Use the information on pages 39–43 to answer the questions. Answers will not be found on any one page, map, or photograph. Use your imagination and thinking abilities to combine information, like solving a puzzle from clues. **❸**

Step 4: Record only the information that relates to your hypothesis under **❹**. (Hint: Reread the problem and your hypothesis again.)

(You will be continuing this exercise on page 45.)

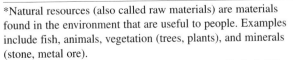

---

*Natural resources (also called raw materials) are materials found in the environment that are useful to people. Examples include fish, animals, vegetation (trees, plants), and minerals (stone, metal ore).

**In First Nation cultures men and women usually had different roles and used different tools for doing specific types of work.

Questions to Guide Research

1. Look at the landform map and photographs on page 38. How did the landforms in the area where the Haida lived affect their culture?

2. a) Look at the climate map and photos on page 39. How might the climate affect them?
   b) How would seasons affect their food supply?

3. How did the way of life that developed depend on the vegetation? (See page 40.)

4. a) What natural resources* were used? (See pages 38, and 40–43.)
   b) How do you think the people used these resources?

5. a) What types of tools** were made and used? (See especially page 43.)
   b) How did making tools help extend the people's control over their environment?

6. a) How did they meet their food needs?
   b) How did the area in which they lived influence the way they obtained their food?

7. a) How did the area in which they lived influence their shelter?
   b) What type of shelter do you think the people had—temporary, portable, or permanent?

8. What resources do you think these people used to make their clothing?

❶ **Problem**	
❷ **Hypothesis**	**Evaluate** (Do step ❺. If your research data support your hypothesis, go to ❼. If your research data disagree with your hypothesis, do step ❻.)
❸ **Research** (Do research. Put your findings in your notebook.) ❹ (Record information that relates to your hypothesis.)	
❼ **Conclusion**	
❽ **Thinking About Thinking**	

Environmental Regions

Landform Regions

Note that the outline colours of the photographs match the colours on the map legend. The numbers refer to the map on page 19. Regions not studied in this book may not have photos.

Geography—
☑ Map
☐ Diagram
☐ Statistics
☑ Picture

Raw Materials from Nature

(Some examples)
earth (clay, mud)
ice blocks
copper, silver (metals)
snow (hard)
stone
tar

Legend:
☐ Innuitian Mountains
☐ Arctic Lowlands
☐ Cordillera
☐ Great Plains
☐ Canadian Shield
☐ Great Lakes and St. Lawrence Lowlands
☐ Appalachian Mountains

Landforms influence what resources are available for meeting basic needs, such as materials for building homes and making tools.

Photographs

1. Hunters
2. Fishers
3. Gatherers and Hunters
4. Hunters and Gatherers
5. Farmers and Hunters
6. Hunters and Fishers

38

Climatic Regions

Note that the outline colours of the photographs match the colours on the map legend. The numbers refer to the map on page 19. Regions not studied in this book may not have photos.

Geography—
☑ Map
☐ Diagram
☐ Statistics
☑ Picture

Legend:
- Arctic
- Subarctic
- Continental
- Maritime
- Semi-arid
- Mediterranean
- Highland

The climate of an area determines what food, water, and materials for clothing and shelter are available to meet life's basic needs. Climate particularly affects vegetation. All regions on this page have four seasons.

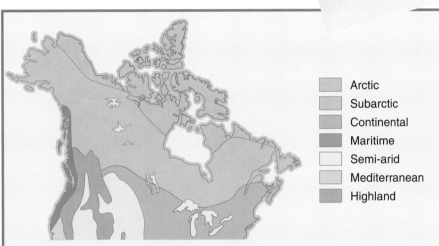

Photographs
1. Hunters
2. Fishers
3. Gatherers and Hunters
4. Hunters and Gatherers
5. Farmers and Hunters
6. Hunters and Fishers

Vegetation Regions

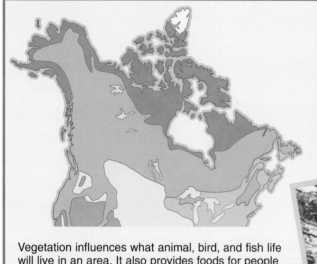

Note that the outline colours of the photographs match the colours on the map legend. The numbers refer to the map on page 19. Regions not studied in this book may not have photos.

Geography—
☑ Map
☐ Diagram
☐ Statistics
☑ Picture

Raw Materials from Nature

(Some examples)
- bark
- berries
- corn husks
- inner bark (of cedar, spruce, birch, willow)
- logs, wood
- plant leaves
- plant roots
- plant seeds
- tree branches, twigs
- vines

- ▨ Tundra
- ▨ Coniferous forest
- ▨ Deciduous–coniferous forest
- ▨ Grassland (prairie)
- ▨ Desert shrub
- ▨ Mediterranean scrub forest

Vegetation influences what animal, bird, and fish life will live in an area. It also provides foods for people and materials for making homes and tools.

Photographs

1 Hunters

2 Fishers

3 Gatherers and Hunters

4 Hunters and Gatherers

5 Farmers and Hunters

6 Hunters and Fishers

Animal Habitats

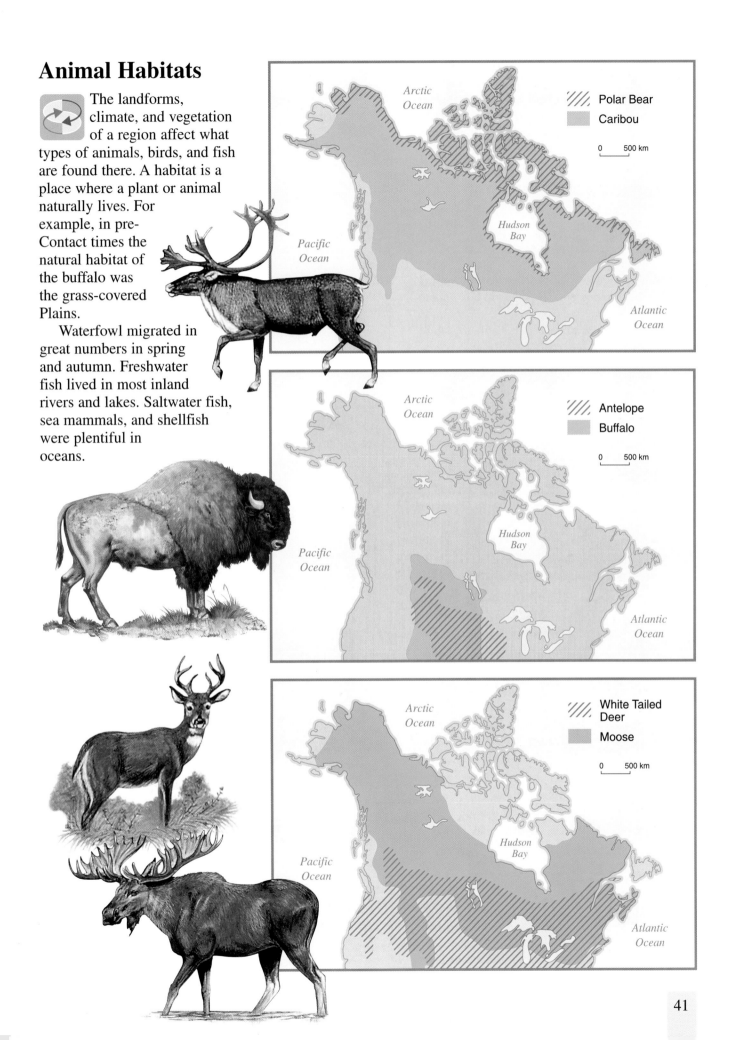

The landforms, climate, and vegetation of a region affect what types of animals, birds, and fish are found there. A habitat is a place where a plant or animal naturally lives. For example, in pre-Contact times the natural habitat of the buffalo was the grass-covered Plains.

Waterfowl migrated in great numbers in spring and autumn. Freshwater fish lived in most inland rivers and lakes. Saltwater fish, sea mammals, and shellfish were plentiful in oceans.

Arctic Ocean

Pacific Ocean

Hudson Bay

Atlantic Ocean

Polar Bear
Caribou

0   500 km

Arctic Ocean

Pacific Ocean

Hudson Bay

Atlantic Ocean

Antelope
Buffalo

0   500 km

Arctic Ocean

Pacific Ocean

Hudson Bay

Atlantic Ocean

White Tailed Deer
Moose

0   500 km

Fur-bearing Animals

Forested regions with cold winters were the habitat of the animals with the warmest fur pelts.

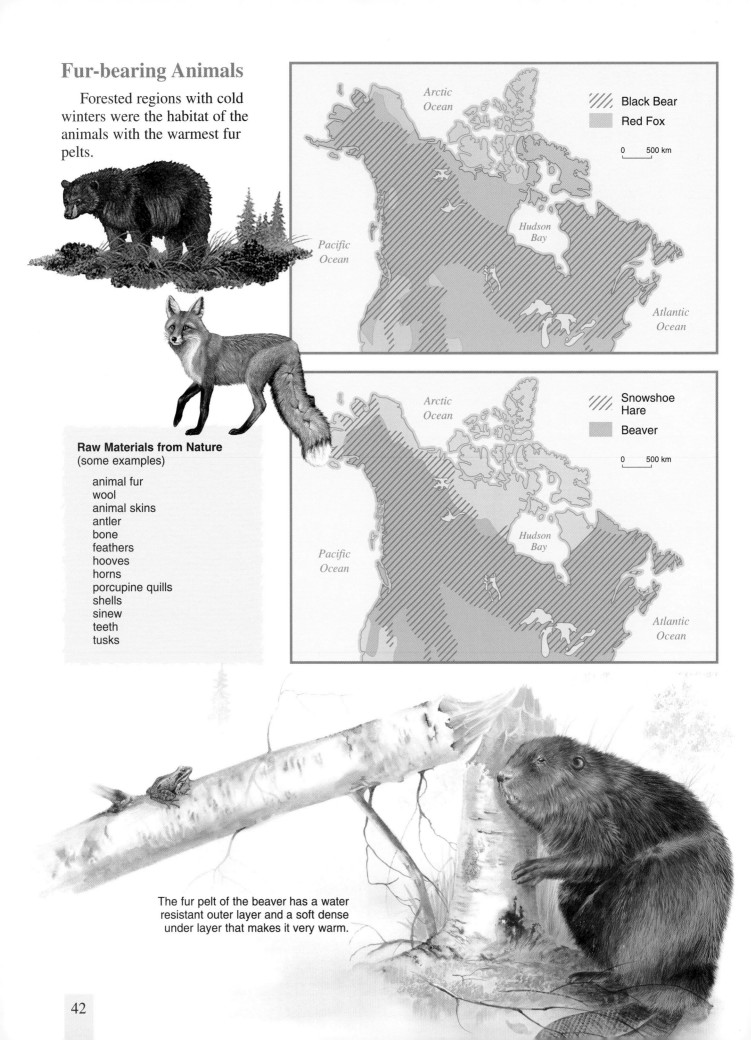

Black Bear
Red Fox

0   500 km

Arctic Ocean

Pacific Ocean

Hudson Bay

Atlantic Ocean

Snowshoe Hare

Beaver

0   500 km

Arctic Ocean

Pacific Ocean

Hudson Bay

Atlantic Ocean

Raw Materials from Nature
(some examples)

- animal fur
- wool
- animal skins
- antler
- bone
- feathers
- hooves
- horns
- porcupine quills
- shells
- sinew
- teeth
- tusks

The fur pelt of the beaver has a water resistant outer layer and a soft dense under layer that makes it very warm.

Resources from Nature

  The technology of a culture includes all the ways people change or use raw materials to make what they need. Raw materials are also called resources. First Nations people used resources from their environment to meet their needs. Plant and animal products, minerals, and other resources served many practical purposes.

Uses of Natural Resources

The First Peoples used resources to create technology to meet their basic needs and make their lives easier or more comfortable. These included tools for killing game, harvesting food, cutting or grinding food, making clothing, and building shelters. Their means of transportation were also important. In the chart below are some examples of uses of resources.

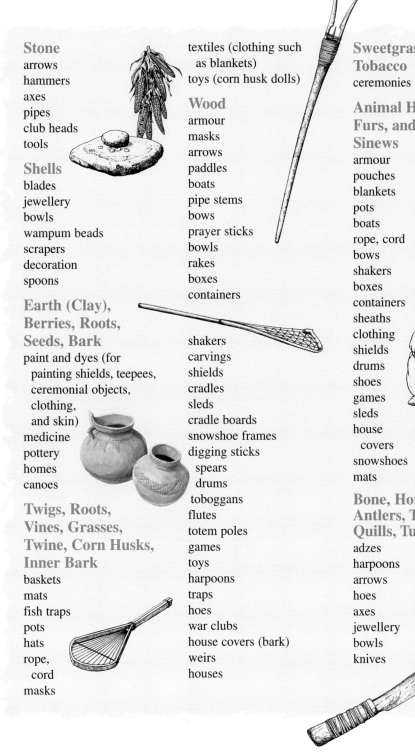

Stone
arrows
hammers
axes
pipes
club heads
tools

Shells
blades
jewellery
bowls
wampum beads
scrapers
decoration
spoons

Earth (Clay), Berries, Roots, Seeds, Bark
paint and dyes (for
  painting shields, teepees,
  ceremonial objects,
  clothing,
  and skin)
medicine
pottery
homes
canoes

Twigs, Roots, Vines, Grasses, Twine, Corn Husks, Inner Bark
baskets
mats
fish traps
pots
hats
rope,
  cord
masks

textiles (clothing such
  as blankets)
toys (corn husk dolls)

Wood
armour
masks
arrows
paddles
boats
pipe stems
bows
prayer sticks
bowls
rakes
boxes
containers

shakers
carvings
shields
cradles
sleds
cradle boards
snowshoe frames
digging sticks
  spears
  drums
  toboggans
flutes
totem poles
games
toys
harpoons
traps
hoes
war clubs
house covers (bark)
weirs
houses

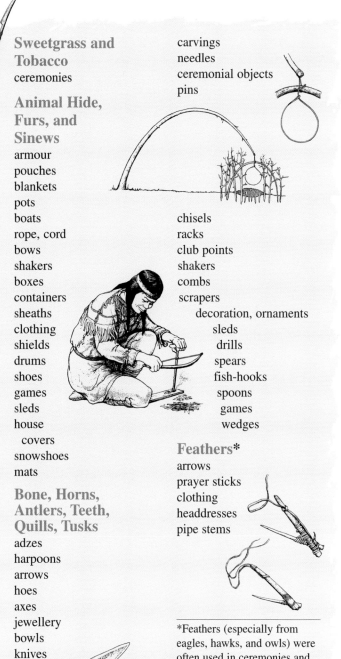

Sweetgrass and Tobacco
ceremonies

Animal Hide, Furs, and Sinews
armour
pouches
blankets
pots
boats
rope, cord
bows
shakers
boxes
containers
sheaths
clothing
shields
drums
shoes
games
sleds
house
  covers
snowshoes
mats

Bone, Horns, Antlers, Teeth, Quills, Tusks
adzes
harpoons
arrows
hoes
axes
jewellery
bowls
knives

carvings
needles
ceremonial objects
pins

chisels
racks
club points
shakers
combs
scrapers
  decoration, ornaments
    sleds
    drills
    spears
    fish-hooks
      spoons
      games
      wedges

Feathers*
arrows
prayer sticks
clothing
headdresses
pipe stems

*Feathers (especially from eagles, hawks, and owls) were often used in ceremonies and offerings. They were considered special and sacred.

43

Learning How to Learn

Thinking as an Archaeologist

Tools, weapons, clothing, and means of transportation are artifacts. The artifacts of a culture include all the objects that people made, using their skills and knowledge.

The following are questions people considered when making an artifact from a natural resource:

- How rare or how common is the material?
- Is the material local or was it traded into the area?
- How rare or common is the skill to work with the material or make the artifact?
- How long-lasting or hard-wearing is the material or artifact?
- How well does the material take a sharp edge and stay sharp?
- How can the material be sharpened?
- Is the material watertight or airtight?
- Can the artifact be made watertight or airtight?
- Will the material or artifact withstand heat or cold?
- What materials and what methods can be used to connect or attach parts together?
- How can the material be cut, shaped, sharpened, or combined with other materials?
- Is the material or artifact used for survival?
- Is the material or artifact used for ceremony?
- Is the material or artifact used to show the importance of the person who has it?

For Your Notebook

1. Re-examine the information on Raw Materials from Nature on pages 38, 40, and 42 for regions in what is now Ontario.
   a) When Aboriginal peoples from what is now Ontario used these raw materials, did they permanently change the environment? Explain.
   b) What else could be added to the lists on page 43?
   c) What raw materials are used/gathered in your community? How does the gathering and use of these materials affect the natural environment?
2. Select three items from page 43. For each indicate
   a) name and description
   b) where, how the item was likely used
   c) what raw materials were used
   d) who probably used this tool (e.g., men, women, hunters, fishers)
   e) what special skills were required to make this item
3. Select two different items from page 43 and answer any five questions from the Learning How to Learn section on the left for each item.

Exploring Further

4. Imagine you are being sent alone to the uninhabited area nearest to your home to survive for a week. Which ten items from the lists of raw materials on pages 38, 40, and 43 would you take? Explain what you would use each item for.

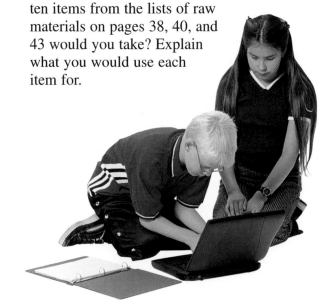

Environment of the Haida*

An Exercise in Problem Solving

Part 2 continued from page 37

The case study that follows provides some information on the relationship between the Haida and their environment. It is not a complete overview of the culture of the Haida. Only information relating to the problem you are solving from page 37 is included.

Review the problem solving model on page 36.

1. Read pages 45–48. Remember the problem you are solving: What part did the environment of the Northwest Coast play in shaping the culture of the Haida?
2. **Steps 3** and **4**: Add to your research notes any new information that relates to the questions you were answering on page 37.

(You will be continuing this exercise on page 48.)

Environment

The ecosystem of the Northwest Coast had great influence on how the people lived.

Landforms
Cordillera Landform Region (see page 38)

- high mountains near coast (ocean), valleys, plateaus, shoreline
- numerous islands
- deep, narrow inlets, swift rivers

Note: The map to the right uses the names that the First Nations prefer to call themselves. Spellings may be different in other books.
*The information in this case study refers to the pre-Contact period. Many First Nations people still have traditional lifestyles.
**See chart on inside back cover.

Climate
Maritime Climatic Region (see page 39)

- warm to mild temperatures and moderate to heavy precipitation**

Vegetation
Coniferous Forest Vegetation Region (see page 40)

- heavily forested area (rainforest)
- cedar is main type of tree
- plentiful plant life

Cedar trees and salmon were the main resources from the region.

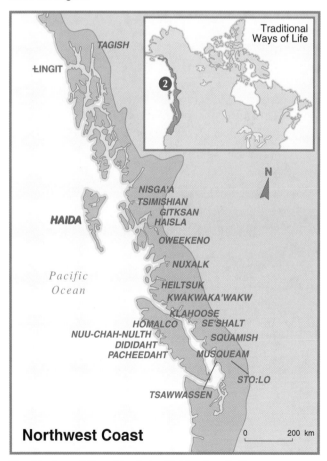

Northwest Coast

The Northwest Coast had plentiful food and other resources. First Nations in this region had similar cultures but a number of different languages. Among the First Nations that lived in this area, trade was common.

The sea and land of the Northwest Coast provided plentiful resources, such as fish, game, and building materials. The Haida, like the Nuxalk people shown above, used cedar canoes for travel and fishing.

Environmental Interaction

  The environment of the Northwest Coast influenced how the people lived. The Haida lived in the environment mainly as they found it. They were careful not to upset the balance of nature. They knew they were just one of the many interconnected parts of nature.

The ocean was the source of much of their wealth, but it was also very dangerous. They respected the power of nature and gave thanks for all that was given to them by the ocean and land.

The Haida people adapted to the land, climate, and vegetation in which they lived. They built their homes along the sheltered beaches of the coast, where it was easy to get food and travel the ocean.

The amount of rainfall in the area and the mild climate affected the type of clothing and housing the Haida had. Cedar bark and goat hair (among other natural resources) were used to make clothing.

Cone-shaped hats were designed to keep off the rain. They built huge canoes from the red cedar tree. Canoes were used to obtain food from the ocean and to trade with other nations.

A typical village consisted of 30 large cedar plank dwellings. Each held several families. Each family had its own area. They shared cooking fires. There were raised wooden platforms for sleeping and storage around the outside walls. Houses and villages were permanent. Possessions such as baskets, storage containers, and furniture were common in the Haida culture.

The Haida obtained abundant food from the ocean and rivers. They also got products from the forest. They only cut as many trees and captured as many fish as they needed for use or trade. The people lived in balance with the environment. The population of the Northwest Coast region was large, but the environment provided plentiful resources. It could easily support many people.

The Haida used the resources available to them. Stone, bone, wood, root fibres, and animal hides were used to make tools. The skills and knowledge for making tools were passed from one generation to the next. Some examples of tools used by the Haida are

- axes and **adzes** (stone with wooden handles)
- chisels (stone)
- knives (bone, beaver teeth, shell)
- sandpaper (shark skin)
- harpoon (wood, antler, shell)
- mortar and pestle for grinding food (stone)

Items not found in the environment were obtained through trade. **Surplus** items were traded. Trade routes existed up and down the coast (including the coastal islands). Traders crossed the mountains to the interior. Shells, hides, furs, blankets, copper, and fish oil were common trade items. The oil from the **oolichan** was an important trade resource. It was burned as fuel for light.

In the painting above the hunter is using a harpoon to hunt a whale.

Cedar, which was plentiful, was the main building material. The home and totem poles above were made by Tlingit peoples, who lived north of the Haida in a similar environment.

Resources from the Ocean and Its Shores

(Some examples)
- birds
- bird eggs
- black cod
- clams
- crab
- halibut
- herring
- mussels
- oolichan (candle fish)
- porpoise
- salmon
- sea lion
- sea otter
- fur seals
- seaweed
- whale

legend
- for food
- for food and oil
- for furs and food

Resources from the Forest

(Some examples)
- beaver
- berries
- bird eggs
- black bear
- cranberries
- deer
- ducks
- elk
- geese
- grizzly bear
- herbs
- huckleberries
- inner bark
- oils
- plants
- roots
- squirrel
- strawberries
- spruce roots
- trees

legend
- for cooking and healing
- for furs and food
- for food
- for building and making things

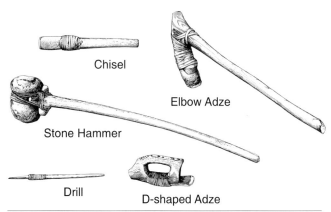

Chisel

Elbow Adze

Stone Hammer

Drill

D-shaped Adze

Adze—a tool for shaping wood
Surplus—more than what is needed for existence
Oolichan—a small, very oily fish used for food and oil

Balance

 Everyone among the Haida knew his or her place and the place of all things in nature. They knew how important they were, and the specific roles they had in life. Female and male Haida of all ages had specific roles and jobs to do. Everyone respected the contributions made by other people. They respected the plants and animals that helped them meet their basic needs. In this way harmony and balance were maintained.

The environment provided generously for the Haida people. Thus, not all people had to work all of the time to make sure they survived. Some people worked as artists. Both women and men had time to decorate their possessions. The Haida developed beautiful art forms. Carvers and painters created ceremonial face masks, canoe **prows**, wooden chests, and bowls. The totem pole, carved from the trunk of a cedar tree, is their most famous art form. Poles often stood at the front of a dwelling and showed the history of the families living in the house.

An Exercise in Problem Solving

Part 3

Remember the problem you are solving: What part did the environment of the Northwest Coast play in shaping the culture of the Haida people?

Steps 5 – 8: Reread what you wrote for 4. Does it support (relate to) your hypothesis? If it does, go on to **Steps 7 and 8** on page 36.

If what you wrote down disagrees with your hypothesis you'll have to form a new hypothesis. Go to **Step 6** on page 36. (Repeat Steps 2, 3, 4, and 5 until your hypothesis makes sense to you and solves the problem.)

The peoples of the Northwest Coast showed their relationship with the environment in their art, ceremonies, and dances. Animals, birds, and fish were carved and painted on homes, totem poles, canoes, containers, and ceremonial clothing. Tlingit longhouses, such as the one shown above, were built in a similar way to those of the Haida.

Canada Revisited

Modern-day artisans from the Northwest Coast create totem pole designs based on traditional symbols of their ancestors. Cedar is still the material most frequently used for totem poles.

Prow—the front part of a boat

Review

The icons on this page are your cue to turn to the Learning How to Learn Appendix (pages 256–265). It contains ideas on how to complete these activities. This icon is a reminder to turn to the Research Model (pages x and xi).

Assessment

1. Complete a self-assessment for one assignment from this chapter.

2.
Section I Presentation Activity
Just a reminder to work on the projects you will use in your presentation. See pages 5, 31, and 262.

Summarizing the Chapter

3. In the preview activity on page 31, you were asked to make a web based on the headings and sub-headings in the chapter. Use a different coloured pen to add details based on what you have learned. Answer the two questions you wrote.

Understanding Concepts

4. Check the organization of your activities for this chapter in your binder:
   - chapter title page, notes, activities, maps, and illustrations in Activities section
   - definitions in WordBook section
   - History Journal writing
   - Learning How to Learn section

5. Here are some of the main ideas from the chapter:
   - interaction between environment and people (environmental interaction)
   - balance

   Do either a) or b)
   a) Create a concept poster about one of the above ideas. Present your poster to the class. (See page 256 for ideas on concept posters.)
   b) Use a web, mind map, outline, or chart to create a permanent set of notes about one of the above ideas. Explain your work to a classmate. (See pages 257 and 261 for ideas.)

6. What does respect mean? Why do you think First Nations people respected the balance and harmony of the land in which they lived?

7. How did a culture (way of life) that developed depend on the kinds of natural resources available?

8. Why do some Aboriginal people say: "Take only what you need from the land?"

Developing Research Skills

9. 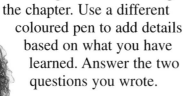 a) Develop a list of questions you could ask an Elder to find out about these topics:
   - how interaction with the environment by his/her people has changed over time
   - how his/her culture has changed and how it has stayed the same over time and why
   b) Why is it important to develop good questions for doing research?

Chapter 3
The Wendat
A Case Study

The information in this chapter refers to the pre-Contact period. Many First Nations people still live traditional lifestyles.

O v e r v i e w

Use this Overview to predict the events of this chapter.

❶ People and Land

The way of life of the Wendat was based on the cycle of the seasons.

❷ Economic Part of Culture

A large population was able to live in semi-permanent villages because of plentiful natural resources and farming.

❸ Social Part of Culture

The Wendat believed in the interconnectedness of all things. They had a matrilineal clan system. Children were part of their mother's clan. Family was important. Elders were respected.

❹ Political Part of Culture

The Wendat had an organized society. Male chiefs represented the people in the Councils and the Clan Mothers provided advice to the Council.

Chapter 3 Focus

Chapter 3 looks at the Wendat people, who lived in North America before the first Europeans arrived. (Many resources may call these people the Huron.) The way of life of the Wendat was based on the cycle of the seasons. The environment had a great influence on how they lived. Refer to pages 38–43 in Chapter 2 for geography information while studying this chapter. Chapter 3 uses basic needs as a way to classify information.

This chapter will focus on the following concepts. It will emphasize environmental interaction, balance, and technology.

Environmental Interaction | Balance | Technology | Cultural Contact | Exploration

Vocabulary

seasonal cycle
communal
trade
clan
matriarchal
extended family
spirituality

values
traditions
customs
symbols
Council meetings
consensus

In narratives, certain words may be written with a capital letter when you don't expect it. This is a sign of great respect for something or someone.

The word Iroquoian is used to refer to a group of nations with related languages and similar cultures. Iroquoian-speaking peoples lived north and south of Lake Ontario in what is now Canada and the United States, and in the valley of the St. Lawrence River. The name Iroquois has been used in many historical sources to refer to the members of the Five Nations Confederacy. They lived south of Lake Ontario in the pre-Contact period. (This alliance became the Six Nations in the 1700s.)

This textbook will refer to the different nations by individual name when possible.

Chapter Preview/Prediction

1. Examine the overview found on the previous page, and the visuals and titles in this chapter.
   a) Based on these, discuss with a partner what you think this chapter is about.

b) Predict answers to the questions in a copy of the Prediction Chart shown below. Put your predictions in the "My Predictions" column.*

Prediction Chart—What Do You Think?		
Questions	My Predictions (fill out now)	What I Found Out (fill out at end of chapter)
1. How did the environment influence how the Wendat lived? How did they interact with and change the environment?		
2. How did the Wendat maintain harmony with nature? How did they respect all living things?		
3. How did the technology the Wendat used affect their way of life?		
4. What contacts were made with other cultures? How did this affect the Wendat way of life?		

Section 1 Presentation Activity

 Use information from this chapter to add to the presentation activity you started on pages 5 and 31 of Section 1. Do either question 1 or question 2. If you selected Wendat, use the information from this chapter.

 Refer to page 262 in the Appendix for presentation ideas to share your learning with others.

*Your teacher may provide you with a full-sized working copy of the Prediction Chart.

51

People and Land

 All forms of life, including people, are influenced by the land, climate, and vegetation of the area in which they live. The Wendat interacted with their environment to meet their needs. Their culture was well-adapted to their surroundings.

The Wendat believed that interconnectedness with nature was important. The people respected all living things. Thus, their way of life helped maintain the balance of nature.

For Your Notebook

1. Locate the homeland of the Wendat people on the maps on the next page and page 19.
2. Use the map on page 53, plus the ones on pages 38–42 to
   a) describe the environment of the Wendat (landforms, climate, vegetation, animals)
   b) describe what knowledge and skills would be necessary for survival in this type of environment.
3. Use the information on the environment you gathered in question 2 to make predictions on how you think the environment affected how the people lived.

This painting by artist Lewis Parker shows a busy day around a Wendat village.

Iroquoian Peoples

The Iroquoian-speaking peoples lived near the Great Lakes and the St. Lawrence River. The map below shows their approximate locations before Europeans arrived in the area. Although the Iroquoian nations had related languages, some groups were in conflict with others. They formed **alliances** to maintain peace and carry on trade. Each nation had a distinct culture (way of life).

This chapter examines the culture and environment of the Wendat nation. The Wendat were an Iroquoian-speaking nation.

See page 19 for information about Traditional Ways of Life.

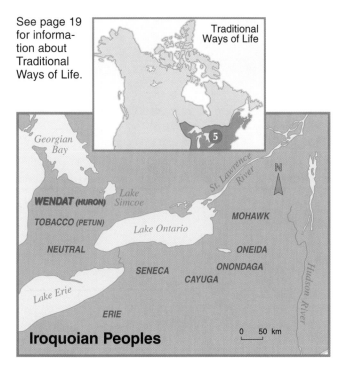

Iroquoian Peoples

Environment

The forest-covered rolling hills of the region where the Wendat lived contained many lakes and small rivers. The environment was able to provide enough food for a large population. The people hunted a variety of animals living in the forest and waterfowl. They also fished. (For information on habitats, see pages 41 and 42.)

Landforms: Great Lakes and St. Lawrence Lowlands Landform Region (see page 38)

- hills, valleys, lakes
- very **fertile** land

Climate: Continental Climate Region (see page 39)

- hot summers
- medium to heavy precipitation*
- cold, snowy winters
- four distinct seasons

Vegetation: Deciduous-Coniferous Forest Region (see page 40)

- mixed forests of many types of trees, including maple, beech, oak, spruce, pine

Iroquois Confederacy (League)	Wendat Alliance
Cayuga Mohawk Oneida Onondaga Seneca	Wendat (Huron) Tobacco (Petun) Neutral Erie

All of the above people were included in the Iroquoian language family. Some other Iroquoian-speaking nations lived farther east.

The people of the Wendat Alliance were mainly in what is now Ontario. The people of the Iroquois Confederacy were in what is now the United States. The Tuscarora lived south of the area shown on the map. They joined the Iroquois Confederacy in the early 1700s.

Alliance—an agreement between nations or groups that benefits those in the union; the League of Five Nations and Iroquois Confederacy both were alliances

Fertile—rich soil; able to grow crops

*See chart on the inside back cover.

53

Seasonal Cycles

 The ways of life of First Nations people were closely tied to seasonal changes. Thus, understanding these changes was important. It was important to know what food and resources were available in different places at different times of the year.

The circle to the right symbolizes the continuous cycle of the seasons. Activities were planned and organized around the seasons.

= Environment

Spring

The Wendat people started in spring to prepare the earth for growing crops. Most of the food for the year ahead was grown in these fields.

Summer

The map below shows a typical Wendat camp during the summer season. In the summer the women, older people, and children moved to small bark shelters in the fields. These temporary summer homes are shown on the map below as ▲. In summer, women weeded crops, gathered herbs and medicines, and made repairs. The children and older people chased away birds and small animals to keep them from eating the crops. The men left the village for hunting, fishing, and trading expeditions.

Autumn

During the autumn, deer were hunted in **communal** hunts. The Wendat mainly hunted deer for their hides and fat. They built triangular enclosures and chased herds of deer into them. Hunters waited there with bows and arrows to shoot them. An illustration is shown on page 66.

Winter

During winter, clothing was made and tools and weapons made and repaired. Winter was also the time for stories, games, dancing, and music. It was the time for creating art and decorating clothing.

For Your Notebook

1. Working with a partner, study the map below. Make a web to record at least 10 things you have learned from this map about the way the Wendat people lived.
2. Record any questions about Wendat life that you cannot answer from the map. As you go through this chapter, look for answers to these questions.

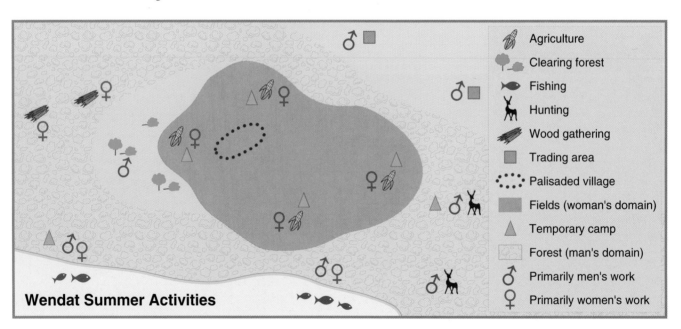

Wendat Summer Activities

Agriculture
Clearing forest
Fishing
Hunting
Wood gathering
Trading area
Palisaded village
Fields (woman's domain)
Temporary camp
Forest (man's domain)
♂ Primarily men's work
♀ Primarily women's work

Communal—activity done co-operatively by a group and the proceeds shared by everyone

Canada Revisited

Symbols: Tribute to Mother Earth

Courtesy of J.C. Hill Elementary School

The mural above, *Tribute to Mother Earth*, created by Onondaga artist Arnold Jacobs, is in J. C. Hill Elementary School in the village of Ohsweken, Ontario.

. . . I have tried to utilize those symbols created by our ancestors. The outside rings represent the four seasons, from spring to winter. The blue ring represents the oceans that encompass the world. The smaller blue circles represent the smaller bodies of Water like the lakes and seas. The wavy blue lines are the rivers that feed the lakes and seas.

The green ring signifies the grass, trees, and other plants that grow on the Earth. The Earth is represented by a reddish brown ring. The reddish-brown colour also symbolizes Native People. The light blue core with four open ends represents the infinity of the Sky.

Within that Sky flies the spiritual eagle, a symbolic messenger to the Creator. Centered above the eagle is the Supporter of Life, our Elder Brother, the Sun (red). Our Grandmother, the Moon (yellow) is there to guide us at night.

The four directions of north, south, east and west frame the eagle. The black colour signifies the power of nature, over which we have no control. The black bars also separate the four winds that regularly affect our lives.

—Arnold Jacobs, an Onondaga artist
living on the Six Nations Reserve in Ontario

For Your Notebook

1. The Wendat planned the year's activities based on seasonal changes.
   a) What seasonal changes in the environment would affect the way the Wendat met their basic needs? (For more information on their environment, review pages 38–40 and page 53.)
   b) 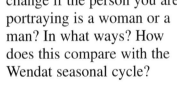 Create a graphic organizer to make notes on seasonal activities by which the Wendat met their physical needs. Organize by season. Whose responsibility is each job? What tools will they need? (See page 257 for information about Charts and Graphic Organizers.)
   c) Much more information about the economic part of the Wendat culture follows on pages 56–69. Add to your chart as you notice references to the seasons.
2. Create a pictorial calendar based on the Wendat seasonal cycle. Copy the circle diagram on page 54 onto a large sheet of paper and illustrate the seasons.

Exploring Further

3.  In pairs, role-play a dialogue between a modern-day outdoor worker and an indoor worker. Describe how their work changes with the seasons. (Examples of outdoor workers are gardeners, letter carriers, bus drivers, road workers. Does your role-play change if the person you are portraying is a woman or a man? In what ways? How does this compare with the Wendat seasonal cycle?

Economic Part of Culture

The economic part of culture deals with meeting physical needs. The Wendat people met their needs in various ways:

- They took resources directly from the environment by hunting, fishing, or gathering.
- They used some resources in their original form and made others into products.
- Their main food supply came from farming.
- They traded resources or products for items not available locally.

Technology

People develop technology to change raw materials into something needed. Technology includes new skills, ideas, and tools for making life easier or more comfortable. For example, the Wendat tanned hides to make them stronger and more flexible. This required knowledge and skill. Women and men had different roles. They had special tools for doing their work. The scrapers and fleshers that women used to prepare hides are examples of technology. The bows and arrows used by men are also technology.

The Wendat used the raw materials available in their environment. They made tools, weapons, containers, and other useful items. They also traded to obtain raw materials not available locally. For example, several types of hard stone used for making tools were widely traded among Aboriginal groups. (See map of the **trading networks** of Aboriginal peoples on page 69.)

The Wendat made clay pottery, birchbark baskets, and stone, wood, and bone tools. Much knowledge and skill are needed to make products such as these.

Trading network—travel routes and contacts with many groups used to trade surplus resources and goods for others that are needed

Homes

The Wendat lived in an environment with plentiful resources and raised food by farming. There was plenty of food for everyone. This allowed the Wendat to live in large groups in semi-permanent villages. The people lived in structures called longhouses. Village size varied from just a few to up to 100 longhouses. All the raw materials needed for the longhouse came from the environment. Most villages were enclosed in a **palisade**.*

Everyone lived very close together, so getting along was very important. Respect, caring, and sharing were important values.

For Your Notebook

1. Review the maps on pages 38–43. What raw materials would the Wendat obtain from their environment to make tools and homes?
2. Examine the illustrations and photographs on pages 57–60, and read the story on pages 61–63. How did the environment influence the kind of shelter the Wendat had?
3. Work with a partner to start a list of the types of work that Wendat women and men did. Add to this list as you go through the chapter.

Each longhouse provided shelter for a number of families, all related through their female members.

Palisade—a wall or fence surrounding a group of buildings
*Archaeologists have recently questioned information about palisades. Some scholars say not all villages had palisades. They say palisade walls were not solid but had openings where people could go through. The reconstructed village shown on pages 57–60 was based on historical information available at the time it was built.

Focus On: A Traditional Wendat Village

The photographs on pages 57–60 were taken in a reconstructed Wendat village near Midland, Ontario. The descriptions were provided by the village.* Refer to the map on this page while studying the photographs. The numbers on the photographs correspond with numbers on the map. They show where the photograph was taken or where the activity described takes place.

The two photographs below illustrate how the palisade was thought to be constructed.

*The text on pages 58–60 has been provided by permission of Huronia Museum and Huron–Ouendat Village, 549 Little Lake Park, Midland, Ontario, L4R 4P4, where the photographs were taken.

Focus On: A Traditional Wendat Village

Inside the Longhouse

Site ❶ Entrance

The narrow winding entrance controls access to the village, protecting its inhabitants from wolves, bears, and unwelcomed people. A surrounding fence, or palisade, also provides protection against strong winds and blowing snow.

Site ❷ Longhouse

Each longhouse accommodates an extended family unit consisting of the female members of a family with their husbands and unmarried children. Approximately 30 people, including grandparents, aunts, uncles, cousins, parents and siblings, live here.

Site ❸ Tool Making

[This site] is used for sharpening and polishing stone tools such as axes, gouges, and chisels.*

Site ❹ Bone Pit (no photo)

The Wendat believe that all natural objects have a Spirit. Although animal bones can be used for tools, bones not in use are protected in a special pit. This respect shown to the Spirits maintains a sacred balance between the human, natural, and spiritual worlds, and promises good hunting in the future for the Wendat.

Site ❺ Sweat Lodge

The sweat lodge is a sacred place for communal prayer used during religious ceremonies and curing rites.** Stones are heated and rolled into the lodge where the Wendat sing and pray to the Spirit world. After each prayer, Water is poured onto the stones, creating an intense heat and steam which cleanses the body and purifies the soul.

Site ❻ Fish Racks

Huge quantities of fish and meat are dried and smoked over an open fire. Fish is consumed daily with corn, beans, and squash in a dish known as sagamite. Meats are usually reserved for feasts and special ceremonies.

Site ❼ Corn Grinding

Over 60% of the Wendat diet consists of corn. This corn is dried in the fall and stored in containers in the longhouse. Dried corn is ground into flour for soups and breads using a wooden mortar and pestle or large grinding stones.

---

*Square brackets mean words have been replaced by a different way of saying something.

**Not all Iroquoian-speaking peoples had sweat lodges.

Site ⑧ Burial Rack (no photo)

Upon death, the deceased is placed on a burial rack usually located outside the village. After four months, the remains are reburied in the village cemetery. Every [10–15] years, the village moves in search of new farm land. Before leaving, a Feast of the Dead ceremony is held to bury all the deceased in a large communal pit.

Site ⑨ [Healer's] Lodge

The [healer] or medicine man is held in high esteem. His powers are revealed to him through dreams, visions, and his contact with the Spirit world. There are four kinds of [healer]: those who control the weather, those who predict future events, those who find lost objects, and those who treat and cure disease. In the lodge are okis, which are objects that possess a special power and assist the [healer] in his work.

Site ⑩ Storage Pits (no photo)

Corn, nuts, and dried meats are stored in underground bark containers.

Site ⑪ Cutting Fire (no photo)

Without the existence of steel or metal, the villagers use fire as a cutting tool. Controlled fires remove larger trees from forested areas. A smoldering fire, maintained inside the village, cuts fallen trees into smaller poles. The ends of the poles are burned to prevent rot and decay.

Site ⑫ Pottery Making

Cooking and storage vessels are made from clay mixed with quartz sand. A firing, or baking, process was developed which causes the quartz to bind with the clay, providing strength and durability. The rims of the pots are decorated using sharp bone or wooden tools. Smoking pipes are made in a similar fashion.

Site ⑬ Corn Field

Agricultural fields surround the village. Corn, beans, and squash are planted together to maximize water and nutrients. Yields of corn, beans, and squash, along with sunflowers used for oil, provide villagers with an abundance of food.

Site ⑭ Lookout Platforms

From the lookout tower, villagers keep watch over the surrounding countryside. In times of war with other First Nation groups, the platforms can be used to defend the village.

Site ⑮ Drying Rack (no photo)

Bears, beaver, deer, and wolf pelts are removed from animals after a hunt. The meat is smoked and the pelts are stretched on a rack to dry. The hair on the hide can be removed using a wood ash and water solution. Animal hides can also be tanned using the brains of the same animal to produce a soft leather.

Site ⑯ Pole Stacks (no photo)

Large numbers of building poles are stored in an upright position in order to preserve space and to keep them dry. The poles provide an emergency building supply to replace longhouses burned or damaged by fire.

Site ⑰ Canoes (no photo)

Two canoe styles are used by villagers. Long distance trading canoes, up to eight metres long, are used to transport goods, such as corn and pelts, throughout the Great Lakes–St. Lawrence River System. Smaller canoes are used for personal short distance transportation, fishing, and recreation.

Moving Day

Fictional Narrative

—Story by writer Phyllis A. Arnold; illustration by Ojibway artist Nokomis

Ever since Tochingo could remember, the Bear Clan had lived beneath the high cliffs, tending crops in the vast fields beyond the village. But last year the crops were weaker than the year before. The group had harvested less corn. This year the women complained even more about how far they had to go to gather enough firewood. A new village site should be selected. Everyone said it was time they moved.

This year several longhouses had been hit by lightning. The Council finally met to decide where they should rebuild the village. Sitting in a circle, the Council opened their meeting with prayers. The decision about moving was discussed for an entire day and long after dusk. Everyone on Council spoke. Each one gave an opinion about the new village. The new area would have to be cleared of trees for the fields. It must have some natural protection such as a cliff.

Tochingo's grandmother was the Clan Mother.* She was a very important advisor. Tochingo's mother was her eldest daughter. Tochingo was

*See family diagram on page 70.

proud that her mother was also asked whether she felt the move was a good idea. When everyone was in agreement it was announced where the new village would be.

Tochingo thought about how much work would be required to build the new village. But she was glad it would happen. It would be much easier for the women to gather firewood. She had never told anyone, but she was always afraid when she was looking for firewood. There were bears in the forest. Her father had once been attacked by a bear while on a hunting party. Just thinking of her father made her sad. Last Summer he had been captured by an enemy war party and had not returned.

The decision about the new location was finally made. Everyone became very busy. After the snow melted and the forest floor was drier, the men worked together to build the new village. Useful materials and poles from the old village were carried to the new village site. But most of the logs came from the new location. First the trees were burnt around the bottom and then chopped down with stone axes. The strongest logs were made into sharp stakes used to build the palisade walls.

Once the walls were completed the men worked together to build the Long-house where the Council meetings would be held, the clan longhouses, the Sweat Lodge, and the communal garbage area. The spring that supplied fresh water was nearby.

The longhouses were made from materials available from the forest. Tall posts were inserted deep into the ground to hold up the walls. Sheets of bark were woven between the posts. Doors were added. Smoke holes were made above each fire. Six families that were related through their mothers shared the longhouse where Tochingo lived. Longhouses were all the same width, but the length varied greatly.

Tochingo was both sad and excited. She and her brothers were moving the family's belongings into their new home. Her mother had told them to enter the longhouse through the east door. They put their things in the cubicle at the second **hearth**, as she had said. Each cubicle was to be occupied by a family, just as in the old village.

Hearth—firepit or fireplace

"Climb up onto the storage platform and hang the food baskets from the rafters, Yocoisse. Mice won't get into them there," said Mother.

Tochingo watched her brother Yocoisse climb nimbly up the large pole. It was a support and leg for the wide storage platform. He carefully stacked the baskets of food on the bark-covered wooden shelves of the high platform. There were sunflower seeds, acorns, beechnuts, dried fish, beans, dried raspberries, blueberries, and cranberries.

From this height Yocoisse could see almost everyone in the longhouse. He watched as his uncle hung a basket up among the ears of corn that were hanging from the roof. He remembered the deer meat his father used to bring home. The other hunters of the Bear Clan helped to provide for their family now that his father was gone. As he looked down he saw the corn soup in his mother's cooking pot far below. It had been simmering all day on the family fire.

Yocoisse's next few loads consisted of his father's snowshoes, bow and quiver of arrows, war club and armor, fishing spears, and bow-drill for starting fires. Next came the pile of deer hides his mother had recently smoked and tanned, a huge pile of rawhide rope, and several coils of spruce roots. Then he brought his mother's clay cooking pots, dried herbs, her scraper, and her flesher.

Tochingo was right behind him with a large pile of soft absorbent sphagnum moss. They used it for her baby sister's cradle-board. Tochingo stayed to look after the baby, and Yocoisse helped the other boys move the fishnets and baskets of dried corn into the communal storage area. They would dig deep pits to store precious foods when the new fields began to yield harvests.

Tochingo was proud of how hard her older brother worked. He had many responsibilities now that their father was no longer with them. He had already attached several woven cornhusk mats to the inside of the outer walls. They would keep out the cold later when the Winter winds blew. Then Yocoisse would climb back up to get the wolf pelts and robes for added warmth.

Just then her mother entered their area of the longhouse. She handed Tochingo a woven basket containing women's sewing tools—needles and an **awl**. Tochingo had learned to sew already, but she would be making her own sewing tools this Winter. Her mother had promised the first good piece of bone from the Autumn hunt. Tochingo would smooth and sharpen her first awl and needle for working leather.

Mother brought in the last basket. It contained their most precious possession—the seeds that would be needed for the Spring planting. Tomorrow she

Awl—tool for punching holes in leather

would begin soaking them in a bed of wet moss and bark outside the longhouse, in the shade.

As Yocoisse arranged the last of the food containers he accidentally knocked down the mats that separated their section of the longhouse from that of his mother's sister. Mats, branches, containers, and baskets of nuts, seeds, and berries all seemed to fall at once.

Everyone laughed and then helped to restore order. Yocoisse found his father's six-holed flute when the containers fell. He climbed up on the high storage platform and played it softly.

That night Tochingo went to sleep thinking about the feast that was soon to be held to thank the Creator for providing them with their new village.

For Your Notebook

1. a) List ways in which Tochingo's family met their basic physical needs.
   b) What technology did they use for building homes, providing food, and keeping warm?

2. Add to the calendar of seasonal activities you started on page 55 as you read further episodes of the story in this chapter.

Food

  The way of life of the Wendat ensured the food supply was regular and plentiful. They hunted, fished, and gathered resources from nature as well as farmed.

Agriculture

The Wendat lived in villages surrounded by fields. The crops gradually used up the **nutrients** in the soil. The result was less food. When that happened, the village would move to a new location. New fields would be created. This happened about every 10–15 years.

Almost all of the farming work was done by women. The women's contributions were recognized. Women of the Wendat had equal **status** with the men. The group depended on the food they produced to survive.

Planting

Land was cleared for fields by the men. They burned around the bases of trees. Then they chopped them down with stone-bladed axes. Shrubs and some stumps were burned. The women planted crops in the ground between the tree roots.

In spring, the women prepared for planting by using digging sticks to loosen the soil. They made holes in the soft ground with bone-tipped hoes. After saying a prayer of thanks, they added the seeds. (See photo 13 on page 60.)

Harvesting and Gathering

The Wendat understood seasonal change, and planned the year's activities carefully. During the summer the women gathered berries, such as strawberries, cherries, blueberries, and raspberries. They also gathered mushrooms, roots, onions, pumpkins, sunflower seeds, and nuts to add to their winter food supply. Herbs were collected for flavouring and medicines. In autumn, crops were harvested and game hunted to add to the supply of food **preserved** for the winter.

The main crops were corn, beans, and squash. These were so important to the diet that they were called the Three Sisters. Tobacco was grown and harvested in the autumn. In some areas, maple syrup was collected and maple sugar made in late winter.

Preserving and Storage

Foods and medicines were dried to keep them from spoiling. Pottery containers, baskets, and boxes were used to store food. Containers were made in many sizes from birchbark, woven bulrushes, or willow branches. Some had lids and others were open.

The corn was picked in the autumn and taken to the longhouse, where it was hung to dry. Then it was stored in bins or pits.

For Your Notebook

1. What methods were used for harvesting and gathering? Who did this work? What tools were used?

Nutrients—food in the soil to grow plants
Status—rank, social position
Preserve—dry, smoke, or otherwise change food so it can be stored without rotting

Air, Water, Sun, and Earth Bring New Crops

Fictional Narrative

Today was the start of Tochingo's first planting with the women. The Clan Mother had said that Grandmother Moon was telling them the time for planting had come. In previous years, Tochingo had worked beside her mother and other women. She and the other children had also chased away the crows from the crops, pulled the weeds, and gathered firewood for the coming Winter. However, during the past Winter Tochingo had become a woman. This year it would be different.

The Sun was shining especially strongly today. The warmth reminded her of the stories she had heard during the Winter. She knew how important the Sun was to farming people.

The women walked together out to the fields. The Clan Mother spoke of how the Earth nourished the people just as a mother cared for a child. She reminded Tochingo that now that she was a woman her contributions in obtaining food were important for the village. The Clan Mother reminded her that she must care for and respect the Earth and the plants she added to the soil, as she herself had been cared for as a child.

When they reached the plot, the Clan Mother said a prayer. She thanked the Sun, the Earth, and the Thunder People for bringing the sacred Water. The Earth was ready for the upcoming seed planting. Tochingo's mother reminded her how everything was interconnected. Their work today would enable the Wendat to live in harmony with the Earth. "Always remember, if you do good your spirit will be strong and good things will happen to you," said Tochingo's mother.

Together the women carried baskets of ashes to their plot. The men had left the ashes when they cleared the fields. Mother patiently showed Tochingo how to plant the corn. First the soil was loosened with a digging stick. Then a hoe made from the shoulder blade of a deer was used to make a hole in the mound. A prayer was said, and the kernels were gently covered with Earth.

"It is good that the sun is hot," said Tochingo's mother. "Corn and beans like hot soil. The seeds will not grow if the soil is cold."

For the next several days the women worked in the fields. Tochingo knew they were planting enough corn to last them up to three years. This was in case they had several years of bad harvests, or their food supplies spoiled or were eaten by the mice.

Next they planted beans. In between the mounds of earth they planted squash and pumpkin.

Tomorrow the Clan Mother would plant the Tobacco. Tobacco was the first plant given to the people by the Creator. It was one of the sacred medicines and was to be used to honour the Creator in ceremonies.* The smoke from the Tobacco carried their prayers to the Creator.

Soon it would be time for the men to leave the village to go hunting and trading. Then the women would move to temporary shelters near the fields so they could tend their crops.**

---

*Other sacred medicines used by First Nations people include sage, cedar, and sweetgrass.

**See map page 54.

Hunting and Fishing

During the summer, the men added to the food supply by doing some hunting and fishing.

Fishing could be done all year round. During **spawning** season nets and **weirs** would be used to harvest large numbers of fish. A fish-hook and line or a spear with an antler point were also used for catching fish. Women preserved the surplus fish. They hung them on wooden racks over the fire to smoke.

During the autumn, deer were hunted in communal hunts. Temporary shelters were built near the hunting area. A herd of deer was driven into a fenced area. Hunters waited there to shoot them

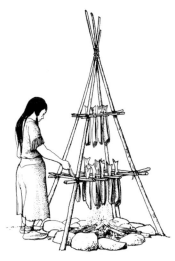

Sturgeon, trout, and whitefish were preserved by smoking.

with bows and arrows, as shown in the picture below. Deer were mainly hunted for their hides and fat, although the meat was also used.

This illustration was drawn by Samuel de Champlain, an early French explorer. It is a primary source. It shows deer being hunted using a fenced area.

History—
☑ Primary Source
☐ Secondary Source
☐ Interpretation
☐ Chronology
☐ Cause and Effect

Food Preparation

Mortars and pestles as shown on the left were used to grind dried or roasted corn into cornmeal. Corn could also be ground between two rocks. (See site 7 on page 59.) This hard work was always done by women.

Once the fine cornmeal was separated from the coarse outer parts, water was added to make a type of flat bread. The bread was baked by wrapping it in corn leaves and putting it under the hot coals in the fire. In early autumn and winter, wild nuts and berries were sometimes added to the bread for flavouring.

Every family always had a pot of corn soup cooking in a pottery container on the fire. Sometimes deer meat, fish, or squash was added to the soup pot. Meats or fish were sometimes roasted over the open fire. Food was also wrapped in leaves and placed in the ashes to cook. Family members ate whenever they were hungry. There were no set mealtimes.

When men were travelling on trading or hunting journeys, they often ate a trail mixture. Corn meal, pounded together with maple sugar and deer fat, made a nutritious product.

For Your Notebook

1. Make a chart to record what foods were obtained by the Wendat, how they were obtained, and who obtained them.

Spawning—fish laying eggs to reproduce
Weir—a fence built across a stream to trap fish

Mortar and pestle—a strong, cup-shaped container and a stone or post used to pound substances to powder

Time to Harvest

Fictional Narrative

In the Autumn, the Clan Mother announced when it was time for the corn harvest to begin. The beans had been harvested a moon earlier. They had already been carried to the longhouse for storage. She organized the activities and gave each of the women and children jobs to do.

The corn needed to be picked and placed in the baskets they carried on their backs. There were also squash and pumpkin to cut from the vines. This Summer's rain and sunshine had been abundant. It had come when needed. The warm Autumn days had lasted for a long time. The harvest was plentiful and the squash were large. Yocoisse and Tochingo's younger brother Sondagua was given the job of hanging the corn to dry. He climbed up the pole and tied the corn to the beams of the longhouse. Mother was arranging a marriage for Yocoisse. He wouldn't be with them to help much longer. Soon younger brother Sondagua would have to take on more chores.

Although the Autumn had been warm, the first frost came early. The Earth was preparing for winter, and this was a reminder to the People to do so as well. Once the corn was harvested and the wild plums and berries picked it was a time for walks into the forest. Sondagua especially liked to walk in the forest with his uncle. His uncle knew so much about the creatures found there. He told Sondagua stories of how the animals prepared for Winter. Above them, a column of migrating geese flew south. Their two lead birds were followed by the other birds in a V–shape clearly visible from below.

The women and children moved from their huts in the fields to live once again in the longhouse.* The men returned from their trading trips. Mother still hoped that news about her missing husband might be heard, but no one knew anything.

The women had made storage containers and baskets from dried bulrushes and birchbark. When the cornhusks from the harvest dried, they too would be made into baskets.

The men of the village were preparing for the moon-long Autumn fishing trip. Sondagua's mother's sister and her husband joined the expedition. Mother remained behind to look after the younger children. A large quantity of fish was needed for the long Winter months ahead. Fish were abundant in the rivers and lakes of the forest. The men would use nets to catch whitefish and lake trout. The women would clean the fish and spread them out on wooden racks to dry. Last year they had returned to the village with their canoes piled high with containers of dried fish and fish oil. The women had boiled some fish in water so the oil floated to the top. They skimmed off the oil and stored it in water-tight containers.

Yocoisse prepared to go with the fishing expedition. He would also be going with the men on the Autumn deer hunt. Soon he would be leaving his mother's fireside—if he killed a deer by himself this year, he would be considered a man. He thought once again about his missing father with sadness, then turned to call to his younger brother to join him.

For Your Notebook

1. Find examples in the story on page 65 and on this page of ways the Wendat people were interconnected with their environment.

*See map page 54.

Clothing

All of the materials used by the Wendat to make clothing came from their environment. Deerskin was the main material used. It was cleaned and tanned by the women to be soft and strong. Pieces were loosely stitched together with sinew or laced together with narrow strips of leather.

Moccasins were cut to fit and carefully made from deerskin. Occasionally the Wendat made moccasins from braided corn husks.

In warm weather, the children and men wore as little as possible. In cooler weather men wore two pieces of leather suspended from a thong around their waist, front and back, leggings, and sometimes a shirt. Women wore a one-piece long dress or a skirt and sometimes a jacket. Fur robes were worn in the coldest weather.

Clothing was decorated with paint or porcupine quill work. Occasionally small beads made from shell were used.

Transportation

The canoe, the tumpline, and the snowshoe were some important types of technology used by many First Nations groups. Europeans who came to live in this country later adopted and used them too.

Summer Travel

The Wendat preferred lightweight canoes for swift travel in summer. The best canoes for trade and travel were birchbark. Where birchbark was not available they used the bark of elm trees. Occasionally they made dugout canoes from hollowed out logs. These were quite heavy and clumsy. Thus they were not used for long journeys. Most often, canoes were acquired through trade with other groups.

A canoe could be built in two or three days by two skilled people. Stakes were driven into the ground to hold the sheets of bark in place. Wood for the ribs was soaked in hot water. The pieces were bent into shape inside the bark within the frame. The bark was sewn to the frame with long strips of spruce root. Then the seams were sealed with hot pine or spruce pitch.

The bark of elm trees could be used to make a canoe if birchbark was not available.

Winter Travel

In winter, Wendat travelled long distances on foot, carrying heavy loads on their backs. They often used a tumpline so they could carry heavier loads. This broad leather strap was worn across the forehead. Long lines wrapped around their bundle or a specially-designed basket.

Snowshoes were made from resources available in the environment. The frames were wood and webbing was **rawhide** strips. Making and repairing snowshoes was a winter activity. Men generally made the frames and women wove the webbing. However, everyone knew how to complete the task if necessary.

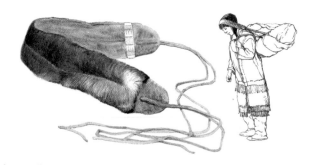

A tumpline made carrying loads easier.

For Your Notebook

1. Review page 43 and the pictures in this chapter. Describe the clothing the Wendat wore. What was it made from and who made it?
2. Use an atlas to do research on waterways in the area where the Wendat lived. In what way would these waterways be useful for the trading network the Wendat maintained?
3. In what ways were the means of transportation used by the Wendat adapted to their environment?

Rawhide—animal hide that is cleaned but not tanned

Trade

 Aboriginal peoples had trading networks long before Europeans arrived on the continent. Their ways of life were adapted to meet most of their needs using local resources. However, some items had to be acquired through trade.

The Wendat women were good farmers, so they often had extra food to trade. The men did the trading. Corn was the main trade product. It was usually exchanged for tobacco, furs, and game.

The Wendat were located between several homelands of Algonquian-speaking groups. (See maps on pages 53 and 85.) The Wendat made great **profits** from acting as **middlepersons**. They traded first with one group, stocking up on goods in return for corn and other produce. Then they traded the goods they acquired with other groups.

Tobacco, hemp fibres, and extra corn were acquired from the Neutral and Petun nations as trade goods. (See map page 53.) Over the winter some of these raw materials were made into products. For example, hemp fibres were woven into sacks and fishnets. Birchbark was acquired from Algonquian peoples farther north. Canoes and furs also came from those groups.

Exploring Further

1. Look at the illustration on page 52. Identify the Wendat longhouses and the Algonquian wigwams. Write a story about the trade that is going on.
2. Look at the trading map below. It appears that some trade goods travelled great distances. How do you think this happened?

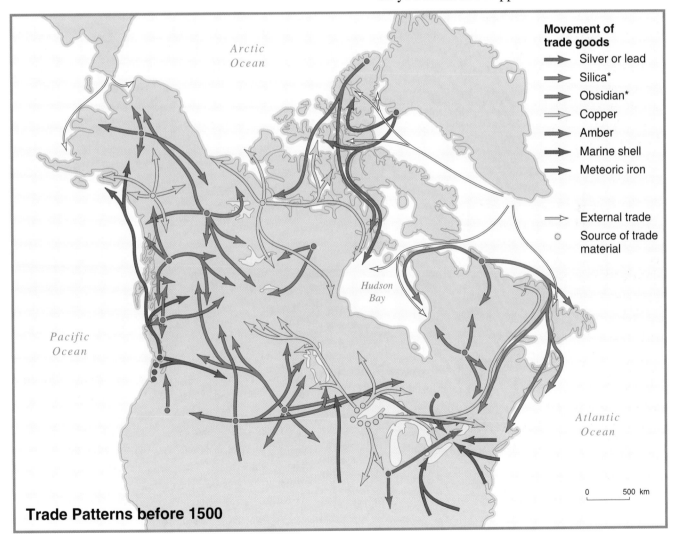

Movement of trade goods
- Silver or lead
- Silica*
- Obsidian*
- Copper
- Amber
- Marine shell
- Meteoric iron

- External trade
- Source of trade material

Arctic Ocean

Hudson Bay

Pacific Ocean

Atlantic Ocean

0   500 km

Trade Patterns before 1500

Profit—when income is greater than expense in a business
Middleperson—a trader who acquires goods to trade to a third party rather than to use

*Silica and obsidian are both hard types of stone that can be worked to create sharp-edged tools.

Social Part of Culture

The social part of culture deals mainly with human psychological needs. The need for love, a sense of belonging, and a sense of identity are important. Communication, spirituality, the arts, and recreation are also psychological needs. Aboriginal people believe that, to be healthy, a person needs to balance the needs of the body, mind, and spirit.

Clans and Family Life

A clan is a group of related families with a common ancestor. Clans were named after animals, birds, and fish from the environment in which the Wendat lived. Among the Wendat, clans traced their **descent** through their mothers. This is called a matrilineal system. Children are part of their mother's clan.

Each longhouse contained people belonging to a particular clan. Most of the people in the longhouse were descended from one woman. This group was an **extended family**. A Clan Mother and her sisters,

their daughters, and adult granddaughters would each have a place at a hearth in the longhouse for her **nuclear family**.*

Women in Iroquoian-speaking cultures were important and powerful. They chose their leader from among themselves. The Clan Mother was often the wisest and oldest woman, the matriarch. She was greatly respected by all the members of the clan.

When a woman's sons became men and married, they moved to live in the longhouse of their wife's clan. Men did not change their clan name, but their children belonged to their mother's clan. A daughter's husband came to live with her.

For Your Notebook

1. Review the family organization in the stories on pages 61, 65, and 67. The diagram below shows the family tree. Compare Tochingo's family with a modern-day family.

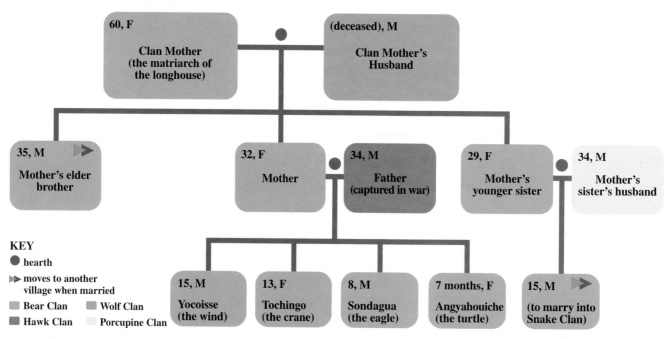

KEY
● hearth
▶▶ moves to another village when married
■ Bear Clan ■ Wolf Clan
■ Hawk Clan ■ Porcupine Clan

In each longhouse lived members of a certain clan and the women's husbands. A Clan Mother was head of the longhouse. Three or more generations lived together. The diagram above shows the family in the stories on pages 61, 65, 67, 72, and 75.

Descent—coming down through the generations from a certain ancestor

Extended family—a family with three or more generations living together: includes "cousins," "uncles and aunts," grandparents, and great-grandparents, not just parents and brothers and sisters

Nuclear family—a wife and husband, or a single parent, and children

*A mother's sisters and a father's brothers were like other mothers and fathers to children. "Aunts," "uncles," and "cousins" are European ideas.

Spirituality

  Aboriginal spiritual beliefs centre on living in harmony with nature.* The Wendat believed everything in nature, including humans and spirits from the world we cannot see, was interconnected. All living things were respected.

Spiritual beliefs were part of everything the people thought and did. They were not separate from daily activities. Many spiritual practices had to do with meeting physical needs, especially food. There were ceremonies used when preparing to hunt, calling to animals to allow themselves to be caught. After the hunt, the animals were thanked for their generosity. The Wendat were a farming people. Spiritual practices connected to planting and harvesting of crops were important.

The Wendat people's relationship with the Creator focused on being thankful for the gifts that they had been given. Corn was a sacred gift from the Creator.

Courtesy of Arnold Jacobs

Onondaga artist Arnold Jacobs, in his painting *Birth of the Earth*, shows the first Woman and the animals coming to create the Earth. This story is told in the narrative on pages 75 and 76.

Symbols

The Wendat people lived in a world rich with symbols. They used symbols in decorating objects, and in ceremonies and stories. Most symbols were considered sacred. They showed connections between the everyday world and the spirit world.

Healing

The Wendat had powerful healers. Some healers specialized in curing sickness. They knew about healing herbs, where to find them, and how to prepare and use them. The healer's job was to cure all kinds of illness of the body, mind, and spirit. A healer also drove away evil spirits and dangers from the spirit world. They spent many years learning their skills and knowledge.

Some ceremonies involved very sacred and powerful masks. Healers who took part in these ceremonies belonged to societies.

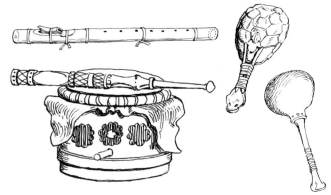

Flutes, drums, and rattles were used in ceremonies and festivals.

Dreams and Visions

The Wendat people considered dreams to be very important. They discussed their dreams with others. The healer gave advice about a person's mental, spiritual, and physical health based on their dreams. The physical and psychological parts of humans were thought to be connected.

At puberty, a boy would go on a Vision Quest to seek a spirit helper for his life. The boy would go alone into the forest to **meditate** and **fast**. As the boy became weaker from hunger, dreams or visions would appear to him. The spirit helper often appeared as a bird, an animal, or an old man. The spirit helper was believed to provide the young man with special powers and direction for his lifetime. In the future, when the boy saw his spirit helper it would bring him a message from the spirit world.

---

*Spiritual practices are difficult to fully understand out of their context. Thus, the sacred ideas and practices of the Wendat will not be discussed in detail in this textbook. Out of respect for beliefs regarding the sacredness of masks, photographs of masks of the Iroquoian peoples do not appear in this textbook.
Meditate—think quietly and deeply, without interruption
Fast—not eat or drink

The Dream

Fictional Narrative

Yocoisse woke from a dream with a clear image of his father. In the dream they had been hunting squirrels in the forest. After his morning prayer of thanks, Yocoisse had his daily bath. Then he helped himself to a bowl of corn soup flavoured with deer meat and several pieces of corn bread with strawberries in it. He did some chores for his mother but the dream images would not leave him, and he felt sad.

Yocoisse gathered up his bow and his father's six-holed flute. "Mother," he said, "I had a dream about father last night. I am going into the forest for several days to think about it. It is time for me to seek guidance from the spirit world. I will fast and meditate. Perhaps a Guardian will appear to me."

His mother nodded silently. She also missed her husband, who had been gone since this time last Summer. She knew that her son's sadness was very deep. He had also been thinking a great deal about the path he would take in life. She hoped that he would receive the gift of a vision that would help him find his way.

As Yocoisse walked through the village he barely noticed the busy activities of the morning. He climbed a steep hill and walked along the ridge above the village. Then he crossed down and over the small valley with the stream in the bottom, into the deep forest beyond.

Yocoisse moved through a stand of beech trees. Between the silver grey trunks the forest floor was almost clear of undergrowth. The deep shade and the heavy layer of old leaves underneath discouraged smaller plants. The light was green. He listened to the gentle wind and smelled the rich scent of dead leaves underfoot.

He came out of the beech wood into mixed trees. He smelled the pitch of a white pine, which had many useful qualities. Pitch, bark, and needles from it were collected for medicine. They helped to heal the winter sickness.

Yocoisse could feel the sacredness of Mother Earth around him. He felt a part of it, but still could not free himself from his sadness. His father had brought him here many times. For hours they had quietly watched and learned from the animals. They had hunted together and his father had taught him the prayers to thank the spirit of the animal for its gift of food. He stressed how important it was to learn and follow the traditions of their ancestors. Yocoisse remembered his father's pride as he acquired each new skill and understanding.

High above Yocoisse an Eagle was hovering in the wind, watching the Earth. His father had told him that the Eagle was the most powerful of all the birds. It was the Eagle that took the Wendat people's messages to the Creator. Seeing an Eagle so early in his journey made Yocoisse feel loved and protected. The Eagle was a powerful Guardian of the Wendat.

Sitting down beside a small stream under a walnut tree, Yocoisse took out his father's flute. He began to play the music his father had taught him. He recalled his dream of the night before. In it, he had been weeping. In the dream his tears had fallen so fast they had become a river that flowed swiftly away from him. The light glinted on the water, but it did not comfort him. He still felt sad.

That night, Yocoisse dreamed again of his father, but mixed into the dream were images of the old man who would become his personal Guardian spirit. In the dream his father walked away from him into the forest, and Yocoisse wept again. The trail became darker, until he could not see. He heard the old man's laughter, cracked and mocking. The old man appeared carrying a heavy pack that was almost bigger than he was. The dim light brightened. The old man beckoned him to follow but Yocoisse could not move.

Once again he woke sad and exhausted. Gradually the sun warmed him. A noisy squirrel chased another around a tree in such a comical way he felt better. He bathed in the stream and then sat down to meditate.

———

Each day Yocoisse sat meditating. Sometimes he walked, deep in thought, always returning to the same place. Each night he dreamed. The old man appeared in many dreams. He was sometimes frightening, sometimes laughing, and occasionally gentle. Once he was angry and waved a stick at Yocoisse. Yocoisse knew the old man was a messenger, but did not understand what he wanted him to learn.

One night in the dream Yocoisse found himself able to move forward. He approached the old man, who handed him the heavy pack. When Yocoisse reached to take the pack from the old man's hand, he noticed that his own hand was larger, a man's hand. And he was taller, much taller than the old man.

The huge pack was smaller than he thought. It was wrapped in deerskin, with brightly painted designs that he could not understand. The old man waved to the brightly lit trail ahead, and disappeared.

———

The next morning Yocoisse awoke refreshed and very hungry. He felt ready to return to the village and his family. He killed a squirrel for food. He was respectful of the squirrel's spirit and thanked it for giving up its life so he could eat. His father had taught him that the creatures were a special gift from the Creator and that all things were interconnected. Yocoisse knew that the spirits of the forest were all around him—on the Earth, in the Water, and in the Sky.

His father had said to him, "Yocoisse, we need the two-leggeds and the four-leggeds, the creatures that swim, and the plants for food. The Wendat depend on them to survive. But they do not need us to survive. In return we must respect all living things. That is why we thank them for giving us the gift of life."

Looking up, Yocoisse saw another Eagle flying high in the Sky. The Eagle would carry his act of honouring the spirits to the Creator. He remembered his father's words about how the creatures contribute to the lives of the Wendat. Suddenly he knew what his life contribution and purpose would be. He

wanted to become a healer who understood the messages of dreams. But he would return to the village to have his own dream explained by the healer there before he began. It was time to return home.

For Your Notebook

1. What connection was there between spiritual beliefs and everyday life?
2. What activities prepared boys for adulthood? Who were their teachers?
3. Compare teenagers in Wendat culture with the culture in which you live. Consider both similarities and differences.

Arts and Recreation
Stories

Stories were used to pass history, spiritual beliefs, values, and traditions from one generation to the next. Storytellers were highly respected for their wisdom and knowledge. This oral tradition allowed children to learn what was important in the culture.

Storytelling was an activity that took place in winter when most people were in the longhouse. Women and men worked quietly, mending and making tools, sewing, or carving. Many just sat and listened while the storyteller created another world for them—a world of the Creator and the First People or of the Trickster and the Animals. Sometimes they heard about how things came to be the way they are in the world today. The Trickster had the powers of both good and bad spirits. Tricksters had the power to change into a living or non-living thing. Different cultures have different names for the Trickster in their stories.

Games and Recreation

It is likely that the Wendat had toys for their children, although no artifacts remain. Toys would likely be made of materials such as corn husks, wood, or small pieces of hide. These materials would decay in time. Children in First Nations cultures were generally treated with love. They were allowed to experiment and experience life, so they learned lessons first hand.

It is known that Wendat people enjoyed games, especially guessing and gambling games. Contests of skill and sports such as racing, archery, snowsnake, double-ball, and lacrosse were also popular.

Snowsnake was played by many First Nations groups. A snowsnake was a wooden rod about two metres long, turned up at one end. Players threw the snowsnake along a path in hard snow, seeing who could make it slide farthest. Record throws could reach nearly a kilometre.

Lacrosse was a very energetic game between teams. Team members passed a hard ball of wrapped leather or wood toward the other team's goal. They used a long stick with a net on the end. Games were very rough and aggressive. They might last all day until the sun went down.

Iroquoian-speaking people refer to lacrosse as the "Creator's Game"—a gift from the Creator. They played it very energetically. It helped them develop strength and quickness, and encouraged co-operation.

Storytelling Time

Fictional Narrative

The temperature dropped and Winter winds blew outside. The people of the entire long-house buried deeper into their wolfhide robes.

Finally the temperature outside got a little warmer. The men mended their fishing nets, snowshoes, and tools and made new ones. Sondagua was learning from his mother's sister's husband how to fasten arrowheads to the shafts. His uncle carefully and patiently showed Sondagua how to balance arrows so that they would travel a long, straight distance. He talked about the need for having inner balance in oneself and a calm spirit as well, if Sondagua wanted to be a good hunter.

Sondagua wanted to be a hunter more than anything. The previous Summer his brother Yocoisse had come back from the forest greatly changed. Now he spent all of his time studying the skills of the great healer who was the best **interpreter** of dreams. Yocoisse wanted to learn the secrets of healing. Sondagua knew he would never give up the thrill of hunting.

Interpreter—someone who understands or explains the meaning of messages that are unclear or in a different language

The boys' sister Tochingo no longer played with the other small girls. She spent her time learning from and working with her mother and aunts. The women repaired and sewed clothing, made baskets, and mended pots and tools. They wove floor mats from dried corn and cattail leaves. Tochingo liked the beautiful designs they made from dyed porcupine quills on moccasins and special clothing best. She also spent a lot of time with her grandmother, the Clan Mother. The Clan Mother knew many stories and jokes. These made the work easier and the time passed quickly.

After the day's work was over, Tochingo and Sondagua sat on mats around the Clan Mother's hearth to hear a story. Their heavy furs provided extra warmth against the Winter cold. Many others joined them. "This is not one of our most ancient stories," said the Clan Mother, "but I have heard it many times so I will tell it. You will hear why this story is important when I tell it." So she prepared herself to speak.

Before this Earth existed, there was only water.

It stretched as far as one could see, and in that water there were birds and animals swimming around. Far above, in the clouds, there was a Skyland. In that Skyland there was a great and beautiful tree. It had four white roots which stretched to each of the sacred directions, and from its branches all kinds of fruits and flowers grew.

There was an ancient chief in the Skyland. His young wife was expecting a child, and one night she dreamed that she saw the Great Tree uprooted. The next morning she told her husband the story.

He nodded as she finished telling her dream. "My wife," he said, "I am sad that you had this dream. It is clearly a dream of great power and, as is our way, when one has such a powerful dream we must do all that we can to make it true. The Great Tree must be uprooted."

Then the ancient chief called the young men together and told them that they must pull up the tree. But the roots of the tree were so deep, so strong, that they could not budge it. At last the ancient chief himself came to the tree. He wrapped his arms around it, bent his knees and strained. At last, with one great effort, he uprooted the tree and placed it on its side. Where the tree's roots had gone deep into the Skyland there was now a big hole. The wife of the chief came close and leaned over to look down, grasping the tip of one of the Great Tree's branches to steady her. It seemed as if she saw something down there, far below, glittering like water. She leaned out further to look and, as she leaned, she lost her balance and fell into the hole. Her hand slipped off the tip of the branch, leaving her with only a handful of seeds as she fell, down, down, down, down.

Far below, in the waters, some of the birds and animals looked up.

"Someone is falling toward us from the sky," said one of the birds.

"We must do something to help her," said another. Then two Swans flew up. They caught the Woman From The Sky between their wide wings. Slowly, they began to bring her down toward the water, where the birds and animals were watching.

"She is not like us," said one of the animals. "Look, she doesn't have webbed feet. I don't think she can live in the water."

"What shall we do, then?" said another of the water animals.

"I know," said one of the water birds. "I have heard that there is Earth far below the waters. If we dive down and bring up Earth, then she will have a place to stand."

So the birds and animals decided that someone would have to bring up Earth. One by one they tried.

The Duck dove down first, some say. He swam down and down, far beneath the surface, but could not reach the bottom and floated back up. Then the Beaver tried. He went even deeper, so deep that it was all dark, but he could not reach the bottom, either. The Loon tried, swimming with his strong wings. He was gone a long, long time, but he, too, failed to bring up Earth. Soon it seemed that all had tried and all had failed. Then

a small voice spoke. "I will bring up Earth or die trying."

They looked to see who it was. It was the tiny Muskrat. She dove down and swam and swam. She was not as strong or as swift as the others, but she was determined. She went so deep that it was all dark, and still she swam deeper. She went so deep that her lungs felt ready to burst, but she swam deeper still. At last, just as she was becoming unconscious, she reached out one small paw and grasped at the bottom, barely touching it before she floated up, almost dead.

When the other animals saw her break the surface they thought she had failed. Then they saw her right paw was held tightly shut.

"She has the Earth," they said. "Now where can we put it?"

"Place it on my back," said a deep voice. It was the Great Turtle, who had come up from the depths.

They brought the Muskrat over to the Great Turtle and placed her paw against his back. To this day there are marks at the back of the Turtle's shell which were made by Muskrat's paw. The tiny bit of Earth fell on the back of the Turtle. Almost immediately, it began to grow larger and larger and larger until it became the whole world.

Then the two Swans brought the Sky Woman down. She stepped onto the new Earth and opened her hand, letting the seeds fall onto the bare soil. From those seeds the trees and the grass sprang up. Life on Earth had begun.

When the Clan Mother finished, Tochingo and Sondagua thanked her for her story. They were both hungry, so they went to their mother's pot for something to eat.

For Your Notebook

1. What problems may arise when a culture relies entirely on oral language for passing on information from one generation to the next?

2. Compare being elderly in the Wendat culture to being elderly in your own culture.

3. Compare either the relationship between mothers and daughters or fathers and sons in the Wendat culture to that in your own.

4.

   a) In pairs, brainstorm a list of effective listening strategies. Think about the qualities of a good listener. Share your ideas with the class. Place your notes in the Learning How to Learn section of your notebook.

   b) How important were good listening skills in Wendat culture? Provide examples.

Story by Abenaki author Joseph Bruchac; "The Earth on Turtle's Back" reprinted with permission from *The Native Stories from Keepers of the Earth*. ©1991 by Joseph Bruchac. Published by Fifth House Ltd. Calgary, Canada.

Political Part of Culture

  The political part of culture deals with humans' group needs. Human beings prefer to live in groups. Social, or group, life requires a sense of order and security. Good leadership and laws are important. Aboriginal peoples were **self-reliant**. They governed all areas of life in a structured manner.

Decision-making

Among the Wendat, society was based around groups of families within a clan structure. A group of related families belonged to a lineage. They were all descendants of one female ancestor. Several lineages were part of a larger group, the clan. The Wendat had eight clans—Wolf, Deer, Bear, Beaver, Turtle, Hawk, Porcupine, and Snake.

The women would meet to bring their concerns and **recommendations** to the Clan Mother. She guided the chief of their clan. The men also met to discuss their concerns and made recommendations to the chief. Each clan had a chief who acted as spokesperson in council meetings.

Decision-making was by consensus. Issues were discussed at great length to come up with a decision that all agreed with and would carry out.

Council Meetings

Villages held Council meetings to settle their problems. Women did not directly take part in this decision-making process. Decisions that affected a village were made by a Council of their local chiefs (or their **representatives**).

Each clan in a Wendat village had three kinds of chiefs: **civil** chiefs, hunting chiefs, and war chiefs. Civil chiefs were concerned with the problems of the people and everyday life. They maintained law and order. They also co-ordinated group activities like feasts, games, and dances. The Clan Mother chose a man as civil chief from among the men within the clan. He was chosen for his wisdom and **diplomacy**. He received advice from the Clan Mother. It was his job to speak for the clan and follow their instructions at the Grand Council meetings. However, if the Clan Mother or the clan was not pleased with the way he carried out his roles and responsibilities, he could be replaced at any time. This ensured that civil chiefs respected their clan's wishes. Hunting chiefs led hunting expeditions. War chiefs were concerned with military matters. Each was called upon at the necessary times when their skills were needed.

Each Nation in the Wendat alliance had its own local chiefs (forming a government) who made decisions affecting individual villages.

Self-reliant—able to look after oneself and make one's own decisions

Recommendation—a suggestion that one favours

Representative—a person chosen to act or speak for others

Civil—having to do with peace, order, and good government of ordinary citizens and their concerns

Diplomacy—skill in dealing with others; skill in managing negotiations between people or nations

Defence, War, and Peace

 The political part of culture also includes the need for group security. One way some groups maintain their security is through military strength.

Physical bravery was valued among Wendat men. This included the ability to withstand pain and to hunt, travel, and fight with little food or physical protection. The people lived in villages with large populations. They were supported largely by farming done by women. The basic needs of the people were taken care of. Thus, large groups of men had time to train as hunters and warriors and take part in raids and war parties.

Iroquoian nations formed political alliances. Two such alliances were the Five Nations Confederacy and the Wendat Alliance (see chart on page 53). Alliances brought peace among the nations in the alliances. This reduced the number of nations that were in conflict with each other. Thus, more of the men were available to carry on hunting and trading activities. They were not needed for defence against war parties or to attack other villages. As trade increased the amount of raiding decreased. Fewer lives were lost, crops burned, and villages damaged. These had put their way of life at risk. However, not all groups formed alliances. Also, conflict over hunting territories and trade arose from time to time. War did not cease completely.

Wampum Belts

Wampumpeak was a word from an Algonquian language meaning "white string." A shortened form of the word was used to describe strings of shell beads that were used by peoples of the Eastern Woodlands.

The shell beads themselves were a trade item. They came from people living along the Atlantic shore. The white beads were more common than the purple ones. Consequently, the purple beads were worth more.

The beads were used to create woven belts or strings that were used as symbols. They were a memory device. That is, they were used to help a record-keeper recall facts and remember them in exact order and detail.

When an important political agreement like a treaty was made between two groups, a wampum belt was woven to record it. The pattern of the white and purple beads reminded the record-keeper of the details of the agreement. Wampum belts are a form of written language.

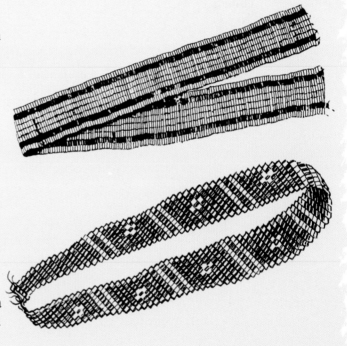

Helped by a memory belt, called a wampum belt, a speaker might tell about an important event.

For Your Notebook

1. a) Define clan.
   b) What is wampum?
2. What kinds of chiefs did the Wendat have? What is the difference between them?
3. In what way were the civil chiefs the same as the people Canadians elect to represent them in government today? How were they different?
4. What part did women take in government?
5. Read page 53 again. What nations were part of the Wendat Alliance? Mark them on a map of Ontario.

Review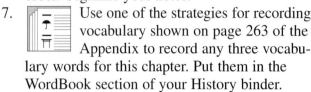

The icons are your cue to turn to the Learning How to Learn Appendix (pages 256–265) for ideas on how to complete these activities.

 This icon is a reminder to turn to the Research Model (pages x and xi).

Assessment

1. Complete a self-assessment for one assignment from this chapter.

2.

   Section 1 Presentation Activity

   On pages 5 and 31 you were asked to begin preparing materials for a presentation showing the relationship between the environment and the culture of the Wendat or Woodland Cree. Work on this now. Refer to page 262 in the Appendix for presentation ideas to share your learning with others.

Summarizing the Chapter

3. At the beginning of this chapter (page 51) you made some predictions. Use what you have learned from studying the chapter to fill in the right hand column of the prediction chart.

4. Refer to "Questions to Talk About" on page 5. Discuss questions 2–4 with a partner, based on what you learned about the Wendat. Record ideas from this discussion in your notes.

Understanding Concepts

5. Create a graphic organizer to show several examples of the interaction between Wendat people and their environment. Show ways the Wendat affected the environment and ways the environment influenced the Wendat.

6. Compare your notebook to that of a partner. Check to see that items are not missing and are in the correct order. Organize your notes.

7. Use one of the strategies for recording vocabulary shown on page 263 of the Appendix to record any three vocabulary words for this chapter. Put them in the WordBook section of your History binder.

8. The chapter overview on page 50 contains some general ideas on how the Wendat lived in the time before Europeans came.
   a) Work with a partner to find examples of each idea as it applies to the Wendat people.
   b) Create a concept poster on one of the above ideas (see Appendix page 256). Present your poster to the class.

Developing Research Skills

9. a) Research means locating usable information on a topic by following an organized series of steps. The research project on pages x and xi involves three main stages: Gathering Information, Examining and Organizing Information, and Presenting Information. As a class, create a list of the steps and activities that might be involved in each of these three stages. Add to your list. Record this in the Learning How to Learn section of your notebook.
   b) Do research on Canada's official national game, lacrosse.

10. Do research to find a Wendat story on one of the following:

   • telling the people how to behave (teaches a lesson)
   • admiring the qualities of an animal or a bird
   • a Trickster or hero
   • a battle between good and evil
   • a story written by an Aboriginal author

Developing Communication Skills

Select at least one question from 11–18:

Reading

11. Read Moving Day on pages 61–63. Imagine that you are a member of a Wendat clan. It has been decided that your village will be moving.

    a) List all of the things you must consider when selecting a new location for your village. Discuss this with a partner.

    b) How were decisions made in the village?

    c) Decide what steps would be required in this type of decision-making. Record your ideas in the Learning How to Learn Section of your notebook.

    d) Use the decision-making steps you listed in c) to come to a decision about one of the following:

       • A new outdoor basketball court will be built on your school grounds. Where should it be located?

       • One of the classrooms in your school will be needed as a new music room. Which one should be used?

Writing

12. Create a character who might have lived in the village on page 52. Write a biography for him or her. See number 1 on page 264 in the Appendix on how to write a biography.

13. With a partner, imagine that you are members of a Wendat clan (boys or girls of your actual age). You have just helped to complete the spring planting. You have some concerns about what the coming seasons hold for the people of your longhouse.

    a) In role, discuss your concerns with each other. What plans can you make to prevent any difficulties? What actions must you take to be sure you continue to live in harmony with nature?

    b) In your History Journal, write about how your ideas about nature and concerns for the future are different from and/or similar to the person you role-played.

14. In the History Journal section of your notebook, tell which person from this chapter you would like to have met. Why do you find this person interesting?

15. If you had been born in a Wendat village 1000 years ago, how would your life have been different? What similarities exist between life now and life then? Select one of the writing forms in the Appendix on pages 264 and 265 to answer the question.

Listening and Speaking

16. Tell a story about some part of life of a Wendat village. You may wish to write out your idea or make notes first.

17. Using your own words, create an audio tape to guide students from site to site in the Traditional Wendat Village (pages 57–60).

Representing

18. Choose a) or b).

    a) Construct a model or a diorama of a Wendat longhouse. If you make a model, construct it so the viewer can see inside.

    b) Construct a model or a diorama of a Wendat village and the surrounding fields.

Applying Concepts

19. Find examples of three of the following from the stories in this chapter.

    a) the people's relationship with the Creator focused on being thankful rather than asking for things

    b) the people traced descent through the women

    c) everyone in the longhouse looked after the children

    d) children learned by watching

    e) the people valued co-operation, sharing, and generosity

    f) the people respected the Sun and the Earth

    g) great efforts were made to respect the sacred teachings, customs, and traditions and pass them on to the next generation

    h) all life is part of a never-ending cycle—all things are interconnected

20. Consider the technology available to the Wendat.
    a) What special technology did they develop to adapt to the challenges of their lives?
    b) What parts of their technology do we still use in Canada today?

21. a) In a group of five, discuss the following: The Wendat lived and worked closely with one another.
    • What are some advantages of this?
    • What kinds of difficulties can arise?
    • How can people deal with these kinds of difficulties?
    • What are some of the skills needed to live and work closely with others?
    b) In what ways would your life change if you lived in a Wendat village?
    c) Record your ideas about working with others in the Learning How to Learn section of your notebook.

22. a) List examples of how the Wendat way of life was based on the cycle of the seasons. Why were the seasons so influential in their lives?
    b) List examples of events in your culture that are based upon the cycle of seasons. How do the seasons influence these activities?

Challenge Plus

23. a) Examine the painting on page 52. Locate the trading areas. These Wendat and Algonquian traders could be considered **entrepreneurs**. Explain.

Entrepreneur—a business person who invests in a business, hoping for a profit but risking a loss

b) Read the definitions of these terms in the Glossary: market, supply, demand, competition, advertising, partnerships, monopoly, profit, trade, prospects.
c) Write the words from b) in a column. Beside each, write one sentence to describe how these modern-day words relate to trade between the Wendat and Algonquian-speaking peoples.
d) What would be necessary to develop and keep a good trading relationship?

24. You have now had the opportunity to complete various projects about the Wendat. This might include projects you completed alone, with a partner, or with the class. An important step in learning is evaluating your work. Complete the following steps alone or with other project participants.
    a) Select one of the projects you completed (e.g., question 13 on page 80).
    b) Review the project guidelines. What was the purpose of the project? What were the required parts? List these items on a piece of loose-leaf with the title, Chapter 3 Self-assessments.
    c) Rate your performance on each of the five requirements according to how well each was done.

    5 = excellent   2 = fair
    4 = very good   1 = needs more work
    3 = average   0 = not completed

    d) Look at your highest scores. Think about why you gave yourself a high score for these items. Under the heading "Successes," list three things you would do again on a project.
    e) Look at your lower scores. Think about why you gave yourself a lower score for these items. Under the heading "Areas for Improvement," list three things you will do to improve your next project.
    f) Put this self-assessment page in the Tools of Learning section of your notebook. Remember to read this page again before you do your next project.

Chapter 4
The Woodland Cree
A Case Study

The information in this chapter refers to the period before European contact. Many First Nations people still live a traditional lifestyle.

O v e r v i e w

Use this Overview to predict the events of this chapter.

❶ People and Land

The environment greatly influenced the way the Algonquian-speaking people lived. They lived in harmony with nature and respected it. The lives of the Algonquian peoples were closely tied to the seasons.

❷ Economic Part of Culture

The Algonquian peoples met almost all of their physical needs with resources from their environment.

❸ Social Part of Culture

The Woodland Cree lived in family groups in winter and gathered in larger groups in summer. Elders had an important role in passing on the culture.

❹ Political Part of Culture

Each family group had a male chief as leader. When family groups met, group decisions were made by consensus among the leaders.

Chapter 4 Focus

In Chapters 4 and 5, you will examine the role of the environment in shaping the way of life of two Algonquian-speaking groups in what is now Central Canada. In Chapter 4 specific examples and stories relate to the Woodland Cree. In Chapter 5 they relate to the Anishinabe (Ojibway). Because the environment had a great influence on how these people lived, you should review pages 38–42 in Chapter 2. Chapter 4 uses basic needs as a way to classify information.

This chapter will focus on the following concepts. It will emphasize environmental interaction, balance, and technology.

Environmental   Balance   Technology   Cultural   Exploration
Interaction   Contact

Vocabulary

game hunters   habitat
Algonquian   patrilineal
migration   community circle
seasonal camp   conflict
economic roles   consensus

Special Spellings

- When referring to the language the Woodland Cree speak, use Algonquian or Algonquian-speaking. (Algonkian is another spelling used in some resources.)
- The Algonquin are one of the Algonquian-speaking nations (see map page 85).

Chapter Preview/Prediction

1. Examine the overview found on the previous page and the visuals and titles in the chapter.
   a) Based on these, discuss with a partner how you think the people met their basic needs.
   b) Predict answers to the questions in the Prediction Chart on this page. Put your predictions in the "My Predictions" column.*

---

*Your teacher may provide you with a full-sized working copy of the Prediction Chart. This chart is available as a blackline master in *Canada Revisited 6 Integrated Unit*.

Prediction Chart—What Do You Think?		
Questions	My Predictions (fill out now)	What I Found Out (fill out at end of chapter)
1. How did the environment influence how the Woodland Cree lived? How did they interact with and change the environment?		
2. How did the Woodland Cree maintain harmony with nature? How did they respect all living things?		
3. How did the technology the Woodland Cree used affect their lifestyle?		
4. What contacts were made with other cultures? How did this affect the Woodland Cree way of life?		

Section I Presentation Activity

Use the information from this chapter to add to the presentation activity you started on pages 5 and 31. If you selected Woodland Cree, use the information in this chapter.

People and Land

 The culture of the Woodland Cree was adapted for living in their environment. The land, climate, vegetation, and animal life of the region influenced how they met their needs.

Two Woodland Cree hunters stalk a small herd of caribou. This ecosystem is more common in the most northerly part of the Canadian Shield.

A group of Woodland Cree hunters have captured a moose in the forest. This ecosystem is common in the central and southern parts of the Canadian Shield.

The Woodland Cree were mainly hunters. They also fished and gathered resources from their surroundings. Moose, woodland caribou, deer, and bear were the large food animals. These animals lived in the forest, widely spread out. The small numbers of animals could not support large groups of humans. Thus, people did not live in permanent villages. Families moved often to find new food sources.

Aside from big game hunting, the Woodland Cree also hunted ducks, geese, and rabbits. They also did some fishing in the many lakes, rivers, and streams of the region. They gathered plants for food and medicines.

The winter and summer lifestyles of the Woodland Cree had some differences. In winter, they lived in small family groups in the forest, far apart from each other. In summer, they formed larger communities for activities such as duck hunting and fishing. At these times, they made group decisions. They also visited, and had celebrations and ceremonies.

The Woodland Cree believed that interconnectedness with nature was important. The people respected all living things. Their way of life helped maintain the balance of nature.

For Your Notebook

1. Review the map on page 85, plus the maps and photographs on pages 38–43.
   a) Describe the environment of the Woodland Cree.
   b) Describe what knowledge and skills would be necessary for survival in this type of environment.
   c) Predict how their environment affected how people met their needs.

Algonquian Peoples

The homelands of Algonquian-speaking peoples, shown below, extended from the Atlantic Coast to the Plains.

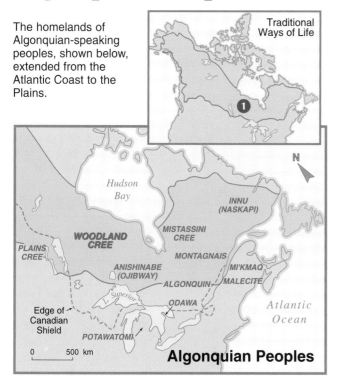

Traditional Ways of Life

Algonquian Peoples

On page 18 you studied various language groups of First Nations people. Notice the homelands of the Algonquian-speaking peoples on this map. The languages in a language group are related but distinct.

This chapter examines the Woodland Cree. They are one of the peoples belonging to the Algonquian language group. Chapter 5 provides a brief case study of another Algonquian-speaking group, the Anishinabe (Ojibway).

The Woodland Cree live the farthest north of the many Algonquian-speaking nations. In the time before European exploration, speakers of Cree **dialects** were found from northern Quebec to the Plains.* The far north of their territory is more like the Arctic. The Woodland Cree there meet some of their needs in ways similar to the Inuit living north of them. In the southern part of their territory, the Woodland Cree way of life is similar to that of the Anishinabe. The paintings on the previous page show different ecosystems in which the Woodland Cree lived.

Dialect—regional variation of a language with some word differences, understandable to people with other dialects
*In modern times, they are found even farther west, as are the Anishinabe.

Environment

  The Algonquian peoples knew they were just one of the many interconnected parts of nature. They lived on the land largely as they found it. They were careful not to upset the balance of nature. Much of the land is coniferous forest ecosystem. Some rocky areas are wet because of heavy snows and poor drainage. **Muskeg** is the ecosystem that results there. Farther north, trees become smaller and the ecosystem is more like tundra.

Landforms
Canadian Shield Region (see page 38)

- rocky outcrops, muskeg, rugged hills and uplands, many lakes and rivers
- swift flowing rivers and streams, especially during spring run-off

Climate
Subarctic Region (see page 39)

- brief summer, but temperatures may be hot on long summer days
- moderate rainfall ⬦⬦⬦⬦
- few hours of daylight in the winter
- long, very cold winters with heavy snowfall**
  ❄ ❄ ❄ ❄ ❄

Vegetation
Coniferous Forest Region (see page 40)

- dense coniferous forests, with some deciduous shrubs
- farther north, area becomes tundra (sparse trees, low shrubs, mosses, and lichens)

Muskeg—boggy land in a forested region, with spongy, waterlogged moss and other vegetation
**See chart on the inside back cover.

Seasons

 The Woodland Cree observed changes in seasons. They noticed the phases of the moon, the length of days, growth of plants, migrations of birds, and many other clues.* This knowledge was essential to carefully planning their seasonal activities.

Winter · Spring · Summer · Autumn

 = Environment

Spring

Late winter was the most difficult time for peoples living in the deep woods. As the days grew longer and warmer, migrating ducks and geese returned from the south. Woodland Cree families travelled toward traditional meeting places.

Travel was difficult as the deep snow softened and grew wet. They stopped often to hunt, because food was in short supply. By the time the duck hunts began, the streams were running high and lakes were clearing of ice.

Fish were swimming up the creeks in great numbers to spawn. Flocks of waterfowl were back. The beaver were active again, so food was plentiful. Birch and maple grew in southern areas. Sapping for syrup was a spring activity, and the syrup was made into sugar.

Summer

During the summer, groups came together for festivals or to make group decisions. This helped people to have a sense of group identity. Religious ceremonies were held. Some law cases were tried and sentences passed on wrong-doers. **Courting**, arranging of marriages, and ceremonies were summer activities.

Summer camps were made in open areas of the forest near lakes and rivers. Fish was a main source of food in summer. Hunting for such a large group of people would have quickly reduced the amount of game in the area.

Autumn

Hunting, gathering, drying, and preserving food for winter were autumn activities. Trading furs for supplies such as wild rice with groups farther south increased the food supply. Individuals who had been away on trading expeditions returned to camp in autumn.

Winter

When the first frost appeared, family groups returned to the forests. Families had traditional hunting, trapping, and ice fishing territories. Groups would be separated by many kilometres. Each hectare of forest supported a limited amount of game. During the long winter months they hunted, fished, and set snares and traps for smaller animals such as snowshoe hare. Snares and traps were checked every day.

During the long winter months, women made clothing from animal skins they had tanned during the summer. They decorated clothing and objects with porcupine quills or dyes. Stories were told during winter work.

If no food was available in a family's area, they were welcome to hunt in another family's territory. Sharing of food and hospitality were essential. A family could starve if its main hunter was injured or killed, so others shared with them.

West Point Museum Collection, United States Military Academy

Exploring Further

1. If you were living in the forest, what would it take to survive during each season? Draw a large circle and divide it into four quarters. Label each season, and write your answers in the appropriate spaces.

---

* The changes of the moon and other changes were used instead of the calendars we use today.
Courting—getting to know someone with the intention of marrying

Kaksekochin

Fictional Narrative

—story by Cree writer/teacher, Laura Okemaw;
illustration by Ojibway artist, Nokomis

Spring was not just the season where all of nature seemed to come alive. It was also the season where the extended families were reunited from their winter camps.

This story is about a boy named Kaksekochin, which means Fast Runner. He was the son of a chief named Wapihesiw, which means White Bird. Kaksekochin had a friend named Chepwaschochin, which means Pointed Hat. His cousin was named Chaychapese, which means He Rides Small.

Kaksekochin rose early. He got dressed in the dark wigwam. As he opened the wigwam flap, he could feel the gentle breeze blowing through the camp. Overhead he could barely make out the V-shaped flock of geese. From a distance he could hear the cracking sound made by the melting, shifting ice. Spring had arrived.

The small Cree camp had come through a long winter. They were almost out of dried meat. The men of the camp were already preparing to go fishing in the stream. Although Kaksekochin was only 12 winters old, he was old enough to help his father, Wapihesiw. Kaksekochin enjoyed fishing. His father turned to hand him his moosehide fishing bag. His friend Chepwaschochin was coming. Both knew it would be a race to see who could catch more fish.

Although the water was ice cold, Kaksekochin and Chepwaschochin did not mind. They were having fun catching enough fish to last a long time.

After some time, Wapihesiw turned to them and said, "Kaksekochin, you and Chepwaschochin go and gather firewood for your mother." The boys ran off into the woods, knowing that they were being given the chance to explore the changes that spring brought.

Summer was coming soon. Kaksekochin's father, as leader, would soon have to decide where to make their summer camp. The next morning he announced that they would be moving to the place they had camped five summers ago. Kaksekochin only remembered a hill beside a river near the woods. Preparations began. They loaded only what was needed into the birchbark canoes.

For three days, Wapihesiw and his people journeyed until they came to the top of the hill. There in the valley, they saw another Cree camp. Kaksekochin heard his mother give a welcoming shout. It was her father's camp. Soon everyone was greeting each other. Kaksekochin saw his cousin Chaychapese.

They had to wait to catch up on all the news. Wapihesiw and his people had to build their summer homes. The men went into the woods to gather poles for the wigwams. When they brought them back, the women and children peeled the bark off the birch. Using the bark, they tied the poles together at one end. Moosehides were placed over the poles, which were slowly raised to form the wigwam. Branches of balsam fir and moss were used to line the floor. *Now* it was time for visiting and exchanging news.

The next day, before dawn, Kaksekochin got up to make the fire outside. Soon the rocks around the fire were red hot.

His mother placed a bag made from a moose's stomach near the fire. The bag was supported by sticks that had one end shoved into the ground. His mother poured water into it from another bag made from animal skin, then carefully placed two hot stones into it. After a long while, and after more hot stones had been added, the water began to boil. Chunks of the meat were placed in the bag, then she added two more rocks to keep the water hot while the meat cooked.

After eating, Wapihesiw told Kaksekochin to help his mother. Wapihesiw was going on a moose hunt. He promised to take Kaksekochin on a hunt when he returned. This made Kaksekochin happy. He wanted to prove to his father that he was no longer a child.

After he helped his mother with the firewood, Kaksekochin got his bow and arrows. He and his friends decided to go on a hunt of their own. Each boy packed a day's supply of pemmican.

It was getting to be mid-afternoon and the boys still had not seen any moose. Just when they were about to give up, Chepwaschochin said, "Look!" There among the bushes stood the most magnificent creature the boys had ever seen.

The boys watched in awe as the moose munched quietly on the short grass and leaves. Kaksekochin tried to remember all the things the hunters said about killing moose. He knew he had one chance. He carefully placed his best arrow in the bow. He slowly stood up, pulling back on the bow string. Just when the moose raised his head, Kaksekochin let the arrow fly. It hit the moose in the neck. At first the moose did not move. Then it slowly took a staggering step forward. Then another. Slowly it swayed to its side. With a loud thud, it fell on the ground. The boys looked down at the magnificent beast just lying there. For a brief moment, the boys felt sadness, knowing the moose had given up its life to feed and clothe their people.

Chaychapese turned to Kaksekochin and said, "Chepwaschochin and I will go back to camp and get someone to help us." While they

were gone, Kaksekochin thought about his childhood. This was the end of life for the moose, and the end of childhood for Kaksekochin. Now he was a hunter, and that meant he was an adult. He said a short prayer, then began cutting up the moose.

After a long while, Chepwaschochin and Chaychapese returned with men to help. When Kaksekochin got back to camp, he was tired but proud as the men set the moose by his father's wigwam. Kaksekochin felt a hand on his shoulder. He heard his father

say, "Meyohsin," which means "it is good."

His mother and several of the women cut up the moose. The meat was shared amongst the people. That night, a feast was held in honour of Kaksekochin. After everyone had eaten, his father stood up and said, "I am proud of my son. Today he showed his skill as a hunter. He has earned his right to join the men on our hunting trips. Tonight he will share his hunting story."

Kaksekochin got up and told his story, describing everything as a storyteller would. When

he finished, the other men stood up and congratulated him. His father smiled proudly.

Exploring Further

1. If you had been born to a Woodland Cree family 1000 years ago, how would your life have been different? Select one of the writing forms in the Appendix on pages 264–265 to answer this question.

NOKOMIS

Economic Part of Culture

   The culture of the Woodland Cree was adapted to the environment in which they lived. They met their physical needs through hunting, trapping, and gathering resources from the environment. They created most of their technology from these resources. They also traded with other groups.

Technology

Woodland Cree men and women used plants, wood, stone, antlers, bone, hides, sinew, and many other natural resources as raw materials. They made homes, clothing, tools, weapons, containers, snowshoes, fish-hooks, and dozens of other products.

The Woodland Cree lived in small, **isolated** groups for half of the year. Everyone had the knowledge and skills for finding, collecting, and making everything they needed. They were active traders, but they could not depend on others for their daily needs. Because the people moved often, they did not have many personal possessions. Everything had to be carried from place to place.

Economic Roles

Men, women, and children all had specific roles they carried out. Women seldom did men's work and men seldom did women's work. However, both could do what was needed in an emergency, or when the men were away from camp.

Economic Roles of Women
- gather wild plants, berries, and other sources of food, medicine, and raw materials
- hunt, snare small animals; fish
- dry meat, fish, berries for winter storage
- prepare meals and tend the fire
- gather bulrushes to weave into mats
- make twine, rope, thread from spruce roots, rawhide, and sinew
- make baskets and containers, wigwam covers, canoe covers, snowshoe webbing
- skin animals, clean and tan hides; stretch furs
- make clothing; decorate items and clothing
- clean and mend tools
- set up and take down wigwam covering
- carry burdens when moving
- plant and harvest summer gardens (some groups)
- pass on skills and knowledge to children

Economic Roles of Men
- hunt large and small game and birds; fish
- trap, snare, stalk, and track animals
- make wigwam frames, snowshoe frames, toboggans, tools, weapons, and canoes
- learn about habitats and movements of game and fur-bearing animals, and forest survival skills
- use weapons for defence and warfare
- trade furs for wild rice and corn
- pass on skills and knowledge to children

Isolated—separated or kept apart

Homes

Wigwams were temporary structures that could be moved easily to a new area. They were about 2.5 by 3 metres in size and housed the members of a family.

The frame was made from young trees. It was covered with sheets of birchbark or hides. When the family moved, the frame was usually left but the covering was taken with them. There were two types of homes. One was a pointed, teepee style. To make the other style, the supports were bent in a curve and both ends of the poles placed in the ground.

The earth floor was covered with evergreen branches. Often, mats woven from bulrushes were spread over the branches. In cold weather fur robes were added over these. There was no furniture. Everyone sat on the floor. A ring of rocks enclosed the fire pit at the centre of the lodge. A hole in the top of the wigwam let out smoke and let in air for ventilation.

In the cold winters, branches, sod, and even snow were heaped around the outside. This gave extra protection from the cold.

Food

The environment determined how the Woodland Cree met their physical needs. Hunters understood that food was limited. Only a certain number of animals could be supported by the habitat. When a habitat had little game, the people moved away until the game returned or increased in population. This helped maintain the balance of nature. It made sure there was enough food in the future.

People living farther south mainly hunted moose, deer, and bear. Those in the north also hunted woodland caribou. The forests were also the home of fur-bearing animals such as rabbits and hares, beaver, and muskrat.

Migratory wildfowl and game birds provided meat and eggs. Fish could be caught in any season, although many Woodland Cree preferred hunting. Some groups were involved in summer gardening. The women also gathered nuts, berries, roots, maple syrup, and honey, as well as plants used for medicine. Foods were smoked and dried to preserve them, and pemmican was made. Pemmican was a compact, nutritious food that was valuable when travelling.

One method of cooking was boiling in the strong stomach from a large animal or in a birchbark container using hot stones.

Clothing

During the warm months, women and girls wore dresses and moccasins made from animal skins. Knee-length leggings were added when the weather got colder. Men and boys wore **breechcloths**, shirts, and moccasins during the warm months. In cold weather, thigh-length leggings were also worn.

Coats and blankets were woven from strips of rabbitskin. Moose or caribou coats, hats, and blankets were made for winter wear. Boots lined with fur were worn over moccasins for extra warmth.

Breechcloth—pieces of material hanging from the waist in front and back

Tanning Hides

In the summer, women tanned hides from large game animals. Tanning made the hides soft and strong. The tanned leather was used for making clothing the next winter. The women spread the skins out flat, hair side down. They fastened them so they would not move. Using a stone flesher, they scraped the hide carefully to remove all fat and tissue. (See tools on page 27.)

Then the hide was turned over and the hair removed with a scraper made of bone. The skin was scraped some more on both sides. This made it an even thickness. Ashes, boiling water, and brains from the same animal were mixed together and rubbed into the hide. This mixture preserved and softened the hide.

The finished hide was stretched on a wooden frame to dry. (See the picture at the bottom right on the previous page.) When dry, it was washed and worked to make it softer. Then it was dried again. Finally, it was hung over a slow, smouldering fire to smoke. Smoking made it stronger and turned it a golden colour.

Transportation

In the northern forest, travel was easiest on foot or by water. In summer people either walked or travelled by canoe. In winter, they wore snowshoes to stay on top of the snow. They carried packs on their backs or pulled loads on toboggans.

The painting on page 86 shows a woman, children, and dogs transporting the family's goods. The man is carrying only his weapon. That allowed him to move quickly to shoot an animal or to protect the family from danger if needed.

The Algonquian-speaking peoples built fine canoes for travel on the swift rivers and many lakes. The canoes were very lightweight. Travellers could **portage** the canoes around stretches of river that had rapids or waterfalls, or from lake to lake. The birchbark cover of the canoes was easily damaged by rocks. Therefore rapids were avoided when possible.

Portage—walk and carry the canoe past rapids or waterfalls or between lakes

Toboggans were usually pulled by humans. A large team of sled dogs would have required too much to eat for the amount of work they did.

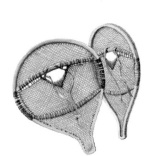

The round, or "bear-paw" snowshoe worked best in soft, deep snow and in the woods. (See painting page 84, bottom.) Long, narrow snowshoes were used on icy, hard snow and in open country.

Trade

Through trade, people were able to get products that were not found in their own territory. The Woodland Cree were able to survive using only local resources. However, they also traded for products from elsewhere. For example, in much of the Woodland Cree territory, birch trees did not grow large enough to make birchbark canoes. Furs were trapped, cleaned, and stretched during winter to trade for other products. Birchbark, copper, arrowheads, wild rice (which grew around Lake Superior in the territory of the Anishinabe), and corn and tobacco from the Iroquoian peoples were products for which the Woodland Cree traded.

For Your Notebook

1. Consider the technology available to the Woodland Cree living in the time before European exploration. What technology did they use to meet the challenges of their environment?
2. Were the Woodland Cree homes moved from place to place or rebuilt at each new campsite? Why?
3. Make a chart that shows men's and women's responsibilities in feeding the family.

Exploring Further

1. Construct a model or diorama of a Woodland Cree summer camp. Include homes and daily activities.

Social Part of Culture

- Family/Clan
- Passing on the Culture
- **Social Part of Culture**
- Arts and Recreation
- Spirituality

 A sense of belonging to family, clan, and group, social roles, and passing along the culture all meet psychological needs. They belong to the social part of culture. The Woodland Cree also sought a healthy balance between body, mind, and spirit. They expressed their spiritual beliefs and values through music, stories, and ceremonies. Leisure and recreation were considered important to a healthy life.

Family and Clan

The family is the main way a culture is passed from one generation to the next. The Woodland Cree lived in small hunting bands of 25–30. A winter hunting band was an extended family that lived in a camp of several wigwams. Everyone was related through **kinship** and marriage.

Children became members of their father's clan at birth. Algonquian nations were **patrilineal**. Members of a clan helped each other and treated other members as brothers and sisters. It was forbidden to marry someone from the same clan. The Algonquian clans were named after animals, fish, and birds that were important to their way of life.

Courtship and Marriage

Family groups came together for fishing and duck hunting in spring. Then young people were able to meet others from different clans. The rules of courting were very strict. A young man would get his parents' permission, then visit a young woman's family to let them know he was serious. Then he had to prove he would be a good provider. Usually he had to kill a moose or deer,

before he was accepted by the family. Young women needed to show they would be reliable and good workers. The couple would live with the man's extended family after they married.

Social Roles

Women and men had social as well as economic responsibilities. Men and women
- made spirituality a part of everything they did
- cared for and taught the children
- passed on their people's beliefs and values
- cared for the elderly
- tried to live in harmony with nature
- participated in ceremonies

Elders

An Elder is a man or a woman who has a great deal of wisdom and knowledge of history, beliefs, traditions, and customs. Elders are respected for what they have learned in life and for their special relationship with Mother Earth and all living things. Traditionally, Elders had an important role in teaching children the stories, history, and values of the people. They acted as advisors to adults. They taught trust, loving others, honesty, sharing, kindness, obedience, and respect for all living things.

Younger people learned the skills and knowledge they needed by watching and helping in daily activities.

Kinship—having some of the same ancestors or being related by marriage
Patrilineal—tracing descent through the father

Passing On the Culture

Woodland Cree children in the pre-Contact period did not attend schools as we do today. Lessons were learned in the forest, the camp, and the wigwam. Children listened to stories around the winter fire. The culture of the Woodland Cree was passed on throughout the four stages of life.

Elderly
Adulthood
Childhood
Puberty

Childhood

Births were welcomed among the Woodland Cree. They were considered a blessing from the Creator. Babies were kept near the mother as she worked. They were strapped to a cradleboard in a soft moss bag.

All of the adults cared for small children if they were in need. Thus, children felt loved and valued. Mothers, aunts, and grandmothers taught daily skills. Children watched adults work and helped whenever they could.

Between the ages of 7 and 14, children learned the skills and activities of adults. Girls learned from women and boys from their fathers, uncles, and grandfathers. Much of the child's education came from watching and playing games that imitated adult life. They did not have to try to do something until they felt confident they could do it. Success rather than failure was important. The child worked hard to understand something before trying it.

Learning how to listen was very important. Children were not sent away during adult conversation, but were expected to remain silent.

Courtesy of Norval Morrisseau and Coghlan Art

The above painting by Ojibway artist Norval Morrisseau is called *Going Herb Picking with Grandfather*.

Puberty

Parents usually taught the practical skills of life. The history, beliefs, and values more often were taught by grandparents and by Elders. When the grandparent felt the child had reached a certain level of knowledge, he or she was sent to an Elder for more education.

Boys often went on a Vision Quest when they reached puberty. A boy went into the forest alone without food for a number of days. He prayed until a spirit, usually in the form of an animal or bird, appeared in a vision. This spirit would then become the boy's guardian throughout life. Guidance and protection would come from the spirit. Sometimes a boy's vision would reveal a special gift or a direction that his life could take. The boy would work at developing that gift throughout life. He would use it to contribute to the community. Girls often married soon after puberty.

Adulthood

Adults continued to learn the practical knowledge and skills of providing for their families and the community. They learned how to be parents from older adults. As they grew older, they developed wisdom and experience. Some studied healing and the spirit world.

The Elderly

Older people were greatly respected. They influenced many of the decisions made by the group. They spent a great deal of time with children, passing on their knowledge.

For Your Notebook

1. Why was it important to Woodland Cree parents that their daughter's future husband be a good hunter?

2. Create a story that shows the stages of the education of a Woodland Cree boy or girl.

Exploring Further

3. Tell a story about some aspect of life of a Woodland Cree person during one of the stages of life.

4. Compare the ways a Woodland Cree family passed on the culture with how a modern-day family does. How are they similar? How and why are they different?

Spirituality

Spirituality was part of everyday life for the Woodland Cree.* Their spiritual practices related to the practical needs of life, such as hunting.

The Elders taught that all parts of the Earth and all forms of life had been made by the Creator. They were all sacred and had a place within the Sacred Circle. This included rocks, lakes, rivers, trees, animals, the moon, thunder, the spirits, and people. If one part was injured then everything would be affected. The people, the natural world, and the world of the spirits were interconnected.

Symbols

Woodland Cree people lived in a world of sacred symbols. Some important symbols included the circle, certain colours, the number four, and eagle feathers. Symbols of animals, birds, fish, or other parts of nature or the spirit world were used to decorate clothing or objects such as drums. A symbol might represent a personal guardian spirit that had appeared in a vision.

The Sacred Circle

There were many examples of the number four and the Sacred Circle in the people's everyday lives.
- The four seasons progress in a circle, returning each year.
- The day and night follow a continuous circle, (dawn, daylight, twilight, darkness) as does the cycle of the moon.
- Life follows a cycle from birth, youth, adulthood, to elderhood.

- Humans are spiritual, physical, emotional, and thinking beings.
- The summer camp was built in a circle, and most lodges were circular.
- The winds flow in a circle around the four directions (east, south, west, north).
- Those attending a ceremony sat in a circle. All in the circle were considered equal, none better than the others.
- The talking circle was round. Everyone had a chance to talk. Decisions were not made until everyone agreed.

"KEEPERS of NATURE"   D. B. Pawis

This image by Ojibway artist Daniel Beatty Pawis uses the circle and several symbols from nature. It shows respect for the traditions and spiritual values of the culture.

*Many of these beliefs are still held today. Spiritual practices are difficult to fully understand out of their context. Thus, the sacred ideas and practices of the Woodland Cree will not be discussed in detail in this textbook.

The Community Circle

The sense of community was important. Everyone had roles and responsibilities. Sharing food and necessities of life was required. An isolated person could easily starve. Everyone had a responsibility for everyone else. Generosity and sharing were highly valued. Everyone worked together and had a say in decisions. This was important for survival and to continue the culture from one generation to the next. All parts of the community circle needed to be strong. If this circle was broken the community would not survive.

Ceremonies

Among the Woodland Cree, many ceremonies were held in summer, when more members of clans were together. Ceremonies took place to mark important events.* Ceremonies showed thankfulness to the Creator. The Sacred Pipe was used in all ceremonies.

The Drum

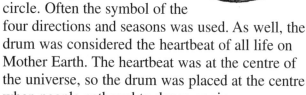

The drum was considered sacred.* Drums were used in spiritual ceremonies, particularly when there was dancing. Drums were round, using the symbol of the circle. Often the symbol of the four directions and seasons was used. As well, the drum was considered the heartbeat of all life on Mother Earth. The heartbeat was at the centre of the universe, so the drum was placed at the centre when people gathered to dance or sing.

The Pipe

The pipe was sacred and very powerful.* It was used in all ceremonies. When the pipe was used a prayer was said and the pipe offered to the four sacred directions.
- First to the East (direction of the sun and new beginnings)
- Second to the South (the direction of the warm wind)
- Third to the West (the direction of the setting sun, giving thanks for good things that have happened)
- Fourth to the North (the direction of the cold wind)

The pipe stem was made of wood. Trees represented honesty. The bowl was usually made from stone, which represented faith. The smoke from the sacred tobacco carried prayers to the Creator.

Gifts

Gifts were given as part of almost all ceremonies.* Sharing and being generous were very important to the Woodland Cree.

Tobacco and Sweetgrass

Sweetgrass and tobacco were sacred.* They were used in ceremonies. In traditional pipe ceremonies, tobacco was smoked to carry a message to the Creator. Today, ritual gifts of tobacco may still be given to a person, particularly an Elder, when asking a favour or for advice. If the person accepts the gift, they agree to help the giver or send them to someone who can help them.

Canada Revisited

Cree artist Dale Auger burns sweetgrass to show his respect for his traditional culture.

---

*Many ceremonies and the use of the sacred symbols of the drum, pipe, tobacco, sweetgrass, and gift-giving continue to be important in Woodland Cree culture today.

Sweat Lodge

A sweat lodge looked like a smaller, lower wigwam. People sat around a circular fire pit. When the stones were very hot, water was poured over them to make steam.

The Woodland Cree used sweat lodges for **purifying** themselves. This often happened before ceremonies or feasts. People cleansed themselves of sickness or evil thoughts and influences. Prayers to the Creator were said and the sacred pipe shared. Sweat lodges were also used as tools for healing, particularly to bring balance to the body, mind, and spirit. **Counselling** and teaching might also take place.

Healers

Those with special powers to contact the spirit world often became healers. These people were believed to have special talents, like the ability to forecast the future. People came to them for advice. Some healers made medicine from roots and herbs to heal the sick. They also used special prayers for healing. Healers were also believed to have the power to injure or destroy.

Arts and Recreation

The Arts*

Among the Woodland Cree no one could be spared from helping meet basic needs. However, people decorated objects like special storage bags and containers when they had extra time, such as in winter. They used both geometric and floral designs. Art gave spiritual power to ceremonial drums, the sacred pipe, and special clothing. Paint, quillwork, and moosehair tufting were used in decoration.

Musical instruments were part of ceremonies and social dancing. People played the whistle, shaker, and hand drum. Singing was also important.

Purifying—making clean; washing away evil
Counselling—when a person with wisdom or training talks to someone to help with a problem
*The Arts include Visual (painting, drawing, carving, decorating), Performance (dance, storytelling), and Music (instruments, singing).

Games and Recreation

Some games were played just for fun, but most were a way to become an expert at a certain skill. Many games were practised for improving eye-hand **co-ordination**, quick thinking, throwing, and strength. Games such as catching a bone ring on a spear helped develop the co-ordination important to a good hunter and fisher. Tug-of-war, wrestling, and snowsnake helped develop strength. Archery was training with the bow and arrow. Foot races were also popular.

Stories

Winter was storytelling time. Both men and women told stories. Some stories were told for entertainment and some were used to teach. Children learned about their family history, about how to act and behave toward other people. Stories were told about the animals, plants, and spirit beings. Stories passed on traditions from one generation to the next. The lesson the story was teaching was never told directly. It was left for the listener to figure out.

Stories told about how the world came to be. There were stories of the origin of the People, how the Thunder came to be, the origin of Fire, and how the Animals got their shapes. Often stories had an animal or bird as the main character.

Stories often involved a character called Trickster.** Trickster was usually part human and part spirit. He was able to turn into other forms, like a rock, an animal, or a stream. He was sly and crafty, and often got into trouble and caused trouble. The story on the next page is about Wesakachak, the Cree Trickster.

Exploring Further

1. Find a story from an Algonquian-speaking people's culture in the library. (See the map on page 85 to find out which nations are Algonquian-speaking.) Tell the story to a friend or classmate in your own words or record your storytelling on audiotape.

Co-ordination—ability to do more than one thing at the same time
**The Trickster in Cree legends is Wesakachak (there are several different ways to spell this name). In Northwest Coast cultures, the Trickster is Raven. Among peoples of the Plains he is Coyote.

Wesakachak

—Cree story "Wīsakecāhk and the Killdeer," illustration by Ojibway artist, Nokomis

Wesakachak was the big brother to all things of Creation. He was a wanderer who made his living by tricking his relatives for a meal. His stories are told during the winter months. Wesakachak is respected as a sacred Being that could change himself or others.

One summer day, Wesakachak was wandering aimlessly, when suddenly he noticed a strange sight. Some killdeer birds were involved in a ceremony. He saw them take their eyes out, throw them in the air above the willows, and then catch them back in their eye sockets.

He thought, "This is an interesting trick." So he approached the birds. "My little brothers, teach me how to do that too."

"No! " replied one bird in a stern voice. "This is a sacred ritual which can be performed only to cure a headache. You can do this four times a year and no more."

Wesakachak walked away wishing the killdeer had not spoken so sharply to him. He thought to himself, "I will fix those birds." He was no sooner out of their sight when he changed himself into an old

Story "Wīsakecāhk and the Killdeer" from *Nēhiyaw Atayokēwina: Cree Legends: Stories of Wīsakecāhk*, edited by Stan Cuthand for Saskatchewan Indian Cultural Centre

man and painted his face red with vermillion. With a stick in his hand and with much moaning and groaning, he walked past the bird who was performing the rite.

"What is the matter old man?" asked the bird.

"Oh, I am miserable and I do not want to bother you with my problems because I will only make you unhappy. You see, I have these terrible headaches. My head feels as if it will split." He began to walk slowly by.

"Wait!" said the bird, "maybe I can help you. Take out your eyes and throw them to the top of these willows, and do not be afraid because they will fall back into place. This can only be done four times a year. Always remember not to abuse this gift. If you use it wisely, it can help you."

Wesakachak groaned pitifully as he took his eyes out and threw them in the air. They fell back into place. He was really pleased with himself, for he did not think such a thing was possible. Quickly he walked away, after assuring the killdeer that the performance had cured him entirely of his headache.

As soon as he saw a bunch of willows, he held his head and began to moan. Again he threw

his eyes up and they fell back into place, then he went on his way. It was a pleasant way of passing time. He kept pretending to have a headache every time he saw willow trees, quickly using the four times he was allowed. Wesakachak was not serious about this sacred rite. As everyone knows this is a dangerous practice. Misfortune usually befalls one who abuses a sacred rite.

Walking along, he again pretended to have a headache. He threw his eyes in the air but much too high. The next thing he knew they dropped on the ground instead of falling back into their sockets.

Wesakachak was blind! He groped around trying to find his eyes, but could not. Every now and then a stick would poke him in the face. While groping for his eyes, Wesakachak heard a fox laughing and teasing him. No animal felt pity for him after all the tricks he had played on them. He called out, "I will make your fur beautiful if you help me." The fox just laughed and walked away.

Wesakachak had to do something! Although he walked slowly he kept bumping into trees. Each time he would ask, "What kind of a tree are you?"

"Oh, I am a birch" or "I am a poplar," they would reply.

98

None of these answers satisfied him, until at last one replied, "I am a spruce."

"Ah, the right one!" cried Wesakachak.

He then collected some dry gum from the spruce. He chewed the spruce gum until it was soft and pliable, shaped it into a ball, and placed it into his eye socket. Then he made the other eye. "Now," he thought, "I will make the fox pay for not helping me."

He came across the fox sleeping on the ground. "Aha," thought Wesakachak, "now is my chance."

He set a fire around the fox and ran away. The fox woke up to find he was trapped. He leaped over the flames, singeing his fur—and that is why the red fox is the colour he is today.

Political Part of Culture

  The Woodland Cree lived in small groups, but they still had group needs. Laws and a form of government were needed for making decisions that were good for all the people.

Clan and Band

The Woodland Cree had many clans. People were loyal to their clan. They had responsibilities to the clan and its other members. People also had responsibility to the band. (Bands were groups of related families that lived and travelled together.) Small bands had just a few families. As many as 100 families might make up a band in areas where food was plentiful. Each band was considered independent and had its own chief. There was no one chief or Council that ruled over all the Woodland Cree. A similar form of band governments is still used today by Cree Nations. You will learn more about band government in Chapter 11.

Leadership

Each band selected a chief. Leaders were chosen because they were respected for their skill in hunting and ability to lead in conflict or war. Leaders did not make decisions by themselves. Most were made by all the adults in the group, using a consensus process. Spiritual leaders guided the decision-making process.

Elders acted as advisors and teachers to the leaders and all the people. They made sure that everyone understood and remembered the customs and laws of the people.

Conflict

Conflict within the community was avoided as much as possible. People lived very close together, especially in winter. Rules of behaviour were quite strict. People were soft-spoken and learned to control their feelings and be respectful. They allowed each other to have personal space. There was little privacy in a wigwam.

If personal conflicts could not be worked out by individuals, the Elders or a community circle would assist. Sometimes issues arose in the community that could not be solved. Then the person involved often left their family group and went to live alone or with another family.

Aggressive or violent behaviour was discouraged. However, the Woodland Cree did go to war if they needed to. If the people became involved in a war with another group they selected a war chief to lead them into battle. The men trained as warriors as well as hunters. Many similar skills were needed.

Canada Revisited

Chief Abel Bosum of the Oujé-Bougamou, a Cree First Nation of Quebec, accepts the 1998 National Aboriginal Award for Community Development. The First Nation led by Chief Bosum planned and built a new, environmentally and people-friendly village after they were moved because of mining and forestry projects in Northern Quebec.

Review

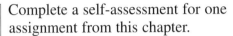

The icons are your cue to turn to the Learning How to Learn Appendix (pages 256–265) for ideas on how to complete these activities.

 This icon is a reminder to turn to the Research Model (pages x and xi).

Assessment

1. Complete a self-assessment for one assignment from this chapter.

2.
Section I Presentation Activity

 Continue with the presentation activity you started on pages 5 and 31: What is the relationship between the environment and the culture of either the Wendat or the Woodland Cree? Refer to page 262 in the Appendix for presentation ideas to share your learning with others.

Summarizing the Chapter

3. In the preview activity on page 83 you were asked to fill in the "My Predictions" column of the chart. Now use what you have learned from reading the chapter to fill in the third column of the chart, "What I Found Out." Share your findings with the rest of the class.

4. Refer to "Questions to Talk About" on page 5. Discuss questions 2–4 with a partner, based on what you have learned about the Woodland Cree. Record ideas from this discussion in your notes.

Generalization—a statement that applies to many specific examples

Understanding Concepts

Do questions 5, 6, 7, and either 8 or 9.

5. The chapter overview on page 82 contains some **generalizations** on how the Woodland Cree used to live. Review the overview, the prediction chart you made for Chapter 4, and any notes you made for this chapter, then do the following activity.

a) On a large piece of poster paper, draw a large circle and divide it into quarters. Label one season per quarter, as the diagram below shows. Because spirituality and community life were central to everything the people did, put them at the centre. Add the environment around the outside, as shown below.

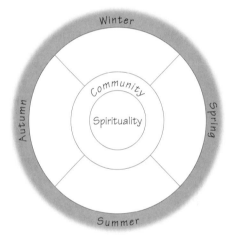

b) Select four generalizations from page 82. Write them around the outer edge of each quarter of the circle. See example below.

c) Write examples for each generalization. Add your own drawings, colour, and designs.

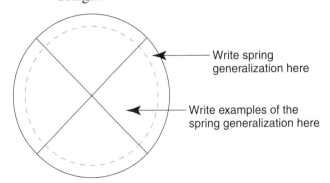

d) Share your circles with the rest of the class.

6. Check the organization of your activities for this chapter in your binder to see that everything is in the correct place.
   - Chapter title page, notes, activities, maps, and illustrations in Activities section
   - definitions in WordBook section
   - History Journal writings
   - Learning How to Learn section

7. Use one of the vocabulary strategies shown on page 263 to record any three of the new vocabulary words for this chapter. Put them in the WordBook section of your History binder.

8. Some of the main ideas from the chapter follow:
   - The seasons influenced the way of life of the Woodland Cree.
   - The Woodland Cree people were big game hunters who used raw materials from the environment to create their culture.
   - The forest ecosystem influenced how the people met their basic needs.
   - The Woodland Cree people interacted with the environment to create a unique way of life.
   - All parts of the community circle must be strong.
   - The beliefs of the Woodland Cree people showed respect for all living things—for the land, the animals, and the people.
   - Most decisions were made by consensus.

   Do either a) or b)

   a) Create a concept poster on one of the seven ideas above. (See Appendix page 256.) Present your poster to the class.

   b) Use a web, mind map, outline, or chart to create a permanent set of notes about one of these ideas. Explain your work to a classmate.

9. Select either a) or b) and find examples in this chapter. Work with a partner to make a mind map that organizes the examples on one sheet of paper. Use simple line drawings and lots of colour. Mind maps are explained in the Appendix on page 261.

a) Environmental Interaction: the environment influences the people and the people interact with the environment.

b) Balance: all living things are interconnected.

Developing Communication Skills

Select at least one question from 10–12:

Writing

10. Select a picture from this chapter. Write a story or tell a partner about it as though you are a person in the scene.

Viewing and Representing

11. In a group of three, create a mural or diorama showing how the Woodland Cree lived. Include activities from all four seasons and all three types of needs (physical, psychological, and group). Show examples of environmental interaction.

Listening and Speaking

12. Talking circles have been used in traditional Aboriginal cultures to solve problems and maintain good community or group relationships. A circle is round, so that all the participants are equal and have an opportunity to speak. Discussions continued until everyone agreed (reached consensus).

   a) How do people sit in meetings in your community? How is it decided who speaks, when, and for how long? How are decisions made?

   b) Are all meetings in your community the same? How do they differ?

   c) Do research to find out more about traditional Aboriginal meetings. In your opinion, which is better? Why?

Applying Concepts

13. Refer to the Chapter Focus on page 83. Notice that Environmental Interaction and Balance have been two focuses of the chapter. Working in pairs or triads, make two webs. One should represent examples of environmental interaction that apply to our world today. The other should represent ways of maintaining balance in nature and human life in our world today.

14. Try to think of as many ideas as you can for how the life of the Woodland Cree might have been different.
    What if . . .
    a) the moose and the deer were herding animals that lived in large groups?
    b) the Algonquian-speaking peoples had invented the wheel but not the canoe?
    Record your answers in the History Journal section of your notebook.

15. Compare the hunting practices and attitudes of the Woodland Cree with modern day hunters (some things to consider are hunting licenses, seasons, age of hunters). See Comparison, page 257. Interview three adults on this topic.

Challenge Plus

16.  Develop a multimedia presentation about a typical day in the life of a Woodland Cree girl or boy.

17. Research newspaper articles on environmental interaction or concerns. Pick one article.
    a) What issue is the focus of the article? (See Critical Thinking on page 258 in the Appendix for information on issues.)

b) What points of view are included in the article?

c) Conduct a survey of ten people to find out their point of view on the issue in the article. Make a graph to record the results of your survey.

d) In your History Journal, record your thoughts about using a survey to find out different points of view on an issue.

Chapter 5: The Anishinabe

Chapter Focus

In Chapter 4 you examined the culture of the Woodland Cree and how the environment had shaped it. Chapter 5 looks at another of the Algonquian-speaking peoples, the Anishinabe (also known as the Ojibway). The Woodland Cree and Anishinabe had related languages and similar cultures. Each was influenced by environment and contact with other groups and trading partners.

Use the information in Chapter 5 to complete one of the three projects on the right. This chapter does not have review questions. The project you do will be used to assess your learning about the Anishinabe.

This chapter will focus on the following concepts. It emphasizes environmental interaction, balance, and technology.

Environmental Interaction   **Balance**   **Technology**   **Cultural Contact**   **Exploration**

Vocabulary

Anishinabe	identity
Ojibway	Thunderbird
watershed	Windigo

Chapter Activity

Use the information from this chapter to complete one of the projects that follow. Make a self-assessment before starting the activity you select. Complete it at the end of the chapter.

Project 1: Make a report on how the Anishinabe met their physical, psychological, or group needs (see pages 22–25).

Project 2: Make a series of visual and written **storyboards** describing activities relating to spring, summer, autumn, or winter.

Project 3: Make a web or mind map using the information from this chapter to show the influence of the environment on how the Anishinabe lived or how they interacted with the environment. Add drawings and colour.

Anishinabe summer camps were usually near a lake for fishing and canoe travel.

Paul Kane, *Indian Encampment on Lake Huron*, c.1845–50, Art Gallery of Ontario

Ojibway has many different spellings. Ojibwa, Ojibwe, and Chippewa are frequently used. Many Ojibway today prefer to call themselves Anishinabe. This is the name used in their stories about the original people. Two stories about the Creation of the First People are told on pages 10–13.

Storyboard—a combination of image, text, and instructions (usually created as a series) to show and tell how a subject will be presented in some other medium such as video

A Case Study

The Anishinabe are an Algonquian-speaking nation. In the pre-Contact period, they lived around the north shores of Lake Superior and Lake Huron and west to the Lake of the Woods.* They were one of the largest and strongest Algonquian-speaking groups. The Anishinabe were expert canoe builders. They travelled widely in their lake and river filled lands. They were well located for trade in all directions.

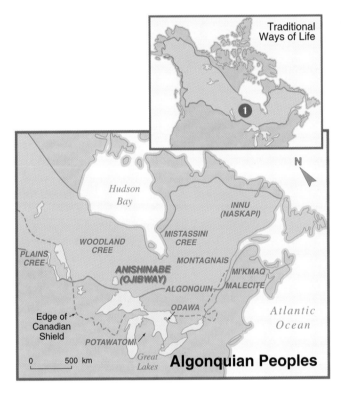

Algonquian Peoples

Environment

Landforms: Canadian Shield region (see page 38)

- rugged, rocky, barren uplands
- boggy wetlands, rivers, streams, thousands of rocky-bottomed lakes
- thin soil, not suitable for agriculture

Climate: Continental (see page 39)

- moderate rainfall** ◊◊◊◊
- cold, snowy winters ❄❄❄❄❄
- warm summers

---

*Like the Woodland Cree, the Anishinabe people later moved much farther west. Today many live on the Plains, as well as in northwestern Ontario.

**See chart on the inside back cover.

Vegetation: Coniferous/Mixed Forest (see page 40)

- coniferous forest; some mixed forest farther south and east
- areas of hardwoods; stands of large maples and birch
- wild rice in wetlands

Economic Part of Culture

   The way of life of the Anishinabe was similar to that of the Woodland Cree. They were mainly hunters. They also fished, trapped, gathered raw materials and food from the environment, and carried on trade.

Like the Woodland Cree, the Anishinabe hunted moose, deer, bear, and many smaller animals and birds. Moose, deer, and bear are fast-moving, alert, and difficult to hunt. They live in small groups that are spread out. Hunting these animals was skilled work. It required much knowledge of the environment and wildlife.

The Anishinabe gathered natural resources from the environment to help meet their needs. This family is collecting maple sap in spring to make sugar.

Seasonal Cycles
Spring (m'nukamik) ① ② ③

Both the animals and the people were hungriest in early spring. New plant growth had not yet started. The stored, preserved food was used up. Snow was melting and wet. The frozen lakes and rivers were not safe for walking on and still not open enough for canoes. Hunters and trappers travelled on foot through the forest.

Tapping maple trees for their sweet syrup was a group activity in early spring. Each family had its traditional sugar bush. Notice the activity in the drawing on page 105.

Autumn (degwagik) ⑦ ⑧ ⑨

Before the frosts began, the Anishinabe hunted game and gathered and preserved food. The season for hunting migrating waterfowl came in late autumn. The traders returned to camp. Many had spent their summers paddling great distances to meet other traders at traditional meeting places. They brought back new goods and any information that could be shared through related languages and signs.

As the frosts began, families got ready to move back to winter camps.

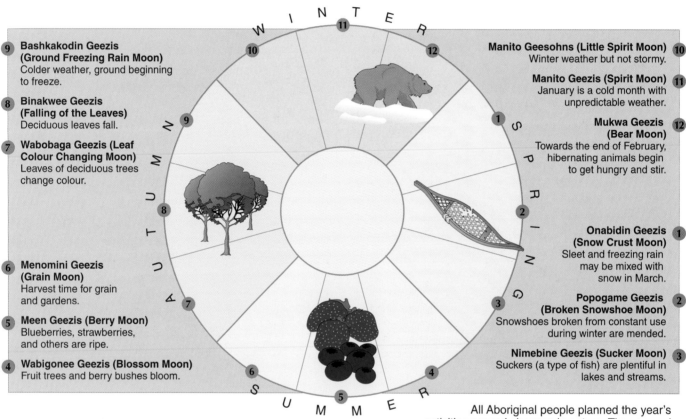

⑨ Bashkakodin Geezis (Ground Freezing Rain Moon)
Colder weather, ground beginning to freeze.

⑧ Binakwee Geezis (Falling of the Leaves)
Deciduous leaves fall.

⑦ Wabobaga Geezis (Leaf Colour Changing Moon)
Leaves of deciduous trees change colour.

⑥ Menomini Geezis (Grain Moon)
Harvest time for grain and gardens.

⑤ Meen Geezis (Berry Moon)
Blueberries, strawberries, and others are ripe.

④ Wabigonee Geezis (Blossom Moon)
Fruit trees and berry bushes bloom.

Manito Geesohns (Little Spirit Moon) ⑩
Winter weather but not stormy.

Manito Geezis (Spirit Moon) ⑪
January is a cold month with unpredictable weather.

Mukwa Geezis (Bear Moon) ⑫
Towards the end of February, hibernating animals begin to get hungry and stir.

Onabidin Geezis (Snow Crust Moon) ①
Sleet and freezing rain may be mixed with snow in March.

Popogame Geezis (Broken Snowshoe Moon) ②
Snowshoes broken from constant use during winter are mended.

Nimebine Geezis (Sucker Moon) ③
Suckers (a type of fish) are plentiful in lakes and streams.

All Aboriginal people planned the year's activities around changes in nature. They named the months, or moon cycles, after some of these events. This calendar has been adapted to fit a modern-day calendar of 12 months rather than having 13 moons.

Summer (neebin) ④ ⑤ ⑥

Small bands gathered into larger communities for summer activities. Many summer activities were social as well as economic. People fished during spawning, when fish are plentiful. Fish were dried, shredded, and packed in bags. Fish oil was collected and sealed in containers.

Gathering went on throughout the summer. Berries, herbs, roots, mushrooms, nuts, and bark were collected when they were ready. The last plant to be gathered in the summer was wild rice. It was an important food and trade item.

Winter (bebohn) ⑩ ⑪ ⑫

In the winter, the Anishinabe spread out into their traditional hunting areas. Their nearest neighbours would be at least 10 kilometres away. Families moved around their area, hunting, checking traps and snares, and ice fishing. They maintained traps and tools, and cleaned and stretched the hides of the animals they trapped.

Wild Rice Collecting

Wild rice grows in fairly shallow (0.5 to 2 metres), slowly-moving water in wetlands. It needs a moderately long growing season. Wild rice is a member of the grass family, not a true species of rice. This nutritious grain has been harvested by Aboriginal peoples for thousands of years.

Harvesting of wild rice was traditionally done from a canoe. The canoe was paddled slowly through the tall grass. The wild rice stalks were bent over top of the canoe with a stick. They were struck with another stick to loosen the ripe kernels, which fell into the canoe. The kernels in the head of a wild rice plant do not ripen all at once. Thus, the people might return to the same place several times to collect newly ripened grain. Some rice was always left to go to seed. To be sure of a good crop the following year, the people always shook some kernels into the water. Thanks was always given to the Creator.

The rice was dried by stirring it in a container near a low fire. Then the grain was separated from the hulls, packed in containers, and carefully stored.

Canada Revisited

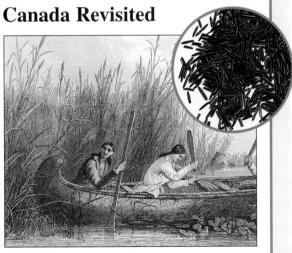

Wild rice harvesting is still an important industry for First Nations in Ontario and Manitoba. Large quantities of wild rice are grown on wetland "farms." Special machinery has been designed for harvesting it.

Technology and Trade

The Anishinabe used many kinds of snares and traps to catch different types of animals. The type of trap depended on the animal. Trappers considered what the animal ate, how it travelled, and what its habits were. How big or dangerous it was and how it might try to escape were also important.

In winter, people walked through forests and across frozen lakes and rivers on snowshoes. In summer, they travelled the waterways in canoes. The canoe and the snowshoe were two important First Nations contributions to Canadian culture.

The Algonquian-speaking peoples built the finest canoes. They traded canoes and rolls of birchbark to peoples that did not have large birch trees in their region. They also traded furs, hides, wild rice, and any other raw materials or products that were surplus to their own needs.

There was a major trade centre for Aboriginal groups at the end of Lake Superior a thousand years ago. It was not a permanent settlement. However, it had a large population in trading season. The region was a source of abundant whitefish and maple sugar.

Fur-bearing animals have their heaviest coats in winter. The best time to trap them is in early spring before they shed their winter hair. The above drawing shows a beaver pond.

Social Part of Culture
Family and Clan

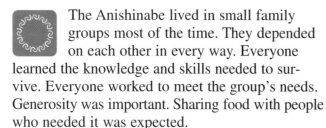 The Anishinabe lived in small family groups most of the time. They depended on each other in every way. Everyone learned the knowledge and skills needed to survive. Everyone worked to meet the group's needs. Generosity was important. Sharing food with people who needed it was expected.

Respect for others was important to group living. Everyone had his or her role. The main hunter, usually the father, was well respected. He was given the most important place in the wigwam. People controlled their feelings and kept their voices low. It was bad manners to show anger in the camp or the home. However, the Anishinabe were brave hunters and fighters when they needed to be.

The Anishinabe had many clans named for animals, birds, and fish. Some of the best known were the Turtle, Deer, Loon, Bear, Beaver, Duck, Eagle, Sturgeon (a large fish), and Watersnake. Belonging to a certain clan was a way of being part of a larger group. Clan membership was an important part of a person's identity.

The Anishinabe were patrilineal. Children became members of the father's clan. When a young man married, he continued to live in his father's family group. A woman did not change clans when she married. However, she went to live with her husband's family group. Members of the same clan could not marry.

Babies and infants were loved and looked after by all. Children worked alongside their parents. They learned new skills by watching until they felt confident to try something. Boys and girls learned their culture's knowledge and skills from parents and adults. Girls learned from their mothers, aunts, and grandmothers. Boys learned from fathers, uncles, and grandfathers. The roles of males and females were different, but families worked together to achieve their goals. Everyone's contribution was respected.

Passing on the Culture

 Children also learned spiritual beliefs and values from parents, other adults, and Elders. They learned by watching, listening, and practising. Recreation was part of education. Snowsnake, wrestling, archery, running, and pin-and-ring games were popular. They developed strength, **agility**, and co-ordination.

The larger summer community was important to the Anishinabe. They met people from other clans, visited, and renewed friendships. They made new friends and looked for marriage partners for their children. People danced, and attended ceremonies, games, and contests. Their group identity was enriched by community events. Sharing a language and customs, ceremonies and beliefs meant they were part of the same nation.

Courtesy of Norval Morrisseau and Coghlan Art

The above painting called *Circle of Life* was created by Norval Morrisseau, an Ojibway artist who lives near Vancouver.

Agility—the ability to move quickly and easily

Spiritual Life

 The spiritual life of the Anishinabe was part of the way they related to the environment. The spirit world and the world of humans and animals were not separate. They believed that a Creator called Kije-Manito had made the people and placed them on the earth. The people gave thanks to animals they hunted and for other resources they collected. They believed that all things were connected.

The stories of the Anishinabe were passed from one generation to the next. Storytellers and Elders explained how the world came to be as it is. Stories are part of what makes a culture **unique**. Aboriginal peoples all describe their origins in story. (Two stories of the origin of the Anishinabe are told on pages 10–13 of this book.) Stories also explained the natural surroundings. Why there is thunder and lightning, or where all the rocks and lakes had come from may be explained in stories. Stories were often about supernatural Beings, or animals with special powers.

The Anishinabe believed that thunder came from a huge bird flapping its wings. Its eyes shot out lightning and rain fell from its eyes. Ceremonies welcoming the Thunderbird back were held before the rain storms of summer began.

The Thunderbird, by the Cree artist, Richard Masuskapoe, shows the spirit of the thunder.

Many Beings from the spirit world were described as helpful to humans. They had to be treated with respect. The Algonquian-speaking peoples also told stories of a frightening spirit called Windigo. The Windigo was dangerous to weak, careless, or unlucky people, particularly in the winter.

Unique—the only one of something; not like others

This painting by Ojibway artist Norval Morrisseau, called *Integration*, shows the interconnectedness of life.

Ojibway artist Blake Debassige's painting called *Bear Feeding* shows the sacred Bear with fish and birds. The painting shows the importance of the animals in the Anishinabe culture.

Political Part of Culture

The Anishinabe, like the Woodland Cree, did not have a central government. Each band was independent and had its own leader. In summer, in the larger community, leaders discussed issues important to all. Some joint decisions would be made. They made agreements about trade, territory, or attack by other groups. Changes facing the Anishinabe as a nation were discussed in these councils. The clan system was an important part of their government.

Note: There is no review section for this chapter. Please refer to the chapter projects on page 104.

Section I Review

Learning How to Learn

Comparison

 Comparison is a tool for examining how two or more topics are the same and how they are different. Comparison is a way to understand and learn about a topic.

Topics can only be compared if they can be described using the same criteria.* For example, it would be difficult to compare "climate" and "moose." However, it would be possible to compare "moose" and "beaver."

Cultures are very complex. It is difficult to compare every detail of two cultures. In this textbook, the headings and sub-headings can help you choose criteria. If the same heading appears in two chapters, it is a way to compare groups. For example, the heading "Environment" is found in the case studies of the Haida, the Wendat, the Woodland Cree, and the Anishinabe. Other related information can also be added to your comparison.

Example:
Compare the environment of the Wendat and the Woodland Cree.

The Wendat	Criteria	Woodland Cree
	Landforms	
	Climate	
	Vegetation	
	Animal Life	

Four assignments follow. Do number 1 and one of 2, 3, or 4. Remember to check page 263 for self-assessment ideas.

1. a) Work with a partner or in a small group and select one topic from the following.

Topics

A. Compare seasonal activities of the Wendat with those of the Woodland Cree.**

B. Compare the environment of the Wendat with that of the Woodland Cree.

C.  Compare how the environment influenced the traditional ways of life of the Wendat and Woodland Cree.

D. Compare a village way of life with a migratory way of life.

E. Compare the ways the Wendat and the Woodland Cree met their physical needs.

F. Compare the ways the Wendat and the Woodland Cree met their psychological needs.

G. Compare the ways the Wendat and the Woodland Cree met their group needs.

---

*Criteria are standards by which something is judged or put into categories.

**The Anishinabe can be substituted for the Woodland Cree but you will need to do extra research.

b) 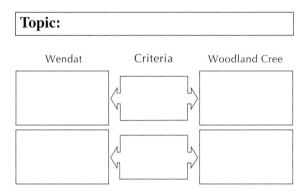 Identify what criteria you are going to use to compare the Wendat and the Woodland Cree. The number of criteria will vary depending upon what you are comparing. Write the criteria on a chart like the one below.

Topic:

Wendat   Criteria   Woodland Cree

Add additional boxes for the number of criteria you are comparing.

c) Show how the items you are comparing are the same and how they are different. Base your comparison on the criteria you identified. (An example to get you started is found on page 257 of the Appendix.)

d) When you have completed your comparison chart, prepare a written or oral report to give to your class.

2.   First Nations people made many contributions to the general way of life in present-day Canada. Prepare a presentation on contributions of the Wendat, the Woodland Cree, or the Anishinabe people. Information about presentations is provided in the Appendix on page 262.

3. Write a story of a day in the life of a young Aboriginal boy or girl. Indicate near the start of your story which First Nation they belong to. Your story must be historically accurate. (See numbers 5 and 7 on page 264.)

4. Select a story and painting from Section I (pages 4–109). Prepare a written review or critique of it. Reviews and critiques are explained under number 13 on page 264.

Section I Presentation Activity

  Throughout Section I you have been working on a presentation that shows the relationship between the environment and the culture of either the Wendat or the Woodland Cree. If you haven't done so already, complete Steps 5/6 of the research model on page xi. Also see the Appendix on page 262 for presentation ideas. Your teacher will give you more information about Steps 7 to 9.

If you haven't discussed self-assessment criteria, do that now. Make an assessment guide and/or get one from your teacher.

Section II

European Exploration

"How many of you watched the launch of the shuttle on TV last night?" asked Mrs. Maziuk.

Many hands shot into the air. Almost everyone had also watched the program on space exploration that had followed.

"It didn't say anything about 'warp speed.' It talked about taking a long time to travel anywhere. Why is that, Mrs. Maziuk?" asked Mark.

Everybody smiled at his comment. "That's just fiction, Mark," somebody said. "Warp drives haven't been invented yet."

"This class should talk about recognizing fact and fiction. Historians need to know how to assess sources of information," said Mrs. Maziuk.

"I know," said Nicole. "Stories are fiction. They often have facts in them but the characters and events are invented. In science fiction the facts are invented too!"

The teacher laughed, then said, "Now let's recall our predictions about what we will study next. Then I will bring up my outline of this Social Studies course."

After the students recalled their predictions, Mrs. Maziuk projected the course outline on the screen.

"Oh, yes—it's European explorers. Here come my ancestors the Vikings," said Niels. The class laughed. He always reminded them proudly of his Viking ancestors.

"We will learn about Petra's too, and then Mark's. We will also look at how European exploration affected Dale and Dani's ancestors," their teacher said.

Questions to Talk About

1. a) What is the difference between fact and fiction?
    b) List types of programs relating to space exploration you watch on TV or read about in the newspaper or in novels.
    c) Mark each item FACTUAL or FICTION.
2. How do you think space exploration will affect you in your lifetime?

File   Edit   Object   Type   Filter   View   Window   Help

Section I **Aboriginal Peoples**	Section II **European Explorers**	Section III **Today and Tomorrow**
• The First People • Environmental Interaction • The Wendat • The Woodland Cree • The Anishinabe	• Early Exploration (the Vikings) • An Age of Exploration • Exploring and Claiming Lands • Exploring and Colonizing Lands • Quebec Colony and the Fur Trade	• Aboriginal People Today • Exploration Today

After Mrs. Maziuk displayed the Social Studies outline, she explained, "We are going to study about the European explorers. They came to Canada during the second **millennium** of the **Common Era**.

"Let's break into six groups. Each group is to discuss the questions on the bulletin board. Each group should choose a recorder to write down the group's ideas. You'll see there are similarities between exploration today and exploration 400 to 1000 years ago. We will also talk about how cultures change when groups come into contact."

Notebook Organization

1. Make a title page in your History binder for Section II: European Exploration.

Exploration
a) What does exploration mean?
b) Record different kinds of exploration.
c) Why do humans explore?
d) Who pays for exploration?
e) What discoveries/ developments in technology are necessary before exploration into unknown territory can occur?
f) What are some of the results of exploration?
g) How is modern-day exploration the same as the European exploration of the second millennium?
h) What challenges does exploration present?
i) When explorers enter a new environment, what effects may their technology have on the environment and its inhabitants?

Millennium—one thousand years
Common Era—CE; equivalent to AD; dates after an agreed-on date

Order of Good Cheer Banquet

Section II Project

 During your study of European exploration your class will prepare and participate in an Order of Good Cheer banquet. The date of the presentation will be decided later. Each of you will make a presentation at this banquet. The presentations will show what you have learned about exploration and colonization before 1660. Include as many of your projects from Chapters 6 to 10 as you can. Ideas for presentations are shown on pages 222, 223, and 262.

As a class you may decide to invite others. Another class, school staff, members of the community, or your parents might come to this special event. Dressing in the clothing styles of the 1600s for the Order of Good Cheer Banquet will make it more authentic. It will also add to the fun.

The Order of Good Cheer

Samuel de Champlain, the famous explorer and colonizer, devised a plan called the Order of Good Cheer. It was intended to keep the colonists busy and entertained. It involved the colonists in food gathering. This guarded the colony's health and provided exercise for them. In his journal Champlain described the Order of Good Cheer.

We spent the winter very pleasantly, and had good fare [food] by means of the Order of Good Cheer, which I established and which everyone found beneficial to his health, and more profitable than all sorts of medicine we might have used. The Order consisted of a chain which we used to place with certain ceremonies about the neck of one of our people, commissioning him for that day to go hunting. The next day it was conferred upon another and so on in order. All vied [competed] with each other to see who could do best and bring back the finest game . . . .

You will learn much more about Champlain in Chapters 9 and 10.

Steps for Planning

1.   As a class, brainstorm for ideas about what to include in the event. Decide together what types of displays and activities you will include. Decide on the types of entertainment you may have at the banquet. Suggestions for a program are shown on the next page.

2. Decide on criteria for assessing your projects and the Order of Good Cheer activity. (See page 263 in the Appendix for ideas.)

3. You may wish to complete an Action Plan once you have looked at all parts of this assignment.

Action Plan

1. Date of Presentation ....

2. Describe what you want your part of the presentation to look like and/or sound like.

   ....
   ....
   ....

3. Plan on paper what tasks have to be done. Assign a completion date for each task.

Task/Person	Completion Date	Done
1.		
2.		
3.		

(add to this list as needed)

Steps for Preparing

- Assign roles and responsibilities. Be sure to set deadlines and to meet as a group often to check your progress. Everyone should begin to practise their parts as soon as possible.
- Finalize the list of displays and presentations and prepare the program.
- Write a script for the Master/Mistress of Ceremonies (MC) and for any other original portions of the program.
- Plan props (including the Order of Good Cheer chain), costumes, sets, supplies, and music. Who will organize, gather, or prepare materials?
- Decide what food and drinks you will serve. They should be as real to the period as possible. Who will prepare the food? Where will you serve it? Who will serve it?
- Create invitations for those you wish to invite. Be sure to invite them as far in advance as possible and ask that they reply

by a certain date, so you can plan properly. (A sample invitation is shown below.)

The honour of your presence and participation is requested at a banquet hosted by Samuel de Champlain, at ____PM on _____, in the dining room at Port Royal. The highlight will be presentations of _____, as well as exhibits created by our talented colonists. Entertainment and refreshments will also be provided.

R.S.V.P.

- Rehearse as a group. Confirm what is left to be done and who will do it.
- Arrange to meet as a class following the event to discuss your program's success, based on the assessment criteria you set.

Sample Program

1. Greeters at the door invite guests to view the projects, which represent European exploration and early colonization in Canada.
2. A drum roll signals the entry into the room of the Master or Mistress of Ceremonies. Samuel de Champlain enters, followed by the person wearing the Order of Good Cheer chain and the rest of the people at the colony.
3. Beverages are served. (French music is played in the background.) Students visit with guests and talk about their lives in the colonies.
4. Drum roll announces the arrival of the entertainers: comedians and storytellers tell jokes and stories based upon life in Canada before 1660.
5. Drum roll. MC announces food will be served.
6. Students who have prepared oral presentations make them now. Be sure someone has been assigned to co-ordinate this.
7. The Order of Good Cheer chain is passed on to the person who will be responsible for the next event.
8. Formal farewells and thanks.

 For more information on the Order of Good Cheer visit http://parkscanada. pch.gc.ca/parks/nova_scotia/ port_royal/english/historye.htm#Cheer

Chronology

Understanding chronology is important in historical thinking. It is one way that historians organize information about history. Chronology involves understanding time, the past, present, and future. Placing events in the order they occurred over time is thinking like an historian.

History—
☐ Primary Source
☐ Secondary Source
☐ Interpretation
☑ Chronology
☐ Cause and Effect

| (Time) | When did an event occur? |
| (Order) | In what order did events occur? |

Some words used in relation to time are *past, present, future, era, epoch, forward, backward, historical periods, historic, prehistoric, geological, modern, ancient, current, annual, generation, eternal, decade, century, centennial,* and *millennium.*

Some words to use when describing time and order are *after, ago, before, during, early, first, last, next, now, old, past, present, since,* and *then.*

Timeline

A timeline is a visual way to show events in the order in which they occurred. Timelines may contain words, numerals, and pictures. There are many ways to make timelines, as the examples on these two pages show.

- John, in the example that follows, used single years to record major events in his lifetime.

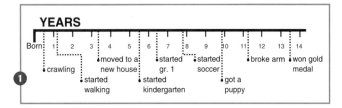

- Taylor showed her life as decades.

Taylor was born on July 1, 1989. On June 30, 1999, she was 9 years old. She was in her first decade. On July 1, 1999, she became 10 years old. She started her 11th year. She was then in her second decade.

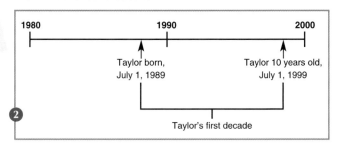

- Timelines may also be drawn in vertical format.

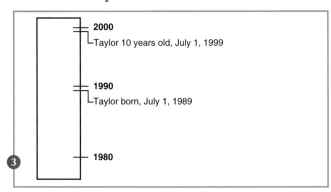

- Taylor showed her great-grandmother's life as decades and as a century.

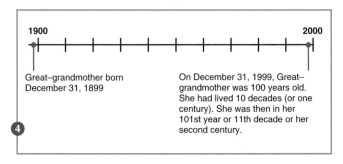

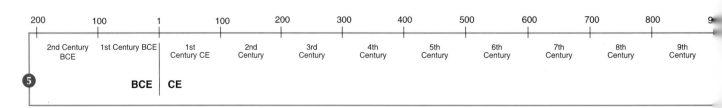

How to Read a Timeline

- Order is important when studying chronology. Events are marked on a timeline in the order in which they occurred. They read from the earliest event to the latest event. (See ❻)

- A sequence of events reads in one direction. However, dates of history can be read in two directions. Events happened and are dated before and after an agreed-on time. For example, in this textbook, we study culture in North America before and after the coming of European explorers (pre-Contact/ post-Contact).

- Some timelines use the Christian system of BC and AD. That system takes the birth of Christ as 1 AD. The previous year was 1 BC. (The actual birth year is slightly different. Scholars do not agree when it was.)

- BCE (Before the Common Era) and CE (Common Era) have the same starting point as BC and AD. BCE and CE are used in this book. Locate these on ❺. Periods are optional (B.C.E., C.E.).

- The initials CE (or AD) are not commonly used when writing dates. For example, Champlain built his fort in 1608, not 1608 CE.

- Events before 1 CE always have BCE (or BC) after them.

- Calendar years are not like birth years (in which you become 1 when the year is over). There was no Year 0, only Year 1, which lasted all year.

- A century is any time period of 100 years. The first century went from the beginning of Year 1 to the end of year 100. (See ❺) A millennium lasts 1000 years. (See ❽)

- Historical events are often referred to by century instead of specific dates. For example, the dates in the 1700s are in the 18th century. (See ❼) Thus, the 20th century went from the beginning of 1901 to the end of 2000. (See ❺)

- Be definite when referring to the past. Rather than say "in the olden days" or "a long time ago," try to date an event at the closest century; for example, the 1st century, the 15th century.

- Certain dates are referred to as turning points or milestones in history. The Age of Exploration lasted from about 1450 to 1600. It included the period of European exploration of North and South America. It was a turning point in Canada's history.

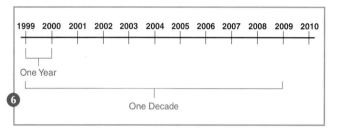

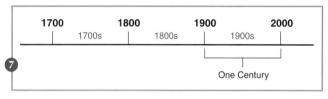

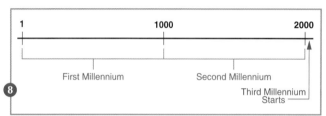

Exploring Further

1.  Begin to create a timeline of European exploration of what is now Canada. Include the explorer's name, the dates that he or she explored, where they explored, and the country for which they explored. As you study Chapters 6–10, add information from that chapter to your timeline. Add challenges faced, personal goals, ambitions, and contributions/effects on Canadian history.

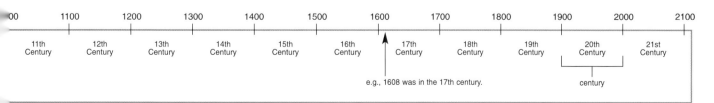

Chapter 6
Early Exploration

Overview

Use this Overview to predict the events of this chapter.

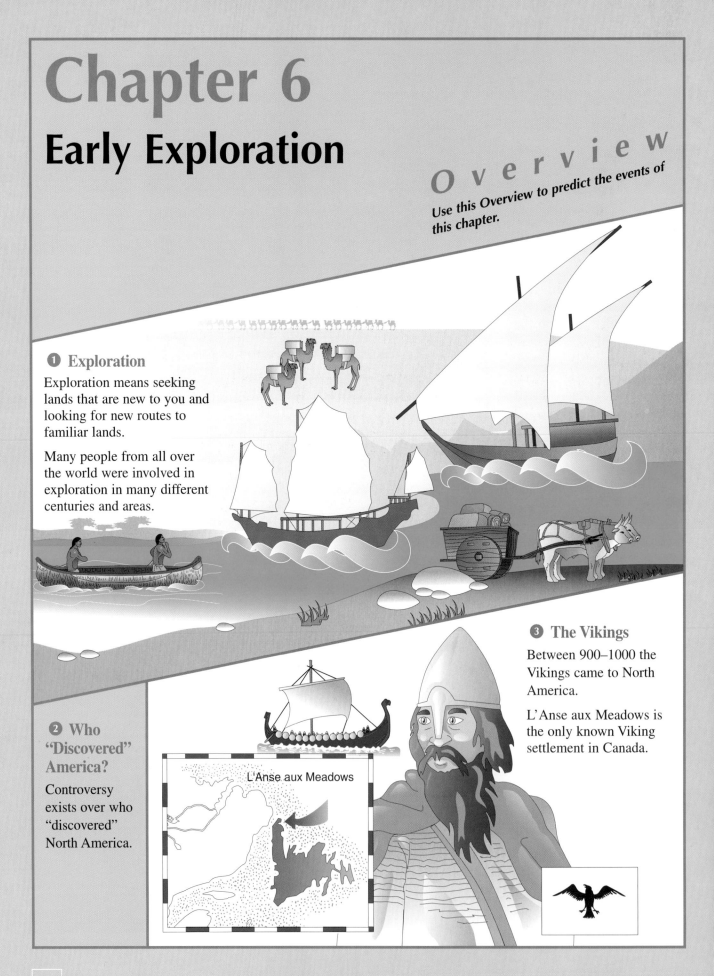

❶ Exploration

Exploration means seeking lands that are new to you and looking for new routes to familiar lands.

Many people from all over the world were involved in exploration in many different centuries and areas.

❷ Who "Discovered" America?

Controversy exists over who "discovered" North America.

L'Anse aux Meadows

❸ The Vikings

Between 900–1000 the Vikings came to North America.

L'Anse aux Meadows is the only known Viking settlement in Canada.

118

Chapter 6 Focus

You started your study in Section I by looking at the origins of the First People. This section starts by examining the origins of the first Europeans who came to what is now Canada. Chapters 6 and 7 focus on what exploration is and how Europeans came to be here.

- This chapter examines how research is carried out. It looks at how historians and archaeologists gather, examine, and organize information.
- You will be involved in several problem solving activities.

A new concept relating to exploration by Europeans is introduced and focused upon in this chapter. Some of the concepts from Section I, The First Nations, also apply.

Environmental   Balance   Technology   Cultural   Exploration
Interaction   Contact

Vocabulary

exploration
discovery
historical interpretation
saga
authentic

archaeologist
artifact
site
archaeological dig

Chapter Preview/Prediction

1. Examine the overview found on the previous page, and the visuals and titles in this chapter.
   a) Based on these, discuss with a partner what you think this chapter is about.
   b) Predict answers to the questions in the Prediction Chart. Put your predictions in the "My Predictions" column.*

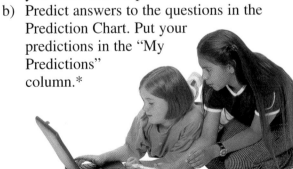

---

*Your teacher may provide you with a full-sized working copy of the Prediction Chart. This chart is available as a blackline master in **Canada Revisited 6, Integrated Unit**.

Check the **Canada Revisited 6 web page for more information about planning this project.

Prediction Chart—What Do You Think?		
Questions	My Predictions (fill out now)	What I Found Out (fill out at end of chapter)
1. In what ways did the coming of Europeans change the balance that existed between the Aboriginal peoples and the environment?		
2. How did the search for new resources affect European exploration? How did new technology affect the European voyages of exploration?		
3. What contacts were made between cultures? What cultural changes occurred as a result of European exploration? Were these contacts positive or negative?		
4. What reasons for European exploration are given?		

Section Activity

Order of Good Cheer Class Project**

On page 114 of this textbook you were asked to prepare for the Order of Good Cheer banquet. Follow the research model on pages x and xi to do research on projects that you will use in your presentation at the banquet. Please see pages 222, 223, and 262 for project and presentation ideas.

Exploration

Defined

 While the Aboriginal peoples explored the lands on which they lived, people across the world were also exploring. They travelled over their homelands and away to other lands. Some journeyed short distances and others thousands of kilometres. Overland and by water, they searched for new places and experiences. **Expeditions** were organized to search for new products to trade and new markets.

Europe was made up of many nations and small states. There was often conflict between them. They competed against each other for power. European countries began to explore more distant places.

Exploration

Seeking lands new to you and looking for new routes to familiar lands.

Fears of the Unknown

Many Europeans thought exploration of places unknown to them was very dangerous. It was said that whirlpools existed in distant waters that were strong enough to sink ships. Some sailors were afraid of drifting too close to the equator, where the water was said to boil. Many sailors believed the Earth was flat. They thought if they sailed too far from the shoreline the ship would fall off the edge. Huge monsters were thought to wait below. Other sailors spoke of sea monsters and of people who lived in lands unknown to them. They imagined creatures with enormous feet and single eyes. Some were said to have faces on their chests.

For Your Notebook

1. Start working on a concept poster on exploration. Include a definition and reasons for exploration.

2. Make a chart like the following to record information about European explorers and their reasons for coming to what is now Canada. (Note: see page 121 for reasons for exploration.)

Name of Explorer	Reasons for Exploration						
	(1)	(2)	(3)	(4)	(5)	(6)	(7)

(add to chart as needed)

Expedition—people sent on a journey for a purpose

Reasons for Exploration

People have always been curious about what was beyond their homeland. Even long ago, groups were rarely completely isolated. Some people were always involved in trade, warfare, or travel for other reasons. Travel by boat was faster than travel on foot, horse, or camel. Rivers and oceans were often used for journeys. Larger loads of goods could be transported by boat than by land.

Sometimes other lands were explored because a country needed new lands to settle on to grow food. Most early exploration was done to obtain new products to trade or sell. Luxuries one did not have in one's homeland were sought after. These would provide a good profit after the costs of the trip were paid. Some European explorers wanted to spread their religion and way of life to the peoples of the world. Sailors and travellers told stories of lands they had visited. These stories appealed to the curiosity of others.

Reasons for European Exploration

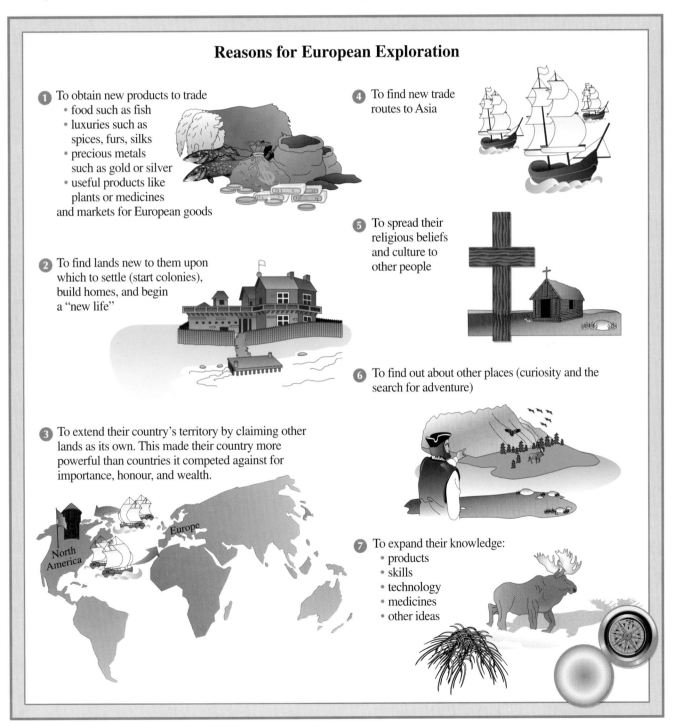

1 To obtain new products to trade
- food such as fish
- luxuries such as spices, furs, silks
- precious metals such as gold or silver
- useful products like plants or medicines

and markets for European goods

2 To find lands new to them upon which to settle (start colonies), build homes, and begin a "new life"

3 To extend their country's territory by claiming other lands as its own. This made their country more powerful than countries it competed against for importance, honour, and wealth.

4 To find new trade routes to Asia

5 To spread their religious beliefs and culture to other people

6 To find out about other places (curiosity and the search for adventure)

7 To expand their knowledge:
- products
- skills
- technology
- medicines
- other ideas

Who "Discovered" America?

An Exercise in Problem Solving

Work in groups of three to carry out this exercise. Follow the steps of problem solving in the Appendix on page 260. You may wish to change your hypothesis after reading the chapter. Submit your conclusion to your teacher at the end of the chapter.

Problem: Who Really "Discovered" America?

In Chapter 1 you read several theories about the first people who came to America. Were these people the "discoverers" of America? Was it Columbus or the Vikings, as the rhyme and cartoon below suggest? Or were there others before them? Take a position in this **controversy** and record your findings.

In 1492,
Columbus sailed the
ocean blue,
But, 500 years before,
Vikings touched our
shore.

"LOOK, ERICKSON, EVERYONE KNOWS I DISCOVERED AMERICA!"

Discover—to find or understand something for the first time
Controversy—disagreement, debate

- Asian explorers explored both overland and at sea. Official records in China tell of Hwui Shan and four other Buddhist monks sailing eastward across the Pacific Ocean. They landed in what is now Alaska in 459 CE. From there they travelled south to Mexico. They named the land Fusang and lived there for 40 years.

A Chinese sailing ship, called a junk

- Polynesian stories tell of sailors being blown off course and reaching South America. Could these people have moved from South America to North America?
- According to Irish stories, St. Brendan, an Irish monk, twice sailed across the Atlantic Ocean to America in 565 CE. He didn't land on the first voyage. Historians think he may have come ashore at Newfoundland (or perhaps Labrador) the second time. Unfriendly people caused him to sail southward to a warm, sunny land he called *Hy Bresail* (Gaelic for Land of the Gods).

In 1976–1977 Tim Severin built and sailed a leather boat from Ireland to Newfoundland. He was retracing St. Brendan's 565 CE voyage. His boat was a replica of an ancient Irish boat.

- Viking sagas (stories) told of sightings of North America in 986. In the years that followed, other Viking sailors landed and established settlements on these lands.

Timeline 1

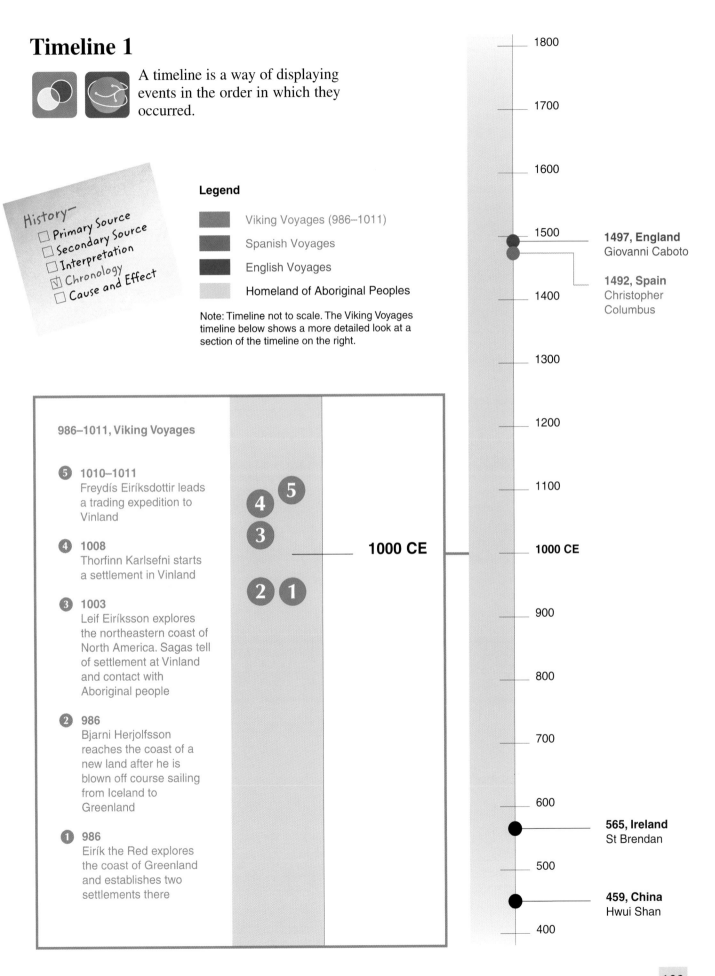

A timeline is a way of displaying events in the order in which they occurred.

History—
☐ Primary Source
☐ Secondary Source
☐ Interpretation
☑ Chronology
☐ Cause and Effect

Legend

▉ Viking Voyages (986–1011)

▉ Spanish Voyages

▉ English Voyages

▉ Homeland of Aboriginal Peoples

Note: Timeline not to scale. The Viking Voyages timeline below shows a more detailed look at a section of the timeline on the right.

1800

1700

1600

1500
1497, England
Giovanni Caboto

1492, Spain
Christopher Columbus

1400

1300

1200

1100

1000 CE

900

800

700

600

565, Ireland
St Brendan

500

459, China
Hwui Shan

400

986–1011, Viking Voyages

5 **1010–1011**
Freydís Eiríksdottir leads a trading expedition to Vinland

4 **1008**
Thorfinn Karlsefni starts a settlement in Vinland

3 **1003**
Leif Eiríksson explores the northeastern coast of North America. Sagas tell of settlement at Vinland and contact with Aboriginal people

2 **986**
Bjarni Herjolfsson reaches the coast of a new land after he is blown off course sailing from Iceland to Greenland

1 **986**
Eirík the Red explores the coast of Greenland and establishes two settlements there

1000 CE

123

The Vikings

Few historical records exist, so it is impossible to know very much about early European exploration. Vikings were probably the first to sail from Europe across the North Atlantic Ocean to North America. The Vikings were from what is now Norway, Sweden, and Denmark.

Good farmland, especially grazing land, was scarce. It was impossible to support a large population there. The Vikings were expert sailors and warriors. They sailed elsewhere to look for land, wealth, or sources of food. They did some trading. They also gained wealth through raiding. Strength and bravery in battle were important Viking values.

After 800 CE the Vikings continually raided the Northern and Western settlements of Europe. They became the most powerful sea-going nation in Europe at that time.

Vikings explored to reach new trading areas. They tried to find and settle lands that were new to them. Vikings reached Iceland around 870. Eirík the Red* started a colony in Greenland in 986. By the late 900s, the Vikings were aware that there were other lands west of their usual travels. They made attempts at settlement in these western lands but did not settle permanently.

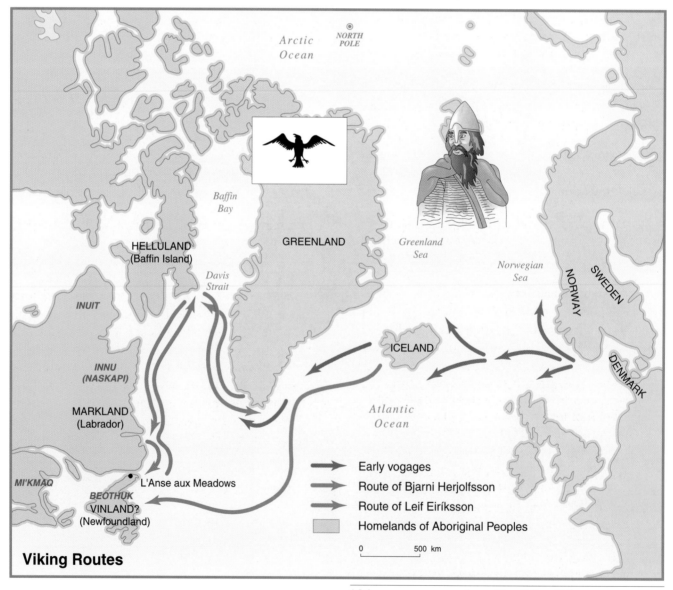

Viking Routes

→	Early vogages
→	Route of Bjarni Herjolfsson
→	Route of Leif Eiríksson
▢	Homelands of Aboriginal Peoples

0   500 km

*Other sources may use the spelling Erik or Eric.

124

Viking Explorers

A modern-day replica of a Viking ship sailing across the Atlantic

Bjarni Herjolfsson

Viking **sagas** report that the first European to see and describe the east coast of North America was Bjarni Herjolfsson. Herjolfsson was on his way from Iceland to the Viking colony of Greenland in 986 CE. He was blown off course into a region of sea fogs. Rather than turn back to Greenland after the fog cleared, Herjolfsson and his crew sailed north along the coast of North America. They did not land.

The Viking sagas give the first European descriptions of the east coast of America:
- a land covered with forests and low hills
- a flat country covered with woods
- a land high, mountainous, and glaciered

Refer to the map on page 124. Historians have wondered whether these lands were Newfoundland, Labrador (now part of Newfoundland), and Baffin Island.

Leif Eiríksson

In the year 1003, a son of Eirík the Red, Leif Eiríksson (Leif the Lucky), sailed from Greenland to follow Herjolfsson's earlier journey. Viking sagas describe Eiríksson as

> tall and strong and very impressive in appearance . . .; a fair-dealing man.

Eiríksson saw the land Herjolfsson described and called it Helluland (Land of Flat Stones). This was probably Baffin Island. A saga describes this land as

> a land without grass, hinterland [lands away from the coast] all great glaciers; a single great slab of rock right up to the glaciers from the sea . . . land barren and useless.

From Helluland, Eiríksson sailed south. The next area he saw was an area he called Markland (Woodland). This was probably Labrador. The area is described in the sagas as
- white sand beaches shelving gently down to the sea
- land of woods
- an open harbourless coast along with long beaches and sands.

The Vikings arrived at the third area after two more days and nights of sailing south. It was named Vinland (Wineland) by Eiríksson. The exact location is not known. The sagas tell us Eiríksson landed and spent the winter here.

Vinland

At Vinland the Vikings built houses of sod supported by a wooden framework. The floors were made of clay. Sections of the floor around the walls were raised. They served as seats and beds. Vinland was used as a wintering-over settlement. The Vikings brought cattle for milk and meat and sheep for wool from Iceland. They caught fish, hunted animals, and picked berries for extra food.

Many Aboriginal people were killed by the Vikings at the first recorded encounter between the two groups. Later the Vikings carried on a small amount of trade with the Aboriginal people. These people could have been the Inuit of Labrador or the Beothuk of Newfoundland. (See the narrative Ashooging and Bjarni on pages 127 and 128.) Furs were exchanged with the Vikings for cloth and possibly some iron tools. However, relations between the groups were often violent.

Eirík the Red's Saga tells of conflict between the Vikings and the local people. The saga says being

> faced with constant fear and strife resulted in [the Vikings] leaving Vinland and returning to Greenland.

Sagas—long poems telling the stories of history, which were passed down as oral tradition

Thorfinn Karlsefni

In 1008, Thorfinn Karlsefni brought 60 people, including five women, to the settlement in Vinland. He also brought some cattle and sheep. The Vikings traded cloth for furs and skins brought to them by the Aboriginal people. The settlement lasted only a few years. While they lived in Vinland, Karlsefni and his wife, Gudrid, had a son, Snorri. Snorri was probably the first child of European parents born in North America.

Freydís Eiríksdottir

In about 1010–1011, Eirík the Red's daughter Freydís led an expedition to Vinland. Under her leadership timber was cut, dried, loaded on boats, and shipped to Greenland.

Freydís Eiríksdottir appears in two sagas, but she is described very differently. Both describe her as wearing men's clothing and show her to be strong, daring, and dangerous. The sagas both say the expedition was successful. However, in one saga, Freydís is leading a business expedition with two of her brothers. The saga says she argued with them, cheated on them, made her husband kill their crew, and took the profits for herself.

In the other saga, Freydís is described as a less important person. She travelled as a member of the expedition, not a leader. However, she is described as leading the Vikings in battle against a group of Aboriginal people. The Vikings were greatly outnumbered, but she was bold and fearless and led them to victory.

Learning How to Learn
Historical Interpretation

Interpretation means trying to understand or explain information that is unclear. Usually historians don't have all the facts about events in history. To understand what most likely happened, historians
- analyse the sources (they try to find out who wrote about or recorded the event or fact and what their point of view was)
- compare different accounts (points agreed on are more likely to be facts)
- look for additional evidence to confirm (prove) their hypothesis

For Your Notebook

1. Compare the accounts about Freydís Eiríksdottir. How might one or the other be confirmed as fact?

Ashooging and Bjarni

Fictional Narrative

—by Joan Clark

Ashooging, a Beothuk boy, stepped back to admire the *mamateek* his mother had just built. She had cut the many tall poles, stuck one end of each into the ground, then tied them together at the top. Then she had pushed clumps of moss between the poles to keep out the cold and rain. She had laid pieces of birchbark on the higher parts of the roof. Between the layers of birchbark was more moss. Around the chimney hole she put clay. It would be a good *mamateek* for their family to live in for the rest of the summer.

Soon it would be time to move inland and build the bigger, stronger *mamateek* that they would share with Demahasit's family for the winter. The winter *mamateek* would be covered with three layers of birchbark with moss and sod between the layers. There would be beams from side to side inside the winter *mamateek*. They could pile dried salmon and caribou meat on the beams.

Ashooging's grandmother put down the piece of caribou skin she had been chewing. When she had chewed the edges enough to make them

Mussels—a type of shellfish
Bakeapples—a type of fruit or berry

soft, she would sew it into leggings for Ashooging to wear in the winter.

"Ashooging, you should go to the place near the sea and pick more of the *abidemashick*. We need the berries to help us to stay healthy through the winter."

Ashooging decided that he would go to the place where the white bones of the killer whale lay on the beach. Now that he had seen twelve summers, he knew that next winter he could be allowed to go on the whale hunt with his father and grandfather. While he was near the sea, he would look for some **mussels**. He would not be able to spear any salmon today as he would not be in his canoe.

Three months ago, when the boat was ready to leave Iceland, Bjarni had told nobody that he was going to sneak aboard. He hid until they were well out to sea, then crawled from his hiding place. Their leader, Karlsefni, had been very angry.

Karlsefni had shouted that the men had been chosen for their strength as oarsmen and woodsmen. They would be bringing back a cargo of wood from the new-found land. It would be heavy rowing when the wind in the sails blew the boat away from the course they

had set themselves across the sea. Why should he feed a boy who was of no use and took up valuable space aboard the boat?

Shamed, Bjarni had made himself useful cleaning up cattle and sheep dung, bailing out rain water, mending sails. When one of the oarsmen fell sick, Bjarni took his place.

Now Bjarni stood alone in this meadow in the new-found land. He thought that these bittersweet berries would please Karlsefni. Getting ready to pick the berries, he unfastened his cloak pin and tossed his grey woollen cloak onto the ground. On top of this he threw his battleaxe.

Standing in the spruce trees, Ashooging watched the pale-skinned, redhaired boy picking the *abidemashick*, the **bakeapples** the Beothuk harvested every summer. Ashooging had never seen white skin or red hair. Was he from the Western Sea, where the Oldest People had sprung from arrows shot to the ground?

Ashooging was an expert with the bow and arrow, already able to bring down a winter caribou. He lifted the bow to his shoulder, fitted it with a stone-tipped arrow, and pulled tight the bowstring. If he let the arrow go, it would pierce the white boy's heart.

What would the People say if he came back to the *mamateek* carrying the head of this red-haired stranger? His father would not like it. Nor would his grandfather, who had never killed a man. Ashooging lifted his bone whistle to his lips and blew three birdlike notes.

Startled, Bjarni looked up from his berry-picking. He saw a boy whose body was covered with a red powder. He had dark eyes and long black hair.

"*Skraeling*!" Bjarni thought. "This must be one of the *Skraelings* the early voyagers spoke of in the sagas." He prayed to the Norse god Odin for courage. He reached for his battleaxe, which was nearby, and lifted it over his head.

"Blue eyes like the sea!" Ashooging thought. "This boy has truly been sent by the sea gods. But the sea gods also send big waves and cruel storms." Ashooging again lifted his bow and arrow.

Each boy stood ready to use his weapon. But Bjarni knew he could not win. "Give me courage," he prayed to Odin. Then he threw his battleaxe on the ground in front of the *Skraeling*.

Ashooging squatted down and picked up the battleaxe. He lifted it over his head to see how

it felt. In his hand it seemed heavy and clumsy. Then he threw it far up the meadow.

Bjarni's fear turned to amazement as he watched the *Skraeling* toss his bow and arrow in the same direction as the battleaxe. He was even more amazed when the *Skraeling* knelt down and began picking berries.

"Then the sagas aren't true," Bjarni thought. "The *Skraelings* are ready to be our friends."

Ashooging put berries into Bjarni's pouch. "To be given berries by the person who spared my life must mean that the god Thor himself has answered my prayers," Bjarni thought. Karlsefni wouldn't be angry at him now, not when he saw so many berries.

Ashooging blew into his whistle, then handed it to Bjarni.

The Beothuk knew it was important to offer a gift to the sea gods. Bjarni blew into the whistle, then laughed when the bird notes tumbled out.

Bjarni pulled the pin out of his cloak and handed it to Ashooging. The Beothuk boy took the pin eagerly. It was green like the sea. The People would be pleased when he brought back this message from the sea.

From the beach Ashooging heard men's voices. The other Vikings from the boat were coming this way. Ashooging ran across the meadow and disappeared into the woods.

Bjarni lifted the whistle to his lips and blew a treble of bird notes into the warm summer air.

For Your Notebook

1. Why do you think Bjarni's first experience with a *Skraeling* was different than the stories he'd heard?

2. a) Think about what each boy will tell his people about his experiences.

   b) Write the next scene to the narrative Ashooging and Bjarni.

Skraeling—name given in the sagas for the Aboriginal people

Viking Sources

How do we know about the voyages of these early Viking explorers? Where do we learn when and where they landed in North America? Historians gathered their data from a variety of places such as

- Viking sagas
- historical maps
- information from local people about the area
- archaeological digs

Sagas

Eirík the Red's Saga was created in the late 12th century (late 1100s). It records voyages made by Leif Eiríksson and his crew. *The Greenland Saga* tells stories of early Viking sightings and visits to the east coast of North America. It was created in Greenland in the late 12th century. Both were oral histories that were later written down. Sagas of early expeditions, such as those by Bjarni Herjolfsson and Leif Eiríksson, provide us with information about these early expeditions. The sagas provide descriptions of lands that Vikings explored.

The stories about Eirík the Red and Leif Eiríksson are very interesting, but are they true? The Norsemen kept few written records at the time the explorations took place. The history of their adventures was told around the fireside. The stories, or sagas, as they were called, were passed down from father to son. All knowledge was passed on in this way. The secrets and the skills of trades and crafts were passed on in spoken form. Accuracy was important, so a good memory was essential among the Vikings, as it was to the First Nations peoples.

Nearly 300 years went by before these sagas were written down. It is not possible to be sure sagas are actual historical records of the voyages or fiction—or even a combination of fact and fiction. As a result, historians look for ways to confirm or prove the information in the sagas. Scientists look for other evidence, such as that from archaeological digs, to support what the stories say.

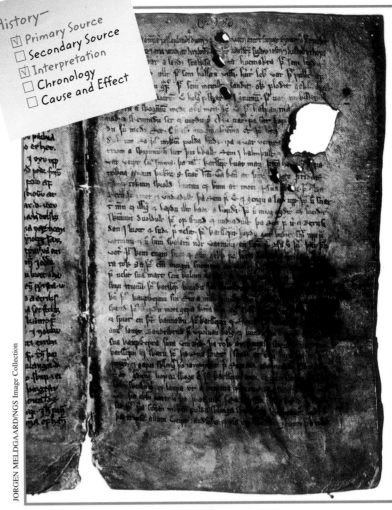

History—
☑ Primary Source
☐ Secondary Source
☑ Interpretation
☐ Chronology
☐ Cause and Effect

JORGEN MELDGAARD/NGS Image Collection

A page from a written account of *Eirík the Red's Saga* describing an encounter between some Vikings and *Skraeling* who were paddling skin-covered canoes

From the sagas we learn that around the year 1000 AD Leif Eiríksson and his crew left Greenland and sailed northward and westward. They went ashore in three places:

- at a land of mountains and glaciers—a land without good grazing grasses. They called this land Helluland, which means flatstone land.
- at an area of trees, low hills, and many sandy beaches. They called this land Markland which means wooded land.
- at an area the sagas called Vinland (Wineland), because one of the crew found grapes growing at their third stop. According to the sagas the group spent the winter at Vinland, building a settlement there. In following years the Vinland settlement continued, but it was eventually abandoned.

Historical Maps

The Vinland Map shown to the right was rediscovered by Yale University scholars in 1965. Many believed it proved the Vikings discovered Vinland. The writing in the upper left says that Vinland was discovered and named by Bjarni Herjolfsson and Leif Eiríksson. The date of Vinland's discovery according to this map was 999 CE.

This map had been studied by earlier scholars and experts. Many believed it was fake. However, recent scientific evidence suggests it may actually be **authentic**.

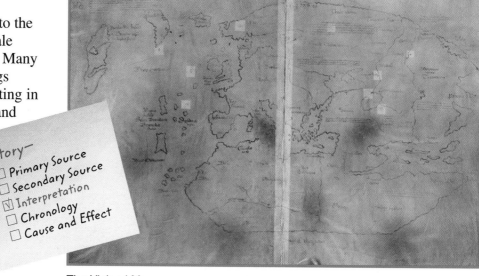

History—
- ☐ Primary Source
- ☐ Secondary Source
- ☑ Interpretation
- ☐ Chronology
- ☐ Cause and Effect

The Vinland Map

Archaeological Sites

Sources such as the sagas are sometimes used to help archaeologists decide where to dig for evidence. Archaeologists **excavate** a site carefully. They make precise records of where they find evidence of past human life. The artifacts from digs are studied to find out where and how the people lived. The evidence from the site is interpreted by archaeologists. They know that new evidence may be found later that shows their interpretation is incorrect. Then they will need to form a new hypothesis.

Archaeology—
- ☑ Site
- ☑ Artifacts

EMORY KRISTOF/NGS Image Collection

A team of archaeologists excavating the L'Anse aux Meadows site

Canada Revisited

Interpretations of artifacts can vary. In August, 1999, an archaeologist from Calgary, Dr. David Kelley, hypothesized that some of the 800 petroglyphs (rock carvings) near Peterborough, Ontario, were probably made by Vikings, not Aboriginal people. Some of the carvings look like a type of writing known to Vikings in the 9th century. There is also a carving of a boat that is similar to a boat on a rock carving in Scandinavia. Dr. Kelley suggests that Vikings may have travelled far inland to trade for copper with the First Nations people in the region.

The Anishinabe consider the petroglyphs and the site to be sacred. The carvings, which include snakes and birds, are mentioned in their stories. Many First Nations people go there to meditate and fast.

Authentic—genuine; proved to be what it seems to be
Excavate—uncover by digging

Problem Solving Using an Archaeological Dig

History—
☐ Primary Source
☐ Secondary Source
☑ Interpretation
☐ Chronology
☐ Cause and Effect

The following paragraphs illustrate how some scientists used an archaeological dig to test their hypothesis. Refer to the problem solving model in the Appendix on page 260 as you read pages 132–134.

The map on page 124 shows where Helluland and Markland were thought to be located. Scientists disagreed, though, over the location of the land the Viking sagas call Vinland.

Nova Scotia, New England, and Minnesota were all suggested as possible locations for Vinland. Most scientists believed Vinland was located farther south because of the wild "grapes" the sagas describe growing there. They reasoned that grapes need a warm climate to grow, so Vinland must be south of Maine.

Sometimes new discoveries about the past result in historians rethinking and rewriting history. Sometimes historians interpret evidence in a different way. This is what Helge Ingstad, a Norwegian explorer and historian, did.

Ingstad asked what if the "grapes" described in the sagas were not grapes at all but large red berries? Besides, he reasoned, the sailing times given in the saga wouldn't have taken the sailors as far south as New England. They probably could only sail as far as Newfoundland, not Nova Scotia or New England. He suggested that archaeologists look north of the areas previously thought to have been Vinland.

In 1960, Ingstad began to do research to test his hypothesis. He revisited the coastal areas northward of New England and searched for sites.

At L'Anse aux Meadows, on the northern tip of Newfoundland, he met George Decker, a local fisherman. Decker showed him what the local people thought was an ancient Aboriginal camp. Ingstad hypothesized that the area could be the site of early Viking houses. Perhaps it was Vinland, he thought.

From 1961–1968 the area was excavated. Archaeologist Anne Stine Ingstad led the dig. Parks Canada was also involved. The remains of buildings were investigated and artifacts studied.*

EMORY KRISTOF/NGS Image Collection

Historian Helge Ingstad working at the dig

The evidence uncovered at L'Anse aux Meadows seemed to indicate that Ingstad's hypothesis about the location of Vinland was correct. No other site of Viking settlement has been found. Vinland probably included the coasts around the Gulf of St. Lawrence. L'Anse aux Meadows was probably Leif Eiríksson's base camp at the northern entrance to Vinland. It is thought to have been the area where boats were repaired.

The excavations and artifacts discovered at L'Anse aux Meadows proved the Vikings had established settlements in North America. The site was dated five centuries before the voyages of Christopher Columbus (1492) and Giovanni Caboto (1497). (See Timeline 1, page 123.)

---

*Pages 132–134 show a map of L'Anse aux Meadows and a description of 12 locations. In 1978 the area was designated a UNESCO World Heritage Site. The photographs are from this reconstructed site.

Focus On: Canada Revisited
L'Anse aux Meadows

In 1960, Anne Stine Ingstad, her team of archaeologists, and Parks Canada excavated a site at L'Anse aux Meadows. They uncovered evidence of eight buildings, a charcoal kiln, and hundreds of Viking artifacts. All date from the 11th century. The site is thought to have been used for repairing boats. The photographs on this page are from a modern day reconstructed site at L'Anse aux Meadows in northern Newfoundland. (The text is taken from a booklet about the site.* Some difficult words are explained at the bottom of the page.)

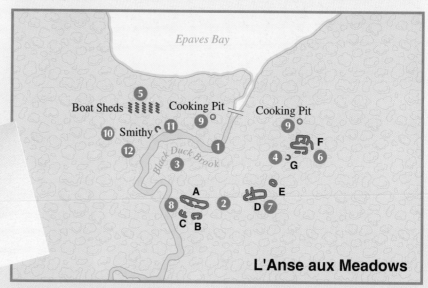

Archaeology—
☑ Site
☑ Artifacts

L'Anse aux Meadows

On the northern tip of Newfoundland lies L'Anse aux Meadows, the only Viking settlement discovered in Canada to date. See also map page 124.

*Site captions and map adapted from Parks Canada.
Marine terrace—a raised area that was an old sea shore
Bog—very wet ground
Sauna—method of cleansing involving heat and steam
Boatshed—building for storing boats

1 Black Duck Brook. A constant supply of fresh water, trout, and salmon.

2 Marine Terrace. Several house sites are situated around the edge of an old sea shore.

3 Bog. What is now a bog in front of the house sites might have been a tidal lagoon in 1000 CE—an ideal place for sheltering boats.

4 "Sauna." The presence of a large number of fire-cracked stones in the fireplace suggests that it may have been a sauna. Saunas were part of old Norse culture and have been found in both Greenland and Iceland.

5 Boatsheds. A series of shallow depressions near the present shore may be traces of Norse boatsheds.

For Your Notebook

1. Draw a quick sketch map of L'Anse aux Meadows like the one shown. Colour it. Use the information from pages 132–134 to add corresponding numbers and facts to the map you've drawn. For example, add #1 to the brook and "fresh water, fish."

2. Draw a sketch or a floor plan of one of the houses, based on the information on these pages.

Exploring Further

3. Describe the technology used by the Vikings at L'Anse aux Meadows. How do scientists know that this was a Viking site and not that of an Aboriginal group such as the Beothuk?

http://parkscanada.pch.gc.ca/parks/newfoundland/anse_meadows/anse_meadowse.htm

Focus On: Canada Revisited
L'Anse aux Meadows **(continued)**

6 **House "F."** Nearly [31 metres] long, this six room house was the largest in the settlement, with typical Norse characteristics such as "long" hearths, **ember** pits, and an indoor cookpit. As with the other large houses on the site, the outer walls curved slightly, a feature of Norse longhouses.

7 **House "D."** This house had three rooms in which were found some iron rivets, a small piece of **smelted** copper and part of a bone needle of Norse type. A smaller structure nearby may have been a separate workshed.

The walls of all the houses in the settlement were of turf [sod], with wooden doorways. The roofs were also turf, supported by timber **rafters**. There were no windows or chimneys, just a hole in the roof to let out smoke. There would have been very little furniture, only a low platform or bench along the inside walls for sitting or sleeping.

LEFT: Three Viking artifacts excavated at L'Anse aux Meadows: part of a stone **spindle** used to spin wool, part of a bone needle, and a needle-sharpening stone

Rafters—wooden cross beams that support a roof

Spindle—tool for spinning wool into thread

Ember—hot coals from a fire

Smelted—heating ore to remove the metal from rock waste

133

8 Houses "A," "B," and "C." Grouped together near the brook, these houses have the same type of hearths and pits as House "F." Two very important items were discovered here: a ring-headed bronze pin of a type common throughout the Norse world in the 9th and 10th centuries; and a part of the shoulder bone of a domesticated pig, an animal otherwise unknown in North America until the 16th century. According to the sagas, the Norse expeditions brought cattle and sheep with them.

11 The "Smithy." This small structure was dug into the bank. Its floor was covered with charcoal, mingled with nodules of bog iron, **slag**, and fragments of iron. This was an ancient blacksmith's shop. **Carbon-14** dates and other evidence leave little doubt that the blacksmith was Norse.

12 Charcoal Kiln. This was probably a kiln for making charcoal for the blacksmith's fires.

Butternuts, like the one found at L'Anse aux Meadows shown above, have never grown in Newfoundland. The farthest north they have grown is northern New Brunswick. Therefore, the Vikings must have travelled farther south.

9 Cookpits. Two large outdoor cookpits were found. While they may also have been used by Aboriginal people they show signs of having first been dug by the Norsemen.

10 Bog Ore Deposit. The Norsemen were skilled at smelting iron from a form of ore found in small nodules [lumps] in bogs. A deposit of this ore lies within a few feet of the house sites at L'Anse aux Meadows.

Smithy—blacksmith shop where iron was worked

Slag—the waste left from ore after the metal is removed

Carbon-14—a method of finding the age of ancient objects by measuring changes in radioactivity

Kiln—oven for heating materials very hot to change them

Review

Assessment

1. Complete a self-assessment for one assignment from this chapter. See page 263 or ask your teacher for ideas.

Summarizing the Chapter

2. Reread the predictions you made on page 119. Fill in the "What I Found Out" column of the prediction chart.

Understanding Concepts

3. Check the organization of your binder according to the description on page 261 of the Appendix. Create a chapter title page if you haven't already done so.

4. Record any three of the following vocabulary terms for this chapter.

exploration	historical interpretation
discovery	archaeological dig
saga	

5. On page 120 you started working on a concept poster on exploration. Complete this assignment now.

6. Create a mind map to show how historians and archaeologists find out about the past.

7. Add the names of the chapter's Viking explorers to the Explorer Timeline you started on page 117.

Developing Research Skills

8.

Order of Good Cheer Class Project

Just a reminder to work on the projects you started on page 114.

Developing Communication Skills

Select at least one from 9–13:

Reading

9. Ask your librarian to help you to locate information about a) or b).
   a) the story of the Brendan voyage (565 CE) and the voyage of Tim Severin in 1976–1977. Did they face similar challenges?
   b) Thor Heyerdahl's modern-day voyages from Peru to Tahiti. What do they tell us about ancient discoveries of America?

Writing

10. Write a story as if you were one of the people in the painting on page 126.

11. Write a hard news story about the archaeological work done by Anne Stine Ingstad. See number 4 on page 264.

Listening and Speaking

12. Thorfinn and Gudrid Karlsefni's child was probably the first child of European parents born in North America. In a group of five, role play experiences of Thorfinn, Gudrid, and three other settlers.

Viewing and Representing

13. Construct a model or a diorama of L'Anse aux Meadows based on the archaeological evidence found by Anne Stine Ingstad and her team of archaeologists.

Chapter 7
An Age of Exploration

O v e r v i e w
Use this Overview to predict the events of this chapter.

❶ An Age of Exploration

An overland trading network existed throughout North, Central, and South America before Europeans came.

Trade goods came overland from Asia to the trading centres of Europe.

When moving goods overland became too expensive, European traders began to seek ocean routes to Asia. European merchants and monarchs provided money for these voyages.

❷ New Ideas

New ideas and developments in technology contributed to an Age of Exploration.

❸ Portuguese Exploration

Portuguese sailors sailed south and then east to Asia.

❹ Spanish Exploration

Christopher Columbus sailed west across the Atlantic Ocean, attempting to reach Asia.

❺ English Exploration

Giovanni Caboto searched for a shorter and cheaper route to Asia by sailing westward from Europe.

❻ Fishing

Caboto's discovery of plentiful fish near Atlantic Canada resulted in fishing vessels coming to the area.

❼ French Exploration

Giovanni da Verrazano found that New Spain and New Found Land were connected to each other but not to Asia. He believed a huge land area existed between the Atlantic and Pacific Oceans.

❽ The Northwest Passage

European explorers searched for a passage through or around North America to Asia.

Chapter 7 Focus

Chapter 6 introduced you to the earliest European exploration in what is now Canada. In Chapter 7 you will continue your study of exploration. You will look at changes that occurred in Europe between 1450 and 1600 that resulted in more European explorers sailing west across the Atlantic Ocean.

Exploration and trade in this chapter primarily focus on activities that affected European people. Keep in mind, though, that exploration and trade were taking place throughout the world (including among First Nations peoples you studied in Section I of this textbook).

This chapter examines how

• timelines and charts may be used as sources of information
• events usually have a variety of causes and results (events bring about change).

The major focus in this chapter will be on the reasons for European exploration of the Americas and the impact of technology.

Environmental   Balance   Technology   Cultural   Exploration
Interaction   Contact

Vocabulary

perspective   monopoly
mariner   investor
charter   claiming lands

Section Activity

Order of Good Cheer Class Project

On page 114 you were asked to prepare for the Order of Good Cheer banquet. Follow the research model on pages x and xi to do research on projects you will use in your presentations and displays at the banquet.

Chapter Preview/Prediction

1. In pairs or small groups, use the overview, the illustrations, maps, and titles in this chapter to predict answers on the prediction chart.* Put your predictions in the "My Predictions" column. The full chart is shown on page 119.

Prediction Chart—What Do You Think?		
Questions	**My Predictions** (fill out now)	**What I Found Out** (fill out at end of chapter)
1. In what ways did the coming of Europeans change the balance that existed between the Aboriginal peoples and the environment?		
2. How did the		

Historical Interpretation

1. When historical events are described from a particular point of view, it is an interpretation of the facts. You will need to read it carefully to be sure of their meaning. Discuss the following questions in small groups.
   a) What does perspective mean?
   b) What perspectives on "discovery" and the "new world" are presented in the following statements?

"In most library references you'll notice statements like 'the Europeans discovered the New World during the Age of Exploration.' They thought that they had discovered it, because *they* hadn't known it was there."

"My ancestors have always lived here. If anyone discovered and explored North and South America, we did! You could say the Europeans explored a land unknown to them. European explorers didn't discover a new world—they 'discovered' another old world."

   c) With which perspective do you agree? Provide reasons.

---

*Available as a blackline master in *Canada Revisited 6, Integrated Unit.*

An Age of Exploration

Trade and Exploration before 1450

Refer to the arrows on the map below and the map on the next page when reading the following.

  Baghdad served as the link between Europe and Asia (China and India).

1. Arab traders brought goods from Asia (red) and European traders brought goods from their homelands (teal) to the trading centre at Baghdad.

Goods were brought from various areas in Asia to trading centres in China and India. From there they were distributed to other trading centres. Arab overland caravans travelled along the Silk Road. This was the overland trading route across Asia. Trade goods from Asia were transported to Baghdad. Baghdad was the Arab centre of trade. By the 9th century Arab traders controlled most of the sea and land trading routes leading to and from this trading centre.

During the 11th and 12th centuries towns and cities in Europe were established as trading centres.

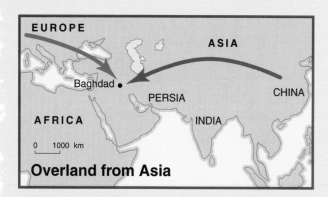

Overland from Asia

Unloading trade goods at Venice

2. From 1095, for the next 200 years, European countries were involved in a series of wars called the Crusades.*

These wars brought many Europeans into direct contact with Eastern (Asian) ideas. They saw products such as silks and spices from India and China. When they returned home they wanted to have these items.

3. The cities of Genoa and Venice became important trading centres. (Refer to map page 139.)

European traders brought goods from their homelands (teal). Merchants obtained products from the local people in the towns and villages of Europe. These products were mostly sent over land or river routes to Venice and Genoa.

Arab traders brought goods (mostly spices) from Baghdad to Venice (yellow).

4. Italian merchant ships carried goods from the cities of Genoa or Venice to various seaports.

European products were sent along the west coast of Europe (mauve), or along overland routes or river routes of Europe (rust), or to Africa (blue) or Persia (black). By the 1400s a flourishing trade had been established. Italian merchants were making huge profits.

5. In 1453, the Ottoman Empire captured the trading centre of Constantinople (later called Istanbul).

The Ottoman Empire placed high taxes on trade goods coming from India and China. Thus, these goods became very expensive to buyers in Europe.

*During the Crusades, Christians from Europe went to the lands of the Eastern Mediterranean to fight a series of wars. The wars with the Muslims were for control of the area which included the ancient Holy Land of Israel and the city of Jerusalem.

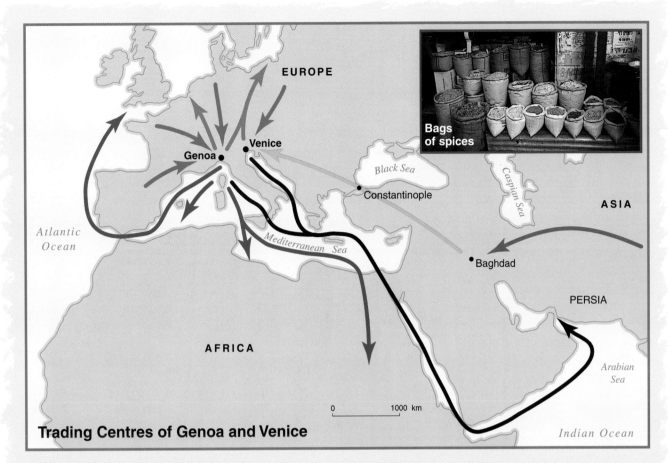

Bags of spices

Trading Centres of Genoa and Venice

Baghdad was a very busy trading centre. Buyers purchased furs and cloth from Europe and precious spices, jewels, silver, gold, pearls, silk, and porcelain from Asia to sell and trade in the market at Baghdad. Refrigeration as we use today was not available. Spices from Asia were used to flavour food, especially old meat.

Exploration after 1450

During the Age of Exploration (about 1450–1600), new ideas and improved methods of shipbuilding made sailing on voyages of exploration safer. Ocean voyages were expensive. As a result, voyages of exploration depended on European kings, queens, and wealthy merchants for financial backing. European monarchs wished to find out more about the world.

They also wanted to gain power and the riches of Asia. They hired mariners to search for a water route to Asia. Portugal and Spain were the first European countries to send ships to seek a route to Asia. England and France sent expeditions soon after. While searching for trade routes, the Europeans also explored North and South America.

Timeline 2

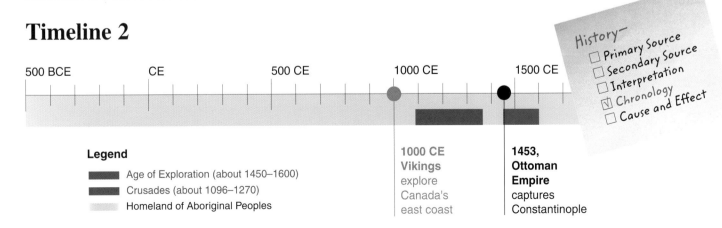

500 BCE CE 500 CE 1000 CE 1500 CE

1000 CE Vikings explore Canada's east coast

1453, Ottoman Empire captures Constantinople

History—
☐ Primary Source
☐ Secondary Source
☐ Interpretation
☑ Chronology
☐ Cause and Effect

Legend

■ Age of Exploration (about 1450–1600)
■ Crusades (about 1096–1270)
■ Homeland of Aboriginal Peoples

New Ideas

During the Age of Exploration, Europeans acquired new knowledge of the world's geography. They made important links with the new ideas shown on the following chart. These developments were made over several hundred years. Europeans used and improved many ideas discovered in ancient times by the Greeks, Arabs, and Chinese.

 The chart on pages 140–142 is designed to show cause and effect. Read the sections of the chart from left to right. Cause and effect is explained in the Appendix on page 256.

Desire for new sea-routes to obtain riches of Asia. Going directly to the source eliminates the middlepersons.

European countries competed for power and wealth.

New Inventions, Ideas, and Interest Lead to An Age of Exploration

New technology (compass, astrolabe, caravel, lateen sail) enabled sailors to navigate better.

Interested monarchs who wanted to increase their wealth, glory, and power paid for expeditions.

Problem *cause*	New Ideas *event or situation*	Result *effect*
1. The boats and ships used by the early explorers needed several improvements for voyages to be safer and more successful.		
a) A type of oar-driven boat (called a galley), had been used in the Mediterranean Sea and by the Norse. It had a single **mast** and square sails. Steering and sailing against the wind were difficult in boats with square sails.	The caravel was the newly designed Portuguese ship. It was small—21 meters in length. Square sails were still used at the front of the ships but two more masts were added. Moveable triangular sails (lateen sails) as used by Arabs were added near the back.	The caravel was an excellent ship for exploration. It needed only 20 sailors to sail it. The arrangement of sails made the ship easier to steer and enabled it to sail against the wind. It was stable in rough seas.

Mast—the long vertical wooden pole used to support a ship's sails

Problem *cause*	**New Ideas** *event or situation*	**Result** *effect*
b) Twin steering oars were not an efficient way to steer a ship on an open ocean. (See visual of Viking ship on page 140.)	The twin steering oars were replaced by a single flat **rudder** mounted at the back of the ship. 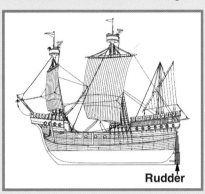 **Rudder**	The rudder made it possible to control direction. Ships could be easily steered from the quarterdeck. The quarterdeck was located between the ship's main mast and the rear of the ship. It was used mostly by the officers, including the captain and **navigator**.
2. **Once the sailors were no longer able to see land they had no accurate method of finding their position at sea. They sometimes became lost at sea.**	The European navigators learned about **latitude** and **longitude** from the ancient Greeks. The mariner's compass had been invented by the Chinese and the Arabs. The **astrolabe** had been invented by the Greeks and was reintroduced to Europe in this period. Both were improved and used more widely by Europeans. The cross staff and the quadrant were also developed for **navigation.**	Navigational tools were available in Europe by Columbus's time (1492). They made exploration much easier. For example, the astrolabe made it possible for sailors to find out their latitude at sea from the position of the sun or stars. The compass helped them know their direction of sailing. The sailors below are using a cross staff and a quadrant to determine position from the angle of the sun.

Rudder—a hinged, flat piece of wood used for steering

Navigator—the person who figures out the location of the ship and sets its course, also known as the pilot

Latitude—one's north–south position (distance north or south of the equator)

Longitude—one's east–west position (distance east or west of 0° at Greenwich, England)

Astrolabe—(ass-troh-layb) an instrument for figuring out latitude position from the angle of the sun or stars

Navigation—the science of figuring out the position of a ship and steering it on a route

Compass

Astrolabe

Problem *cause*	New Ideas *event or situation*	Result *effect*
3. **Trading ships were often attacked by pirates. People were killed and the ship's cargo often stolen.**	Cannons were added to ships. 	Ships were easier to defend, although pirates continued to be a danger. In some countries such as England, the monarch (Queen Elizabeth I) encouraged and even supported pirates that attacked ships from other European countries.
4. **Books were copied slowly and carefully by hand.**	The printing press was invented by Johann Gutenberg. Type (alphabet letters) was used to form words.	Books were made faster and cheaper. Many copies of a book could be made. Knowledge and ideas spread, especially stories of travel and explorations.
5. **Maps were in an early stage of development in Europe.** Accurate maps of the world's oceans had not been made. Large parts of the world as we know it today were unmapped.	In 1521, Ferdinand Magellan's ship completed a round-the-world trip. (See map inside back cover.)	European sailors explored more of the world and learned about the lands from the inhabitants. New information was added to the maps and corrections were made to existing maps. More accurate and useful maps became available for sailors. This helped bring about more voyages of exploration. Maps were made by explorers to record where they had been and to mark trade routes.

Pierre Descellier/National Archives of Canada/NMC 40461

Exploring Further

1. Explorers' descriptions of the region shown in the map above were used by a European map-maker several years later to create this map. How can you tell that the map-maker had never been to the region? What does this say about the difference between primary and secondary sources? Where are the lands shown on this map?

2. Pretend you are a newscaster reporting on one of the inventions on pages 140–142. OR create a magazine ad or a radio or TV commercial to sell one of them.

3. Create an invention "Hall of Fame." Include at least three of the types of technology described on pages 140–142. Tell why the technology was so successful.

4. Brainstorm as a class. What problems require solutions (new technology or inventions) today? Individually, select three. What kind of solution is needed? What will the result be in society or the world?

Portuguese Exploration

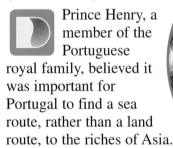
Portugal concentrated on developing trade routes through the world's oceans. They hoped that a sea route would be faster, easier, and cheaper to maintain than the overland route. The Ottoman Empire controlled Baghdad and the overland trade routes. They charged taxes for coming through their territory from India and China. This added to costs. If the Portuguese had their own sea routes they would no longer have to pay middlepersons for trade goods from Asia. They could get them directly from the source, and sell them to the rest of Europe.

Prince Henry

(1394–1460)

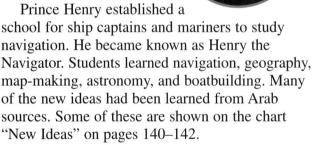
Prince Henry, a member of the Portuguese royal family, believed it was important for Portugal to find a sea route, rather than a land route, to the riches of Asia.

Prince Henry established a school for ship captains and mariners to study navigation. He became known as Henry the Navigator. Students learned navigation, geography, map-making, astronomy, and boatbuilding. Many of the new ideas had been learned from Arab sources. Some of these are shown on the chart "New Ideas" on pages 140–142.

The Portuguese Sail South and East

By 1460 Portuguese mariners had established a sea route down the west coast of Africa. Ships from Portugal continued to sail further south along the western coast of Africa. Eventually Bartholomew Diaz's ship rounded the Cape of Good Hope. In 1498 Vasco da Gama reached India by sea.

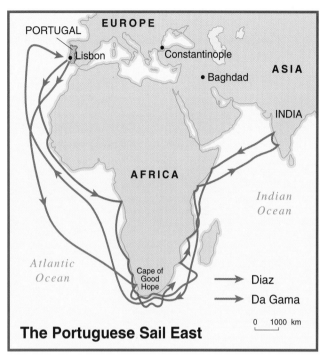
The Portuguese Sail East

Archive Photos

Prince Henry's school of navigation contributed to the skills of mariners. The sea routes established by Vasco da Gama and the mariners that came after him opened up new trade routes. Portugal grew wealthy from goods traded in Asia and Africa.

Around the World

In 1519, Ferdinand Magellan led an expedition of five ships westward. He was seeking the islands off the east coast of the Asian continent on behalf of Portugal. He took the stormy and dangerous route south around the tip of South America. The expedition reached the Philippine Islands in 1521, where Magellan was killed in a conflict. One of his ships continued on and returned to Portugal. Magellan was the first European to reach Asia by sailing west. His ship's round-the-world route is shown on a map inside the back cover of this textbook.

143

Spanish Exploration

An Exercise in Decision-Making

In this part of the chapter you will be asked to make a decision on an issue. Decision-making is explained on page 259 of the Appendix.

Spain in 1490

This activity should take approximately three class periods. In the first two classes you will do the role-play and fill out the decision-making chart. In the third you will explain the monarchs' decision and reasons to the rest of the class.

Your teacher will divide your class into groups of seven students. Role-play cards follow for Christopher Columbus, King Ferdinand, Queen Isabella, and the Naval Advisor. Each group should select these four and the following:

- scribe: one person to record the monarchs' decision on the decision-making chart. (See Appendix, page 259.) This person is to work with the king and queen.
- group leader: one person to lead the group through the decision-making process.

- spokesperson: one person to speak for the group (You will explain the results of the role-play to the rest of the class.)

Periods One and Two

1. Read and become familiar with your role card. Carry out the suggestions on it. Scribe, group leader, and spokesperson prepare the decision-making chart.
2. a) Columbus should present his ideas to King Ferdinand and Queen Isabella while the rest of the group listens and makes notes.
   b) King Ferdinand and Queen Isabella should consult with the Naval Advisor to discuss Columbus's request.
3. The entire group, except for Columbus, should fill out the decision-making chart. You will also prepare a short summary of the alternatives and consequences discussed and Ferdinand and Isabella's decision. The person playing Columbus should research the historical events of Columbus's explorations in the library and report the findings to the class.

1. Christopher Columbus

You are the Italian mariner Christopher Columbus. You believe the world is round and that if you sail west from Europe you will reach Asia. But a sea voyage such as the one you want to take is very expensive. You want to present the idea of sailing westward to King Ferdinand and Queen Isabella. Consider the following before you meet them:

- What are your reasons for wanting to sail west? Why don't you sail south and east like the Portuguese have been doing?
- Why should the Spanish monarchs finance your voyage?

2. King Ferdinand and Queen Isabella

Under your leadership Spain has become an important nation. Your army and navy are powerful. The Roman Catholic Church has great influence in your country and you wish to help it grow.

You are about to meet the mariner Christopher Columbus. You have heard he is seeking money to finance a voyage to Asia. Before you meet with Columbus you should consult with the Naval Advisor. You must decide:

- Should your country become involved in Columbus's idea? Why or why not?
- Where will the money to finance the voyage come from?

3. Naval Advisor

As a mariner, you have sailed most of the world's known oceans and seas. You made several long and dangerous voyages to the lands of Asia. You are especially interested in adding to your country's knowledge of the world and have drawn several maps yourself. You are an experienced navigator. You know how latitude and longitude work and how to use a compass and astrolabe. You now advise the king and queen about sea travel, trade, and security.

Period Three

1. The spokesperson from each group should explain the group's decision and reasons to the rest of the class. Columbus should report the historical findings researched.

Thinking About Thinking

2. a) In your groups discuss the decision-making process you used. Did all participants agree with the decision? Why or why not? What would you do differently next time?
    b) Record in your History Journal your reaction to this decision-making exercise.

Christopher Columbus
The Spanish Sail West
1492

  Sailing on behalf of Spain, Columbus crossed the Atlantic and landed on an island he called San Salvador in 1492. Columbus made three more voyages to the Americas. He was the first to incorrectly call the Aboriginal peoples that he met Indians because he thought he was in the Indies.

Columbus's initial voyage had long-lasting effects on both the people of the Americas and on Europeans. Some of these effects are shown on the chart on pages 147–149.

In the next 12 years, over eighty voyages were made to the Americas from various parts of Europe.

As a result of Spain's voyages to the Americas, the country became more powerful. The Spanish treasury grew as gold, silver, and other treasures (especially from Mexico and Peru) were added. However, the Aboriginal peoples of Central and South America suffered greatly. Great numbers died, and their ways of life changed forever.

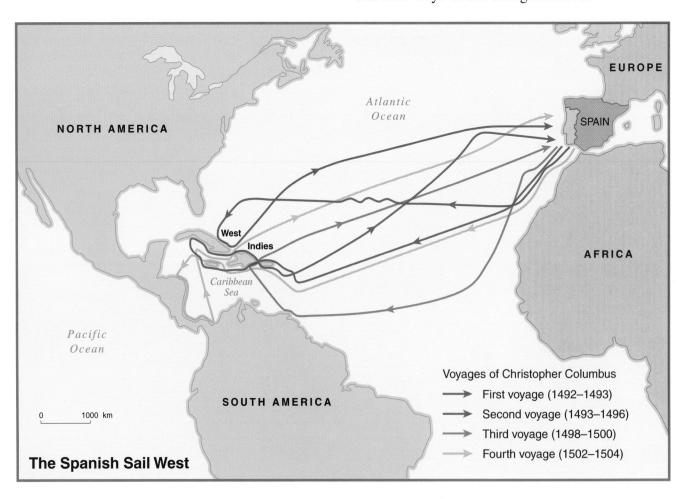

The Spanish Sail West

Voyages of Christopher Columbus
→ First voyage (1492–1493)
→ Second voyage (1493–1496)
→ Third voyage (1498–1500)
→ Fourth voyage (1502–1504)

Effects of Westward Expansion

Events	Effects
In the Treaty of Tordesillas* (1494) the Pope granted all lands east of 46° West longitude to Portugal. All lands west of this line were granted to the Spanish. The line ran from the North Pole to the South Pole.	This imaginary line divided the Americas and resulted in Spain and Portugal having a monopoly. A monopoly is a right to buy and sell granted to a country, a group, or a person that excludes others from buying and selling. The Treaty gave Spain and Portugal control of the Americas.

The English, French, and Dutch refused to recognize the Treaty of Tordesillas. However, they left Central and South America to Spanish and Portuguese control. They concentrated on seeking a more northerly route to Asia. Almost immediately King Henry VII of England **sponsored** an Italian mariner, Giovanni Caboto (John Cabot), to sail westward. This northern route they sought came to be referred to as Northwest Passage. (It will be your next area of study, along with information on Giovanni Caboto.)

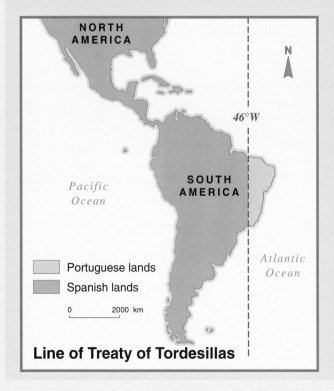

Line of Treaty of Tordesillas

NORTH AMERICA

N

46°W

Pacific Ocean

SOUTH AMERICA

Atlantic Ocean

Portuguese lands

Spanish lands

0   2000 km

History—
☐ Primary Source
☐ Secondary Source
☐ Interpretation
☐ Chronology
☑ Cause and Effect

---

*Tordesillas—pronounced tor-day-see-yahs
Sponsored—supported an activity with money or a guarantee of backing

Events	Effects
Columbus's expeditions were followed by other explorers, adventurers, missionaries, and settlers.	The Spanish found vast quantities of gold and silver in South and Central America. The Aboriginal people were forced to work in the mines, where thousands died. The Spanish took most of the Aboriginal people's treasures.
Without realizing it, the Spanish, and later other Europeans, brought European diseases (smallpox, diphtheria, measles, mumps, and typhus) to the Americas. Some diseases were also introduced to Europe from America. **America ← Europe**	The Aboriginal people had not built up resistance to European diseases. The diseases became **epidemic** among the Aboriginal people. The population of the Aboriginal people in the Americas was reduced by 50% to 90% between 1500 and 1900. Thousands died as groups came into contact with Europeans or European diseases.
Sugarcane was introduced to Hispaniola, an island in the West Indies. **America ← Europe**	Sugarcane was grown using the plantation system. Slave labour was used to work the huge farms. **Deforestation** resulted from clearing space to grow crops.
Explorers, scientists and settlers discovered species of plants unknown in Europe. They took back seeds and cuttings to start new plants. 	New foods and flowers were introduced into Europe from the Americas. Potatoes, corn, tomatoes, peppers, cacao (from which chocolate is made), turkeys, vanilla, beans, squash, pumpkins, avocado, peanuts, pecans, cashews, pineapples, and sunflowers are examples. These foods added variety to the daily diet of the people. Some eventually became staples in European homes. Flowers such as dahlia, marigold, and poinsettia were also taken to Europe. **America → Europe**
As settlers came to the Americas they brought with them familiar plants and foods. They grew some for their own use and raised crops in large farms for sale in Europe. Some weeds were introduced by accident. 	Over time, foods such as coffee, wheat, rice, barley, cabbage, turnip, lettuce, peaches, pears, lemons and oranges, bananas, and olives were introduced to the Americas by Europeans. Flowers such as the gladiola, lilac, carnation, daffodil, tulip, daisy, and two weeds, crab grass and dandelion, were also introduced from Europe. **America ← Europe**

Epidemic—disease quickly spreading among many people
Deforestation—loss of natural forests due to cutting down or burning

Events	Effects

In 1493, Columbus sailed from Europe with 17 ships full of animals. There were horses,* cattle, pigs, sheep, goats, chickens, and donkeys. All were unknown in the Americas. Other explorers also brought animals. The Spanish re-introduced the horse to the Americas.

America ⟵ Europe

Horses gave the Spanish advantage over the people in the Americas. The Spanish also had the skills and knowledge of raising and caring for the animals they brought. Horses were traded or escaped. They soon spread north and south from the West Indies. The horse greatly changed the way of life of the American people, especially that of the people who lived on the plains.

Europeans possessed firearms. Muskets and cannons were superior technology of warfare. They were weapons of mass destruction rather than single combat.

Guns, along with horses, made the "conquest" easier for the Europeans. The Aboriginal peoples were unfamiliar with the noise of guns. Damage and injuries could occur from a distance. Guns replaced the need for hand-to-hand combat.

For Your Notebook

Read pages 147–149 and answer the following:

1. a) Make a spider definition and/or a concept poster for the term monopoly.

   b) Which European countries claimed a monopoly on parts of North and South America?

   c) How would a monopoly help make a country richer?

2. In triads carry out a think-group-share:

   a) Record an hypothesis of how the line drawn in the Treaty of Tordesillas would affect areas of the world that England, France, and the Netherlands could explore.

   b) Discuss whether you think it was acceptable to divide up lands like this. Consider the rights of Aboriginal peoples that lived in these lands.

   c) Record an hypothesis as to why the Pope didn't include the Aboriginal peoples in the Treaty of Tordesillas when he made his 1494 decision.

3. Did Columbus discover America? Explain your reasons for your answer.

4. List your favourite meals. Which ones use foods that originated in the Americas?

5. Which of the changes listed on pages 147–149 do you think had the greatest effect on the people living in the Americas?

Optional

6. Use a chart like the following to record information about Columbus.

Christopher Columbus	
Country explored for	
Reasons for exploration	
Where explored	
Personal goals, ambitions	
Challenges faced	
Contributions/effects on Canadian history	

*Archaeologists believe the horse was originally from the Americas and migrated to Asia via the Bering land bridge during an Ice Age. Horses later became extinct in the Americas.

English Exploration

An Exercise in Decision-Making

Before starting this activity review the steps of Decision-making in the Appendix on page 259.

England in 1496

  Your teacher will divide your class into groups of five students. Role-play cards follow for King Henry VII, Giovanni Caboto (John Cabot), and three English investors. Each group should have one of the investors take the role of group leader to lead the group through the decision-making process. Another of the investors should take the role of group spokesperson to explain the results of the role-play to the rest of the class. The third investor should act as group recorder to record the group's decision on a chart. Caboto and the investors should also fill in a decision-making chart.

Periods One and Two

1. Read and carry out the suggestions on your role card.
2. a) Role-play the meeting between Caboto and the English investors. King Henry is not part of this discussion.
   b) The investors' group recorder should fill in the decision-making chart. Prepare a short summary of the alternatives and consequences discussed and the final decision.

Periods Three and Four

1. a) Role-play the meeting between King Henry VII and Caboto. The investors should also take part in this meeting.
   b) The recorder should fill in the decision-making chart with the group. (See page 259.)
   c) When not involved in this activity, King Henry and Caboto can be carrying out research on Caboto in the library.
2. The king should explain his decision to the rest of the class.
3. As a class discuss Evaluation. Then fill in Step 6 on the decision-making chart. (See page 259.)

1. Henry VII, King of England

You are about to meet with an Italian mariner Giovanni Caboto and a group of English merchants. Your advisors have informed you that Caboto is seeking financial backing for a voyage to Asia. You are not prepared to finance his voyage. He is also requesting that you grant him a monopoly to control trade in any areas he lands upon. Before meeting with Caboto, decide the following:
- Do you want the English to become involved in world exploration, especially in finding a westward route to Asia?
- Should Caboto lead the first English voyage?
- Will you grant Caboto a royal **charter** to claim lands and a monopoly to control buying and selling in areas he explores?

Charter—written permission from a king or queen

2. Giovanni Caboto

It is the year 1496. Your Italian ancestors have for centuries been using the overland routes to China and the East Indies. These routes are now controlled by the Ottoman Empire. Goods moved along this route are now very expensive. You believe there is a cheaper way to get the goods the people of Europe want. You are aware of the voyages made by Christopher Columbus. You believe that the world is round. Therefore, you believe you can reach Asia by sailing westward from Europe. You think a more northerly route than the one taken by Columbus might be shorter. You have asked merchants in other countries to finance a voyage westward but were unable to find investors. You have decided to go to Bristol, England, to see if merchants or other investors there will help you. You've heard English money is available for expeditions. You are also looking for a monarch under whose flag you can sail. Make sure you have a clear understanding of the following before you meet with King Henry VII:

- What are your reasons for wanting to sail west? Why don't you sail east like the Portuguese?
- Where do you plan to sail? What route will you take? What are your reasons?
- What will your investors gain if they finance your voyage? What will the English monarch gain if he grants you permission to sail for England?

3. English Investors from Bristol

For decades your businesses and investments have made money from trade. Many products have come overland from China. Since the Ottoman Empire has controlled trade at Constantinople it has been very expensive to obtain goods from Asia. You are looking for another way to obtain these trade goods. You know that Portuguese mariners have sailed around Africa's Cape of Good Hope and east into the Indian Ocean. Other investors from Bristol have financed expeditions to Iceland and to the areas west and south. They have made money trading English goods to Iceland, then bringing dried cod from the Grand Banks back to England. You believe a western sea route exists. It will be faster, easier, and less expensive than financing eastern overland trading expeditions. You have a large amount of money to invest in an expedition to the west. If the king will give Caboto a royal charter to claim lands and a monopoly to control buying and selling you will make a profit.

Giovanni Caboto*

Giovanni Caboto thought the world was round. He believed he could reach the riches of Asia by sailing northwest across the North Atlantic Ocean. Caboto was granted a charter by King Henry VII of England to trade in these lands. His voyages were funded by merchants in Bristol, England.

The explorer Giovanni Caboto was sent by Henry VII, King of England, to look for a shorter route to Asia. Caboto sailed west from England across the North Atlantic. (The drawings of Caboto are based on imaginings. No known portrait of him exists.)

1497 and 1498 Voyages

On June 24, 1497, Caboto and 18 men sailing a ship named the *Matthew* landed somewhere on the east coast of North America. They probably landed on the island that Caboto named New Found Land. Or, they may have landed on Labrador or Cape Breton Island. Caboto claimed the land for England. He then sailed southward along the coast for about three weeks. He landed from time to time, then returned to England. Caboto, like Columbus, believed he had reached Asia, not a continent between Europe and Asia.

King Henry VII sent Caboto to explore further in 1498. Caboto disappeared on this voyage. Many considered him a failure because he did not return with riches as the Portuguese and Spanish had done. Caboto's son, Sebastian, made two more voyages

to the area of what is now Atlantic Canada. However, the English lost interest in North Atlantic exploration for many decades.

Giovanni Caboto landed in Atlantic Canada at a place he called *Buona vista* [happy sight]. It was the first recorded European landing in what is now Canada since the Vikings had sailed there 500 years earlier. Caboto's expeditions were the earliest English-financed voyages of exploration into the region. He discovered a rugged, rocky land and uncountable numbers of fish in the ocean off the coast. In later years, Caboto's maps and diaries were lost without trace. There is no proof of where he landed, whether on Newfoundland, Labrador, or elsewhere.

Caboto's Contributions

The *Matthew* encountered great schools of fish. After Caboto's visits, Basque** and other fishers began coming in greater numbers to the shores of eastern Canada to fish. Many other explorers eventually journeyed westward from Europe following the northwest route that Caboto reported after his first voyage. Some sources credit Caboto as the "discoverer" of what we call Canada.

---

*The English version of Giovanni Caboto is John Cabot.

**Basques lived along the Atlantic coastlines at the border between France and Spain. They were expert fishers and whalers.

Canada Revisited

500th Anniversary Voyage

On June 24, 1997, a replica of Giovanni Caboto's ship the *Matthew* sailed into the harbour at Bonavista Bay, Newfoundland. The event was part of the 500th anniversary celebrations of the explorer's arrival on the shores of Atlantic Canada.

Cheering crowds, hundreds of small boats, the news media, and many famous people watched the small wooden ship and its crew arrive. Queen Elizabeth II, Prince Philip, and Prime Minister Jean Chrétien were all present to celebrate the **re-enactment** of the historic event.

The *Matthew* had been at sea seven weeks. The crew experienced floating icebergs, storms, and fog. It was a different kind of sailing than the modern-day sailors had been used to. It gave them great respect for the skills of the early explorers.

The explorers had sailed an unknown ocean without the technology, safety equipment, or even the food and clothing of today.

In the summer of 1997, a replica of Caboto's ship *Matthew* crossed the North Atlantic under sail. The ship had no motor, although it did have modern navigational and safety equipment.

Statue of Giovanni Caboto in Bonavista Bay, Newfoundland

This graphic was designed to commemorate Caboto's voyage.

Re-enactment—to show a past event again, using actors

Fishing

The first European industry in what is now Canada was fishing. Later the fur trade became an important industry. Europeans came to recognize that these lands could be a source of wealth. These two industries supplied important raw materials, but they did not need permanent European settlements.

By the late 1400s fishing vessels were common in the waters to the north and west of Europe, especially near Iceland. Religious rules forbade the eating of meat on certain days of the week. Thus, fish was an important food in most homes in Europe. Codfish was the most sought-after fish because of its taste and its large size.

Fishers were always looking for new fishing areas to satisfy this market. Caboto's report of the great quantities of cod near the New Found Land caused great excitement. He reported seeing an abundance of cod. There were so many that they could be gathered in baskets dipped into the water. Soon the "codfish lands" near Newfoundland's Grand Banks were the destination of most of Europe's fishing vessels.

French, Basque, Spanish, Portuguese, and English fishers all fished the Grand Banks. It is estimated there were about 300 English fishing ships around Newfoundland during this period.

Fishing was considered a seasonal activity. The ships returned to Europe as the winter approached. At this time European countries had no permanent settlements in North America. Fishing stations were set up on shore for cleaning and preserving fish. Nearly all people working in this industry at that time were men. Fish were either caught from small rowboats or from the main ship's decks. Cod were either salted or dried to preserve them for the long voyage to Europe.

Preserving Methods
Dry Fishing

Most English fishers used a method called dry fishing. This method required on-shore fishing stations to dry the fish. The process is shown below and in the diagram on page 155.

Above: Cod drying on racks

Whalers working at an Atlantic fishing station

Canada Revisited

Selma Barkham was an historical geographer working for Public Archives of Canada who began searching for sites used by the Basque whalers in Newfoundland in the 16th century. Her work led to the discovery in the 1970s of the world-famous Basque whaling site at Red Bay, Labrador. Three ships were uncovered by underwater divers. The site is now a National Historic Site.

For Your Notebook

Use the illustration above to learn about an early fishing station and dry fishing. Match a number in the illustration to each of the following statements.

a) Fish were caught in deeper water by hooks attached to lines and b) taken in rowboats to the processing area on shore.

c) The fishers were working in cold climates.

d) Processing fish was done by first removing and throwing away the insides (except the liver).

e) Salt was added to preserve the cod.*

f) The fish were carried to the shore, where in g) excess salt was washed off.

h) Oil was removed from the liver, wastes were put into troughs i) and the oil into barrels, as shown in j).

k) The fish were laid out on platforms to dry. These platforms were called flakes. It took about ten days to dry the fish so they were ready to ship to Europe.

Wet Fishing

Some ships were equipped for doing processing on board. This was called wet fishing. The fish had their heads and insides removed and then were preserved in salt. Salt was expensive and not easily available. Spanish, Portuguese, and some French fishers used the wet fishing method. They seldom went ashore.

Basque Whalers

Whaling in the waters of what is now Atlantic Canada was also a profitable industry. One method was to drive whales into shallow water to kill them. Harpoons were used in deeper water. Once the whale was landed on shore the blubber was removed, cut into cubes, and boiled. The valuable oil was poured into barrels. The oil was taken by small boats to the ships in the harbour which then took it to Europe. Whale oil was used as a source of fuel for light.

*Too little salt resulted in a rotten cargo before the ships reached Europe; too much salt burned the fish.

French Exploration

Giovanni da Verrazano

1522

Francis I, King of France, met with Giovanni da Verrazano, an Italian navigator. Verrazano was convinced that a huge land area existed between Europe and Asia. Verrazano had sailed many times from various French ports into the North Atlantic. He had also fished in the codfish-land (known today as the Grand Banks) off the coast of New Found Land.

King Francis I was aware of the riches to be made from the trade of spices. Spices had been brought back from a round-the-world expedition led by Magellan. The king was anxious to get involved in sea expeditions to Asia. However, he was a Roman Catholic ruler. He knew he ought to honour the Pope's decision recorded in the Treaty of Tordesillas.* The Treaty did not give the French any rights to territory in the Americas. However, the king decided to ignore the treaty and sponsor Verrazano's voyage as an expedition for France.

Exploring Further

1. Pretend you are King Francis I. Write a journal account of your meeting with Giovanni da Verrazano. Tell why you decided to make his voyage an official French expedition. Journal writing is explained on page 264 in the Appendix.

In 1524, Giovanni da Verrazano travelled along the eastern coast of North America from Florida to the New Found Land. He was taking a risk, as this area was claimed by Spain and he was sailing for France. Upon returning home he reported to King Francis I that New Spain and the New Found Land were connected to each other but not to Asia and Africa. He believed that a huge land area (North America) existed between the Atlantic and the Pacific Oceans. He believed he had found a route to Asia through this "new" land mass. This possible route became known as the Northwest Passage.

Exploring Further

Read page 157 before answering the following.

1. Write a letter to the king of France from the point of view of Giovanni da Verrazano. Try to convince the king to finance your next voyage of exploration.

2. Imagine you are a sailor on one of the early voyages searching for a northern route to Asia. Write a weekly journal account. Include your duties, daily work, and innermost thoughts, fears, and dreams.

3. Work with a partner to do the following.

   a) Make a web or mind map of the information on these pages.

   b) Locate the following in an atlas: Chesapeake Bay, Hudson River, Bay of Fundy, Gulf of St. Lawrence, Hudson Strait.

   c) Explain why early mariners might think the above waterways were a passage around or through North America to Asia.

4. Many cod fishers and whalers had visited the waters near Newfoundland. Why do you suppose they didn't attempt to search for the passage to Asia?

---

*See page 147 for information on the Treaty of Tordesillas.

The Northwest Passage

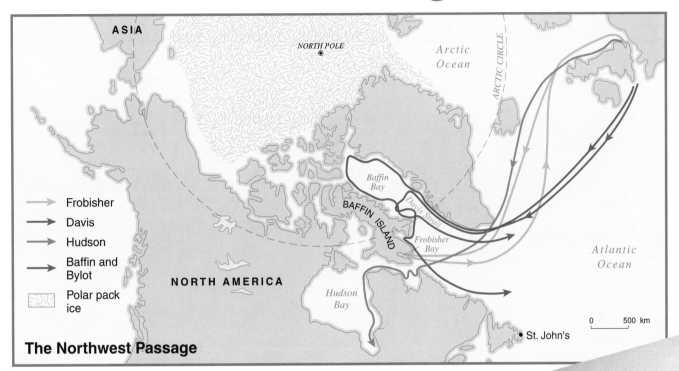

The Northwest Passage

Map legend:
- Frobisher
- Davis
- Hudson
- Baffin and Bylot
- Polar pack ice

 During the 1500s Spain and Portugal controlled the southern routes that they hoped would take them to Asia. Thus, England and France were forced to look for a more northerly route. They needed to go around or through the western land mass between Europe and Asia. Some explorers who searched for a Northwest Passage are shown on the map and chart.

English Failures to Find the Northwest Passage		
Date	**Explorer**	**Area Visited**
1576–1578	Martin Frobisher	Made three attempts to find Northwest Passage. Explored area of Baffin Island. Explored and named Frobisher Bay.
1583	Humphrey Gilbert	At St. John's, Newfoundland, attempted the first English colony in the Americas.
1585–1587	John Davis	Made three attempts to find a Northwest Passage. Explored and named Davis Strait.
1610–1611	Henry Hudson	Explored Hudson Strait and Hudson Bay.
1615–1616	William Baffin and Robert Bylot	Explored and named Baffin Bay area while looking for Northwest Passage.

Henry Hudson

In 1610, an English captain named Henry Hudson sailed his ship, the *Discovery*, through the waterway now known as Hudson Strait. He reached what is called Hudson Bay. He believed that he had found the western ocean that would take him to China. He sailed to the south end of Hudson Bay and was trapped there by the ice of winter.

That winter Hudson's men suffered from starvation and **scurvy**. When the ice was gone in the spring, Hudson said that he wanted to explore farther. This caused his crew to rebel. They put Hudson, his son, and several others into a small boat. Several of the men who remained on the *Discovery* died on the way back to England. Eight survived and returned to England. No one knows the fate of Henry Hudson and the men cast adrift in the small boat on Hudson Bay in 1611.*

Scurvy—a disease common among sailors who did not get enough vitamin C in their diet, which is found in fruits and vegetables.
*One story which has some support is that Hudson, his son, and the others landed on the shores of James Bay. Hudson and the first mate soon died. Hudson's son was adopted by the Woodland Cree. He moved around with them and married a Cree woman. They have descendants in Ontario today. There is a birchbark scroll at a small fur trading fort near Ottawa that reports this story.

History—
- ☐ Primary Source
- ☐ Secondary Source
- ☑ Interpretation
- ☐ Chronology
- ☐ Cause and Effect

Review ● ● ● ● ● ● ● ● ● ● ● ● ● ● ● ● ● ● ●

Assessment

1. Complete a self-assessment for one assignment from this chapter. See page 263 or ask your teacher for ideas.

Summarizing the Chapter

2. Reread the predictions you made on page 137. Fill in the "What I Found Out" column of the prediction chart.

Understanding Concepts

3. Check the organization of your binder according to the description on page 261.

4. The European countries believed that they had the "right" to supervise, control, and take anything they wanted from the people living in areas they explored. Often this included the land upon which the people of the Americas lived. Often it included the people themselves.
   a) Do you agree with this perspective (point of view)? Why or why not?
   b) Discuss your perspective with several friends.

5. In what way(s) did each voyage of exploration studied in this chapter result in more knowledge and a better understanding of the world?

6. Record three of the following vocabulary items for this chapter:

   Age of Exploration   investor
   monopoly   Northwest Passage
   sponsor

7. Create a concept poster for the Age of Exploration, monopoly, or the Northwest Passage.

8. Add names from this chapter to the Explorers Timeline you started on page 117.

9. Discuss the following as a class. Caboto is often credited with the "discovery" of Canada. When the word discovery is used this way, Caboto's voyage is looked at only from the European point of view. What about the Aboriginal people who had lived there for centuries? What about the stories of the voyage of the Irish monk St. Brendan? Or the Vikings? Or the many fishers who visited the east coast of what is now Canada? Might the people who had lived on Greenland and Iceland for years have sailed westward to Canada? Did Caboto really discover this land? What do you think? Give reasons for your answer.

Developing Research Skills

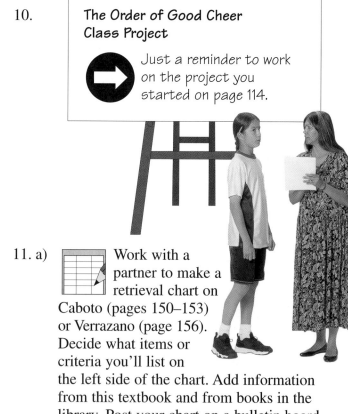

10.
   The Order of Good Cheer Class Project

   Just a reminder to work on the project you started on page 114.

11. a) Work with a partner to make a retrieval chart on Caboto (pages 150–153) or Verrazano (page 156). Decide what items or criteria you'll list on the left side of the chart. Add information from this textbook and from books in the library. Post your chart on a bulletin board and exchange ideas with other students.
    b) Add what you learned on chart-making to your history binder under "Learning How to Learn."

12. Carry out research to find out more about whaling in the northwestern Atlantic during this time period. Find out more about whaling today and compare.

Developing Communication Skills

Select at least one of 13–17:

Writing

13. Imagine yourself living at a time when almost everybody believed the world was flat. In your History Journal, write out what you would say if you were Columbus, trying to convince unbelievers that the world is round.

Listening and Speaking

14. Imagine that Giovanni Caboto could have been present for the re-enactment of the sailing of the *Matthew* to Newfoundland. With a partner, role-play the conversation he might have with a reporter as they watch the celebration take place.

15. Was Caboto's voyage successful? Work with a partner to gather information which either supports the "Yes" side or the "No" side. Another team of two will gather evidence for the opposite answer. Present your ideas to the other team. Listen to their ideas. Once all ideas have been shared, discuss and compare the evidence. Which side had the strongest evidence?

Viewing and Representing

16. Your teacher will divide your class into four groups: Spain, Portugal, France, England. Each group should prepare and present a series of **tableaux** to represent the exploration activities of each country. Be prepared to answer questions about the country your group is presenting.

17. Study the picture of Genoa on page 138 at the top right. Compare this city to a present-day city near where you live and to a Huron village (as described in Chapter 3).

Tableau—participants represent a scene by taking positions and not moving; tableaux can be based on a picture, story, or idea.

Applying Concepts

18. In the Learning How to Learn section of your binder:

   a) Use a diagram to show two examples of cause and effect in events in your life.
   b) Find a news clipping or article about a recently improved piece of technology or a new invention. What problem led to this new technology or invention? What may some results of this discovery be?

19. Discuss the following questions and then find a way to share your ideas in a visual format (such as an illustration or poster).

   a) What types of things might have to be taken along on the ships for survival?
   b) What kinds of problems do you think the early explorers might encounter?
   c) Do any of the above apply to modern day exploration?

20. Early expeditions and trade between America and Europe meant new foods became available to people on other continents. How has technology (e.g., transportation, refrigeration, communication) affected what foods and products are available today? What foods and products would you not have access to if it were not for such developments in technology?

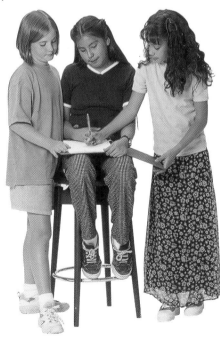

Chapter 8
Exploring and Claiming Lands

O v e r v i e w

Use this Overview to predict the events of this chapter.

❶ Early Navigation

Early maps and navigational tools were different from those used today.

❷ Jacques Cartier

Sent by the king of France, Francis I, Jacques Cartier made three voyages to modern-day Canada. He was searching for a short route to Asia.

1534

Cartier had his men place crosses at various locations to show that France claimed the area of modern-day Atlantic Canada and the Gulf of St. Lawrence.

1535–1536

King Francis I sent Cartier to explore farther up the St. Lawrence River. He sailed as far west as modern-day Quebec City and Montreal. Many men died from scurvy over the winter.

1541–43

Cartier searched for the riches of the legendary Kingdom of Saguenay. Cartier and Jean Francis de Roberval attempted to establish a permanent French settlement.

❸ Results

When two cultures meet they affect each other.

Chapter 8 Focus

Chapter 7 introduced you to world-wide exploration carried out by several European countries. Chapter 8 focuses on the voyages of the French explorer Jacques Cartier. The chapter examines how the French struggled to meet their needs in a new environment. It looks at exploration and claiming lands, and how people from different cultures affected each other when they met.

This chapter
- relies on a variety of primary sources of information
- provides you with critical thinking and decision-making exercises to examine what may happen when different cultures meet.

The major focus for this chapter will be the concepts of technology, cultural contact, and exploration. The minor focus will be environmental influences and balance. This is a good chapter to look at differences in how the First Nations people and the French saw these ideas.

| Environmental Interaction | Balance | Technology | Cultural Contact | Exploration |

Vocabulary

claiming lands   cultural contact
interpreter   monopoly
scurvy

Chapter Activity/Note Making

 Use a fishbone graphic organizer such as the one below to make notes of the chapter.

Chapter Preview/Prediction

In pairs or small groups, use the overview, the illustrations, maps, and titles in this chapter to predict answers on the prediction chart.* Put your predictions in the "My Predictions" column. The full chart is shown on page 119.

Prediction Chart—What Do You Think?		
Questions	My Predictions (fill out now)	What I Found Out (fill out at end of chapter)
1. In what ways did the coming of Europeans change the balance that existed between the Aboriginal peoples and the environment?		
2. How did the		

Section Activity

The Order of Good Cheer Class Project

Use the information in this chapter to add to the Section Activity you started on page 114.

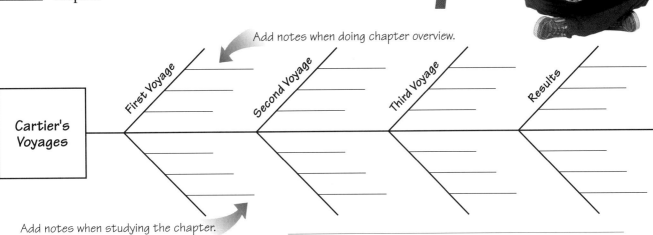

Add notes when doing chapter overview.

First Voyage

Second Voyage

Third Voyage

Results

Cartier's Voyages

Add notes when studying the chapter.

*Available as a blackline master in *Canada Revisited 6, Integrated Unit.*

Early Navigation

Geography—
- ☑ Maps
- ☐ Diagram
- ☐ Statistics
- ☐ Picture

An Imaginary Conversation Between Three Sailors

Xavier and his friend André are about to apply for positions on Cartier's ship. They have heard Cartier is hiring sailors for a voyage westward to Asia. They have both attended navigational school and sailed in small boats all their lives. Marcel, a man from their fathers' village, has been to the Americas many times as a fisherman. He is willing to share some things that his years of experience as a sailor have taught him. He will test them on what they know.

Scene 1

Marcel

André, your father tells me you two young men want to sail with Captain Jacques Cartier on his next voyage.

André Yes, Sir. Will you help us prepare for an interview with him? Tell us what you've learned over the years about sailing the deep oceans far away from land.

Marcel (Laughing) It's impossible to tell you everything I've learned. But let me start by seeing what

you two young men know. Xavier, tell me what you know about maps.

Xavier The top of a map should point to the direction north. The bottom of the map is south, the left west, and the right east. We also learned how to use a compass and the compass rose on a map to follow a direction.

Marcel reaches for several maps and starts to unroll them.

For Your Notebook

1. Work with a partner. Pretend you are Xavier and André. Study the Planisphere map below.
   a) Share five things this map tells about what European people knew about the world in 1527.
   b) Locate a compass rose on the map.
   c) Check the timeline on pages 123 and 139. What explorers and countries were involved in exploration by 1527?
   d) What knowledge would round-the-world explorers like the captains on Magellan's ships have provided to the map-makers? (See map on inside back cover.)

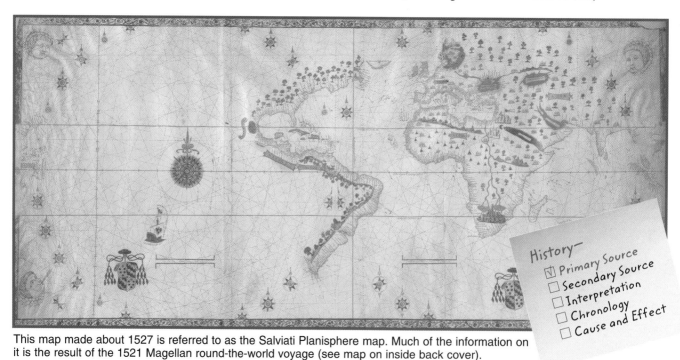

History—
- ☑ Primary Source
- ☐ Secondary Source
- ☐ Interpretation
- ☐ Chronology
- ☐ Cause and Effect

This map made about 1527 is referred to as the Salviati Planisphere map. Much of the information on it is the result of the 1521 Magellan round-the-world voyage (see map on inside back cover).

Scene 2

Marcel   Tell me what you have learned about winds and ocean currents.

Xavier   Years ago when ships tried to sail south and east around the western coast of Africa to Asia they found this very difficult to do. They were forced to sail in the direction of the currents and winds. For example, the Canaries Current forced them to travel south and west, not south and east as they wanted.

André   Once their ship crossed the Equator the pattern of currents and winds changed. The Benguela Current took them north and then west.

Xavier   Differently designed ships helped solve this problem. A different steering system using a rudder was developed. Ship builders also borrowed the design of the lateen sail from the Arabs. These triangular shaped sails help ships navigate into the wind. It was easier to sail in the direction they wanted to go.

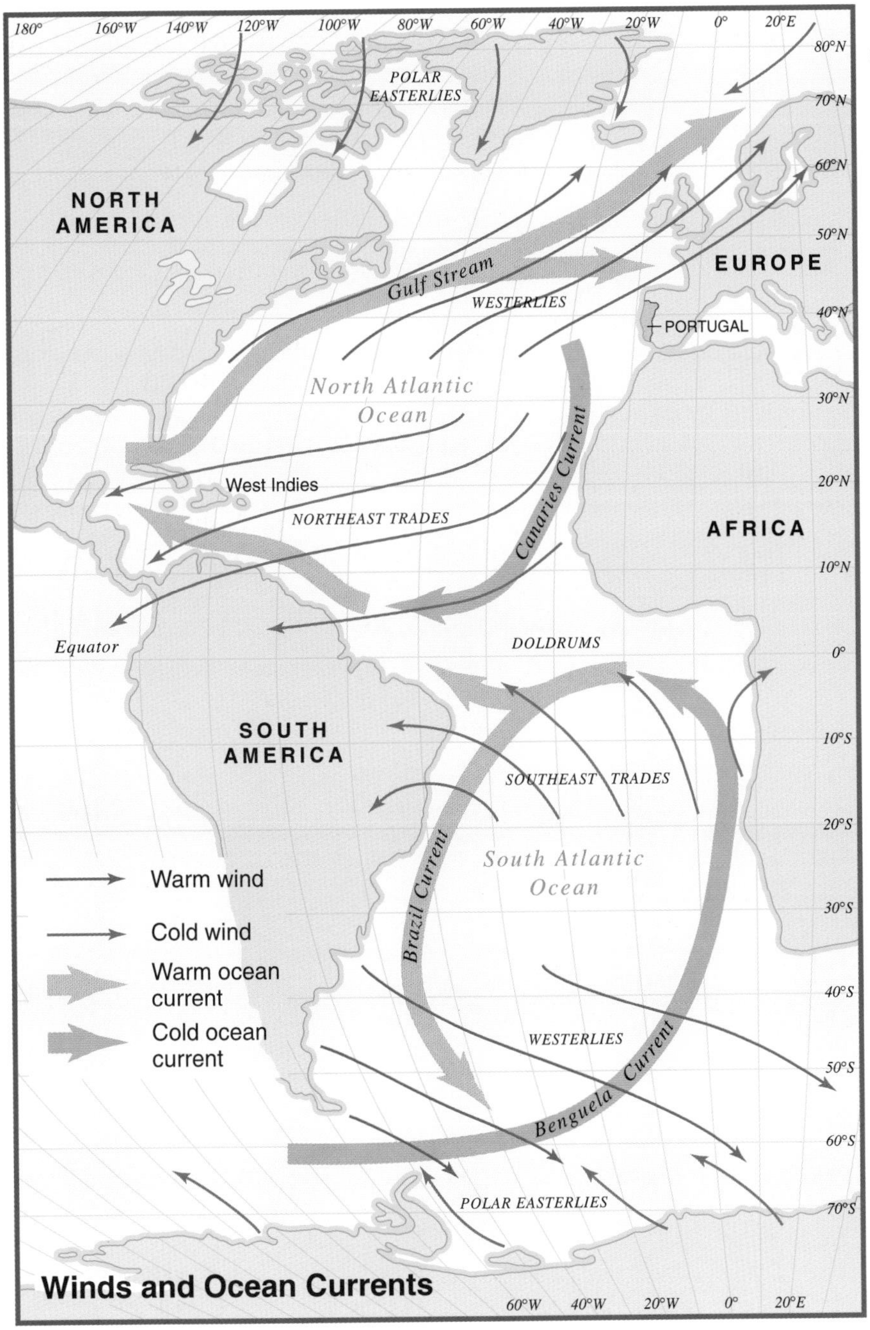

Winds and Ocean Currents

Legend:
- → Warm wind
- → Cold wind
- ⇒ Warm ocean current
- ⇒ Cold ocean current

Challenge Plus

1. Refer to the map to the left while answering the following questions.

    a) If a ship sailed from Portugal and then set a course west at 20°N latitude, in what direction would the ocean currents take it? At what area in America would it likely land? In what way do you think the ocean currents influenced where Columbus landed in what is now called the West Indies?

    b) If a sailing ship left the West Indies and sailed with the current, in what direction would it naturally go?

2. How did winds and water currents influence where the western Europeans sailed?

3. How did early sailors use technology?

163

Scene 3

Marcel What did you learn about finding the ship's position while at sea?

Xavier Ships can easily get lost once they leave port and lose sight of land. Without landmarks or instruments for navigation, sailors can't tell where they are and which direction is which.

Marcel We always use the sun to tell what basic direction we are sailing. If the rising sun is starboard then we know we are sailing north. You know where starboard is, don't you?

Xavier Yes, the right side of the ship when you face in the direction you are sailing.

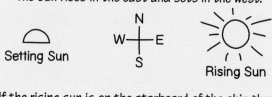

The sun rises in the east and sets in the west.

Setting Sun — N W—E S — Rising Sun

If the rising sun is on the starboard of the ship then the ship is sailing north.

Left (port) | Right (starboard)

If the rising sun is on the port of the ship then the ship is sailing south.

Right (starboard) | Left (port)

Marcel Navigators also use the stars at night to help find the ship's location. The **North Star** is always directly north, however it is higher or lower in the sky at different latitudes. The farther south we sail the lower the North Star appears in the sky. I only crossed the Equator once. It was a clear night and the stars were bright but the North Star could not be seen. It was below the horizon. It can only be seen in the Northern Hemisphere. That's the half of the globe north of the Equator.

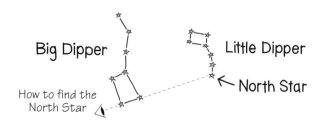

Big Dipper — Little Dipper — North Star

How to find the North Star

André But on cloudy days and nights sailors can lose their way. It is impossible for them to know where they are unless they can fix their latitude and longitude readings.

Marcel And . . . ?

André After the clouds clear they take readings and use maps to figure out where they are.

Xavier Maps use a **grid** system to show the exact location of a place on the Earth's surface. The grid is made up of two sets of imaginary lines. They're called latitude and longitude. They are used for reference.

Marcel Most sailors don't know about latitude and longitude. Will you draw these sets of lines for me? Also tell me what you've learned about these imaginary lines.

André The **parallel** lines that go across are called latitude. Latitude is numbered in degrees north or south of the Equator. The Equator is numbered 0°.

Xavier Maps also have imaginary long lines that run from North Pole to South Pole. They are farthest apart at the Equator and meet at the poles. They are called longitude.

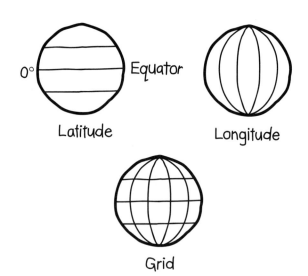

0° — Equator — Latitude — Longitude — Grid

For Your Notebook

1. Locate latitude and longitude lines on the map on page 163.

North Star—A bright star found directly above the North Pole, used by sailors to determine the direction they were sailing; also called the Pole Star or Polaris

Grid—lines of longitude and latitude marked on a map, used to figure out the exact location of a place
Parallel—always the same distance apart

Scene 4

André   Marcel, did you use a cross-staff and astrolabe when you were young?

Marcel   When I was a young sailor we usually figured out our position by sailing north and south using the stars. Then we sailed west or east until we hit land. On my first trip to the West Indies we sailed south until the butter melted —butter melts when you get to the warm lands near the Equator—then we sailed west. Once we learned how to use a cross-staff and an astrolabe to calculate latitude we could find our position more easily while at sea. Longitude is still very difficult to calculate. In spite of everything we know, sailing depends on the captain's skill and experience, particularly with winds and currents.

Xavier   How did you know when you were approaching land?

The astrolabe consists of a heavy brass ring with a ruler for sighting along attached at the centre. An astrolabe is used to determine latitude position. A quadrant, such as the one in the photograph on page 141, was used in a similar way.

Marcel   We carefully watched the sea. If we saw only the albatross we knew we were far from land.* If the water appeared full of lots of objects from land—trees, branches, wood—we knew land was near. When we saw gulls, terns, and sparrows we knew land was near. When our Captain thought we were approaching land he had the men lower a rope with a weight on it. Close to shore the weight attached to the end of the rope reached the ocean bottom. We could tell how deep the water was by measuring the length of rope. We learned this from experience. Now, I think you are both ready for your interview with Captain Cartier. You learned quite a bit at that school for navigators!

Exploring Further

1. What questions do you think Cartier asked André and Xavier? In groups of three, role-play Cartier's interview with André and Xavier. Does Cartier give them positions on his ship? Why or why not?

Using a cross-staff and astrolabe

---

*The albatross is a large seabird that can remain in the air for long periods without landing. They can be found far from shore.

Jacques Cartier

 Jacques Cartier was a French explorer who sailed from France to search for a western route to Asia. Money for the voyage came from the French king. Cartier made three voyages to modern-day Eastern Canada. He came into contact with First Nations people there.

Much of what you will learn about Cartier is from excerpts from his journal.

In this painting, Jacques Cartier is claiming the land for the king of France in 1534. On his second voyage in 1535–36 he sailed as far west as present-day Quebec City and Montreal.

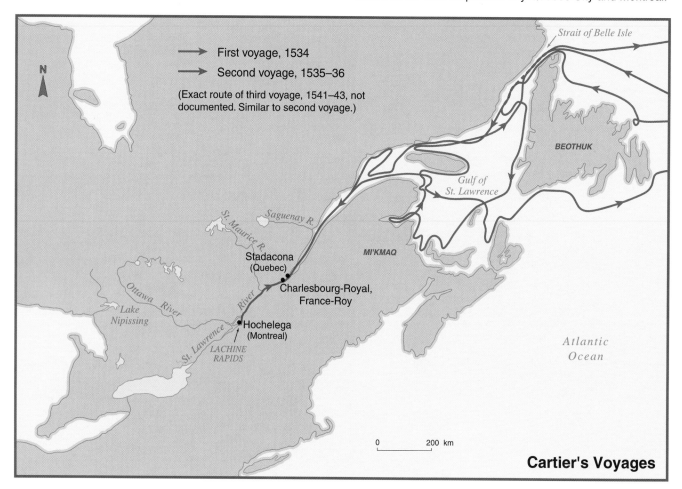

Cartier's Voyages

First Voyage

1534

On April 20, 1534, Jacques Cartier set sail with two ships from St. Malo, a port in northwest France. He was sent by Francis I, the king of France, to

- travel through the Strait of Belle Isle
- travel to the Sea of Asia
- discover lands rich in gold and other precious things.

Learning How to Learn

Thinking as an Historian

Cartier's journal is the first written record we have of the European exploration of Atlantic Canada. It is a primary source. Most sea captains (if they could read and write) kept a log of their explorations. A log is like a journal. Logs were often used by early writers as references for books published about the explorers. In the next few pages you will find excerpts from *The Voyages of Jacques Cartier*, published in 1924 by H.P. Biggar. As part of his research, Mr. Biggar studied the original French log of Jacques Cartier and translated it.

You may see words in square brackets in the text of a primary source. These indicate information that this textbook's authors have added to make your reading easier. Three periods are used to indicate missing text. Not all the text of the original is included.

The maps and illustrations in this chapter, unless marked, are secondary sources. They are not from Cartier's journal.

For Your Notebook

1. Identify each of the following as primary or secondary sources: *The Voyages of Jacques Cartier* by H.P. Biggar; this textbook; Cartier's 1534 journal.
2. When reading pages 167 to 170 you will notice some numbers. Match these numbers to their locations on the map on page 168.

Jacques Cartier's Account of Francis' Land

1 . . . we set forth from the harbour and port of St. Malo [France] with two ships of about sixty tons' burden each, manned in all with sixty-one men, on April 20 in the said year 1534; and sailing on with fair weather we reached Newfoundland on May 10, sighting land at Cape Bonavista in latitude 48° 30 [degrees longitude not stated] . . .

2 . . . And on the twenty-first of the said month of May we set forth from this harbour with a west wind, and sailed north, one quarter north-east of Cape Bonavista as far as the isle of Birds . . . [latitude 49]

3 . . . We made our way among these islands, and at the end of the thickest portion of them, we found a good harbour . . . which was named St. Anthony's [52°N 56°W] harbour . . . .

4 And further on, about a league or two, we came to a small very deep passage with the land running south-west and with very high shores. It is a good harbour; and a cross was set up there . . . .

. . . the land should not be called the New Land [as Caboto had said], being composed of stones and horrible rugged rocks; for along the whole of the north shore, I did not see one cart-load of earth and yet I landed in many places . . .

History—
- ☑ Primary Source
- ☐ Secondary Source
- ☐ Interpretation
- ☐ Chronology
- ☐ Cause and Effect

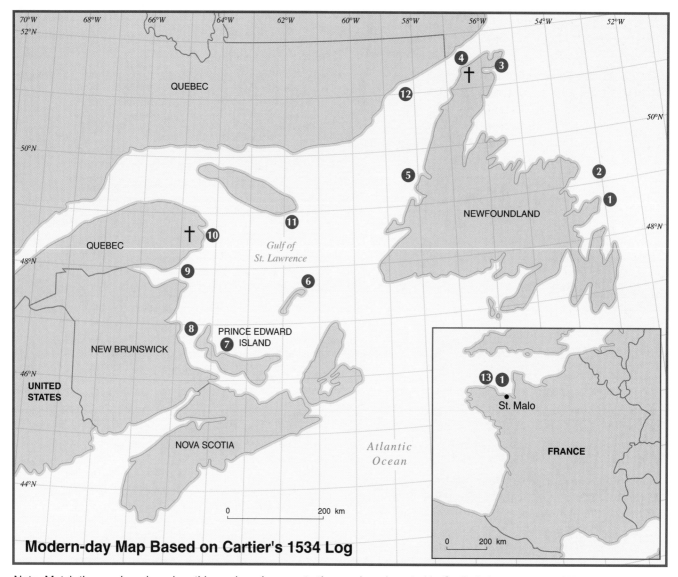

Modern-day Map Based on Cartier's 1534 Log

Note: Match the numbers in red on this modern-day map to the numbers inserted in Cartier's log on pages 167 to 170.

. . . In fine I am rather inclined to believe that this is the land God gave to Cain. There are people [Beothuk] on this coast . . . who wear their hair tied up on top of their heads like a handful of twisted hay, with a nail or something of the sort passed through the middle, and into it they weave a few birds' feathers. They clothe themselves with the furs of animals, both men and women . . . .

5 . . . the sixteenth of the month [of June], we ran along this coast to the south-west . . . when we come to a region of very high and rugged mountains . . . .

6 . . . until the twenty-fourth of the said month [June 24] we had stormy weather, head winds and overcast sky to such an extent that we could not get sight of land until St. John's day when we saw a head-land to

the south-east of us [south of the Madeleine Islands] . . . .

7 And pursuing our course we came in sight of what had looked to us like two islands, which was mainland.

All this coast is low and flat but the finest land one can see, and full of beautiful trees and meadows . . . .

. . . a man came into sight who ran after our long-boats along the coast, making frequent signs to us to return towards the said [First Nations] point. And seeing these signs we began to row towards him, but when he saw that we were returning, he started to run away and to flee before us. We landed opposite to him and placed a knife and a woollen girdle [sash, belt] on a branch; and then returned to our ships . . . .

8 . . . we saw that this [entrance to North-umberland Strait] was a bay . . .

9 . . . we coasted along the north shore [of Chaleur Bay] in order to find a harbour, and entered a small bay and cove completely open to the south . . . . we caught sight of two fleets of [First Nations] canoes that were crossing from one side to the other, which numbered in all some forty or fifty canoes. Upon one of the fleets reaching this point, there sprung out and landed a large number of [First Nations people], who set up a great clamour and made frequent signs to us to come on shore, holding up to us some furs on sticks. But as we were only one boat we did not care to go, so we rowed towards the other fleet which was on the water.

And they [on shore], seeing we were rowing away, . . . came after our long-boat dancing and showing many signs of joy, and of their desire to be friends, saying to us in their language: *Napou tou daman asurtat*, and other words, we did not understand . . .

. . . and [we] waved to them to go back, which they would not do but paddled so hard that they soon surrounded our long-boat with their seven canoes. . . . And when they had come alongside our long-boat, we shot off two fire-lances which scattered among them and frightened them so much that they began to paddle off in very great haste, and did not follow us any more . . . .

. . . The next day [Tuesday, July 7] . . . As soon as they saw us they began to run away, making signs to us that they had come to barter with us; and held up some furs of small value, with which they clothe them-selves. We likewise made signs to them that we wished them no harm, and sent two men on shore, to offer them some knives and other iron goods, and a red cap to give to their chief. Seeing this, they sent on shore part of their people with some of their furs; and the two parties traded together . . . .

10 . . . On the twenty-fourth of the said month [July], we had a cross made thirty feet high, which was put together in the presence of a number of the [First Nations people] on the point at the entrance to this harbour, under the cross-bar of which we fixed a shield with three fleurs-de-lys, and above it a wooden board engraved in large Gothic characters, where was written, LONG LIVE THE KING OF FRANCE

We erected this cross on the point in their presence and they watched it being put to-gether and set up. And when it had been raised in the air, we all knelt down with our hands joined, worshiping it before them; and made signs to them, looking up and pointing towards heaven, that by means of this we had our redemption, at which they showed many marks of admiration, at the same time turning and looking at the cross.

When we had returned to our ships, the chief, dressed in an old black bear-skin, arrived in a canoe with three of his sons and his brother; but they did not come so close to the ships as they had usually done. And pointing to the cross he [the chief] made us a long harangue [speech], making the sign of the cross with the two of his fingers; and then he pointed to the land all around about, as if he wished to say that all this region belonged to him, and that we ought not to have set up this cross without his permission.

And when he had finished his harangue, we held up an axe to him, pretending we would barter it for his fur-skin. To this he nodded assent and little by little drew near the side of our vessel, thinking he would have the axe. But one of our men, who was in our dinghy [small boat], caught hold of his canoe, and at once two or three more stepped down into it and made the [First Nations people] come on board, they were assured by the captain that no harm would befall them, while at the same time . . .

. . . every sign of affection was shown to them; and they were made to eat and to drink and to be of good cheer. And then we ex-plained to them by signs that the cross had been set up to serve as a land-mark and guide-post on coming into the harbour, and that we would soon come back and would bring them iron wares and other foods; and that we wished to take two of his [the chief's] sons away with us and afterwards would bring them back again to that harbour. And we dressed up his two sons [Dom Agaya and Taignoagny] in shirts and ribbons and in red caps, and put a little brass chain round the neck of each, at which they were greatly pleased; and they proceeded to hand over their . . . [clothes] to those who were going back on shore. To each of these three, whom we sent back, we also gave a hatchet and two knives at which they showed great pleasure. When they had returned on shore, they told the others what happened. About noon on that day six canoes came off to the ships, in each of which were five or six [First Nations people], who had come to say good-bye to the two we had detained, and to bring them some fish. These made signs to us that they would not pull down the cross, delivering at the same time several harangues which we did not understand.

11 . . . We sailed along the coast [of Anticosti Island] . . . we assembled all the captains, pilots, masters and sailors to have the opinion and advice as to what was best to be done. . . .

12 . . . we decided by a large majority to return home . . . .

13 . . . We had such favorable weather that we reached the harbour of St. Malo whence we had set forth on September 5 in the said year [1534].

For Your Notebook

1. Europeans had been fishing the waters around Newfoundland for many years before Cartier sailed there. Find proof from Cartier's journal that Cartier and his men were not the first Europeans the First Nations people had seen.
2. a) Define cultural contact (see page 171).
   b) On Cartier's first two voyages to North America he met several groups of First Nation people. What items were exchanged between the groups?
   c) How did Cartier treat the First Nation people he came into contact with on his first voyage?
   d) How did the First Nation people treat Cartier?
3. In your History Journal, react to Cartier taking Dom Agaya and Taignoagny back to France. For example, are you in favour of this or not? Should Cartier have done this?

In this painting, Dom Agaya and Taignoagny are being taken back to France on Cartier's ship. They are shown here wearing European clothing.

An Exercise in Critical Thinking

On his first voyage in 1534, Cartier explored the area around modern-day Atlantic Canada. Cartier had his men place a cross on the Gaspé Peninsula. It read "Long live the king of France," thus claiming that the French now controlled that part of North America.

Refer to the section on Critical Thinking in the Appendix on page 258. Reread Cartier's journal for July 24 **10**.

1. People often see situations differently. Cartier and the First Nations leader had different points of view about the cross.*
Follow the three steps on Critical Thinking to record information on the above situation.
Either copy the chart or ask your teacher for a copy.
2. You have read Cartier's point of view on raising a cross. Write a story about the event from the point of view of the First Nations leader.

---

*It is believed that the people encountered by Cartier on the Gaspé Peninsula were Iroquoian-speaking people from Stadacona, where modern-day Quebec City is located.

Cultural Contact

When people from two cultures meet, they affect each other. The people often exchange objects or ideas with one another. Often one culture has a stronger influence on the other. Conflict often occurs.

For Your Notebook

1. What were Cartier's goals? Did he achieve them?
2. Use the map on page 168 to review where Cartier went on his 1534 voyage.
3. Discuss the meaning of cultural contact. In small groups predict how the First Nations and the Europeans (the French) would affect each other.

Claiming Lands

  As lands in the Americas were explored, rulers from the various European countries claimed them. This was usually done by an explorer setting up a huge cross and/or flag of his home country in the earth of the land. The cross was a sign to other European countries that the land had been claimed.

By claiming these lands the European rulers believed they also obtained the right to control all the trade in the area. This was known as a monopoly. Control was thought to extend beyond the land and its resources. It also affected the First Nations people who had been living there for thousands of years.

Second Voyage

1535–1536

 Cartier took the two young men, Dom Agaya and Taignoagny, with him when he returned to France. Dom Agaya and Taignoagny learned French and were valuable as interpreters. They told the king about the vast riches in the Kingdom of Saguenay in their homeland. The French wondered whether this could be the lands of Asia they were looking for.

In 1535 King Francis I sent Cartier to explore Newfoundland and farther up the St. Lawrence to look for riches. Cartier was told to spend at least a year in the Americas.

Stadacona

  Dom Agaya and Taignoagny were with Cartier when he sailed once again to Atlantic Canada. The ship passed through the Strait of Belle Isle, and along the north side of Anticosti Island. These waters were quite familiar to Cartier. (See map page 166.) Upon entering the St. Lawrence River, Cartier followed the directions of Dom Agaya and Taignoagny. At the place where the St. Lawrence gets narrower Cartier dropped anchor. The Iroquoian-speaking Stadacona people called this location "Kebec." It was the home of Dom Agaya and Taignoagny. There they received a warm welcome from their father Chief Donnacona and the people of their village.

Cartier at "Kebec." Cartier's ship the *Grand Hermine* was 24.2 m long and 7.6 m wide. (Measure out this distance to see its size.)

The journal entry that follows describes Cartier's plans.* Refer to the map on page 166 while reading the following.

> . . . it was told us by the two [young men] whom we had captured on our first voyage . . . that two days' journey from this cape and island, began the kingdom of the Saguenay, . . . and that thence came the copper they call *caignetdazé* . . .
>
> . . . The two assured us that this was the way to the mouth of the great river of Hochelaga and the route towards Canada, and that the river grew narrower as one approached Canada; [this narrow point was called *kebec* meaning "where the stream is obstructed"] and also that farther up, the water became fresh, and that one could make one's way so far up the river they had never heard of anyone reaching the head of it. Furthermore that one could only proceed along it in small boats . . .

History—
- [✓] Primary Source
- [ ] Secondary Source
- [✓] Interpretation
- [ ] Chronology
- [ ] Cause and Effect

At Stadacona, Chief Donnacona (Dom Agaya and Taignoagny's father) tried to discourage Cartier from travelling westward up the St. Lawrence River. Another Iroquoian-speaking group, the Hochelagans, lived upriver from Stadacona. Some historians believe Chief Donnacona thought the Europeans might become valuable future trading partners. They think he wished to control the inland trade of European goods.

European trade goods like iron tools were valuable. European fishing boats in the St. Lawrence area had been the only supply until then. The various First Nations peoples had been trading with each other since long before the arrival of the Europeans to North America. Their trading patterns involved many nations and great distances. (Refer to the map on page 69 to review these patterns.) Chief Donnacona's people could have developed a monopoly, whereby other people would have to trade with them to get the goods of the French.

---

*Note: The journal entries on pages 172 and 173 were not written by Cartier but by one of his crew.

Hochelaga

  Cartier continued up the St. Lawrence River to Hochelaga, which was located where the present city of Montreal now stands. (See map page 166.) There Cartier repeatedly heard *"Aguyase"* (welcome). Cartier and some of his men climbed to the top of the hill behind Hochelaga. Cartier called this area Mont Réal (Royal). In spite of the beautiful view Cartier was disappointed. The rapids he saw upstream meant that the St. Lawrence was not a passage through a large land area. It was a river flowing out of one. Asia seemed to be nowhere in sight. The rapids prevented his boats from going farther west. The journal entry on October 2 describes the area:

> . . . During this interval we came across on the way many of the people of the country, who brought us fish and other provisions, at the same time dancing and showing great joy at our coming. And in order to win and keep their friendship, the Captain [Cartier] made them a present of some knives, beads and other small trifles, whereat they were greatly pleased. And on reaching Hochelaga, there came to meet us more than a thousand persons, both men, women and children, who gave us a good welcome . . .

> . . . we marched on, and about half a league [about 2.5 km] thence, found that the land began to be cultivated. It was fine land with large fields covered with the corn of the country, which resembles Brazil millet, and is about as large or larger than a pea. They live on this as we do on wheat. And in the middle of these fields is situated and stands the village of Hochelaga, near and adjacent to a mountain, the slopes of which are fertile and cultivated, and from the top of which one can see for a long distance. We named this mountain "Mount Royal." The village is circular and is completely enclosed by a wooden palisade . . .

> . . . The Captain showed them some copper, which they call *caignetdazé*, and pointing towards the said region, asked by signs if it came thence? They shook their heads to say no, showing us that it came from the Saguenay, which lies in the opposite direction. Having seen and learned these things, we returned to our long-boats, . . .

History—
- ☑ Primary Source
- ☑ Secondary Source
- ☐ Interpretation
- ☐ Chronology
- ☐ Cause and Effect

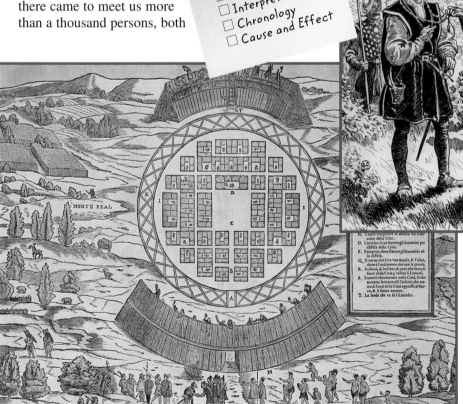

ABOVE: In this drawing, artist C.W. Jefferys gives an interpretation of the above journal entry.

LEFT: A drawing of Hochelaga, by a European artist. He had probably never visited Hochelaga but based his drawing on his knowledge of medieval Europe and Cartier's journal.

Exploring Further

1. Think–Pair–Share: Examine the drawing of Hochelaga on page 173. How accurate is it, based on what you know about the way of life of the Iroquoian peoples? How do you know if pictures provide true information? What questions can you ask yourself when looking at a picture to gather information? Discuss this with your classmates. Record your ideas in the Learning How to Learn section of your notebook. Do either question 2 or 3.

2. Pretend you were with Cartier as you climbed to the top of Mount Royal. In a letter home to France describe what you saw. Use what you learned earlier about the Iroquoian people, plus what Cartier wrote in his journal.

3.  The people of Hochelaga told Cartier of another river that led to a series of freshwater lakes farther to the west. The French probably wondered whether this route led to the Western Sea and Asia. Write an account in your History Journal as if you were with Cartier and had just seen these rivers and lakes. In a modern-day atlas, identify the river and fresh water lakes that Cartier heard about.

Back in Stadacona

The people of Stadacona were no longer as friendly to the French. Cartier had kidnapped Donnacona's two sons on the first voyage. He had also gone to Hochelaga despite their protests. Many historians believe that Chief Donnacona felt the French were trying to take over their territory. Other historians disagree. They believe the First Nations people had a different belief about land ownership—that the land was not theirs to own but to be shared by all. Still other historians believe that Chief Donnacona wanted to control the trade that could result from the goods and technology of the French.

History—
☐ Primary Source
☐ Secondary Source
☑ Interpretation
☐ Chronology
☐ Cause and Effect

Exploring Further

1. With which historical interpretation of what Chief Donnacona thought (see pages 172 and 174) do you agree? Discuss as a class.

An Exercise in Decision-Making

Since it was already October Cartier considered whether they should return to France or spend the winter at Stadacona. You are to act as advisors to Cartier. Work in pairs or triads. Consider the following and then decide what you will advise Cartier. (Note: you don't have to write answers for the following, just discuss them.)

- The autumn weather at Stadacona was beautiful—hot and sunny. Would winter in Stadacona be the same as at St. Malo in France, where winters were mild (-7° to 4°C)?

- Where would you spend the winter if you remained? What type of shelter would you have? Is your clothing adequate for winter? (Notice visuals in this chapter.) Would building a fort for protection cause Chief Donnacona to react in a negative way?

- Do you have enough food? What would you do if you ran out of food?

- There was tension between the French and the people of Stadacona. Will the Stadaconans be friendly or will problems occur for the French?

Optional

 Role-play an imaginary conversation between Cartier and his advisors about the above decision.

Winter at Stadacona

Since it was too late in the year to sail to France, Cartier decided the group should spend the winter at Stadacona. A small fort had been built by Cartier's men. It was to be used as protection and shelter for the coming winter.

The winter of 1535–1536 was very difficult for the French. The weather was much colder than they were used to in France. In December, as the following primary source shows, a dreadful disease occurred.

From Cartier's Journal: Second Voyage (1535–1536)

History—
☑ Primary Source
☐ Secondary Source
☐ Interpretation
☐ Chronology
☐ Cause and Effect

1535: In the month of December we received warning that the **pestilence** had broken out among the people of Stadacona [modern-day Quebec] to such an extent, that already, by their own confession, more than fifty persons were dead. Upon this we forbade them to come either to the fort or about us.

. . . the sickness broke out among us accompanied by the most marvellous and extraordinary symptoms; for some lost all their strength, their legs became swollen and inflamed, while the sinews contracted and turned as black as coal. In other cases the legs were found blotched with purple-coloured blood. Then the disease would mount to the hips, thighs, shoulders, arms, and neck. And all had their mouths so tainted, that the gums rotted away down to the roots of the teeth, which nearly all fell out.

The disease spread among the three ships to such an extent, that in the middle of February, of the 110 men forming our company, there were not ten in good health so that no one could aid the other, which was a grievous sight considering the place where we were. For the people of the country who used to come daily up to the fort, saw few of us about . . .

Our Captain,* seeing the plight we were in and how general the disease had become, gave orders for all to pray and . . . had an image and figure of the Virgin Mary carried across the ice and snow and placed against a tree about a bowshot from the fort, and issued an order that on the following Sunday, mass should be said at that spot . . .

After this the disease increased daily to such an extent that at one time, out of the three vessels, there were not three men in good health, so that on board one of the ships, there was no one to go down under the quarter-deck to draw water for himself and the rest.

And already several had died, whom from sheer weakness, we had to bury beneath the snow; for at that season the ground was frozen and we could not dig into it, so feeble and helpless were we. We were also in great dread of the people of the country, lest they should become aware of our plight and helplessness. And to hide the sickness, our Captain, whom God kept continually in good health, whenever they came near the fort, would go out and met them with two or three men, either sick or well . . . and the Captain had the sick men hammer and make noise inside the ship with sticks and stones, pretending they were calking [repairing the ship].

Exploring Further

1. During the winter months of the second voyage Captain Cartier and Chief Donnacona spent many hours together. Donnacona's sons acted as interpreters.
   a) Write up three questions they may have asked each other.
   b) Exchange these with a partner, who is to write a possible answer.
2. Pretend that you are in charge of health care aboard one of Cartier's ships. Write up the symptoms of the disease in your journal and make your diagnosis. What do you think should be done? Write up your report and give it to Cartier (your teacher).

Pestilence—plague; a serious disease that was usually fatal
*The text printed here is made up of Cartier's original journal published in Paris in 1545 plus those from various sources that have been added over the past four hundred years.

From Cartier's Journal (continued)

One day our Captain . . . on going outside the fort to walk up and down on the ice, caught sight of a band of [First Nations people] approaching from Stadacona, and among them was Dom Agaya whom he had seen ten or twelve days previous to this, extremely ill with the very disease his own men were suffering from . . . . The Captain, seeing Dom Agaya well and in good health, was delighted, hoping to learn what had healed him, in order to cure his own men.

. . . Dom Agaya replied that he had been healed by the juice of the leaves of a tree and the dregs [the remaining parts] of these, and that this was the only way to cure sickness.

Help For the French

The disease Cartier and his men encountered was scurvy. This was a disease common among people who did not get enough vitamin C in their diet. Vitamin C is found in fresh fruit and vegetables. Sailors often got scurvy when on long journeys.

The people of Stadacona, under Dom Agaya's direction, helped the French recover from this disease. They gave Cartier about ten branches from a local tree. They instructed him to grind the bark and the leaves and then to boil this mixture in water. The sick were to drink this tea every two days. They were also to place the boiled mixture of bark and leaves on the affected parts of their bodies. The Stadaconans also arrived daily at the fort with fresh venison and fish. The food helped the sick men regain their strength.

An Exercise in Decision-Making

Select one of the following:
1. Discuss with a partner:
    a) Did Cartier make a wise decision when he would not allow the people of Stadacona to mix with the French? Why or why not?
    b) Why did Cartier pretend that all was well and have his men act as if they were going about their daily chores?
2. Pretend you were a sailor on one of Cartier's ships. Would you follow the advice of Dom Agaya? Why or why not. Explain in paragraph form.

Historians think the cure for scurvy that the Stadaconans shared with the French was a tea made from the bark and needles of the white cedar tree.

The Kidnapping

In the spring when the French were ready to sail home to France, Cartier began to plan how he could take Chief Donnacona back with him. Dom Agaya suspected what Cartier intended to do. However, Cartier told him that the king had told him not to bring back any adults to France. Cartier offered to transport Donnacona to Newfoundland and leave him there. In spite of Cartier's promises the people who came to the French fort the next day were cautious. The situation that followed is described in *The Voyages of Jacques Cartier*.

> . . . At this the Captain issued his orders for the seizure of Chief Donnacona, Taignoagny, Dom Agaya and two other headmen, whom he pointed out and he commanded that the others should be driven away . . . . when the above-mentioned had been captured and the rest had all disappeared, the chief and his companions were placed in safe custody . . . .

History—
☑ Primary Source
☐ Secondary Source
☐ Interpretation
☐ Chronology
☐ Cause and Effect

The next day the people of Stadacona tried to get their chief back, but Cartier refused. He took the prisoners to France with a promise that they would be returned in a year's time. He wanted Chief Donnacona to help him convince King Francis I of the value of what he had found.

A Land Rich in Resources

Iron Pyrites

Cartier did not find the riches that King Francis wanted. What he thought was gold turned out to be iron pyrites. What he thought were diamonds were quartz crystals. Cartier had also seen other resources—fish, furs, trees for timber, and fertile land to plant crops. He wondered if these would be enough to interest the king and the business people in France in financing further expeditions to search for a route to Asia.

> The whole country on both sides of this river [the St. Lawrence] up as far as Hochelaga and beyond, is as fine a land and as level as ever one behold. There are some mountains visible from the river, and into it several tributaries flow down from these. This land is everywhere covered and overrun with timber of several sorts . . . There are a large number of big stags, does, bears, and other animals . . . is rich in every kind of fish that anyone remembers having ever seen or heard of . . . .

—from Cartier's Journal

Exploring Further

Do two of the following:

1. 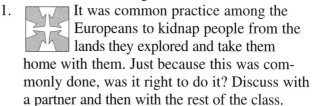 It was common practice among the Europeans to kidnap people from the lands they explored and take them home with them. Just because this was commonly done, was it right to do it? Discuss with a partner and then with the rest of the class.

2. Pretend you are Cartier. Prepare a speech asking King Francis I for financing for another voyage. Include your accomplishments in Canada.

3. Pretend you are advisors to King Francis of France. You have just read descriptions of New France from Cartier's "report" of his second voyage. You have listened to Jacques Cartier's request to the king for funding. In small groups, decide what you would recommend to King Francis. Should the king fund an expedition to colonize New France?

4. 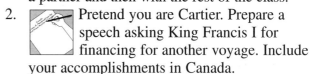 Record your thoughts on a) and b) in the Learning How to Learn part of your History Journal.

   a) School textbooks often refer to Cartier as the discoverer of the St. Lawrence River. Do you agree with this statement? Why is a statement such as this misleading? How could it be interpreted?

   b) Think–Pair–Share: In the years that followed, European explorers often described the land as hostile, inhospitable, and lonely. What do these terms mean? How might First Nations people living in such a place describe the land?

5. a) What is the difference between a strait and a river? Show this in a drawing.

   b) Use a modern-day atlas to prove that what Cartier thought was a strait through the Americas was actually a river—the St. Lawrence River.

Jacques Cartier approaches King Francis I requesting money for a third voyage to the St. Lawrence.

Third Voyage

1541–1543

 King Francis I appointed a French nobleman, Jean Francis de Roberval, to lead the third expedition to the St. Lawrence. Jacques Cartier went as the chief navigator.

King Francis I was interested in more than a voyage of exploration like Cartier's earlier voyages had been. He wanted to **colonize** the lands Cartier had earlier claimed for France. If French colonization was to be successful people from France would have to move there to make their homes. As part of his duty to colonize, Roberval was instructed to build churches. The king wanted Roberval to spread Christianity on behalf of the Roman Catholic Church.

Few people were interested in moving to New France. The king released some people from prison to move to the colony because colonists were needed.

Charlesbourg-Royal

In 1541, Cartier set sail for the St. Lawrence with five ships of colonists and supplies. Roberval was to meet them there. After sailing to Newfoundland, Cartier continued up the St. Lawrence River until he reached Stadacona.

When the people from Stadacona saw Cartier they approached his ship. They were probably anxious to see Chief Donnacona and the others from their village who had sailed with Cartier to France five years ago. However, they were disappointed.* Cartier did not tell them the truth about Chief Donnacona.

Construction began almost immediately on a fort and shelter for the winter. The settlement was called Charlesbourg-Royal. The French continued to search for the riches of the Kingdom of Saguenay. During the winter there was fighting between the Stadaconans and the French. In the spring Cartier abandoned the Charlesbourg-Royal settlement and set sail for France.

On his return voyage to France (spring of 1542) Cartier stopped in St. John's harbour, Newfoundland. He took on a supply of fresh water and wood for the crossing of the Atlantic Ocean. There he met Roberval and 50 colonists on their way to Francis' Land. Roberval ordered Cartier to sail westward up the St. Lawrence with him, but Cartier refused. During the night, without Roberval's knowledge, Cartier ordered his ship to set sail for France. Once back in France, Cartier's diamonds and gold were analysed and proven to be false. Not only were Cartier's treasures worthless, but to King Francis I the land seemed worthless also.

France-Roy

Roberval sailed westward up the St. Lawrence without Cartier. Near Stadacona the French constructed a fort that they named France-Roy. Nearby a settlement was built.

The winter of 1542–43 was extremely difficult for Roberval's men. Over 50 died of scurvy. In the spring of 1543, Roberval and several of the men on the ship set out in one of the ship's smaller boats to locate the diamonds, gold, and the Kingdom of Saguenay. They still hoped to find a passage to Asia that Cartier had told them about. At Lachine they were unable to pass through the rapids. Thus, they were unable to continue their voyage westward to Asia.

In 1543, Roberval abandoned France-Roy and returned to France. The French did not explore this area until the 1600s. You will learn about later French exploration in Chapter 9 when you study Champlain.

Colonize—create settlements in a new land in order to control the use of the land and trade on behalf of another country
*According to historical records, Chief Donnacona died while in France. Little is known of the other captives.

Results

Cultural Contact

History—
☐ Primary Source
☐ Secondary Source
☑ Interpretation
☐ Chronology
☐ Cause and Effect

The First Nations peoples had different values, spiritual beliefs, languages, technology, and social and political organization than the early Europeans who met them. The groups found it very difficult to understand one another.

When very different cultures meet there are usually misunderstandings. People may not know how to interpret what they observe the other group doing. They may not trust each other and there may be conflict. People who live in one culture all their lives often believe that their culture is the best. They are used to their culture and it meets their needs. A strong group may try to force the other group to change. Or they may try to control, drive away, or even wipe out the other group.

Some French men learned First Nations languages. They reported that the First Nations people generally regarded themselves as superior to the French in every way except in certain technology: metal tools, weapons, and cloth. The French thought they were superior to the First Nations people. They said so repeatedly in their journals. Each group accepted ideas and technology from the other that helped them meet their needs in the environment. However, neither respected most of the other group's way of life or beliefs. This meant that conflict often occurred. In time, the Europeans became stronger than the First Nations and outnumbered them.

First Nations Contributions to European Colonists
• survival skills such as hunting local animals, trapping, canoeing, and snowshoeing
• guiding and geographical knowledge of the area
• remedies for illnesses such as scurvy
• fresh food

European Contributions to First Nations
• European technology (metal tools such as knives, axes; weapons such as muskets; metal cooking pots; blankets, clothing)

Cartier's Achievements

In spite of the failures of Cartier's three voyages, he made contributions to Canada's history. He was the first European to explore the St. Lawrence River. His journals contain descriptions and maps of bays, coves, rivers, including water depth. These added greatly to Europeans' knowledge of present-day Atlantic Canada and the St. Lawrence River. He proved that Newfoundland was one island.

Cartier recorded information about the climate, fertile land, great forests, and waters full of fish. He showed that the area could be a home for future French settlers.

Cartier gathered information on the places, people, and customs of the First Nations. These were written down and passed on to future generations. They are some of the earliest written descriptions of Canada's First Nations people.

Cartier spent the winters of 1535 to 1536 and 1541 to 1542 in North America, learned how difficult it was to survive in a Canadian winter, and returned to France.

For Your Notebook
1. Working in groups of three make a large group web or mind map defining and providing examples of cultural contact.
2. Think–Pair–Share: In your opinion did the items traded result in a fair exchange? Did one side gain more than the other? Look at this issue from two points of view: an early European explorer and someone from a First Nation. Record your ideas in your Thinking Journal.

Exploring Further
3. Post a large chart in your classroom. As you progress through this history book add examples of cultural contact.

Review

Assessment

1. Complete a self-assessment for one assignment from this chapter. See page 263 or ask your teacher for ideas.

Summarizing the Chapter

2. Reread the predictions you made on page 161. Fill in the "What I Found Out" column of this chart.

3. Complete the fishbone note making activity you started on page 161 if you haven't done so already.

Understanding Concepts

4. Why were the French interested in exploring lands new to them? How did the French indicate they had claimed an area?

5. Explain what is meant by "claiming lands" from the points of view of someone from a First Nation, the king of France, and Cartier.

6. a) Cartier's journal for the Third Voyage describes the people from Stadacona as hostile. Is this a fair description on Cartier's part?
   b) Describe the situation from the point of view of the people of Stadacona.
   c) Why is it important to look at an issue from several points of view?

7. In what ways did each European voyage of exploration add to geographic knowledge at the time?

8. Check the organization of your binder according to the description on page 261.

9. Record any three of the following vocabulary for this chapter.

   interpreter   colonize
   superior   cultural contact

10. Create a concept poster for cultural contact, claiming lands, monopoly, or primary sources.

11. Add names from this chapter to the Explorers Timeline you started on page 117.

Developing Research Skills

12.

The Order of Good Cheer Class Project

Use the information in this chapter to add to the Section Activity you started on page 114.

13. Carry out research on one of the following topics:

   a) Research how the Beothuk or Mi'kmaq peoples lived.
   b) Imagine an interpreter is available. Take the points of view of a Mi'kmaq leader and of a Beothuk leader. With a partner, prepare speeches to each other describing the coming of Cartier.
   c) Does scurvy exist today? Why or why not? How is it treated?
   d) Why did Cartier think iron pyrites was a metal and quartz crystal was a precious stone?
   e) Cartier found iron pyrites, not gold. Where in modern-day Ontario and Quebec is gold mined?
   f) Why was Cartier unable to travel up-river beyond Montreal? What did the Canadian government do (approximately 400 years later) so that large ships could travel this route?

Developing Communication Skills

Select at least one question from 14–21:

Reading

14. Read tourist brochures which describe historic and present-day Montreal. How does this type of information compare to that which is found in an encyclopedia? In Cartier's journal?

Writing

15. Pretend you were with Cartier on one of his voyages. Write at least six journal entries of what you saw, heard, felt, or experienced.

16. There are two parts to this activity. Part One: Write an historical story about some event that occurred on one of Cartier's voyages. Use Cartier's journal as reference material. Write the story from the point of view of the First Nations people. (See number 5, page 264.)
Part Two: Exchange your story with someone else in the class. Rewrite the event described in the story from the point of view of a French explorer.

17. As the king of France, you have been asked what criteria you will use to select an explorer to seek a western route to the lands of Asia. List these criteria in your History Journal.

Listening and Speaking

18. Select a partner. One of you, acting as Cartier, should explain to the king of France why the settlement you tried to establish in 1541 failed. The other, as king of France, should respond.

19. Imagine you are Cartier. Practise reading several passages of your journal. Create an audio tape of how Cartier himself might have read it.

20. Reread page 178. Pretend you are Cartier. Prepare a speech on what you will tell the people of Stadacona about their chief.

Viewing and Representing

21. Select an issue or situation that occurred during Cartier's visit to what is now Canada. Create a visual to show how the First Nations people and the French viewed the situation differently.

Applying Concepts

22. a) Do you think Cartier extended thanks to the First Nations people for helping cure the colonists of scurvy?
    b) Imagine you were a member of Cartier's crew. Would you express your thanks to the people of Stadacona? If so, what suitable way could you do so? If not, why?
    c) What ways are there to express thanks or appreciation to someone who has assisted you?

Challenge Plus

23. Cartier visited both Stadacona and Hochelaga. There he saw villages different from the French town of St. Malo. Pretend you are Cartier and have just visited these two villages. Write a journal entry describing the village at Hochelaga and how the people live. (Hint: Refer to Chapter 3 and to the visual of a European city on page 138.)

24. Select an issue from this chapter and prepare it as an editorial or a letter to the editor. See numbers 10 and 11 on page 264.

Chapter 9
Exploring and Colonizing Lands

❶ Colonization

For years Europeans considered North America an obstacle that stood between them and Asia.

Eventually Europeans began to consider North America as an important area for trade and colonization.

Many European countries established colonies in the Americas. They did this for a variety of reasons.

Colonies were the sources of raw materials and a market for finished goods.

North America

Europe

Asia

The people of the First Nations traded raw materials such as furs to the French traders.

In 1604, a colony was started in Acadia.

❷ French Colonization

In the early 1600s, the French government granted trading monopolies to individuals and companies in the area of the St. Lawrence River and the Atlantic coast.

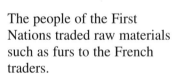

St. L...

A C A D I A

Chapter 9 Focus

This chapter will focus on French exploration and colonization along the Atlantic coast in an area called Acadia. You will learn about these concepts through following the activities of the explorer Samuel de Champlain.

The major focuses for the chapter are technology, cultural contact, and exploration. The minor focuses are environmental interaction and balance.

Environmental Interaction | Balance | Technology | Cultural Contact | Exploration

Vocabulary

mercantilism
colonization
settlements
colony
finished goods
mother country
charter

industry
economy
illegal traders
trading company
supply
demand

Mercantilism

Mercantilism was an economic theory popular in Europe during the Age of Exploration. It related to world exploration, establishing colonies in other lands, and protecting industry in the European country. Mercantilism can be summarized as follows:

- A country's wealth is based on the amount of gold and silver it has.
- A country increases its silver and gold by selling more goods to other countries than it buys from them.
- The government regulates all foreign trade (imports and exports) so more gold and silver enter the country than leave it.

Chapter Preview/Prediction

1. a) Working alone or with a partner, preview the chapter's overview, visuals, titles, and subtitles.

b) Using a large sheet of paper, make an introductory web or mind map on colonization. Use the words in italics in the following questions, the overview on page 182, and the chapter titles to do this.

c) As you read through this chapter use the following questions as a guide to complete your web or mind map.

1. What is colonization? (*meaning*)
2. How was *mercantilism* connected to colonization? What were some advantages and disadvantages of this system?
3. Why did colonization come about? (*reasons*)
4. What does colonization reveal about the *policies of the mother country*? About life in that country?
5. What were some *results* of colonization?
6. How might the *First Nations people* have felt about colonization?
7. How does colonization relate to *you*? To our world today?

Section Activity

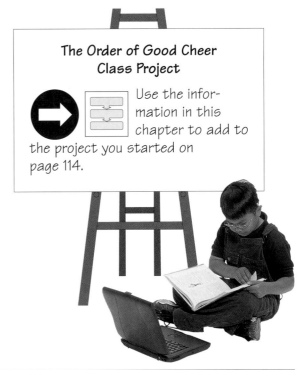

The Order of Good Cheer Class Project

Use the information in this chapter to add to the project you started on page 114.

Policy—a chosen plan of action that guides future decisions

183

Colonization

Defined

   Colonization involves one country bringing another region under its direct control by creating permanent settlements.

Reasons for Colonization

  European countries started colonies for many reasons.

Reasons for Colonization

1 European countries competed with each other for power. Colonies were started so the mother country could obtain wealth from the colony. Once large enough, colonies became markets for goods made in the mother country.

2 Countries in Europe started colonies so they could control newly claimed lands. This prevented people from other countries moving there. Armies, navies, forts, and settlers were ways of protecting colonies.

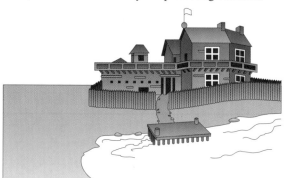

3 Many European nations wanted to start colonies so they could attempt to **convert** Aboriginal people to Christianity.

4 Many settlers moved to the colonies because land was plentiful and inexpensive. In some colonies it was easier to own land than in the mother country.

5 Many settlers moved to colonies where they could practise whatever religion they wished.

6 Some people moved to the colonies for personal reasons. Some reasons were to get away from family, neighbours, enemies, the law, or for adventure.

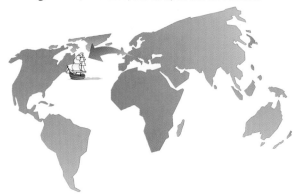

Convert—change people's beliefs to one's own

Colonization and Mercantilism

Europeans explored and claimed lands new to them before they started colonies in North America.

During the 1500s and the 1600s many European countries wanted to be powerful. One way for a country to be powerful was to have wealth in the form of gold and silver. Countries became wealthy through profit. They could get raw materials from their colonies and make them into finished goods. Then the goods could be sold to other nations. This is part of mercantilism, a popular European theory. The largest profit was made by countries who spent the least on raw materials and sold the finished goods for the highest prices. Mercantilism is explained on page 183.

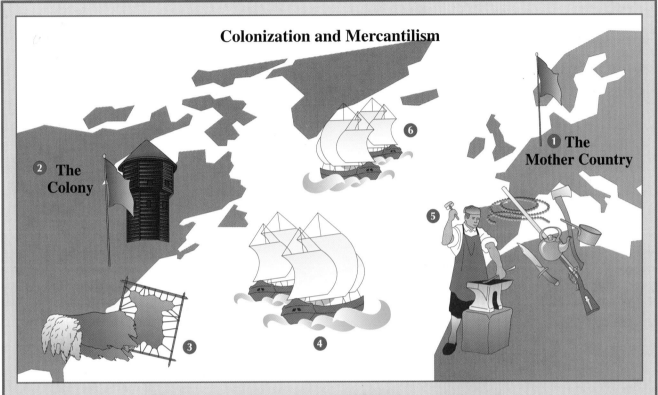

Match the numbers in the following with those on the diagram.

1 Countries in Europe (the mother countries) started colonies in North America, Africa, Asia, and Australia.

The mother country had direct control over how the colonies were run. It decided on the type of government for them. Europeans believed their way of life was superior to the ways of First Nations peoples. Many thought that everyone in the colony should share the culture of the mother country.

2 The colonies had lands that Europeans needed to explore before they could settle there.

3 Settlements in the colony were expected to provide raw materials and cheap labour. Workers were needed to collect, process, and transport raw materials.

4 Then the raw materials were shipped to the mother country in Europe.

5 The raw materials were made into finished products in the mother country.

6 Finished goods were shipped to other nations and colonies. They were sold at much higher prices than raw materials.

Exploring Further

1. In groups of three or four create a concept poster for either colonization or mercantilism.

2. Create a mind map, web, paragraph, poster, collage, or mobile that shows the reasons for colonization.

Territorial Claims

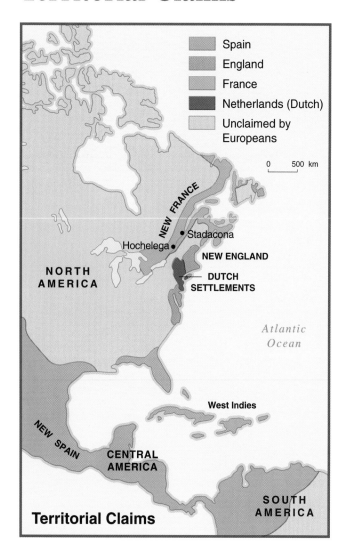

Map legend:
- Spain
- England
- France
- Netherlands (Dutch)
- Unclaimed by Europeans

0   500 km

NEW FRANCE
• Stadacona
Hochelega •
NEW ENGLAND
NORTH AMERICA
DUTCH SETTLEMENTS
Atlantic Ocean
West Indies
NEW SPAIN
CENTRAL AMERICA
SOUTH AMERICA
Territorial Claims

Spanish

Columbus and other Spaniards explored the islands in the West Indies, Central America, and South America. Colonies were established. Soon the area was known as New Spain. The Spanish took vast quantities of gold, silver, emeralds, pearls, and religious art treasures back to Spain.

English

In the early 1600s, English merchants formed trading companies to obtain raw materials from the eastern coast of what is now the United States. Individuals or groups of business people invested money in these companies. Some colonists went to America to get free land. Some went to be able to worship as they pleased.

French

French fishing ships continued to land at the Grand Banks of Newfoundland. Ships went to what is now Atlantic Canada and the St. Lawrence area to trade for furs. However, the French were more interested in exploring what is now the southern United States and South America. After the French supply of furs from Russia was cut off by warfare in Europe, France became more interested in North American furs.

Dutch

In 1609, the Dutch started settlements on the island of Manhattan (where New York City is currently located) and along the Hudson River valley. They developed the fur trade there. Iroquois traders brought beaver pelts to the Dutch to trade for guns, ammunition, and other goods from Europe.*

Portuguese

By the 1550s, Portugal had about 50 bases along the coasts of Africa and Asia. These bases were used as places for trading goods. Forts were built to house military forces. This helped the Portuguese maintain power and control in the areas they explored and colonized. The Portuguese did little exploration in the Americas except for Brazil.

First Nations Territory Changes

When the Europeans came to the St. Lawrence River valley during the 1500s, First Nations groups as far west as the Great Lakes were affected. First Nations groups competed for trade in European goods. Tools with iron blades like axes were sought after by First Nations people. The Iroquoian peoples around Stadacona and Hochelaga controlled the trade and acted as go-betweens. First Nations farther inland wished to deal directly with the Europeans. Historians think they made war on the St. Lawrence Iroquoians. The St. Lawrence Iroquoian-speaking people left the area. The Montagnais and Algonquin moved into the area around Stadacona and Hochelaga and by 1600 controlled it. The villages of Stadacona and Hochelaga were abandoned.

---

*The Dutch concentrated most of their efforts in Asia. The Dutch East India Company organized and controlled exploration in the islands off the east coast of Asia.

French Colonization

The French king decided colonies were needed to protect the riches of the fur trade in New France from other European countries. He granted trading monopolies to individuals and companies that promised to help start colonies in New France. Colonies would make the French claim more secure. (Read the chart below for information on how French trading monopolies worked.)

Exploring Further

1. In groups of three or four, create a concept poster to explain how trading monopolies work.

Trading Monopolies

1 The French king and his government controlled the French mercantile system. See page 183 for a definition of mercantilism.

2 The French king granted fur-trading monopolies to individuals and/or companies. Usually the king did not invest money in the expedition. The company that received the monopoly financed it. Traders who were not part of the company with the monopoly were not allowed to trade in the area.

CANADA

3 Trading companies controlled the French fur trade in New France. The people of the First Nations supplied furs (the raw materials) to the French traders. The companies traded goods made in France to the First Nations people in return.

4 Ships carried the furs to France, where they were in demand. Beaver pelts were made into the felt hats popular at the time.

5 In return for this trade monopoly, the French king required the companies to establish forts and bring out colonists and missionaries at their own cost.

French Trading Monopoly

 In 1603, King Henry IV granted a fur-trading monopoly in New France to Pierre Du Gua de Monts. Samuel de Champlain was part of this expedition. De Monts received an exclusive right to the fur trade in this area for 10 years.* In exchange he was expected to do the following:

• Explore the St. Lawrence area as a possible place to start a colony
• Make peace with any First Nations people in the area and convert them to Christianity
• Look for gold and other precious metals

De Monts decided to settle in Acadia instead of the St. Lawrence area. It was farther south than the St. Lawrence area. He hoped that the climate there would be more favourable to colonists in the winter. The fur trade in the St. Lawrence area would be carried out from their base in Acadia.

Port Royal

They selected a location on an island in the Ste. Croix River at the entrance to the Bay of Fundy. It was not successful. The small, isolated island had no protection from the cold winds. No fresh water was found on the island. The land was unsuitable for agriculture. The settlers had a difficult winter and many suffered from scurvy.

The next year the group moved across the bay and established Port Royal. (See pages 190 and 191 for a diagram of the habitation at Port Royal and illustrations.) Two winters were spent at this location.

Champlain organized an activity called the Order of Good Cheer to help the colonists get through the winter. (It is described in Champlain's own words in the Section II project on page 114.) The men living in the habitation took turns hunting to provide food for banquets. They ate together and often provided entertainment for each other to keep spirits up. When spring came, the colonists planted crops.

The First Nations people of the region were Mi'kmaq, an Algonquian-speaking people. (See map page 85.) The Mi'kmaq were friendly to the French and traded their surplus furs for French goods. The kindness, hospitality, and guidance of the Mi'kmaq in the area helped the settlement succeed. Membertou was the Mi'kmaq chief and healer. He was greatly respected, and often visited the habitation. Chief Membertou became a Christian and was the first North American to be baptized in his own country.

Even though the colony seemed successful the fur trade was not. It was difficult to control the monopoly over the entire St. Lawrence region from the Bay of Fundy. Many traders were trading illegally for furs in the area. The French king cancelled de Monts' monopoly. De Monts was forced to abandon the Port Royal settlement in 1607. Chief Membertou protected and cared for the habitation for three years until the French returned.

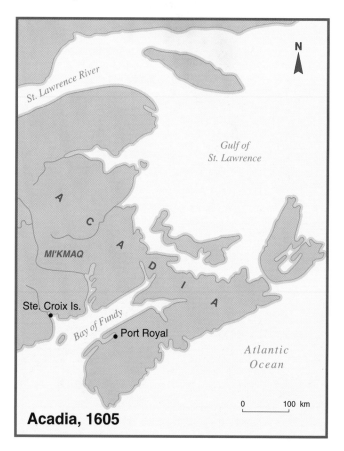

Acadia, 1605

Exploring Further

1. As you progress through this history book add examples of cultural contact to the chart in your classroom you started on page 179.

---

*Everyone else who traded in this area was considered to be involved in illegal trading.

 For more information on de Monts and other individuals involved in colonization, visit the *Canada Revisited 6* Homepage.

For more information on Port Royal and the Order of Good Cheer visit http://parkscanada.pch.gc.ca/parks/nova_scotia/ port_royal/english/historye.htm#Cheer

The Beaver

For nearly 300 years, fishing and the fur trade were important business activities of the Europeans in what is now Canada. During the years of the fur trade, the beaver was the most important fur-bearing animal. Others were also trapped for furs. The beaver pelts were of fine quality. They were in great demand in Europe.

The Canadian beaver had thicker fur than those found farther south in what is now the United States. The colder Canadian winters caused the beaver to grow a rich fur coat. Streams, ponds, and rivers in the northern part of North America were abundant. They provided the perfect habitat for beaver, as well as transportation for the fur traders.

The beaver pelt consisted of two layers. There was coarse guard hair on the outside and soft velvet-like fur formed an inner layer.

Traders explored north and west from the area of Acadia and the St. Lawrence. They searched for more furs and furs of better quality. The costs of transporting furs from New France to France were high. However, huge profits could be made from the fur trade. The fur trade could not have been as successful as it was without the involvement and contributions of First Nations people.

In the Trading Room at Port Royal. The Mi'kmaq brought their furs to the French to trade for European goods.

Clerical
(18th century)

Continental
(1776)

The D'Orsay
(1820)

Millions of beaver pelts were sent to Europe to be made into fashionable felt hats for gentlemen.

Exploring Further

1. Make a web or mind map of the information on this page. Use vocabulary such as raw materials, finished goods, supply, and demand in this web.
2. What if . . . there hadn't been any beaver in what is now Canada? Would Canada's history have been different?
3. Create a stamp to honour the beaver and its effect on Canadian history.

In 1939–40 Parks Canada reconstructed Port Royal. Canadian artist C.W. Jefferys's illustrations give an interesting account of life at Port Royal (as seen on these pages). Use the visuals on these two pages to answer the questions on page 191.

Habitation at Port Royal

1. Workmen's dwellings
2. Area and platform for cannon
3. Storeroom
4. Quarters for Champlain and de Monts
5. Blacksmith's shop
6. Palisade
7. Bakery
8. Kitchen, dining room
9. Storage space for boat equipment

A play called *The Theatre of Neptune* was created to greet one of the investors, Jean de Poutrincourt, in Port Royal in 1606. Marc Lescarbot (a Paris lawyer who spent a year at Port Royal) wrote the play. Both Mi'kmaq and French were involved. Neptune, the god of the sea, appeared in a bark canoe to welcome Poutrincourt. The investor was surrounded by the performers who praised the leaders of the colony in French and then in Mi'kmaq. Trumpets and cannon completed the welcome.

For more information on Port Royal visit http://parkscanada.pch.gc.ca/ parks/nova_scotia/port_royal/ english/On_linee.htm

Focus On: Port Royal

Exploring Further

1. Examine each picture closely.
   a) Use the diagram on page 190 to decide where each scene is located.
   b) Write a caption for each picture that describes the scene.
2. Write a story as though you were one of the people in one of the paintings.
3. Choose any one person from this chapter. In your History Journal, write a description of that person. Tell what kind of person you think he or she must have been and why you think so. What did that person look like? How did he or she behave? How did others react to that person? What contributions did he or she make to Canadian history?

Louis Hébert the Apothecary

In the Governor's House

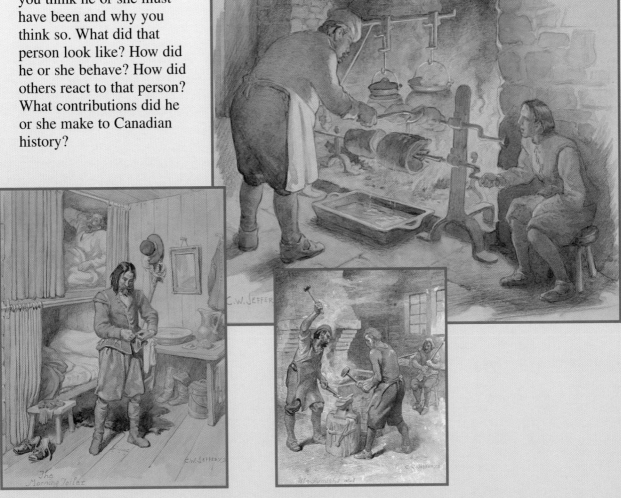

The Morning Toilet

Blacksmiths and

Review

Assessment

1. Complete a self-assessment for one assignment from this chapter. See page 263 or ask your teacher for ideas.

Summarizing the Chapter

2. If you haven't done so already, complete the Chapter Preview/Prediction activity (web/mind map) and questions you were assigned on page 183.

Understanding Concepts

3. Use the chart on page 185 to help you write a paragraph to describe the relationship between exploration, colonization, and monopoly.

4. a) Explain how voyages of exploration were inspired by a belief in mercantilism.
   b) Why would colonization be essential to maintain authority over newly claimed lands?

5. Answer the following from the point of view of the mother country, the European colonists, and the First Nations people.
   a) What are the advantages of colonization?
   b) What are the disadvantages and difficulties?

6. Check the organization of your binder according to the description on page 261.

7. Record any vocabulary from this chapter that you don't know the meaning of.

8. Add names from this chapter to the Explorers Timeline you started on page 117.

9. Create a concept poster about the ideas on the chart above right.

Struggle for Power

Desire for Power

• need for wealth (gold and silver)

Mercantilism

• need for colonies
• need for wealth (gold and silver)

Exploration

• seeking other lands

Colonization

• claiming other lands
• settling and controlling other lands
• trading based monopoly

Developing Research Skills

10. **The Order of Good Cheer Class Project**

 Add information from this chapter to the section activity you started on page 114.

11. Discuss the following question with your classmates. Record your ideas in the Learning How to Learn section of your notebook.*

Usually, you do not need or cannot use all information available from any one resource. How do you know what information to record?

Developing Communication Skills

Select at least one question from 12–17:

Reading

12. Ask your librarian to recommend fiction resources about the Mi'kmaq.

Writing

13. Use one of the ideas on pages 264 and 265 to record your ideas on the following.
   a) How would your life have been different if you had come to Acadia or New France with Champlain?
   b) What might a First Nation person have said about colonization at Port Royal
      • upon first encountering the colonists?
      • one year later?
      • 10 years later?

14. a) Select an issue from this chapter and write up the conflicting points of view about it.
   b) Interview five people (including adults) to find out their view about the issue. (See number 21 on page 265.) OR
   c) Prepare a questionnaire about the issue and give it to at least 10 people. (See number 20 on page 265.) Show the results on a chart or graph.

Listening and Speaking

15. You are a talk show host in a program called *Canada Revisited*. Your guests are a French fur trader, an English fur trader, and someone from a First Nation. You should discuss how each guest views the struggle for control over territories. Present your show to the class. After the class has listened to the discussion, have them choose which group they would support. Discuss their choices.

16. Pretend you are an actor in Lescarbot's *Theatre of Neptune* at Port Royal. (See page 190 and number 6 on page 264.) Perform for your class.

Viewing and Representing

17. Create a design/plan for a habitation on paper and/or build a habitation using cardboard.

Applying Concepts

18. a) Look at the Canadian nickel. What is the significance of the beaver on this coin?
   b) Do research to find out when it was decided that a beaver should appear on Canadian nickels.
   c) Imagine that you were part of the committee deciding what image or person will appear on a new Canadian coin. What person or image do you think should appear on the coin? Why?

19. Define each of the following business terms: entrepreneur, competition (as in business), market, profits. Find examples from this chapter for each term.

---

*Note: This question doesn't require you to actually do the research. It just asks you where you would look. The question focuses on sharing ideas of how to gather, examine, and organize information.

Chapter 10

Quebec Colony and the Fur Trade

O v e r v i e w

Use this Overview to predict the events of this chapter.

❶ The Quebec Colony

In 1608, Champlain founded the colony of Quebec for France. A habitation was built and the fur trade started in the area.

Champlain and the French formed alliances with the Montagnais, Algonquin, and Wendat Nations. They competed against the Five Nations Iroquois Confederacy and the Dutch (and later the English).

Two fur trading networks developed:
- one using the St. Lawrence/ Ottawa River route
- one using the Hudson River water route

Quebec

Port Royal

St. Lawrence R.

Hudson River

N

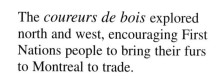

The *coureurs de bois* explored north and west, encouraging First Nations people to bring their furs to Montreal to trade.

❷ The Fur Trade

The Wendat acted as go-betweens to obtain furs from other First Nations peoples.

❸ Strengthening the Colony

Champlain worked to make Quebec colony self-supporting. He focused on
- developing the fur trade
- trying to bring settlers to Quebec

- bringing in religious orders to convert First Nations people to Christianity.

❹ Catholic Missionaries

The Roman Catholic Church was involved in the religious life of the French colonies. The church started the first schools and hospital and brought missionaries to the colony.

❺ The Fur Market

First Nations people came to Montreal each summer to trade furs.

❻ The English Enter the Fur Trade

After 1665, a third trading network developed around Hudson Bay when the English entered the fur trade. The Hudson's Bay Company was formed in 1670. It involved more First Nations people directly in the fur trade.

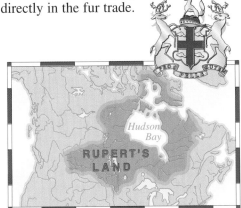

❼ Contributions of the First Nations People

The contributions of the First Nations people were necessary for the fur trade to succeed.

Chapter 10 Focus

In the last chapter you studied French exploration and colonization at Port Royal in Acadia. Champlain was one of the French colonists at Acadia. He was a map-maker and manager. This chapter looks at Champlain's activities in the Quebec colony. Major focus is on the fur trade north and west of Quebec. You will continue to study about the early contacts between the French and the First Nations people.

All five concepts will be examined, but this chapter focuses on Technology, Cultural Contact, and Exploration.

Environmental Interaction

Balance

Technology

Cultural Contact

Exploration

Vocabulary

alliance (ally)	religious order
network	Jesuits
go-between (middleperson)	convert
	Huronia
independent	consequence
self-supporting	contributions
missionary	

Chapter Overview/Prediction

Use the overview, Timeline 3, the chapter's titles, and the visuals to predict what this chapter is about. Fill out the "My Predictions" column of the prediction chart before continuing. For a complete version of this chart see page 119.

Prediction Chart—What Do You Think?

Questions	My Predictions (fill out now)	What I Found Out (fill out at end of chapter)
1. In what ways did the coming of Europeans change the balance that existed between the Aboriginal peoples and the environment?		
2. How did the		

History—
☐ Primary Source
☐ Secondary Source
☐ Interpretation
☑ Chronology
☐ Cause and Effect

Section Activity

Order of Good Cheer Class Project

Add information from this chapter and/or do additional research to add to the project you started on page 114.

Timeline 3

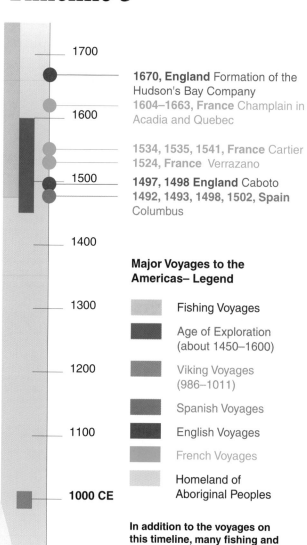

1700

1670, England Formation of the Hudson's Bay Company
1604–1663, France Champlain in Acadia and Quebec

1600

1534, 1535, 1541, France Cartier
1524, France Verrazano

1500

1497, 1498 England Caboto
1492, 1493, 1498, 1502, Spain Columbus

1400

Major Voyages to the Americas– Legend

1300
Fishing Voyages

Age of Exploration (about 1450–1600)

1200
Viking Voyages (986–1011)

Spanish Voyages

1100
English Voyages

French Voyages

1000 CE
Homeland of Aboriginal Peoples

In addition to the voyages on this timeline, many fishing and exploration voyages were made to the Americas every year.

900

Timeline not to scale.

196

Cultural Contact

Research Project

 Use the ideas on this page to guide you through the following issue: **Which group of people influenced the culture of the other most during European exploration and early colonization—the First Nations or the French?** Examine the issue from the points of view of the First Nations people and the French.

Work in triads and follow the research model on pages x and xi. Each group should research the same issue and share results at the end. Select a chairperson. Everyone in the group is responsible for making his or her own notes. At the end of the chapter each group will make a collective presentation.

Gathering Information

1. Understanding what you are to do
 Write the issue you are studying in your notebook. Refer to page x for more direction.

2. Planning the Project
 Ideas for planning a project are on page x. (See page 115 for a sample Action Plan.)

3. Locating the Information
 For ideas on where to locate additional information that is not in this textbook, see page xi. Find out more information on the issue from the point of view of
- the First Nations people
- the French

4. Recording the Information
 For ideas on recording information see page xi.

Examining and Organizing the Information

 5. Examining the Information

 6. Organizing the Information

These steps are difficult to separate and are often done at the same time.
- Divide your information into two categories: information that relates to First Nations people and information that relates to the French.
- Make two charts to record your information. Add pictures, colour, and captions to make the charts interesting. Title the charts First Nations Point of View and French Explorers Point of View.
- Decide on an answer to the research question.

Communicating the Information

7. Preparing the Presentation
 Decide how you wish to communicate your research findings to others.

- See appendix page 262 for presentation ideas.
- Work with your teacher to establish criteria for judging your presentation.
- Prepare your presentation. (Use an "Action Plan" to organize yourself. See page 115 for an example.)

8. Sharing the Presentation
 Practise sharing your presentation. Show it to another group for feedback before you share it with others.

9. Assessing What You've Done
 • Judge how effective your presentation was, based on the criteria you have selected.
- Think about the project and your presentation. What would you do differently next time? Record these ideas in the Learning How to Learn section of your History Journal.

The Quebec Colony

1608

In the St. Lawrence Area

 Pierre du Gua de Monts had a fur trade monopoly in the French colonies. However, he could not stop illegal traders from trading furs with First Nations people. Champlain wanted to move the French colony to a new location. He convinced de Monts to let him start a colony in the St. Lawrence River valley. He thought he could better control their monopoly there.

Champlain picked a site near what had been Stadacona. He thought it gave the best protection. De Monts and Champlain wanted to have security against attack by other European forces and First Nations groups that opposed them. Quebec seemed to be a natural fortress. It was protected by a cliff at the back and on the other three sides by water. The land seemed to be good for growing crops. Settlers would need to grow food to survive.

The site also seemed to be a good base for exploring westward. The French still hoped to find the Northwest Passage to the riches of Asia. The area had good access by river to the fur-producing regions. The Iroquoian-speaking peoples who had lived there when Cartier kidnapped Chief Donnacona had left or been driven away. The area around the Quebec site was not inhabited.

The winter of 1608–1609 was difficult for the colony. The men suffered from scurvy and almost starved to death. (Twenty out of twenty-eight died.) When spring came the supply ships brought food to the starving men. It also brought news that the king had cancelled the fur trade monopoly. In spite of this, de Monts wished to keep the colony going for one more year. He had obtained enough money from other investors to do this.

Champlain knew the investors would expect profits from the money they had invested. He knew that money would come from the sale of fur pelts in France. Champlain began to make plans for expanding the fur trade. He wanted to ensure that a greater supply of furs would be brought to Quebec. One way to do this was through alliances with some of the First Nations.

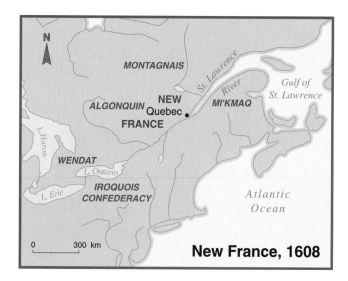

The habitation built by Champlain and his men in 1608 served as both living and working space. This drawing was made by Champlain.

History—
☑ Primary Source
☐ Secondary Source
☐ Interpretation
☐ Chronology
☐ Cause and Effect

For Your Notebook

1. a) De Monts and Champlain were choosing a site for a new colony. What factors did they consider?

   b) In the narrative Moving Day on page 61, the Wendat chose a new site for a village. Compare the process they went through in making their choice.

Alliances

 When two groups agree to join together to do something that benefits both, they form an alliance. Alliances were formed to carry on peaceful trading or to have support in war.

Historians do not agree on the extent of warfare among First Nations peoples before European contact. At the time Champlain was starting the colony at Quebec, the Wendat, Algonquin, and Montagnais were allied. They competed with the Five Nations Iroquois living south of the St. Lawrence Valley for trade.

The Algonquin asked Champlain for military support. He agreed because he depended on them to bring furs for trade.

The Iroquois Confederacy

The Iroquois Confederacy (also called the League of Five Nations) dates from before the arrival of the Europeans. Many historians say it began in the 1400s. A man called the Peacemaker and his helper Hiawatha* founded the Iroquois Confederacy. The Confederacy brought peace to the Mohawk, Oneida, Onondaga, Cayuga, and Seneca. The Tuscarora joined the League much later, in the 1700s. After that, the League was called the Confederacy of Six Nations. All of these nations are members of the Iroquoian language family. Their cultures were similar in many ways.

The Confederacy Council was made up of 50 chiefs. It met once a year in the autumn at the homeland of the Onondaga Nation. Each nation had one vote, thus all were considered equal. Council decisions had to be agreed upon by all. Consensus had to be reached not only among the leaders of each nation, but also among the Five Nations.

*This is a different Hiawatha than the one featured in Longfellow's poem.

Economic Alliances

Economic alliances with local First Nations people were essential for the French. Champlain was allied with the Wendat, Algonquin, and Montagnais. They were a large group of traders who had other trading alliances in place. They agreed to include the French in their trading network. They also supplied the French with furs, food, and canoes. They acted as guides and interpreters for the French and often saved their lives.

Political Alliances

Champlain made the trading alliance political when he agreed to help the Wendat to invade the territory of their Iroquois enemies. The French joined their side against their enemies, the Iroquois Five Nations and the Dutch colonists along the Hudson River.

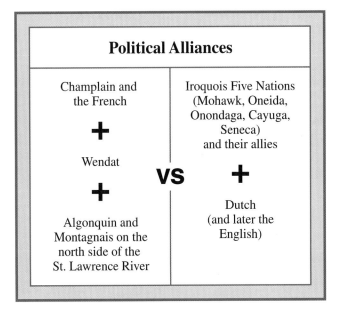

Political Alliances	
Champlain and the French **+** Wendat **+** Algonquin and Montagnais on the north side of the St. Lawrence River	Iroquois Five Nations (Mohawk, Oneida, Onondaga, Cayuga, Seneca) and their allies **+** Dutch (and later the English)

VS

For Your Notebook

1. Make a web or mind map to record information on this page.

2. Use the information on this page to show cause and effect.

Exploring Further

3. As you progress through this history book, add examples of cultural contact to the chart you started on page 179.

1609 Battle with the Iroquois*

  Champlain travelled the Richelieu River to a place he called Lake Champlain with a war party of Montagnais, Algonquin, and Wendat. There Champlain, the other Frenchmen, and their First Nations allies made a raid on the Mohawk.** The raid was successful largely due to surprise and the French firearms. (The Iroquois were unfamiliar with the noise of muskets.)

Three Mohawk chiefs were killed in this battle. This was the main reason the Iroquois became bitter enemies of the French for many years. The

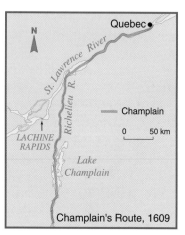

Iroquois Confederacy controlled the south shore of the St. Lawrence River above the Lachine Rapids. The French had to seek other routes to the fur territory or risk their trading canoes being raided by Iroquois along the river.

For Your Notebook

1. Read Champlain's description of the 1609 battle and examine the diagram below.
   a) How do you think this battle affected future relations between the French and the different First Nations groups?
   b) What value do you think the Iroquois would place on the weapons (guns) of the French? Predict how this could affect history.

The following primary source is from Samuel de Champlain's book, *Voyages and Explorations*.

As soon as we were ashore they [Champlain's First Nations allies] began to run about 200 paces toward their enemy, who were standing firmly and had not yet noticed my companions, who went into the woods with some [First Nations people]. Our men began to call me with loud cries; and, to give me a passageway, they divided into two parts and put me at their head, where I marched about twenty paces in front of them until I was thirty paces from the enemy. They at once saw me and halted, looking at me, and I at them. When I saw them making a move to shoot at us, I rested my arquebus [musket] against my cheek and aimed directly at one of the three chiefs. With the same shot two of them fell to the ground, and one of their companions, who was wounded and afterward died. (I put four balls into my arquebus.) When our men saw this shot so favorable for them, they began to make cries so loud that one could not have heard it thunder. Meanwhile the arrows did not fail to fly from both sides. The Iroquois were much astonished that two men had been so quickly killed, . . .

As I was loading again, one of my [French] companions fired a shot from the woods, which astonished them again to such a degree that, seeing their chiefs dead, they lost courage, took to flight and abandoned the field . . . .

History—
☑ Primary Source
☑ Secondary Source
☐ Interpretation
☐ Chronology
☐ Cause and Effect

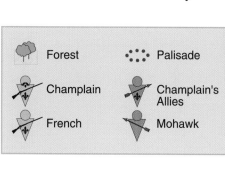

🌳 Forest		⋯ Palisade	
Champlain		Champlain's Allies	
French		Mohawk	

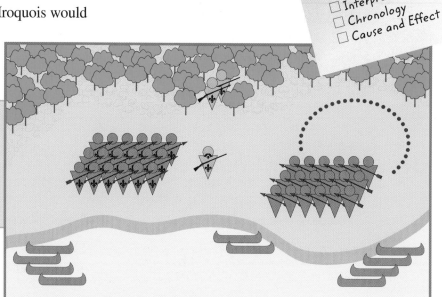

*When Iroquois is used this way in this textbook it refers to the Five Nations Iroquois.
**The Mohawk were part of the Iroquois Confederacy.

This diagram is based on Champlain's drawing of the battle.

More Battles with the Iroquois

 In 1610, Champlain was reminded that he had agreed to help a war party of Montagnais fight the Iroquois (see chart page 199). At the mouth of the Richelieu River, Champlain and his allies captured a Mohawk camp. War with the Iroquois continued for many years.

The following sketch by Champlain shows a 1615 battle with the Iroquois. Champlain was wounded in that battle and spent the winter with the Wendat in a village with 200 longhouses. He was able to learn a great deal about the Wendat way of life during this time.

History—
☐ Primary Source
☐ Secondary Source
☐ Interpretation
☐ Chronology
☑ Cause and Effect

Champlain chose to side with the people north of the St. Lawrence instead of the Five Nations Iroquois. This affected French expansion in North America for many years. Champlain's 1609 and 1610 victories strengthened the French alliance. However, the Five Nations Iroquois Confederacy became an enemy of the French for almost 100 years.

When the Dutch set up trading posts on the Hudson River, the Five Nations traded there. By the 1640s, the Iroquois had guns that they had received in trade with the Dutch on the Hudson River. Thus the Five Nations had an advantage when they later invaded the territory of the Wendat, who had few firearms.

In 1664, the English captured the Dutch colony. After that, the Five Nations traded with the English. The Iroquois attacked the French fur trading canoes, their farms, homes, and forts. Several treaties were made between the Iroquois and the French, but war broke out over and over. As a result two trading networks developed:
- one using the St. Lawrence and Ottawa Rivers
- one using the Hudson River

History—
☑ Primary Source
☐ Secondary Source
☐ Interpretation
☐ Chronology
☐ Cause and Effect

The arquebus was an early form of firearm. It was very loud but not very accurate. This drawing of himself was done by Champlain as part of his drawing of the battle with the Mohawk in 1609.

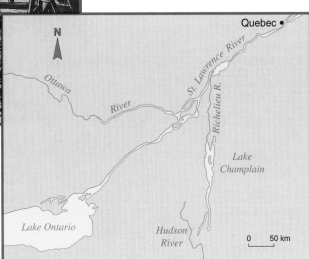

For Your Notebook

1. Use the information on this page to create a chart of the causes and results of the 1609 and 1610 battles.

The Fur Trade

   In the next few years, Champlain understood better the vastness of what is now Southern Ontario. The threat of Iroquois attack was ongoing. He concentrated on making the settlement secure. He continued to have trouble getting enough money to support the Quebec colony. He also wished to bring over **missionaries**, and also settlers to further develop the fur trade.

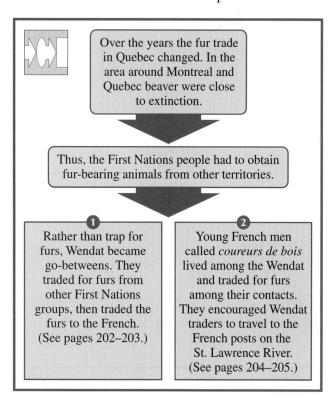

Over the years the fur trade in Quebec changed. In the area around Montreal and Quebec beaver were close to extinction.

Thus, the First Nations people had to obtain fur-bearing animals from other territories.

1 Rather than trap for furs, Wendat became go-betweens. They traded for furs from other First Nations groups, then traded the furs to the French. (See pages 202–203.)

2 Young French men called *coureurs de bois* lived among the Wendat and traded for furs among their contacts. They encouraged Wendat traders to travel to the French posts on the St. Lawrence River. (See pages 204–205.)

Wendat Obtain Furs for the French

1 Long before Europeans came, the Wendat had trading links with many First Nations. Trading patterns are shown on page 69 (in Section I) and on page 203.

Champlain became part of this trading network. Later other Frenchmen established alliances with the Wendat. Furs were traded for European finished goods. Those goods were then traded for furs from First Nations in the interior.

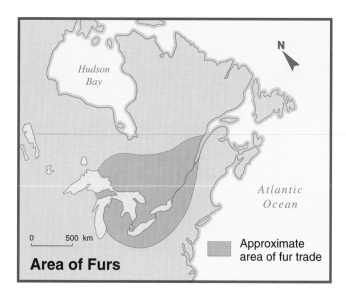

Area of Furs

Hudson Bay

Atlantic Ocean

0   500 km

Approximate area of fur trade

The increased demand for furs caused over-trapping. Once trappers had reduced the animal population in an area they moved into other territories. First Nations competed for territory and trade. More powerful groups forced other groups to move farther west and north.

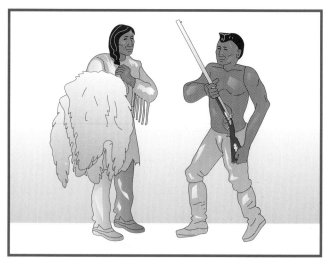

The First Nations peoples living in what is now Ontario had been trading with each other for centuries. The Wendat continued to use this trading network.

For Your Notebook

1. Make notes on pages 202–205.
2. What were the consequences of over-trapping for the environment? What were the consequences for the First Nations people?

Missionaries—people who bring their religious beliefs to people who do not share them

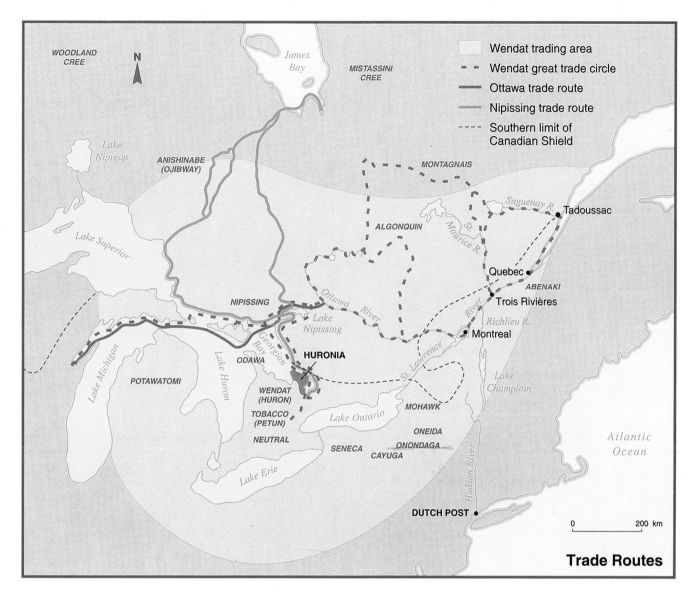

Trade Routes

Legend:
- Wendat trading area
- Wendat great trade circle
- Ottawa trade route
- Nipissing trade route
- Southern limit of Canadian Shield

The Woodland Cree, Anishinabe, Montagnais, and Algonquin brought furs from the forests of the Canadian Shield to the Wendat traders (go-betweens). On the shores of northern lakes such as Lake Nipigon, the Wendat traders bartered the European trade goods for the furs brought by the Algonquian-speaking peoples from the North. Furs from the Canadian Shield reached Montreal via the rivers marked on this map. A popular route was across Georgian Bay to Lake Nipissing down the Ottawa River to Montreal.

For Your Notebook

1. To be successful, the fur trade required co-operation between First Nations people and Europeans. Provide examples to prove this statement.
2. Refer to the above map as you examine the Wendat trading routes. Other trading routes are also shown on the map.
   a) Describe the boundaries of the Wendat trading area to a partner.
   b) What types of products did First Nations people trade before the arrival of Europeans?
3. How did Champlain become part of the existing trading network?

Exploring Further

4. Working in a group of five or six, prepare and present a series of tableaux to show how the Wendat obtained furs for the French.
5. Pretend you are with a Paris (France) newspaper and have just visited the Quebec colony. Write an article for your readers on the French fur trade. Include how the French trading system depended on the trading network and co-operation of the First Nations.

The Coureurs de bois

("runners of the woods")

   ❷ It was safer for the French to have furs brought to them when Iroquois attacks on canoes carrying furs and trade goods were frequent. Trading centres were established at Quebec, Trois Rivières, and Montreal. However, higher profits could be made by French men who went into the interior themselves to bring back beaver pelts.

During peaceful times, more and more young French men were attracted to the high profits and challenges of the fur trade. These men became expert canoeists and businessmen. They were sources of information for the Quebec officials and French government. They were known as *coureurs de bois* ("runners of the woods").

During their fur-trading expeditions, the *coureurs de bois* travelled far into the interior of the country. They explored inland and encouraged First Nations to journey to Montreal to trade their furs. Many also hoped to find the Northwest Passage—a new and shorter route to the riches of Asia.

The French developed trading alliances with many groups of Algonquin and Wendat. Trading between First Nations was usually done through family contacts. To become part of this family trading system, young *coureurs de bois* lived with a band during the winter. They adapted easily to the First Nations way of living. They often married First Nations women and became part of their nations. In this way friendship and trust developed between the First Nations people and the French traders. These qualities were valued in future trading sessions.

Exploring Further

1. Select a partner. Each of you writes a journal entry for Champlain on some of his thoughts about the *coureur de bois* system. Share your entries with each other.

The *coureurs de bois* expanded the fur trade and explored farther and farther into the interior of the country. They did a great deal to extend French control over a large amount of inland territory. The painting shows Champlain and Étienne Brûlé, a *coureur de bois*.

Étienne Brûlé

In 1610, Samuel de Champlain arranged for Étienne Brûlé to live with some Wendat people. Brûlé was a teenager at the time. Champlain wanted him to learn the Wendat language and customs.

Brûlé explored many areas previously unknown to the French. He was probably the first European to see Lakes Ontario, Erie, Huron, and Superior. Brûlé lived with the Wendat for 20 years.

Jean Nicollet

Another *coureur de bois* whose name is found in history books was a young French man named Jean Nicollet. On a fur-gathering journey in 1634 he came upon an enormous lake that had not previously been noted by a European explorer. It was Lake Michigan, one of the Great Lakes.

Nicollet expected to find the Northwest Passage or Western Sea leading to Asia. On his travels he carried with him a magnificent Chinese robe to wear at the Chinese court when he got there. He never had a chance to wear it, however, for he never reached China. But he did explore many areas unknown to the Europeans. He met many First Nations peoples. He persuaded some of them to bring their furs to the French settlement of Trois Rivières, built along the northern bank of the St. Lawrence River.

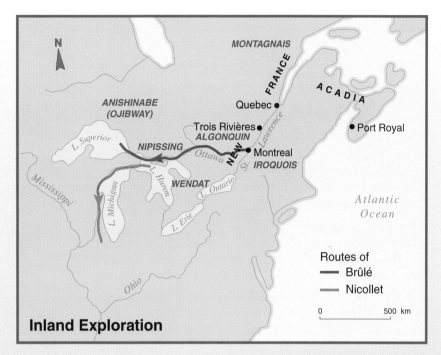

Inland Exploration

Exploring Further

1.  Write a story about an imaginary incident, such as a surprise encounter between a lone Five Nations Iroquois man and a Wendat man travelling with a *coureur de bois*. Write from the point of view of one of the First Nations people. Then write about the same incident from the point of view of the *coureur de bois*.

2. a) Discuss with a partner how each of the following people might have reacted to Brûlé or Nicollet coming into their camp: a Wendat woman, an Algonquin woman, an Elder, or a youth about your age.
   b) With your partner, take turns in the roles of the people listed in 2a. Ask and answer questions they might have had.

Samuel de Champlain

The Father of New France
(1567–1635)

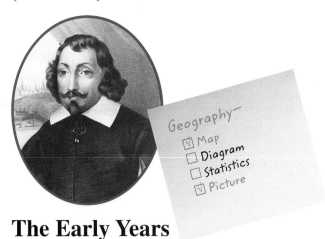

Geography—
☑ Map
☐ Diagram
☐ Statistics
☑ Picture

The Early Years

Little is known of Champlain's boyhood except that he grew up in a French seaport. His father was a sea captain and his grandfather a fisherman. He probably learned from them how to sail and to respect the sea. He probably taught himself the skills of navigation and map-making while aboard his father's ship. As a young man Champlain served in the French army. This experience was also of great value. In the army he learned military **tactics**.

Champlain commanded a Spanish ship sailing to the West Indies. He saw the great Spanish empire in North America. He learned there how colonies were built, organized, and managed. His interest in geography led him to record his observations on the West Indies. He was a skilled map-maker, illustrator, and writer. Therefore, he was able to make interesting, detailed records of his travels. This information about new lands and natural resources was useful to the people on the expedition. It was also valuable to the king and the investors.

King Henry IV of France was very impressed with Champlain's report on the West Indies. This report, in addition to his past military record, resulted in Champlain becoming the Royal Geographer on French expeditions to what is now Canada.

Champlain's Accomplishments

Champlain contributed to the history of Canada in many ways. His policies in North America tended to focus on four general areas.

Policies

1. Champlain knew that exploration was important to the fur trade. Without a prosperous fur trade, the monopoly would be taken away by the French king. With a prosperous fur trade, money would be available for colonization.
2. Champlain was interested in discovering a water route (called the Northwest Passage) through North America to Asia. He thought that the St. Lawrence might lead to the salt water in the west that linked New France to Asia.
3. Champlain set up military alliances with the First Nations who were trading partners of the French. These people became go-betweens in the fur trade. Much later, the French expanded to the Rocky Mountains. By continually pushing the fur trade inland into the interior of the continent, the French were able to obtain great quantities of furs.
4. Champlain made many efforts to bring Christian **religious orders** to New France to do missionary work.

Contributions

 Champlain helped to build settlements in New France at Ste. Croix Island, Port Royal, and Quebec. He worked to create a strong foundation for New France. The colony survived (with government help) long after his departure because of his efforts.

Champlain was able to see the potential of the St. Lawrence Valley for a colony. Eventually a profitable business empire extending far to the west was built. The colony was the entrance to the richest fur territory in North America.

Champlain was a navigator and map-maker. Some of his maps are very accurate. He was an explorer, geographer, and naturalist. Through him

---

Religious orders—groups of people who live under a set of religious rules that govern their way of life; members are usually nuns or monks

---

Tactics—skills and ideas used in planning

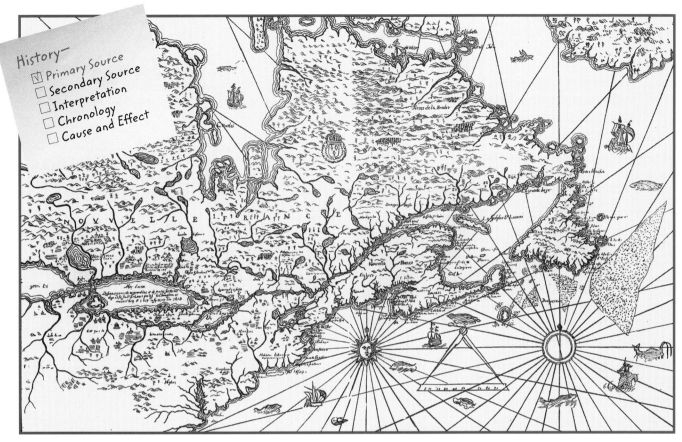

Champlain drew this map in 1632.

we have learned a great deal about the French colonies and their people. Through his efforts, religious orders came to New France.

For 30 years Champlain struggled against uncertainty. The trade monopolies and government financial support for the colony could be cancelled at any time. The threat of attack by the Iroquois and the Dutch was ongoing.

When Champlain died in 1635, the settlement he had founded was slowly becoming an important community. Samuel de Champlain is often called the "Father of New France" because of the contributions he made in the fur trade and the efforts he made to establish permanent settlements there.

Canada Revisited

The 1998 Canada Day edition of *Maclean's* put Samuel de Champlain at the top of their list of the most important Discoverers and Inventors in Canadian History.

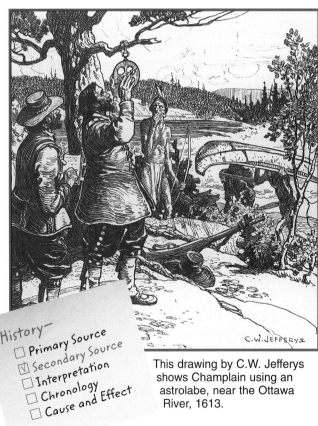

This drawing by C.W. Jefferys shows Champlain using an astrolabe, near the Ottawa River, 1613.

Strengthening the Colony

 By 1618, the fur trade had become a very profitable business. Fifteen to twenty thousand beaver skins (pelts) per year were shipped to France. Champlain also continued working to make New France secure and self-supporting as a colony. He urged his superiors and the investors in France to provide supplies, soldiers, and colonists (especially farmers).

Security

The Wendat were continually under attack by their enemies, the members of the Iroquois Confederacy. Few of the Wendat had muskets to defend themselves against attack. The French refused to trade guns to First Nations people who had not accepted the Roman Catholic religion.

By the mid-1600s the Iroquois were trying to control more of the fur trade. They tried to get the Wendat to take the furs they had obtained from the north and west to the Dutch rather than the French. The Iroquois attacked fur **brigades** on the Ottawa River as they headed for Montreal. They also attacked the French settlements along the St. Lawrence and the Wendat villages.

> They [the Iroquois] are merely small troops well armed, which set out incessantly, one after the other, from the country of the Iroquois, in order to occupy the whole great River [St. Lawrence], and to lay ambushes [surprise attacks] along it everywhere; from these they issue unexpectedly, and fall indifferently upon the Montagnais, Algonquins, Hurons [Wendat], and French. . . .

(from *Jesuit Relations*, report by Father Vimont 1642, 1643)

History—
- ☑ Primary Source
- ☐ Secondary Source
- ☐ Interpretation
- ☐ Chronology
- ☐ Cause and Effect

Colonists

Many fur traders did not want settlers in New France. They believed settlers would hamper the fur trade. However, Champlain believed settlement was essential. In 1616, he persuaded the Hébert

Brigade—group of canoes carrying trade goods and supplies

family to come to New France to become farmers. Later a few more families arrived. Farmers could grow food for the fur traders and other workers in the colony. If settlers learned how to shoot and defend themselves, they could defend the colony from Dutch or Iroquois attacks.

The population at Quebec grew very slowly. After 20 years, the Quebec colony had only about 100 European people. This number included missionaries, *coureurs de bois*, fur trade clerks, craftsmen, and about 20 families of settlers.

In 1620 Champlain brought his 22-year-old wife, Hélène Boullé to this small outpost. They had been married when she was very young. She had remained in France for the first years of the marriage. Unlike her husband, Madame de Champlain was not suited to life in New France. She returned to France after four years and became a nun. She remained in a convent for the rest of her life.

The artist has shown the young Madame de Champlain arriving in Quebec.

Missionary Efforts

Members of the Récollet and Jesuit orders were sent to New France. Their missionaries worked hard to convert the Wendat people. Only a small percentage of the First Nations people were converted to Christianity. However, in some villages many became Christians.

For Your Notebook

1. How did Champlain try to make the colony self-supporting?

Catholic Missionaries

The artist has shown Paul de Maisonneuve and the settlers at Ville-Marie.

  Several religious orders, both men's and women's, came to New France in the 1600s.* It was the Jesuits who carried out most of the missionary work.** Their main goal was to convert First Nations people to the Roman Catholic faith. Members of other religious orders were involved in education and health care in the colony.

Many missionaries were interested in exploration. They also tried to understand the cultures of the First Nations peoples. Jesuit priests lived among various First Nations, especially the Wendat. They learned the languages and wrote about what they saw of First Nations customs and spiritual beliefs.

The Jesuits established Ste. Marie in Huronia in 1634. Huronia was the name given by the French to the entire area where the Wendat people lived. Ste. Marie was their first fortified mission. This means that it was protected by a palisade. Several missions were built in the area. From Ste. Marie the missionaries visited their other missions. Much of what we know of how the First Nations people lived has been based on the *Jesuit Relations* letters, journals, and reports.

The first group of nuns arrived in 1640. Women's religious orders lived and worked in the European settlement. They set up the first schools and hospitals.

Under the leadership of Paul de Maisonneuve, the Société de Notre-Dame de Montreal founded a Catholic Mission at Ville-Marie (Montreal) in 1642. It was continually threatened by Iroquois attacks.

In 1648–1649, the Iroquois began attacking and destroying Wendat settlements. Thousands of Wendat died in these attacks. The Jesuit Missions in Huronia were especially vulnerable to Iroquois attacks. In 1649, a number of Jesuits, including Jean de Brébeuf and Bariel Lalemant, were taken prisoner and killed by the Iroquois at the Mission of Saint-Ignace.

The combination of disease and war finally destroyed Huronia. The remaining Wendat (approximately 500) retreated. The Christians went to Christian Island. Others went to what is now the United States. Some starved during the following winter; others were adopted into other First Nations.

Huronia, 1639-1649

For Your Notebook

1. What types of work did members of religious orders carry out in New France?

---

*The *Canada Revisited 6* homepage provides more information on the Roman Catholic Church. See information on page ix on how to reach the *Canada Revisited 6* homepage.

**The Jesuits were called the "Black Robes" by the First Nations.

Focus On: Disease Among the First Nations

The *Jesuit Relations* reported that the first missionaries of New France were welcomed by the Wendat as part of their alliance with the French. However, this changed.

- The missionaries expected the Wendat to change their culture (including their spiritual beliefs) to that of the French.
- European diseases spread among the Wendat. The diseases were thought to have come from the black robes (the clothing) worn by the Jesuits. Tens of thousands of people died from smallpox, tuberculosis, and measles. This was nearly half the Wendat population. In its weakened state the Wendat nation was vulnerable to Iroquois attack.
- In the end, Huronia was destroyed and the Wendat nation disappeared. The small number that survived disease and war were scattered. Most were adopted into other groups.

The European explorers came from countries that were very unsanitary compared to the way the people of the First Nations lived. Regular bathing was not common in Europe, but was important to First Nations people. Poor nutrition and unsanitary conditions were common in Europe, as was disease. Over the years, the Europeans had built up some resistance to common diseases like smallpox, measles, and typhus. Smallpox is a highly **contagious** disease. Tens of thousands of First Nations people throughout North and South America died from smallpox.

The primary source that follows is a description of smallpox in a colony of what would become the United States. However, the effects on the First Nations people in New France were much the same.

History—
- ☑ Primary Source
- ☐ Secondary Source
- ☐ Interpretation
- ☐ Chronology
- ☐ Cause and Effect

This spring also, those Indians that lived about their trading house there, fell sick of the small pox and died most miserably. . . .

. . . The condition of this people was so lamentable [terribly sad] and they fell down so generally of this disease as they were in the end not able to help one another, no not to make a fire nor to fetch a little water to drink, nor any to bury the dead. But would strive as long as they could, and when they could procure no other means to make fire, they would burn the wooden trays and

This illustration shows a family with smallpox with their desperate relatives, who are weeping and praying. It illustrates an epidemic in 1634, described by William Bradford.

dishes they ate their meat in, and their very bows and arrows. And some would crawl out on all fours to get a little water, and sometimes die by the way and not be able to get in again. But of those of the English house [Plymouth colonists], though at first they were afraid of the infection, yet seeing their [First Nations people's] woeful and sad condition and hearing their pitiful cries and lamentations, they had compassion on them, and daily fetched them wood and water and made them fires, got them victuals [food] whilst they lived; and buried them when they died. For very few of them escaped, notwithstanding they did what they could for them to the hazard [danger] of themselves.

—William Bradford
History of Plymouth Plantation

Contagious—easily spread from one person to another (How this occurred was not understood at the time.)

The Fur Market

First Nations peoples came to Montreal each summer to trade furs. In spite of the threat of Iroquois attack, Montreal became the centre of the fur trade.

Furs obtained by First Nations peoples were traded for European goods. The pictures and chart on this page show examples of trade goods. Iron or steel tools and firearms were especially important. The French "bought" the furs at a low price and sold them in Europe at a high price. For example, a European gun worth $3.00 was traded for beaver pelts worth $50.00. However, trade goods brought from France were in limited supply, and importing them was risky and costly. The French could charge high prices because there was little competition in the market.

The fur trade introduced First Nations peoples to European goods. These items gradually changed their lives. As time went on, many of them became dependent on these trade goods. Although sharpened stone and shell blades had been used for thousands of years, iron tools were sharper and did not break. Trading patterns that had developed among First Nations changed because of their wish to trade with Europeans for iron tools, especially axes.

In 1665, one beaver pelt purchased: 0.9 kg of gun powder or 1.8 kg of lead or 8 wooden-handled knives or 12 iron arrow-heads or two swords or two axes.

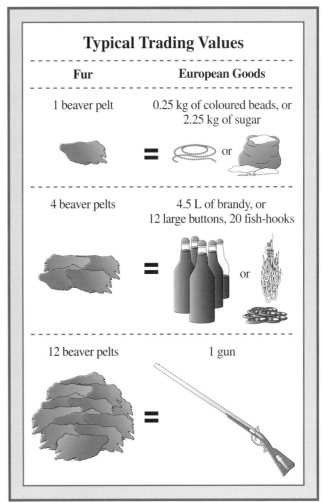

Typical Trading Values

Fur	European Goods
1 beaver pelt	0.25 kg of coloured beads, or 2.25 kg of sugar
4 beaver pelts	4.5 L of brandy, or 12 large buttons, 20 fish-hooks
12 beaver pelts	1 gun

For Your Notebook

1. Create a visual chart for the information in the caption of the painting on the left.

The English Enter the Fur Trade

Radisson and Groseilliers

Pierre Radisson and Chouart des Groseilliers were two French *coureurs de bois* who had a great impact on the fur trade in Canada. When they applied for a licence to trade in the country beyond Lake Superior, the governor of New

Pierre Radisson

France would not grant it. They had to promise to give him a large share of their profits. They refused. They decided to go farther west and obtain furs without a fur-trading licence.

In 1659, they left Trois Rivières in secret to trade in the area north of Lake Superior. This land was not well known by French explorers and fur traders. There Radisson and Groseilliers found Anishinabe (Ojibway) and **displaced** Wendat and Odawa willing to trade enormous quantities of furs. They wanted metal axes and kettles, and other European trade goods. When Radisson and Groseilliers returned to New France they were fined for trading without a licence. Their valuable load of furs was **confiscated**.

Radisson and Groseilliers were convinced of the potential of this northern fur area. They went to England to meet with Charles II about the rich fur-trading country. They hypothesized that this area could be reached easily by sailing a ship through Hudson Strait and then south into Hudson Bay and James Bay (see map on page 214). The Woodland Cree and other northern nations living in the region would be able to bring furs down the rivers that flowed into Hudson Bay. Radisson and Groseilliers believed that this plan would bring profits to investors.

Displaced—moved by force from a place formerly occupied
Confiscate—to seize or take away; to claim in the name of the government

An Exercise in Decision-Making

England in 1665

Students Involved

 Break your class into groups of seven students. One student should take the role of King Charles II. Another should be Prince Rupert. The third student should act as court secretary. He or she will chair the meeting and record information on the decision-making chart and/or any other documents. The other students should take the roles of Radisson, Groseilliers, and English investors who are interested in the fur trade.

Periods One and Two

Role-play a meeting in England between King Charles II, his cousin Prince Rupert, Radisson, and Groseilliers. Read Question 1 before proceeding with the role play.

1. a) **Radisson, Groseilliers, and two English investors:** Before you present your ideas to King Charles II, make sure you have a clear understanding of the following:
   - Why do you (Radisson and Groseilliers) no longer want to trade for furs in New France?
   - What is the country like beyond Lake Superior? the people? the availability and quality of furs?
   - Think of reasons why the English should get involved in the fur trade.
   - Try to think of the questions King Charles II may ask you and figure out your answers before you talk with him.

- You may wish to draw a map of North America to present to the king. Remember maps in the 1660s were very different from maps we use today.

b) **Prince Rupert**: Your cousin King Charles II of England will be asking your advice on the issue Radisson and Groseilliers will be presenting to him. Do some research to find out about New France, the fur trade, and English explorers who had searched for the Northwest Passage.

c) **King Charles II**: You are somewhat familiar with the Hudson Bay, as the English have done some exploration by ship in this area while looking for the Northwest Passage (see chart page 157). Do research to find out about New France and the fur trade.

d) **Court secretary:** Prepare a decision-making chart similar to the one on page 259.

Periods Three and Four

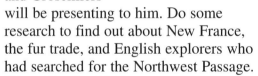

1. a) King Charles II, Prince Rupert, Radisson, Groseilliers, the investors, and the Court secretary meet. Radisson and Groseilliers and the investors present their idea and their supporting arguments.

b) King Charles II meets with Prince Rupert. Prince Rupert provides background information on Radisson and Groseilliers' ideas.

c) King Charles II and Prince Rupert use a decision-making model to help make their decision. The court secretary fills in the chart. Radisson and Groseilliers work on question 2, which follows.

Decision-making Chart

2. Everyone involved prepares a written record of the event.

a) Radisson and Groseilliers each write a journal account, or a formal letter to the king.

b) Prince Rupert writes a formal report for the king's records of what was said and what decisions were made.

c) King Charles II dictates a report to the court secretary of the meeting and the results.

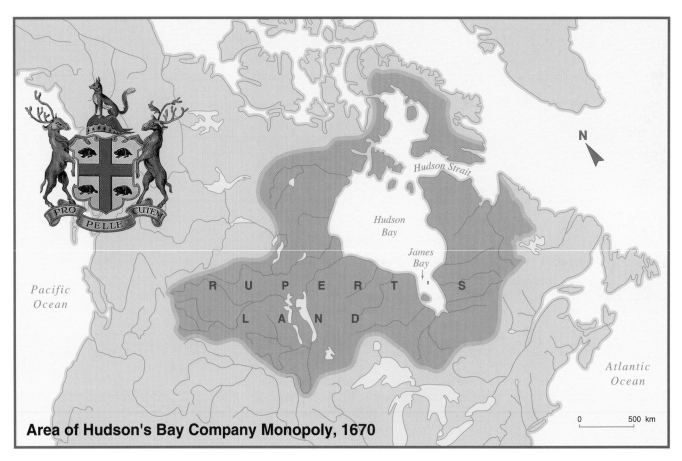

Area of Hudson's Bay Company Monopoly, 1670

Formation of the Hudson's Bay Company

   The English decided to participate in the fur trade in North America. They saw it as a way to increase their power and influence and make profits.

The Hudson's Bay Company was formed by a group of English investors. These men persuaded King Charles II of England that profits from the fur trade in the northern part of North America would be huge. They asked him for a charter and exclusive trading rights (a monopoly) on a large tract of land. The land would be controlled by the Hudson's Bay Company.

King Charles II agreed. On May 2, 1670, he granted a charter to "The Governor and Company of Adventurers Trading Into Hudson's Bay." The charter was granted in the name of Prince Rupert, the king's cousin. As a result, the Hudson's Bay Company land became known as Rupert's Land. The charter gave the investors a monopoly over the trade in all the territory whose rivers flowed into Hudson Bay (as the above map shows).

The English acted as if the land were uninhabited. However, there were many First Nations that made their homes in Rupert's Land. The Hudson's Bay Company officials did not talk to them about taking over their lands, or consider how this might affect them.

The Hudson's Bay Company forts were built at the mouths of the main rivers flowing into Hudson Bay. The Hudson's Bay Company was dependent on the First Nations peoples for the interior trade. First Nations trappers and people acting as go-betweens brought furs by canoe to the forts for trading. These furs were exchanged for European goods. These were then traded for more furs from other First Nations.

An Exercise in Critical Thinking

A Woodland Cree Trader

We already have trading relationships with the French and other First Nations. This competition from the English will mean changes to our trading patterns. The English expect many more furs for their trade goods than the French do.

Captain of a Hudson's Bay Company Ship

Often the goods we trade are inexpensive to make. However, it costs us a lot to transport them from England to the Hudson's Bay Company posts in Rupert's Land. We need to cover our costs. It's dangerous too. If the ship gets caught in the ice, we will lose everything.

Hudson's Bay Company Investor

Yes, we made tremendous profits—up to 1000% after expenses. But often it takes three to four years before we get back our return on our investment. We have to charge high prices for the trade goods to cover the financial risks.

1. Do you agree with any of these people's point of view? Consider the positive and negative changes that will result from the presence of the English. Use a Critical Thinking model for this activity, such as the one on page 258.

2. Pretend you live in Rupert's Land. With a partner or in a small group discuss or role-play your reaction upon hearing that English traders are setting up trading forts near the Hudson Bay. Through an interpreter, have a conversation with these three people.

For Your Notebook

1. Did King Charles II have the right to give the land that became known as Rupert's Land to the Hudson's Bay Company?

Exploring Further

2. Both First Nations women and men acted as interpreters in the fur trade.
   - What would an interpreter do during trade negotiations?
   - What challenges would such an interpreter face?
   - What listening and speaking skills would such an interpreter need?
   - How can you relate these ideas to the listening and speaking you do in school?

3. Find out what percentage of profit business people usually like to make. Compare this with the profits made by the Hudson's Bay Company.

Contributions of First Nations People

The contributions of the First Nation peoples were essential to European exploration and the fur trade in the history of Canada. The fur trade was the main business activity during the 1600s in what is now Canada. It was an important industry for 300 years. From the start, the First Nations peoples played an important part in this trade.

The "know-how" of the First Nations people saved the lives of countless Europeans in those early days of exploration and trade. The fur trade would not have existed without them. They were the principal labour force for the trade and supplied all of the knowledge about trapping, the environment, and travel routes.

The early explorers and fur traders found survival in the Canadian environment difficult. To them the environment was hostile. They called it a "wilderness." They were in constant danger of being injured, starving, freezing, drowning, or being killed by animals. The First Nations understood this environment. It was not a wild place (wilderness) to them. They willingly shared their skills and knowledge with the Europeans and helped them survive.

First Nations and Metis people trapped and transported furs for European fur traders.

First Nations people showed the Europeans how to "live off" the country. They provided the fur traders with much of their food.

First Nations people taught the newcomers how to live comfortably by wearing properly-made skin and fur clothing. Women made mitts, moccasins, robes, leggings, and carrying pouches for them.

Metis—persons whose parents were First Nations and European. The Metis culture was a mixture of First Nations and European ways of life.

The explorers and fur traders quickly adopted the canoe as a speedy mode of travel.

First Nations people taught the Europeans how to make snowshoes, sleds, and toboggans to travel in deep snow.

First Nations people also acted as go-betweens in the fur trade. They traded with other First Nations people to get the required furs. Some acted as interpreters for the Europeans. They also acted as guides. Later in the west this role was often filled by Metis people.

Guides showed explorers and fur traders the best trails and canoe routes.

Focus On: The Role of First Nations Women in the Fur Trade

The journeys of some European explorers were remarkable achievements. The key to their success lay in their ability to live and travel with the people of the First Nations. Help was given to them, much of it by First Nations women.

The fur trade in Canada is often associated with men. Historians write about hunters, trappers, fur traders, *coureurs de bois*, voyageurs, explorers, and employees of fur-trading posts. From these accounts, it appears that the fur trade was an all-male world. It actually was not. First Nations women and women of mixed ancestry (Metis) were deeply involved in various aspects of the fur trade. Some were traders, others served as guides and interpreters. Their skills in the preparation of pelts, food, and clothing were essential.

Women prepared the animal furs and skins. They knew efficient ways of stretching, scraping, and preserving the hides. Comfortable clothing was made from tanned skins and warm furs. Many European explorers and traders found this clothing more suitable than clothing they brought from Europe.

The European men who were involved in the fur trade lived lonely and difficult lives. Young French fur traders often  married First Nations women. When the woman learned her husband's language, she could act as his interpreter. She also introduced him to her relatives with whom he could trade. A wife also taught her husband about survival in the cold winters. For winter travel, she equipped him with warm clothing, a toboggan, and snowshoes.

A First Nations family making maple sugar

Children of mixed First Nations and European parents were called Metis.

Mixed marriages sometimes caused cultural problems on both sides. While the women thought they were married for life, the European men often did not. Some European husbands returned home to Europe or central Canada. However, many of the marriages were happy and lasted a lifetime.

These couples and their Metis children and descendants had the perfect combination of knowledge and skills. They were the backbone of the fur trade. You will learn more about the contributions of the Metis people in Grades 7 and 8.

European women were seldom mentioned in the history books of this time period. If European women came to North America at this time, their individual contributions are lost forever.

For Your Notebook

1. The products listed in the caption at the bottom of page 211 changed the lives of First Nations men. Describe the changes that metal cooking pots, as shown in the picture to the left, made to women's lives.

Timeline

History—
- ☐ Primary Source
- ☐ Secondary Source
- ☐ Interpretation
- ☑ Chronology
- ☐ Cause and Effect

1 French trade for furs along Atlantic Coast and in St. Lawrence River area

2 French government grants fur trading monopolies in Acadia and in St. Lawrence

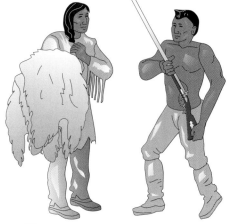

3 Wendat act as traders for the French

4 Montagnais, Algonquin, Wendat, French vs Iroquois Five Nations, Dutch

5 Iroquois become enemy of the French for almost 150 years

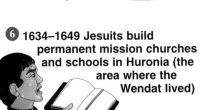

6 1634–1649 Jesuits build permanent mission churches and schools in Huronia (the area where the Wendat lived)

7 1653 French *coureurs de bois* replace the Wendat as go-betweens in the fur trade

8 1670 Formation of Hudson's Bay company (the English enter the fur trade in Canada)

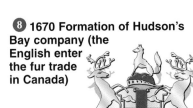

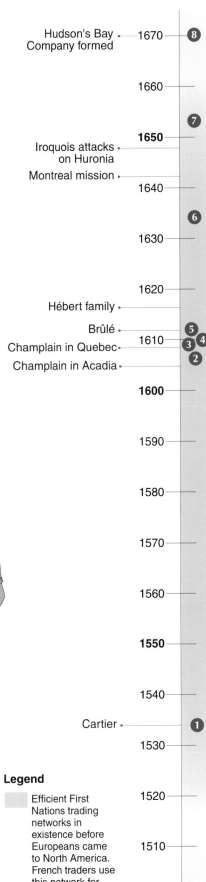

Hudson's Bay Company formed	1670	**8**
	1660	
		7
	1650	
Iroquois attacks on Huronia		
Montreal mission	1640	
		6
	1630	
	1620	
Hébert family		
Brûlé		**5**
Champlain in Quebec	1610	**3** **4**
Champlain in Acadia		**2**
	1600	
	1590	
	1580	
	1570	
	1560	
	1550	
	1540	
Cartier		**1**
	1530	
	1520	
	1510	
	1500	

Legend

[shaded bar] Efficient First Nations trading networks in existence before Europeans came to North America. French traders use this network for trading activities.

Timeline not to scale.

Review • • • • • • • • • • • • • • • • • • •

Assessment

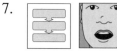 Complete a self-assessment for one assignment from this chapter. See page 263 or ask your teacher for ideas.

Summarizing the Chapter

1. Reread the predictions you made on page 196. Fill in the "What I Found Out" column of the prediction chart.

Understanding Concepts

2. Do either a) or b).
   Work with a partner. Create a large mind map to show
   a) Aboriginal–European interaction with the environment. How did Iroquoian involvement in the fur trade affect the above? Consider the availability of beaver.
   b) the three fur trading networks that developed at this time.

3. What contributions did First Nations people make to the fur trade?

4. Use a "spider" chart to record definitions for alliance and contributions.

5. Use the information in Chapters 9 and 10 to find examples of alliances. Create a concept poster of alliances.

6. Add names from this chapter to the Explorers Timeline you started on page 117.

Developing Research Skills

7. If you haven't done so already complete the research activity you started on page 197. Your teacher can give you some ideas on how to make a presentation.

8. On page 197 you had the opportunity to use the Research Model. Record the following in the Learning How to Learn part of your History Journal.
   a) Which steps in the Research Model did you find the most difficult? Why? How might you change your approach next time? What skills do you wish to develop?

b) With which steps did you feel most successful? Why? What will you continue to do on your next research project?

9.

Order of Good Cheer Class Project

Add information from this chapter to the section activity you started on page 114.

Developing Communication Skills

Select at least one from 10–14:

Writing

10. Was Champlain rightfully called the "Father of New France"? Write a newspaper editorial to persuade others of your point of view. (See 10 on page 264.)

11. Write a poem or song to portray early European–First Nations interactions or First Nations contributions to the fur trade.

Listening and Speaking

12. Discuss the following with your classmates. "The First Nations people gradually became dependent on the European trade goods. . . ." How did this happen? Over what period of time do you think it happened? Was it a positive or a negative change? Why?

220

13. Which person from this chapter would you like to have met? Explain to a friend why you find that person interesting.

Viewing and Representing

14. Decide how the people listed on the following chart might react to the idea of expanding the colony of Quebec. Record your ideas in a chart like the one below.

Should the colony of Quebec be expanded?			
	Advantages	Disadvantages	Suggestions
Fur trader			
Mohawk person			
Wendat person			
Potential colonist			
Roman Catholic priest			

Applying Concepts

15. a) What qualities were required for a fur trader to be a good business person?
    b) What makes a successful business venture?
    c) What steps do business people (entrepreneurs) take today to help make businesses a success?
    d) Did Champlain take any of the actions you listed in b)? Could he have tried any of the other ideas to expand the fur trade and make sure a greater supply of furs was brought to Quebec?

16. Respond to this question in your History Journal: Does competition hurt or help business ventures? How do business people respond to competition? Use historical and present-day examples.

17. Many First Nations peoples suffered and died from European diseases passed to them by colonists.
    a) Were any precautions taken to avoid the spread of disease when Europeans first arrived?
    b) What steps were taken once the spread of disease began?

c) Do you think First Nations peoples passed any diseases to Europeans?
d) What regulations and precautions are in place today for travellers going to another country?

Challenge Plus

18. Do either a) or b).
    a) Present a sequence of tableaux to show the steps in trade involving a go-between.
    b) Why were "go-betweens" (middlepersons) important to the expansion of the fur trade?
    c) Think of examples of "go-betweens" in society (our economy) today. What purpose(s) do they serve? Are there any similarities between go-betweens (middlepersons) in the fur trade and middlepersons in today's society?

19. What are the characteristics of a business? Create a web which shows the fur trade as a business.

20. a) When there is a high demand for a product, such as there was for fur-felt hats in France, how would the following be affected?
    - raw materials needed to make the product
    - number of people involved in related trade
    - profits
    - prices
    - competition
    b) Will prices and profits be higher or lower as the needed resources are gradually used up?
    c) Explain how a) and b) relate to "fads" today. Use an example in your explanation.

Section II Review

1. As a class discuss the questions on page 113.

2.
    Order of Good Cheer Class Project

    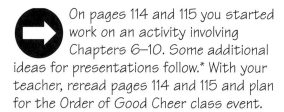
    On pages 114 and 115 you started work on an activity involving Chapters 6–10. Some additional ideas for presentations follow.* With your teacher, reread pages 114 and 115 and plan for the Order of Good Cheer class event.

Some Presentation Ideas

If you don't already have a presentation topic, select from among the following:

1. If Canada Had TV a Millennium Ago!
    Most of Canada didn't have television until the 1950s. Let's pretend, though, that there was television a millennium ago. Pretend you are part of an on-the-spot TV newscast crew. Work in groups to prepare and share with your classmates one of the following events:
    * Vikings returning home from Vinland
    * Beothuk meeting Vikings
    * Caboto returning to England and reporting on the huge quantities of fish
    * fishing vessels returning from the Grand Banks with a cargo full of fish
    * a whaling vessel returning to a European port
    * Cartier raising the French flag on Gaspé Peninsula

    * Mi'kmaq reacting to French coming to Gaspé Peninsula
    * the completion of the habitation at Port Royal (or Quebec)
    * Mi'kmaq helping the French
    * Jesuits describing their missions in Huronia
    * Wendat describing the missions in Huronia
    * Wendat reaction to the French wanting to trade furs for metal goods
    * huge profits being made from furs from the colonies
    * the latest in felt hats—a fashion statement!
    * Radisson and Groseilliers's meeting with King Charles II
    * colonists leaving France for the Quebec colony
    * a newsworthy event that you choose

2. Instead of using a topic in number 1 as an on-the-spot newscast, turn it into one of the following:
    a) a radio, TV, or newspaper interview of a person from history
    b) a brochure for an **adventure tour** of the colonies in North America. The year is 1650.

3. Prepare a newspaper, magazine, or TV commercial or ad for
    * fur hat styles
    * clothing styles
    * sailors for a voyage to the St. Lawrence area with Champlain
    * volunteers from a First Nation to return to Europe with an explorer
    * metal-bladed knives and tools
    * bilingual Iroquoian–French speakers to work as interpreters
    * settlers to move to Acadia or to the Quebec colony
    * workers on a fishing or whaling vessel
    * workers with fur traders at Quebec, Trois Rivières, or Montreal

4. Write three journal entries from either point of view:
    * you are the character
    * you have just met the character
    For example, you could be Champlain writing in his journal, or someone who just met

---

* Presentation, as used in this book, refers to the communication of information in visual, oral, or written forms. See page 262 in the Appendix.

Adventure tour—an organized holiday trip

Champlain. Other ideas: a Viking, a Basque fisher, an explorer searching for the Northwest Passage, a Jesuit priest in Huronia or a nun in Quebec, someone on the League of Five Nations Council, a Wendat fur trader, a Wendat woman who lives in Huronia, a young Wendat girl living in a convent in Quebec

5. Write a letter home as if you were living in Port Royal, Quebec, Montreal, or Huronia. For example, you could pretend you came to Quebec (or Port Royal) with Champlain, or to Montreal with Maisonneuve, or were a fur trader such as Brûlé, Nicollet, Radisson, or Groseilliers. Other ideas include settlers such as Marie Hébert or Louis Hébert; or be Champlain writing to his wife, Hélène Boullé, or Hélène Boullé writing to her husband, Champlain.

6. Pretend you are someone from Canadian history (before 1663). Make up a fictitious timeline of your life.

7. Imagine you are with one of the European explorers. Create a set of postcards from some of the places you have visited. Draw a picture on one side of the postcard highlighting a place of interest. Write a message on the reverse side describing the scene or some experience you had. Include three facts and three impressions or personal feelings.

8. Create one of the following about a North American expedition or colony: board game, puzzle, skit, radio show, song, or rap. Include at least 10 facts in it.

9. Encourage Europeans to settle in Acadia or the Quebec colony. Create one of the following:

booklet	pamphlet
display	travel brochure
magazine article	poster

10. Write a story that starts with the sentence: If I had been born as Marie Hébert (or some other person you studied about in Section II) my life would have been different.

11. a) Pretend you are Champlain and are looking for the "perfect" location to start a colony. Describe what you are looking for.

   b) Describe what qualities your colonists should have in order to survive and help the colony grow.

12. From the point of view of a Wendat fur trade go-between, draft a sales speech you would make to a Woodland Cree person describing the benefits of a steel-bladed axe compared to a traditional stone axe or a metal cooking pot compared to a birchbark container.

13. Write an e-mail to one of the famous people you've studied about this year. Tell them why you admire them or ask them three questions to which you would like an answer.

14. Pretend you are writing for a French newspaper and describe the instructions for the game of lacrosse.
   OR
   Pretend you are broadcasting on radio a game of lacrosse. Your listeners have never heard of the game before.

15. Work with a partner to create the final summaries from both sides of an imaginary legal case being tried. Choose one of the following. Each of you defends one side:
   • Freydís Eiríksdottir versus her brothers
   • Dom Agaya versus Jacques Cartier

Today and Tomorrow

The drive north from the city to the reserve where Dad grew up took a day and a half. I had forgotten how much of Ontario was forest, rock, and lakes! Dad didn't stop for lunch because he said Grandmother would have food waiting for us. After we got there, it seemed like visitors dropped in at my grandparents' house all afternoon. Several people commented on how much Dani and I had grown. As if we wouldn't have! We hadn't been there for two years.

It took a few days to get used to being there, but the freedom was great. There were lots of cousins to play with and we could go anywhere we liked. Grandmother always had food ready, so there often wasn't a set time for meals. Mom and Dad drank tea and visited all day, and they were pretty relaxed about bedtimes.

One day my grandfather asked, "How would you like to go fishing with me, young Dale? Tomorrow we could go out in the canoe for the day."

"That would be great," I said. I really liked canoeing, but I didn't know my grandfather very well. I wondered what it would be like.

The next morning at 4:30 Grandfather woke me up. He didn't say much, which was fine with me because it was the middle of the night as far as I was concerned. When we had the canoe on the lake he gave me a cup of hot chocolate and a biscuit. He told me that his grandfather used to take him fishing when he was my age, and it was an important part of his education.

I caught my first fish that afternoon! I caught three in all and Grandfather caught eight. He taught me a prayer of thanks to say after I took each fish off the hook. He said we must always show respect for the beings that feed us.

"Is that one of the traditional ways, Grandfather? Does everybody still do it?" I asked him.

"There's nothing wrong with the old ways," he said. "People still need to understand they are part of everything. If they had more respect, we wouldn't have pollution in the lakes and the animals disappearing from the land."

He seemed upset, so I thought I would change the subject. I mentioned that I had learned in school about a theory that thousands of years ago our ancestors had come from Asia across the Bering Strait, which was dry land at the time because of the ice age. "Isn't it amazing that they might have come all that way, and spread all over North and South America, right to the tip?" I asked him.

He looked at me in silence, then said, "Our people have always been right here. This Mother Earth was made for us and we were put on it by the Creator. We were the original people." He paused. "I think it is time for you to spend some time with an Elder to learn more about your people's ways." He didn't say any more about it. We fished a little longer and then started home.

I was surprised to find out in a few days that my parents had agreed to go back to the city without me so that I could stay several more weeks. My father said it was a great opportunity. He said his visits with a very wise Elder at my age had helped him figure out what path he wanted to take in life.

The next day, after they left, my grandfather gave me an old birchbark basket decorated with porcupine quills and a small turtle carved from wood. "These are for you," he said. "They were my grandfather's. The turtle stands for patience.

It will take a long time for you to learn the traditional ways of our people. You must be patient like the wise turtle."

He also gave me a jar of maple syrup and a package of tobacco as a ritual gift for the Elder. He instructed me carefully in what to do and say. That afternoon I rode my cousin's bike to a white house near the ball diamond. The Elder's wife greeted me with a big smile and hug. She showed me where the Elder was sitting in the shade behind the house.

He nodded to me and said he knew that I was coming. I took the gifts out of my backpack and offered them to him. As I had been instructed, I said, "In the Name of the Great Spirit, Mother Earth, and the Grandfathers, will you help me learn about the old teachings of our people?"

He accepted the tobacco and syrup and nodded, and pointed to a seat beside him. I knew that I must be silent until he spoke. All I could hear were the crows in the forest behind the house and children playing farther away. Suddenly the Elder looked at me with a twinkle in his eye.

"You know what a satellite is?" he asked.

I couldn't have been more surprised. "Sure, "I said. "Satellites are machines that circle around the earth. They have computers on them that record and pass on information to different places on earth and in space."

"There is a satellite dish at the recreation centre. People can watch television from all over." He was silent for a long moment. "Everything is connected," he said. "But sometimes it's hard to know how some things fit in the Creator's plan. It's hard to know how to keep in balance."

The crows were making a lot of noise, fighting over something they had found. "Yes, Grandfather." I didn't know what else to say.

"The old ways have many things to teach us about being in balance, and not running this way and that way. You live in the city. I see on the television that people in the city run around all the time. There are also things that you should learn from your ancestors that will help you live better than that. There are also things that you should learn about belonging to your people."

Some friends in my class had families with different

traditions. They talked about how they had to balance their families' traditions with what they learned in school or saw on TV. It was hard for them to feel like they really belonged. "But Grandfather," I said, "I'm confused about the different ways of explaining things. I think I would like to be a scientist. I would like to explore new ideas, maybe go to new places. How can I do that and also learn about the old ways of our people? I'll just be more confused."

"Ah," he said, "I see that there are many things for you to learn. We will explore many surprising places together— before you get to explore out in space with the satellites!" And he laughed his quiet laugh.

Chapter 11
Aboriginal People Today

O v e r v i e w
Use this Overview to predict the events of this chapter.

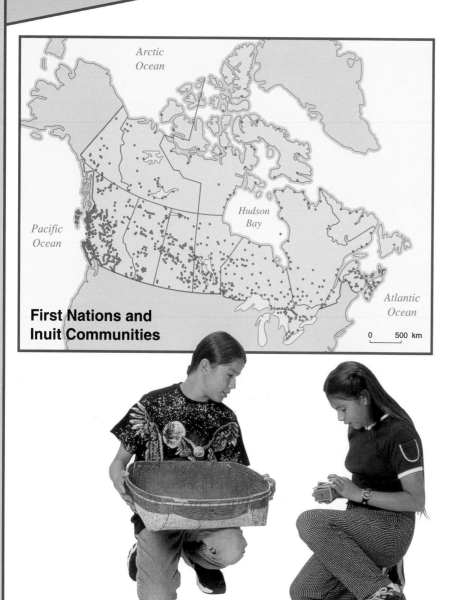

First Nations and Inuit Communities

Arctic Ocean

Pacific Ocean

Hudson Bay

Atlantic Ocean

0   500 km

❶ **The Aboriginal Peoples**

In 1982, the Canadian government defined Aboriginal to include Indian (First Nation), Inuit, and Metis people. Aboriginal people live in all regions of Canada.

❷ **Contributors and Contributions**

Many foods, medicines, technologies, and words used in Canada today have come from Aboriginal cultures. Aboriginal musicians, actors, artists, storytellers, scholars, athletes, dancers, and politicians are well-known to Canadians.

❸ **Economic Part of Culture**

Aboriginal people today struggle to balance traditional values with meeting their economic needs. The majority live in urban centres.

❹ **Social Part of Culture**

Family continues to be important and Elders are still part of passing on the culture. Issues arise from the need for balance between traditional cultures and Canadian culture.

❺ **Political Part of Culture**

Aboriginal people are seeking more power to govern themselves. Many land claims are being negotiated with the federal and provincial governments of Canada.

Chapter 11 Focus

Section I of the textbook focused on pre-Contact cultures of Aboriginal peoples. Section II described contact with Europeans during early exploration and colonization. Four hundred more years of history passed before the present day. You will study those years of history in Grades 7 and 8.

Chapter 11 looks at Aboriginal peoples (First Nations, Inuit, Metis) today. You will look at contributions they made in the past, and people who are making a difference now. You will study challenges and changes in the economic, social, and political parts of First Nations cultures today.

This chapter will focus on the following icons. Emphasis will be on balance and cultural contact.

Environmental   Balance   Technology   Cultural   Exploration
Interaction   Contact

Vocabulary

Indian Act   majority
treaty   reserve
Status Indians   levels of government
Non-Status Indians   self-government
Treaty Indians   band council
minority   First Nation government

Pre-reading Activity

From what you have studied in this book so far and from looking at the chapter titles and visuals, make a list of contributions of Canada's Aboriginal people. Add to this list as you go through this chapter.

Of all the teachings
we receive
this one is the most
important:
Nothing belongs to you
of what there is,
of what you must take,
you must share.

–Chief Dan George,
Excerpt from *My Heart Soars*.
©1989, Hancock House, 19313 Zero Ave.
Surrey, B.C. V4P 1M7.
Reprinted with permission.

Chapter Activity

 This chapter does not have review activities. Instead you are to prepare a presentation on one of the following topics. Projects may be done individually, in pairs, or in small groups.

1. Traditional and Modern-day Aboriginal Music: Listen to both traditional music and music of today. Discuss types of music, instruments, and singing. Is the focus of the songs the words or something else? Who are well-known Aboriginal musicians today?

2. Aboriginal Poets: Identify a poet from the past or a poet of today and describe his or her work. Do the poems tell a story, describe a feeling, deal with an issue or challenge? In what ways (if any) do the images and rhythms relate to Aboriginal cultures? What values are expressed in the poetry?

3. Aboriginal Storytellers: Select a storyteller, a writer, a filmmaker, or a playwright. How does the person's work reflect his or her traditional culture? What themes does he or she present? What does his or her work offer to an Aboriginal audience? to a non-Aboriginal audience?

4. Aboriginal Visual Artists: Select an Aboriginal visual artist. Research the artist's background. What themes does he or she often show in art? Describe ways in which the artist's work expresses her or his traditional culture.

5. Aboriginal Actors: Select an Aboriginal actor and research his or her background. What opportunities did he or she have? What are the actor's goals? What does the actor feel were obstacles to success? How does the actor relate to his or her traditional culture?

6. Nunavut: Research Canada's newest territory.

7. Lacrosse: Research Canada's official national game.
   • www.lacrosse.ca
   • www.ontariolacrosse.com

8. Aboriginal Activists and/or Leaders in the 20th Century: Research a person who has worked for change.

9. Issues Faced by Aboriginal People Today: Choose an issue and research its origins. Include different points of view about possible solutions.

The Aboriginal Peoples

In 1982, the **Constitution Act** gave an official definition of Aboriginal that includes Indian, Inuit, and Metis peoples of Canada.

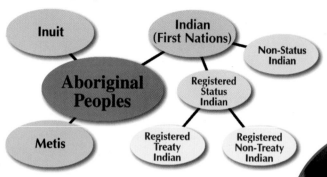

Who the Aboriginal People Are Today

According to the 1996 Canadian census* there were 28 528 125 people in Canada. Of this number, approximately 3%, or 799 010, were Aboriginal.

Aboriginal Population (1996)	
First Nations	554 290
Inuit	41 080
Metis	210 190
Total	**799 010****
Non-Aboriginal Population	27 729 115
Total Population of Canada	28 528 125

■ Non-Aboriginal Population: 27 729 115

■ Aboriginal Peoples (First Nation, Inuit, Metis): 799 010

Constitution Act—the Act (law) passed by the Canadian Parliament in 1982 that defined the country of Canada, the form of its governments, its official languages, and the rights of its citizens, including the Aboriginal peoples. The Constitution Act replaced the British North America (BNA) Act of 1867, which had created Canada.

*The census is a detailed official count of the people of a country. Statistics Canada: http://www.statcan.ca

**This total is slightly less than the numbers of First Nation, Inuit, and Metis people added together. This is because some people told the census they belong to more than one group.

Government Definitions

Indian [First Nations]
Status and Non-Status Indian

Status Indians are listed in a government of Canada register and given a number and card. They have certain rights and restrictions under the **Indian Act**. People who have First Nations ancestors but are not registered under the Indian Act are called Non-Status Indians. (See web to the left.)

Before 1985, if a Status Indian woman married a Non-Status Indian, she and her children lost their status. Aboriginal women worked hard to get this law changed. Mary Two-Axe Earley, shown on the left, was the first woman to be reinstated as a Status Indian under the Indian Act.

Treaty Indian

The ancestors of many First Nations people signed treaties with the government of Canada. They are often called Treaty Indians. They are registered under the Indian Act. All Status Indians are not Treaty Indians. The government of Canada does not hold treaties covering all the lands where once only Aboriginal peoples lived.

Inuit

The Inuit are the people of Canada's North. Most of them live in the new territory of Nunavut, the Northwest Territories, northern Quebec, Labrador, and the Yukon Territory.

Metis

The Metis are people who have both European and First Nations or Inuit ancestry. Many trace their ancestry to the time of the fur trade. They are recognized by the Canadian government as Aboriginal, but do not receive the legal benefits of Status Indians.

Indian Act—an Act passed in 1867, changed many times since then, which outlines the relationship between the Government of Canada and First Nations people. It states who is covered under the terms of the Act. Inuit and Metis people are not covered by the Indian Act.

Where They Live

First Nations, Inuit, and Metis people today live in all parts of Canada. They live on **reserves** and off-reserve in rural areas. Others live in small towns and villages. In some places, Aboriginal people are the **majority** of the population. Recently, many more have moved to larger towns and cities. They are usually a **minority** in cities. The map on the right shows locations of First Nations and Inuit communities across Canada.

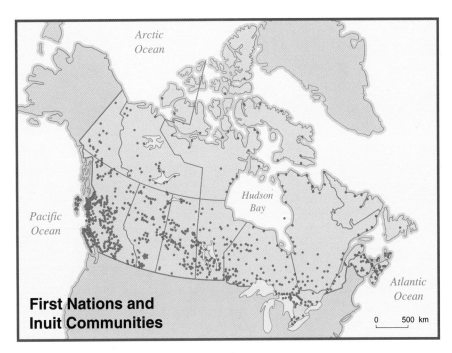

First Nations and Inuit Communities

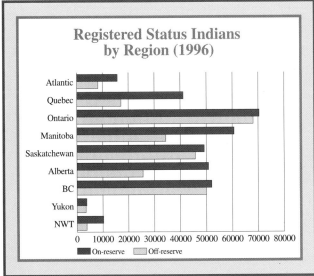

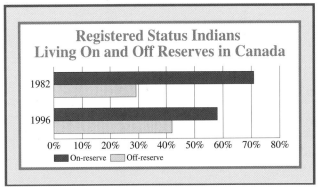

Canada's First Nations off-reserve population is expected to continue to grow faster than its on-reserve population.

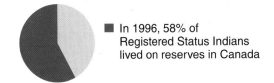

In 1996, 58% of Registered Status Indians lived on reserves in Canada

Aboriginal Languages Today

Aboriginal people in Canada speak 53 distinct languages. Many of these languages are spoken by very few people today. These languages are in danger of becoming extinct. Aboriginal people are working to keep their unique cultures and languages from disappearing.

For Your Notebook

1. Record in your WordBook any definitions from this page that are new to you.
2. Copy the web on page 228. Use the information from that page to add details to the web.
3. What does the bar graph Registered Status Indians Living On and Off Reserves in Canada tell us about population changes of these First Nations people?
4. Why is it important to keep Aboriginal languages from disappearing?
5. What can Aboriginal peoples do to keep their unique cultures and languages from disappearing?

Reserve—land set aside under the terms of a Treaty or by the government; only members of a First Nation may live there
Majority—largest group in a total population
Minority—smaller group, less than half of a total population

Why I'm Proud to be Aboriginal

—by Cheyenne Corcoran, Dene Nation
(Grade 6)

My mother, Carole Corcoran, is the person I have chosen for my Aboriginal hero. I have chosen my mother because she has had a tough life, but through it all she kept going without quitting. My mother was the first woman elected to our Band Council. She worked hard to make the Band Council give housing to single mothers. She started the first school on our reserve. She had to face many hardships because she was the only woman on the Band Council. She was brave and stood up for what she thought was right. I consider this an act of heroism.

What inspires me about my mother is that she left her family to go to university and got her degree in Law so she could get a good, successful job. I am proud of my mother because she did not quit. My mother was the first person from our family and our Band to get a university degree.

My mother was born in Fort Nelson, BC. She moved to Vancouver in 1985 to go to university. It was important for her to get an education so she could teach her children the importance of education. The hardest thing of all for my mother was when she moved to Vancouver with my sister and me. My dad had to move to the Northwest Territories. We only saw him at Christmas and in the

©Mokakit Education Research Association based at Kainaiwa Board of Education, P.O. Box 240, Standoff, AB. T0L 1V0. First published in Theytus Books' *Courageous Spirits: Aboriginal Heroes of Our Children.*

summer. My brother also lived away from us. He lived with his grandparents because they wanted him to stay with them in Fort Nelson. Three years after my mother started Law school I moved to the Queen Charlotte Islands to live with my dad. He had a job as the school principal there. My mother was in Vancouver by herself until she graduated in 1990.

In October, 1990, the Prime Minister of Canada asked her to work on a special commission on the future of Canada. For eight months she travelled across the country, meeting all kinds of people. It was a very hard job because a lot of people didn't like the Prime Minister and his government. With her busy job she did not have very much time to go home. In 1991 we moved to Prince George. My mother had to go back to Vancouver to take a two and a half month legal course in August. She came home in November, 1991. She has been an articled law student ever since.* She will finish her training in July, 1992, and then she will become a lawyer.

My mother has received many job offers from the government, First Nations groups, and other law firms. She is not sure where she wants to work next. She would like to help the Aboriginal people get self-government. Self-government is people who control their own actions.

My mother also wants us to have respect and recognition for our Aboriginal heritage when we

*This essay was written in 1992.

grow up. My mother has taught me that Aboriginal people have not been treated like Canadians. The governments of Canada have forced most Aboriginal people to live in terrible conditions on Reserves. Aboriginal people have been treated very badly. Until the government realizes this, the Aboriginal people will not have a chance to make better lives for themselves. She says that she will never be proud to be a Canadian citizen until Aboriginal rights are recognized.

The most important thing that my mother has taught me is that no matter how hard things are, you never give up. Even though our family was split up for seven years, when we didn't have very much money or when we had family problems, she never gave up her hopes that she could accomplish her goals.

One special moment that I value in my memory about my mom is when she graduated from Law school. It was a special day. My grandparents, some of my aunts and uncles, my brother, my dad and I were all there to see her graduate. I was proud of my mom and I knew my family was too.

My mother influences me in many ways. She has helped me to see that it is important to get an education and go to university. Most important of all is the way she makes me proud to be an Aboriginal person and to fight for my rights. I think the world needs more people like my mom because she fights and fights without stopping. She is unique and she gives me a lot of wisdom.

Contributions and Contributors

Yesterday and Today

   The technology and foods of Aboriginal peoples helped European explorers and settlers survive. The explorers learned of many foods from them. They also used plants, medicines, tools, clothing, and means of transportation that were first used in Aboriginal cultures. They learned many skills from Aboriginal people. Many of these contributions are part of modern life in Canada. For example, snowshoes, moccasins, and mukluks are commonly used today. The pictured items are just a few examples.

Foods like corn, squash, pumpkins, beans, tobacco, maple syrup, wild rice, beef jerky, and saskatoon berries are produced for sale by Aboriginal groups and by others. They are also used at home. Many medicines are made from materials used first by Aboriginal people.

The English language identifies many contributions of Aboriginal groups. For example, the word toboggan came from the Mi'kmaq and kayak is a word in Inuktitut. Many names of places across Canada come from First Nations words.

1 Toboggan
2 Parka
3 Canoe
4 Kayak
5 Lacrosse
6 Arts and crafts

People Who Make a Difference

Historical People

Aboriginal people have been part of the changes that have shaped the nation we live in today. Many historical figures made a difference. There have been political and military leaders, artists, and people in many other fields.

You will study the history of Canada after 1600 in Grades 7 and 8. Thus, this textbook will not describe these important historical figures. This brief list is provided if you wish to research their contributions on your own.

- Big Bear (Plains Cree)
- Molly Brant (Mohawk)
- Crowfoot (Cree/Blackfoot)
- Gabriel Dumont (Metis)
- Garakontié (Onondaga)
- Handsome Lake (Seneca)
- Hiawatha (Onondaga or Mohawk)
- Pauline Johnson (Mohawk)
- Rev. Peter Jones (Mississauga)
- Membertou (Mi'kmaq)
- The Peacemaker (Wendat)
- Gerry Potts (Metis)
- Louis Riel (Metis)
- Catherine Sutton (Mississauga)
- Tecumseh (Shawnee)
- Kateri Tekakwitha (Mohawk)
- Thanadelthur (Chipewyan)
- Thayendanegea/ Joseph Brant (Mohawk)

Louis Riel   Thayendanegea

(detail) William Berczy, Thayendanegea, (Joseph Brant), Acc.#5777, National Gallery of Canada, Ottawa

 Visit the *Canada Revisited 6* homepage for more information about the people in the lists on pages 232–235.

People Today

Aboriginal people contribute to all parts of Canadian culture. Many have had to overcome great disadvantages in their lives. **Discrimination**, poverty, and difficulty getting training or work have been barriers to success for many.

The people shown on pages 232–235 are known because of their talents, determination, courage, **sacrifice**, and dreams. They serve as examples and **role models** for young people. (These lists just give examples. Add names to your own lists of Aboriginal people who make a difference.)

Musicians

Some composers, performers, and conductors are

- Susan Aglukark (Inuit)
- John Kim Bell (Mohawk)
- Lee Cremo (Mi'kmaq)
- Barbara Croall
- Kashtin (Innu)
- Robbie Robertson (Jewish/Mohawk)
- Buffy Sainte-Marie (Plains Cree)
- Shania Twain (Ojibway)

Susan Aglukark received an Aboriginal Achievement award in 1994 and two Juno awards in 1995. She performs in Inuktitut and English, and is an active role model in her community.

Discrimination—being treated unfairly because of belonging to a certain group
Sacrifice—giving up something in order to accomplish something important
Role model—an adult who sets an example for young people of how to behave

Visual Artists

The works of many artists are found throughout this textbook. Their art shows their thoughts and feelings about their cultures. Some examples of painters, sculptors, printmakers, architects, photographers, and mixed-media artists are

- Kenojuak Ashevak (Inuit)
- Jackson Beardy (Cree)
- Douglas Cardinal (Metis)
- Fred Cattroll (Cree)
- Robert Davidson (Haida)
- Blake Debassige (Ojibway)
- Stanley R. Hill (Mohawk)
- Arnold Jacobs (Onondaga)
- Alex Janvier (Chipewyan)
- Joshim Kakegamic (Cree)
- George Littlechild (Cree)
- Jim Logan (Metis)
- Nokomis (Ojibway)
- Norval Morrisseau (Ojibway)
- Daphne Odjig (Ojibway)
- Pitseolak (Inuit)
- Jane Ash Poitras (Cree)
- Aoudla Pudlat (Inuit)
- Bill Reid (Haida)
- Joane Cardinal Schubert (Blackfoot/Metis)
- Allan Sapp (Cree)

The designer of the Museum of Civilization in Hull, Quebec, and many other public buildings is architect Douglas Cardinal. He is of Metis background.

Actors

Actors perform roles on television, stage, and film. In the past, many Aboriginal roles were performed by non-Aboriginal actors. This is no longer common. Some examples of Aboriginal actors are

- Tantoo Cardinal (Metis)
- Graham Greene (Oneida)
- Tom Jackson (Cree)
- Margo Kane (Cree)
- Tina Keeper (Cree)
- Cody Lightning (Cree)
- William Lightning (Cree)
- Annick Obomsawin (Abenaki)
- Jay Silverheels (Mohawk)
- Gordon Tootoosis (Cree)

Daphne Odjig was the first Aboriginal woman artist to be widely known in Canada and elsewhere. Her work has influenced many other painters.

Alex Janvier is an Alberta painter whose work has been displayed in art galleries in many parts of the world.

Tina Keeper and Tom Jackson are shown here hosting the 1998 National Aboriginal Achievement Awards. They have both performed in Canadian television series such as *Big Bear* and *North of 60*, as well as in movies. They are role models for younger performers because of their talent and determination.

Storytellers and Scholars

Storytellers create and perform stories for listeners. The list below includes storytellers who write books, make films, create plays, and write poetry. Some examples are

- Edward Benton-Banai (Ojibway)
- Maria Campbell (Metis)
- Gil Cardinal (Metis)
- Phyllis Cardinal (Cree)
- Beatrice Culleton-Mosionier
- Olive Dickason (Metis)
- Chief Dan George (Salish)
- Basil Johnson (Ojibway)
- Lenore Keeshig-Tobias (Ojibway)
- Michael Kusugak (Inuit)
- Alanis Obomsawin (Abenaki)
- Ruby Slipperjack (Ojibway)
- C. J. Taylor (Mohawk/Metis)

Athletes and Dancers

Both athletes and dancers develop their bodies' skill, strength, and co-ordination. Some examples of Aboriginal athletes and dancers are

- Ron Atcheynum (Plains Cree)
- Angela Chalmers (Metis)
- Alex Decoteau (Cree)
- Rene Highway (Cree)
- Waneek Horn-Miller (Mohawk)
- Tom Longboat (Onondaga)
- Alwyn Morris (Mohawk)
- Ted Nolan (Ojibway)

Political Activists and Legislators

Political activists are women and men who work to bring about political changes. They want changes in governments or laws. Legislators are people who are elected and work as part of a government to create or change laws. Some examples are

- Jack Anawak (Inuit)
- Ethel Blondin-Andrew (Dene)
- Matthew Coon Come (Cree)
- Tagak Curley (Inuit)
- Walter Dieter (Plains Cree)
- Mary Two-Axe Earley (Mohawk)
- George Erasmus (Dene)
- Phil Fontaine (Anishinabe)
- James Gladstone (Cree/Metis)
- Elijah Harper
- Roberta Jamieson (Mohawk)
- Rosemarie Kuptana (Inuit)
- Harry Laforme (Mississauga)
- Len Marchand (Okanagan)
- Ovide Mercredi (Cree)
- Zebedee Nungak (Inuit)
- Murray Sinclair (Ojibway)
- Ralph Steinhauer (Cree)

Phil Fontaine, National Chief of the Assembly of First Nations

Tom Longboat was a marathon runner born in 1887 on the Six Nations reserve near Brantford, Ontario. In 1998 he was chosen by *Maclean's* as Number 1 on their "Stars" list of the 100 Most Important Canadians in History. He is seen as one of the finest Canadian athletes ever. He is in Canada's Sports Hall of Fame.

Jack Anawak, a Cabinet Minister of the first government of Nunavut, checks into his office via satellite phone.

Students, use our web site to send us names of other people who are making a difference.

Aboriginal Media

Aboriginal newspapers, magazines, radio, television, and internet web sites are ways of passing on the culture. They help to keep languages and traditions alive. They show Aboriginal points of view. Some Aboriginal programs are found on national and local stations. The Canadian Broadcasting Corporation (CBC) North* Service has broadcast programs in First Nations languages and Inuktitut in the North for many years. The Aboriginal People's Television Network (APTN) is the first cable network in Canada with all-Aboriginal programs. APTN went on the air in 1999.

Aboriginal People's Television Network

Windspeaker is a monthly newspaper which is read across Canada. The *Aboriginal Voices* magazine is sold in both Canada and the United States. Other magazines and newsletters are created for local audiences. Web sites on Aboriginal subjects can be read around the world. Many First Nations have their own web pages.

Canada's National Aboriginal News Source

National Aboriginal Achievement Awards

Since 1994, achievement awards have been given each year by the Aboriginal community. They celebrate people who have taken on challenges and achieved successes in many areas. These people often put the needs of others ahead of their own. They have made great contributions to their communities and to Canada. Many of the people listed on the previous pages have received awards.**

Each year, between 12 and 14 awards are presented. Awards categories have included Architecture, Arts and Culture, Business and Commerce, Community Service, Environment, Education, Film and Television, Health Services, Heritage and Spirituality, Law and Justice, Medicine, Science and Technology, Sports, Public Service, Women's Rights, a Youth Recipient, and a Lifetime Achievement award. The categories can vary from year to year. More than one award can be given in a category. New categories are created if someone's contribution is unusual but important.

John Kim Bell is a musician, composer, and orchestra conductor. He is also a television producer, and a business person. He created the National Aboriginal Achievement Awards.

Aboriginal Associations and Institutions

Aboriginal people have created many organizations that help them achieve their goals by working together. A few examples are

- Assembly of First Nations
- First Nations Technical Institute
- Gabriel Dumont Institute
- Inuit Tapirisat
- Metis Settlements General Council
- National Association of Friendship Centres
- Native Canadian Centre of Toronto
- Native Women's Association of Canada

---

*CBC North web site is http://www.cbcnorth.cbc.ca/
**Recipients of each year's awards are listed on web pages. See http://www.westindies.cibc.com/aboriginal/98recipients.html

Economic Part of Culture Today

   Aboriginal people struggle to balance their traditional values and cultures with meeting their needs in life today. Their homes, food, clothing, and the ways they work to meet these needs reflect how they relate to their environment. Their technology has changed a great deal.

1. Some Inuit, First Nations, and Metis people still make a living trapping, hunting, and fishing. Many forest habitats have been logged or industries developed in them. They no longer support enough animals for people to make a living by trapping. Fewer markets for furs have also affected this traditional way of life.

2. Governments have put limits on fish catches. Today, there are fewer fish in the ocean and in many lakes and rivers than ever before. This has affected traditional ways of life based on fishing.

3. Most Aboriginal people use modern technology and materials and styles for clothing and housing. Traditional clothing may be used for ceremonies or special occasions. Clothing like mitts, moccasins, parkas, and mukluks are worn by most Canadians to keep warm. Modern-day homes of Aboriginal people are in different styles but still must suit the environment.

4. About one-fifth of Canada's Aboriginal people live in seven large Canadian cities.* For example, an estimated 16 100 live in Toronto. Winnipeg has the largest number, an estimated 45 750. Saskatoon has the highest percentage of their total population, 7.5%.

*Statistics on pages 236 and 237 are from Statistics Canada, 1996 Census, and from Basic Department Data, 1997, DIAND. For detailed information check these web sites: Statistics Canada at http://www/statcan.ca/Daily/English/980113/d980113.htm and DIAND Publications at www.inac.gc.ca

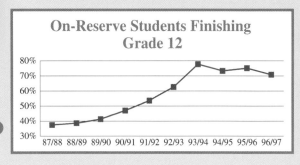

On-Reserve Students Finishing Grade 12

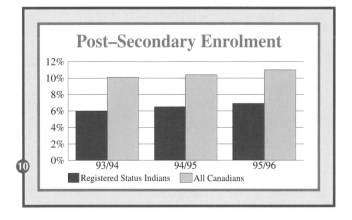

Post–Secondary Enrolment

⑤ Many Aboriginal groups worry about industries being developed on their lands. Oil, gas, mining, and hydroelectric projects are common on or near Aboriginal peoples' lands. Creating jobs is important, but so is preserving the environment. The land must be passed on to future generations.

⑥ Guiding and tourist camps use the knowledge and skills of people who live on the land. Bands are involved in a variety of businesses. Farming, ranching, processing fish, making furniture and clothing, and arts and crafts are examples.

⑦ Many reserves start their own businesses and develop their own natural resource industries rather than deal with outside companies.

Post-secondary—after high school; university, college, or technical school

⑧ Aboriginal people use many forms of transportation in making a living. Automobiles, snowmobiles, and airplanes are common. Airplanes are used for travel and transport in the vast spaces of the Canadian Shield and the Arctic. Canoes and snowshoes are used mainly for recreation today.

⑨ First Nations children on reserves are remaining in school longer. More finish high school. Native teachers and curricula have made a difference. Many go on to university and other training. Some return to their home communities, and others remain in the city.

⑩ There are Aboriginal people working in law, medicine, government, universities, the arts, entertainment, and most other fields.

Economic Issues

The **standard of living** on reserves varies a great deal. Some reserves are well-off and others very poor. When Aboriginal people move from a reserve to the city they may face economic challenges. Living comfortably in the city can be expensive. People with low incomes and those who are unemployed find it hard to live well. People may also face discrimination.

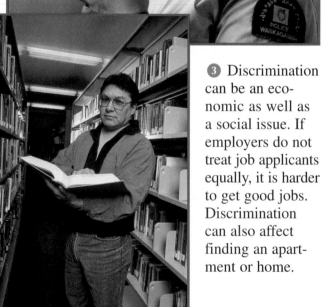

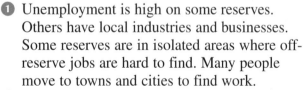

❸ Discrimination can be an economic as well as a social issue. If employers do not treat job applicants equally, it is harder to get good jobs. Discrimination can also affect finding an apartment or home.

❶ Unemployment is high on some reserves. Others have local industries and businesses. Some reserves are in isolated areas where off-reserve jobs are hard to find. Many people move to towns and cities to find work.

❷ Some people living on reserves, or in rural communities, run small businesses out of their homes. They sell their products to people both on and off the reserves.

❹ Even a good job may not last forever. Employers sometimes reduce staff, or businesses stop operating. When a person loses a job, finding another job can be difficult.

❺ Not all people complete their education when they are young. Adult education and evening classes help people return to school while working or raising families. Retraining or learning new skills helps people to get better jobs.

Standard of living—the cost of providing basic needs

Social Part of Culture Today

Having a sense of belonging and being loved are important psychological needs.

1. Many Aboriginal children learn knowledge, skills, customs, and beliefs of their traditional culture. They also learn the shared culture of Canada. It can be difficult for them to balance these values.

2. It is important for Aboriginal languages to be kept alive. Language is part of identity. It is the most important way of passing on culture. Some traditional ideas cannot be explained in other languages. Ideas may be lost or changed in another language.

3. Elders spend time with children to help pass on the culture. They teach traditional knowledge and share the wisdom they have gained in their lives. Learning traditional values helps develop a sense of identity. Sharing and generosity are still important values. If a family has enough for their needs they are encouraged to help others. Elders also are asked to advise leaders and councils when making decisions that affect the people and the land.

4. Recreation is an important part of health and social life. Speed, co-ordination, strength, and enjoyment can be practised in traditional games such as lacrosse and snowsnake, as well as modern games like hockey. Games help teach the important traditional value of co-operation.

5. Media such as radio, television, newspapers, magazines, and the internet help keep Aboriginal languages alive. They also build group identity. The media share news, ideas, and music that are of interest to their listeners, readers, and viewers.

Celebrations and Powwows

Aboriginal groups have a variety of gatherings that are important to their cultures. Some are sacred and cannot be attended by outsiders. These are part of the groups' spiritual practices. There may be a number of different festivals and events during the year.

Gatherings such as powwows are more public social events. Friends and outsiders may be invited to attend.

① Powwows today are important for passing on the culture. They help people keep a sense of group identity. People go to powwows to get together with relatives and friends they don't see often. Visiting, singing, dancing, drumming, games, and contests can be part of a powwow.

② Dancers may go to more than one powwow in the summer. Some powwows have dance competitions. Others don't allow them. Dancers of all ages wear specially-made clothing. It is based on traditional ceremonial clothing. A mixture of modern and traditional materials are used to create these outfits.

③ Metis traditional dancing is usually fast and exciting. Metis dancers do many kinds of jigs. Jigs use quick footwork to keep in time with the lively fiddle music.

Social Issues

Aboriginal people have not been treated well in Canada. As a result, there are many problems in Aboriginal communities today. You will learn more about the background of these problems in your Grade 7 and 8 history classes.

Social problems can occur in any group, not just among Aboriginal people. Family problems, drug and alcohol abuse, violence and other problems occur everywhere. Poverty makes these issues more difficult.

Aboriginal people balance belonging to their own culture with belonging to the general Canadian culture. Many have experienced discrimination. They have not been accepted for who they are. Many work to balance a sense of identity as Aboriginal people and Canadians.

❶ Close family ties are important in Aboriginal cultures. Many families have suffered from poverty and other problems. Earlier in this century, many families were divided when children were sent to residential schools. Children have been put in foster homes when their families had trouble coping with problems.

❷ When people move to a town or city from a rural area or a reserve, they may feel lonely and cut off from their community and culture. They are used to knowing everybody. They have always had relatives nearby and been involved in events. Friendship Centres provide meeting places for Aboriginal people living in an urban environment.

❸ Many Aboriginal people speak and understand more than one language. This street sign is in English, Cree, and French. Many Aboriginal languages are no longer being learned or used.

❹ Harmony with the environment and maintaining the balance of nature are still important values. Conflicts can arise with industries that threaten the environment. Hydroelectric dam projects, logging, mining, oil drilling, and tar sand development are often found in areas where many Aboriginal people live.

❺ Since European settlement, many Aboriginal people have converted to Christianity. Many stopped practising their traditional beliefs. Some people today combine both Aboriginal and Christian practices. Practices like the sweet-grass ceremony, the sweat lodge, the **potlatch**, and the sacred pipe ceremony are being used more often today than earlier in this century. Aboriginal people are recovering these traditions and passing them on to the next generation.

Potlatch—a large gathering to celebrate an event, at which the guests are given gifts; traditional among peoples of the Northwest Coast

Political Part of Culture Today

Government, laws, leadership, and security are group needs. Aboriginal people have held very little power to govern their own lives since European colonization. They have been governed by laws made by other governments. Their traditional leaders were not recognized. Groups had little control over their own security. They struggled to keep or to get back the lands they had once lived on and controlled.

During the last two decades of the 20th century, Aboriginal groups have worked to bring about changes. Across Canada, hundreds of demands are being brought to the government of Canada. Most have to do with self-government and **land claims**.

Aboriginal leaders have formed organizations so they can work together for change. The Assembly of First Nations is a national organization. It involves a Council of Elders. They offer guidance and advice to leaders and groups across the country.

Political Issues

Treaties

Treaties are official agreements between nations or groups. Before 1867, treaties were made between First Nations groups and the British government. Canada became a nation in 1867. After that, treaties were made between First Nations and the Canadian government.

- Not all groups in Canada have signed treaties with the government. Not all parts of Canada have been covered by treaties.
- In the past, under the terms of treaties, First Nations groups agreed to share the land with settlers in return for certain treaty benefits.
- Most Status Indians who have treaty rights also have membership in a First Nation. There are 608 First Nations in Canada.

Some examples of treaties include

- Robinson–Huron Treaty (1850)
- Robinson–Superior Treaty (1850)
- Treaty 8 (Alberta, 1899)
- Treaty 9 (Northern Ontario, 1905)
- James Bay and Northern Quebec Agreement (1975)

Treaty Rights

Treaty rights are what will be received by one group for giving up or sharing something else with the other group. Examples include land, money, goods, mineral rights, and hunting and fishing rights. Benefits could be received in a single payment, over a certain period, or forever.

John Lucas, *The Edmonton Journal*

Elder Jean Potskin holds sweetgrass for Elijah Harper, former MLA from Manitoba, to light at National Aboriginal Day celebrations in 1999. The Elder's family had signed Treaty 8 in Alberta one century earlier. The Treaty 8 lands were homelands to Cree, Chipewyan, and Beaver nations, and also many Metis communities. Because Metis people are not covered under the Indian Act, they were not included in the treaty and received no treaty benefits.

Reserves

Reserves are lands set aside for the use and benefit of First Nations people only. Reserves vary greatly in size. Ontario has many small reserves, whereas western provinces have fewer, larger ones. There were 2406 reserves in Canada in 1997. As land claims are settled, these numbers will change.

Land claim—proposal to a government from an Aboriginal group asking for the return of formerly occupied or controlled lands or payment for them

Self-government

Self-government is the power of the members of a group to govern the group. Self-government allows people to control their own affairs. In the past many decisions affecting Aboriginal groups were made by the government of Canada. Some were made by the provinces or territories.

Because of the Indian Act, First Nations governments had little power, except over local issues. Now groups are seeking more power to govern themselves. They wish to control their reserves and councils. They also want their own social, family, and medical services, schools, housing, laws, and police forces.

Services must be paid for. The First Nation government, the government of Canada, and the province or territory share the costs of services and responsibilities for them. Some First Nations have more income than others. They may get it from use of their land, natural resources, and local businesses. Some groups struggle with poverty and unemployment. Social problems often go with them. These are challenges they must find ways of meeting.

Band Councils

First Nations governments may be called band councils. They are made up of a chief and council. Councils are groups of men and women who are elected by the people of the band or First Nation to represent them. Council members and the chief make decisions affecting the people on the reserve they represent.

On reserves, band councils control monies taken in and how they are spent. Responsibilities include housing, education, health care, recreation, and local laws for the community. Challenges occur as the people attempt to keep their identity and meet their needs in the modern world.

Land Claims

Land claims are issues about the ownership of land on which Aboriginal people originally lived or that they controlled. Some Aboriginal lands were given up under treaties. Vast areas of Canada were never covered under treaties. Aboriginal peoples were often displaced by settlement or natural resource development.

The media often focus on land claims. Between 1993 and 1997, the Canadian government settled 67 claims, involving 85 First Nations. Total payment amounted to $342 million. Approximately 482 000 hectares of land were made into reserves.

In some regions no treaty was ever signed with the government. Other land claims involved settlements to meet treaty promises that a past government did not keep. Federal, provincial, territorial, and Aboriginal governments are involved in land claims. These disputes can take decades to settle. Not everyone agrees with the decisions.

The Metis people struggled to get their own homeland for many decades without success. In Alberta in 1938, twelve Metis settlements were established.

Pages 244 and 245 look at two examples of land claims. The Nisga'a claim for land was originally made in the nineteenth century. The Inuit government and territory of Nunavut were created April 1, 1999. There are hundreds of other negotiations for self-government and land claims under way. More arise each year.

Nunavut

On April 1, 1999, Nunavut was officially created as a new political region of Canada. It was the largest land-claim agreement in Canadian history. It covers one-fifth of the land area of Canada. (See map at the back of this textbook.) Under the agreement, Nunavut was formed. Nunavut means "Our Land" in Inuktitut. The agreement included land, mineral rights, financial payments, and self-government.

The Inuit people elected their first all-Aboriginal government.

After 30 years of political activity by Inuit leaders like Tagak Curley, the Inuit of the Eastern Arctic reached an agreement with the government of Canada.

The Legislature has 19 elected members. It operates under a consensus form of government. The first Premier is an Inuit lawyer, Paul Okalik.

Capital	Iqaluit (formerly Frobisher Bay)
Population	27 219 (85% Inuit)
Languages	Inuktitut/English

The town of Iqaluit is the new capital of Nunavut.

The Nisga'a Treaty

Treaties were never signed for the lands occupied by First Nations in mainland British Columbia while the province was being settled by Canadians, Europeans, and Americans. The Nisga'a chiefs from the Nass Valley in northwestern British Columbia asked the government in 1887 for title to their land. They wished to legally claim the lands they had always lived on (see map on page 45). They wanted to prevent settlers from moving onto their lands. However, they were not given reserve lands.

Over the years, the Nisga'a continued to press the government for an agreement. They got few results. They sent a petition to the British government in 1913. Finally, in 1969, they began a court case against the British Columbia government.

After a long process, a settlement was reached in 1999. Land, monies, and some powers of self-government were given to the Nisga'a First Nation. In return, the Nisga'a gave up title to much of the land they had originally controlled.

The Honourable Jane Stewart, Minister of Indian Affairs and Northern Development, looks on as a Nisga'a drummer celebrates the signing of the treaty in 1999.

The Metis

Some Metis people live on the land or in separate communities called Metis Settlements. Others live in small towns where they make up the majority of people. However, most Metis people live scattered among the general population of towns and cities.

It is difficult for the Metis people to preserve their unique culture, which developed in the days of the fur trade. After the fur trade became less important, many Metis people lost their employment. Political events in Western Canada in the nineteenth century resulted in economic and social hardship for them. (You will learn more of their history in Grade 8.)

Organizations such as the Metis National Council and provincial organizations are one way Metis people work together to achieve their goals and maintain their culture.

Metis people are working to recover their traditional culture. The lists of Aboriginal people who make a difference (pages 232–235) contain many names of Metis people. Research and teaching of Metis history is one of the features of the Gabriel Dumont Institute in Saskatchewan. It is the first Metis-run college in Canada.

Complete the list of contributions and the projects you started on page 227.

Chapter 12
Exploration Today

O v e r v i e w
Use this Overview to predict the events of this chapter.

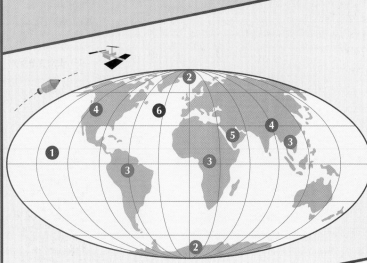

Note: The above numbers are referred to later in this chapter.

Of Planet Earth
1. The Earth's Oceans
2. The Polar Regions (North Pole and South Pole)
3. Tropical Forests
4. Mountains
5. Hot Deserts
6. Below the Earth's Crust

Into the Solar System

 Competition: The First Era of Space Exploration

 Co-operation: The Second Era of Space Exploration

Exploration Today

Defined

Exploration means seeking places new to you and looking for new knowledge of places that are known.

Reasons

Exploring the unknown is part of human culture, based on meeting physical, psychological, and group needs. Exploration involves
- seeking challenge and adventure
- expanding knowledge
- discovering new places
- seeking power and control
- obtaining wealth and resources
- countries competing against each other

Explorers Past and Present

"One small step for man . . . one giant leap for mankind." These words were spoken by Neil Armstrong, the first person to walk on the surface of the moon. The date was July 20, 1969. Events such as this do not just happen by chance. They are the final result of many years of hard work. Today, we strive to increase our knowledge of other worlds—worlds beyond the planet Earth. We seek to settle new lands, establish trade, and control the development of new nations to come.

The oceans and lands of planet Earth represented the mysterious unknown for early explorers. Now only the extremes of Earth remain to be explored—the deepest seas ❶, coldest polar ice ❷, thickest forests ❸, highest mountains ❹, hottest deserts ❺, and deep beneath the surface of the earth ❻. Outer space represents unknown territory for astronauts and scientists. The reasons for exploring territory that is unknown to us are much the same today as in the times of the Aboriginal peoples or in the Age of Exploration.

Chapter 12 Focus

In Chapters 6 to 10 you studied European exploration of planet Earth. Our emphasis was on Canada's east coast and the lands along inland waterways that lead to the east coast. This final chapter in the book will look at human exploration in the late 20th and into the 21st century:
- on planet Earth
- into the solar system

These two areas are shown on the map on page 246.

The chapter will look at the following concepts. The emphasis is on the concepts of technology and exploration.

Environmental Interaction   Balance   Technology   Cultural Contact   Exploration

Vocabulary

challenge	co-operation
extreme	international
competition	astronaut
aquanaut	

Chapter Preview

Examine the map on the previous page. In which two areas is exploration still going on today? Make a web to show these areas.

Chapter Activity

1. In pairs or triads, brainstorm and record challenges that have been faced by explorers of planet Earth. Include the challenges faced by Aboriginal peoples as well as the early Europeans. Share these with your classmates.

2. Solve the following problem by using the information in this chapter and what you know about modern-day space exploration.* Problem: What challenges do modern-day space explorers have and how do they overcome these challenges?

3. Compare challenges faced by the early explorers of Canada with those faced by space explorers today. Use a chart similar to the following. Add to it as needed.

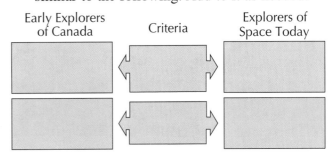

Early Explorers of Canada   Criteria   Explorers of Space Today

4. Review the definition of exploration and reasons for exploration on pages 120 and 121. Create a Venn diagram showing the ways early exploration and exploration today are the same and different. (See page 258 for information about Venn diagrams.)

Timeline 4

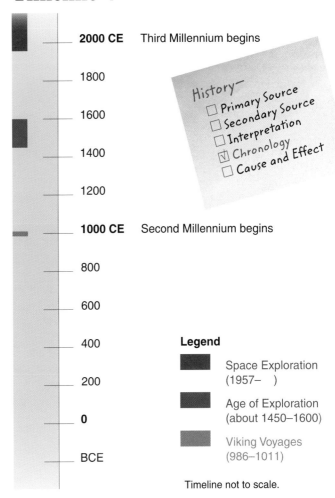

2000 CE	Third Millennium begins
1800	
1600	
1400	
1200	
1000 CE	Second Millennium begins
800	
600	
400	
200	
0	
BCE	

History—
☐ Primary Source
☐ Secondary Source
☐ Interpretation
☑ Chronology
☐ Cause and Effect

Legend

Space Exploration (1957–)

Age of Exploration (about 1450–1600)

Viking Voyages (986–1011)

Timeline not to scale.

Humankind is entering the third millennium of the Common Era (CE). People are still curious about the unknown and wish to explore.

---

*When recording information on space exploration include facts only, not fiction that you've seen or read in movies, TV, or books.

Of Planet Earth

 Human exploration of planet Earth is continuous. Even after we have seen and lived in a place we study it to understand it more deeply. Scientists are now studying the most **extreme** places on Earth. Humans cannot live in these places without technology to protect and help them. It will be important to understand how life survives in extreme places if human life on earth is threatened by changes in climate.

The Earth's Oceans

Many have called the oceans our final **frontier**. Humans have explored all Earth's land areas, but we know little about the depths of the oceans. Early diving expeditions often explored wrecked ships. They were usually looking for buried treasure. The first official scientific expedition to explore the ocean's bottom was carried out by divers on the *Challenger*, a British ship, in 1872.

Over the years, diving vehicles and equipment became more advanced. With each advance in technology, divers were able to explore deeper than before. Scientists learned how to overcome challenges such as deep-water pressure and cold. Inventions such as the aqualung helped provide divers with a supply of air underwater.

Great amounts of knowledge have been gathered about the lands and life forms at the bottom of the oceans. Scientists and aquanauts such as Jacques-Yves Cousteau have done a great deal to further our knowledge of deep-sea diving and what lies beneath the ocean's waters.

Modern-day research submarines carry out hundreds of scientific experiments. Universities and naval research groups from many of the world's countries are also exploring the oceans. Most of the money required to pay for research expeditions comes from foundations. Foundations carry out activities that benefit humankind. Individuals and businesses give money to foundations to help the search for new knowledge that may have economic or social value.

The research submarine Alvin is being lowered into the Pacific Ocean from the deck of the Atlantis to study the ocean's floor. The water pressure is too great for humans to be outside the submarine even in protective clothing. Robotics are used to take samples.

Exploring Further

1. Carry out research to find out more about under-water expeditions. Some areas to explore are
   - scientific expeditions
     Check the internet: some key words are

undersea	oceanographic
deep sea	exploration
marine	research

     Check the National Geographic Society's homepage (www.nationalgeographic.com) for modern day expeditions.
   - contributions and work done by underwater pioneers such as Jacques-Yves Cousteau
   - shipwrecks such as the Titanic (1912 collision with an iceberg), pirate ships (especially in the Caribbean), merchant ships in the Mediterranean
   - shipwrecks in the Great Lakes

Extreme—farthest away from the moderate range; extraordinary
Frontier—at the boundary of known or settled lands

The Earth's Land Areas

Polar Regions

Explorers searched for the Northwest Passage without success in the 1500s and 1600s. Eventually many expeditions were made to the Northern Arctic in the 1800s. (See ❷ on the map on page 246.) Scientists were interested in mapping these northern lands and studying the rocks, climate, and wildlife. The first recorded trip to the North Pole was made in 1909 by Robert Peary, an American Navy officer. He was guided by four Inuit men: Oogueah, Ootah, Egingwah, and Seegloo.

Roald Amundsen, four companions, and 52 dogs made the trek to the South Pole, arriving December 14, 1911.

Explorers competed to see who would be the first to reach the South Pole. (See ❷ on page 246.) The honour went to the team of Norwegian explorer Roald Amundsen in 1911. Robert Scott of the British navy arrived at the South Pole shortly after Amundsen.

Mapping and the collection of scientific data in the Arctic and Antarctica continues today.

Tropical Rain Forests

The world's rainforests are rapidly being cut down or destroyed. The most damaging deforestation is taking place in the Amazon rainforest. (See ❸ in South America on the map on page 246.) Scientists estimate that as many as five million kinds of plants and animals may live in the world's rainforests. This is 50% to 80% of all the living things on earth. This storehouse of plants and animals can be used for human benefit. Valuable medicines can be made to treat diseases. Food production could be improved to feed the world's people.

When the rainforests are destroyed the possible benefits of the plants and animals are lost to the world's peoples. There is an impact on the world's climate as well. Many scientists are doing research in the world's rainforests in case they change or disappear.

Mountains

Most of the Earth's mountains are in such remote areas that few people have visited them. (See ❹ on page 246.) Very few of them have been climbed.

Today individuals and groups continue to climb high mountains. Some do it for the challenge, others to carry out scientific experiments.

"I feel no great elation at first, just relief and a sense of wonder. Then I turn to Tenzing and shake his hand . . . . He throws his arms around my shoulders, and we thump each other, and there is very little we can say or need to say."

—Sir Edmund Hillary
National Geographic Society

In 1953, New Zealand's Edmund Hillary and his guide Tenzing Norgay reached the top of Mount Everest, the world's highest mountain.

Deserts

Scientists continue to do research in the hot deserts of the Earth. (See ❺ on page 246.) About one-third of the Earth's surface consists of arid (dry) or semi-arid conditions.

The deserts contain valuable minerals and vast supplies of oil. Scientists are also concerned about understanding the effects of climatic changes on the desert. During the 1990s, hundreds of thousands of kilometres of good agricultural land each year were lost because of the expansion of deserts.

Into the Solar System

Competition: The First Era of Space Exploration

 Space exploration in the early years focused first on the challenge of whether humans could successfully put an artificial satellite into orbit. Later the United States and what was then the Soviet Union competed to be the first to send human beings into space. The desire to discover and visit new worlds beyond ours and the search for adventure were part of this quest.

In 1957 Sputnik I, the first artificial satellite, was launched by the Soviet Union.* The event started a "space race" between the Soviet Union and the United States. Each challenged the other for "firsts." The USA sent up Explorer I in 1958. The Soviet Union was also the first to send a human into space—Yuri Gargarin in 1961. Alan Shepard was the first American into space later that year. In 1962, John Glenn became the first American to orbit the Earth.

In 1961, President Kennedy challenged Americans with "landing a man on the moon and returning him safely to the Earth" before the end of the 1960s. In 1969, Neil Armstrong and Edwin Aldrin landed a lunar module on the moon. Millions

"That's one small step for man . . . one giant leap for mankind."

—Neil Armstrong

The lunar landing mission was carried out with Apollo II.

of people around the world watched the live TV coverage of this historic event. The two astronauts walked on the surface of the moon, planted the American flag, and collected rock samples and moon dust. Many believed that being first to land on the moon gave the Americans control of space.

The American flag was planted on the moon in 1969.

*Not all space launches are included on this page—only major milestones in history.

Valentina Tereshkova, of the Soviet Union, was the first woman in space. In 1963, the Soviet cosmonaut orbited the Earth 45 times.

Results of the Space Race

The space race brought power, importance, and knowledge to the winners in the early years. Space exploration continued. Space stations were built, the space shuttle invented, and materials found in space were examined. The competition also provided humankind with new technology:

- satellites to monitor weather, the ozone layer, and the environment
- satellites to observe military actions of other countries (spy satellites)
- satellites to map the world
- telecommunications satellites to provide instant/live global communications for TV, news events, the internet, fax, and telephones
- satellites to gather data on the solar system
- scientific equipment to study larger planets in our solar system to see if they will support human life. Telescopes in space, such as the Hubble Space Telescope, photograph and collect data in space. They send the information to scientists on Earth for further study.
- special tracking systems such as Global Positioning Systems (GPS) aid pilots, sailors and soldiers, and shipments of goods
- special space clothing (spacesuits) to use in extreme conditions
- food and drink (freeze-dried or dehydrated) to use in extreme conditions

Today space exploration is done by many countries and thousands of individuals and businesses.

Co-operation: The Second Era of Space Exploration

  Competition in space is being replaced by co-operation among many of the world's countries. The goals are much the same. Explorers wish to go farther, stay longer, and learn more about space. Sixteen nations are building the International Space Station under the leadership of the United States. The space station will consist of a giant science laboratory in space that will orbit the Earth. Scientists

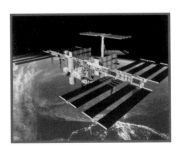

from many nations will live and work in this station. Experiments will focus on how the space program can benefit the people of planet Earth. The station will carry out medical research and research on technology.

Roberta Bondar is Canada's first woman astronaut. She is only one of many astronauts from

other countries who have participated in missions launched by the United States. Technology developed by other countries, such as Canada's robot arm, has also been used on American space missions.

Space exploration is very costly. In the early years it was paid for by the governments of the countries who controlled the program. Space exploration in the future may be paid for and controlled by private businesses.

After his second trip in space, astronaut John Glenn said, " . . . we are only at the beginning of our space quest . . . there is so much more to explore and to learn . . ."

For Your Notebook

1. a) What reasons are given for space exploration?
   b) In what ways are they the same as reasons given for European exploration of planet Earth?
   c) In what ways are they different?
2. Do you expect to see space colonization within your lifetime? Why or why not?

Challenges

Space exploration has had a variety of challenges. As humans explore farther into space, more will arise. These will be met just as the Aboriginal peoples and the European explorers met their challenges.*

❶ Rockets were first invented by the Chinese in ancient times. Modern rocket technology was developed to meet the challenge of the pull of gravity. An object must travel 40 200 kilometres per hour to escape Earth's gravity. Saturn V, shown above, is the largest rocket ever built. This three-stage rocket was designed, tested, and built by NASA in the United States.** It was used to launch the spacecraft Apollo to the moon.

❷ Using rockets to send satellites and probes into space was very costly. The space shuttle was invented to reduce these costs. The shuttle returns to Earth like an airplane, so the shuttle and the equipment that launches it may be used over and over.

❸ Space travel involves immense distances. Therefore, humans must be able to live in space for long periods of time. Space stations are being built as places for astronauts and scientists to live and work. The costs of building space stations are huge. Many people from many countries are working together on these projects. They also exchange with each other what they learn about space.

❹ Scientists carefully monitor the astronauts to study the effects of long and short periods of space travel on the human body. Many of their discoveries are being used back on Earth, for example, in health care. Space travel affects many parts of the body, such as bones, muscles, and bodily fluids. Weightlessness results in space motion sickness. These are new problems to be solved. In 1962, John Glenn was the first American to orbit the Earth. In 1998, Glenn once again went into space. Comparisons with his first trip gave scientists information about aging and space travel. (John Glenn is shown at the top centre of the group photo on page 251.)

*See timeline page 247.
**NASA stands for National Aeronautics and Space Administration. The web site for the Kennedy Space Center is http://www.ksc.nasa.gov/

5 Specially-designed clothing is needed to survive in space. Space suits contain an antenna for communication and a portable life-support system with oxygen and cooling controls.

6 Specialized vehicles have been designed. The Soviet-built *lunokhod* was controlled from Earth by remote control. The Mars Pathfinder and the robot microrover Sojourner have been used to move about on the surface of planets and moons. The Canadarm shown in the photo, is a robotic arm that is controlled from within the space shuttle. Specialized equipment is used to gather and send back information to Earth. Some examples are television cameras, robots, probes, and scientific instruments.

7 Living conditions in space are a special challenge, especially on long voyages. Weight and space restrictions on spacecraft are a special concern. There is little room for belongings. Weightlessness is also a problem. Specially packaged freeze-dried and dehydrated (water removed) foods have been developed because they take up less room. Other concerns relate to using the toilet, receiving enough oxygen, disposing of body wastes, keeping clean, sleeping, exercising, and having fun while in space.

8 Rocks and minerals found on planets and moons have value for science. They can give information about the Earth's history. Many explorers hope to return with discoveries such as diamonds, gold, or minerals that are rare on Earth.

9 Making space travel safer is a challenge. Humans cannot survive in space without protection and technical support. Exploration of unknown areas has always been dangerous. Liftoff and return to Earth are the most dangerous parts of space travel. The first experiments on the effects of weightlessness and survival in space involved mice, rats, chimpanzees, dogs, plants, and insects. Spacecraft with no crews such as space probes and landers record images of objects in space. They carry out scientific research. They have provided us with vast amounts of knowledge about the solar system. The new knowledge is applied to future space travel and often to life on Earth as well.

In Conclusion

A Review Activity

Creating a Bulletin Board

Your study of Canadian history has been divided into three sections: The First Nations, European Exploration, and Today and Tomorrow. While working with these topics, you have been using five social studies concepts: environmental interaction, balance, technology, cultural contact, and exploration. To review what you have learned, work with your classmates to create a Canadian history bulletin board display.

 As a class, discuss what elements might create a meaningful and appealing bulletin board display. Discuss self-assessment criteria. Keep these ideas in mind as you prepare your part of the display.

Part 1: Prepare to Share

Environmental Interaction   Balance   Technology   Cultural Contact   Exploration

1. Break into groups of three to five students. Each group will be assigned one of the five concepts.

2. Brainstorm for examples from Canadian history that relate to your concept. Think about people, places, events, and ideas. Use the questions that follow as a guide. Write down as many examples as you can. Look through your notebook and the textbook to add to your list of examples.

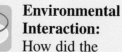

Environmental Interaction: How did the environment influence the ways of life of Aboriginal peoples? How did they interact with and change the environment?

Balance: How did Aboriginal people maintain harmony with nature? How did they respect all living things? In what ways did the coming of Europeans change the balance that existed between Aboriginal people and the environment?

Technology: How did the technology used by Aboriginal people affect their way of life? How did the search for new resources affect European exploration? How did new technology affect the European voyages of exploration?

When explorers enter an area new to them, what effects may their technology have on the environment and the people living there?

Cultural Contact: What contacts did Aboriginal peoples make with other Aboriginal peoples? How did the cultural contact affect their ways of life?

What contacts were made between Aboriginal cultures and European cultures?

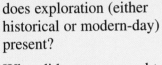

Exploration: What changes occurred as a result of European exploration? Were these changes positive or negative? How is modern-day exploration the same as (and different from) European exploration during the Age of Exploration? What challenges does exploration (either historical or modern-day) present?

What did a person need to become an explorer in the Age of Exploration? Consider background, education, personality, and behaviour.

Do present-day explorers share these characteristics? Are they different in any ways?

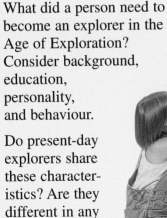

Part 2: Plan with Your Concept Group

1. Brainstorm with your group for effective ways to present these ideas on the bulletin board. Record your ideas.
2. Decide which examples of the concept you wish to display. Who will create the visual/written representation for each example?
3. Decide what materials are needed. Plan a layout. Where will items be placed and how much space is available?
4. Set completion deadlines. When will you assemble all the parts on the bulletin board? How much time will be needed to do so?

Part 3: Create Your Display

1. With your concept group, discuss how each example on your display represents your concept. Include a title and a drawing of your concept.
2. Decide how you will explain your display to the class. Practise presenting and answering questions.

Part 4: Present Your Concept

1. Tell your classmates about your display.

Part 5: Connect the Concepts

1. 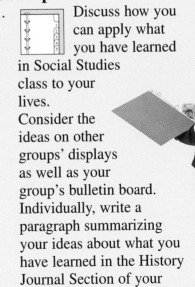 Discuss how you can apply what you have learned in Social Studies class to your lives. Consider the ideas on other groups' displays as well as your group's bulletin board. Individually, write a paragraph summarizing your ideas about what you have learned in the History Journal Section of your notebook.

Appendix

Learning How to Learn

(SKIMM™)

On the following pages you will find a variety of ideas to help you with your assignments. Use these organizers as sample formats. Add to them or delete as needed.

Brainstorming

Brainstorming is a strategy for coming up with as many ideas about a topic as possible. After the ideas have been listed, you can choose the best one(s).

Suggestions for Brainstorming

1. Write down all ideas. Do not evaluate or criticize ideas as they are mentioned.
2. Quickly add ideas to the list. Don't reflect whether the idea is "good" or not. Unusual and fun ideas should be added to your list.
3. Sometimes thinking about one idea leads to another. Add to, subtract from, join, and change ideas to come up with new ones. The more you have, the better.
4. Reflect about your ideas and choose the best.

Cause and Effect

A cause is something that makes an event or situation occur. The event or situation then leads to other effects (results).

Use a diagram similar to the one below to show cause and effect.

Cause → Event → Effect(s)

Concept Poster

Concept posters are a fun way to learn, remember new information, and share what you've learned with your classmates. Concept posters may be done individually, in pairs, or as a small group. A concept poster is more than a visual display. To create one, follow these steps:

Steps for Creating a Concept Poster

Step 1:
1. Review information about the concept in your textbook and your notebook.
2. List examples of the concept (historical, current, and possible future examples).
3. Brainstorm to decide what the examples have in common. Look for patterns, links, and connections.

Step 2: Plan and create a presentation to represent your ideas and examples about the concept. You could include any of the following: picture (photo, drawing, map, or diagram), skit or tableau, music/song/sound effects, words (spoken or on paper), objects/models.

Step 3: Present your concept poster to your classmates. You may either tell them what concept you are presenting or have them guess.

NOTE: Registered™ 1996 Arnold Publishing Ltd. SKIMM™ (Skills, Models, and Methods) Learning How to Learn—the techniques of assigning questions/activities written in a textbook or digital presentation and referring users to an appendix or glossary (print or digital) for suggestions on how to carry it out—has been registered as a trademark by Arnold Publishing Ltd. All copy used in SKIMM™

(Learning How to Learn), including the icons, is protected by copyright. © 1996, 1998, 1999 Arnold Publishing Ltd.

 An expansion of SKIMM™ (Learning How to Learn) is available on the Arnold Publishing internet site.

Charts and Graphic Organizers

Charts are also referred to as diagrams, tables, or graphs. They are used as a quick way to organize and record information.

Retrieval Charts

Title		
Criteria	A	B

List items or criteria you are describing.

Record important information as it relates to the criteria.

Flow Chart

Flow charts are diagrams of ideas in sequence (order). Flow charts can show classification, relationships, possibilities, or choices.

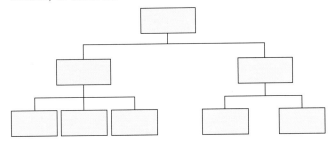

Steps for Classifying

Classification is a commonly used thinking tool. To classify, you gather together ideas, events, or items and arrange them into groups that have common characteristics. Each of us thinks differently, so there are many ways to classify information. The flow chart above shows one way to do this. (Look at the flow chart sideways or upside down to see other ways to use it.)

1. Randomly list items or examples.
2. Identify and label groups (categories) based on their characteristics.
3. Sort into groups based on similarities.
4. (optional) Record information on a graphic organizer.

Comparison Chart

This thinking tool is used to show how something is similar to and different from something else.

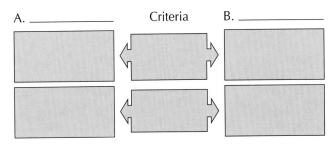

Another style of chart used for comparison is the Venn diagram shown on page 258.

Steps for Comparing

1. Identify what you are comparing.
2. Identify what criteria you are going to use in comparing. The number of criteria will vary depending upon what you are comparing.
3. Show how the items you are comparing are the same and how they are different, based on the criteria you identified.

Example

Step 1: Identify what you are comparing.

A. Woodland Cree   HOMES   B. Wendat

Step 2: Identify what criteria you are going to use in comparing.

Step 3: Show how the items you are comparing are the same and how they are different, based on the criteria you identified.

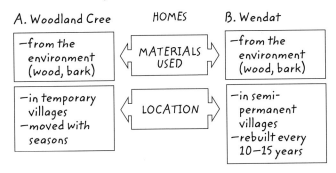

Charts and Graphic Organizers (continued)

Venn Diagram

Topic: _____

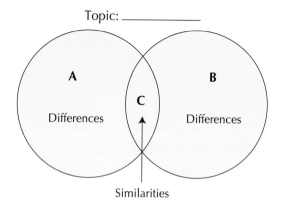

A
Differences

C

B
Differences

Similarities

Steps for Using a Venn Diagram
1. Identify the topic. Then, identify what two people, places, objects, or ideas (subjects A and B) you are comparing.
2. Identify (and keep in your mind) what criteria you are going to use to show differences. In circle A write words or descriptions about subject A, according to the criteria you selected. Do the same for subject B in circle B.
3. In the central space C, randomly list ways in which A and B are the same.

Fishbone

The fishbone chart is a method of note making. Each of the "large bones" is a main idea related to the title. The "smaller bones" are details (sub-ideas) relating to the topic. Increase or decrease the number of main ideas and sub-ideas as needed.

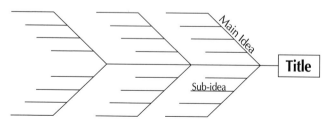

Main Idea

Sub-idea

Title

Issue—a problem or question for debate. An issue is often written as a question that uses the word "should." There is often not a definite answer to an issue. Refer to page 259 under Decision-making for more information about issues.

Critical Thinking

Not everyone thinks the same way as you do. Everyone has a point of view or viewpoint. Different people and people from different cultures have different ideas, beliefs, priorities, goals, and ways of doing things. They have different customs and traditions. Thus they have different ideas of what they think is important. When thinking critically, you are examining ideas, situations, and statements. You are trying to "step out" of your point of view to look at the situation or **issue** from the perspective of another person or persons.

Steps for Critical Thinking

Step 1: Identify the issue and examine the information you already have about this issue.

Step 2: Identify the various people who will have different points of view on the issue.

Step 3: Try "stepping out" of your own point of view and thinking about what one or more of the other people might think about this issue. It might help to ask yourself these questions.
• Why does a person think the way she/he does?
• Why does a person think his or her way is best?

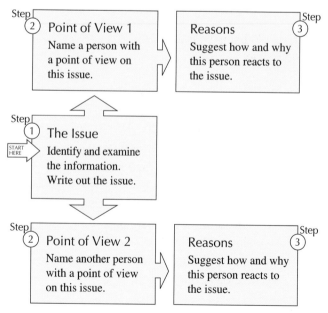

Step 2 — Point of View 1 — Name a person with a point of view on this issue.

Step 3 — Reasons — Suggest how and why this person reacts to the issue.

Step 1 — The Issue — Identify and examine the information. Write out the issue. START HERE

Step 2 — Point of View 2 — Name another person with a point of view on this issue.

Step 3 — Reasons — Suggest how and why this person reacts to the issue.

The above chart may include as many points of view as needed.

Decision-making

Decision-making is a process used to resolve an issue. Issues are a problem or question for debate. They are often written as a question using the word "should." For example, Should students be allowed to wear whatever they like to school? There is often not a definite answer to an issue. A person must choose from several alternatives. As a result, opinions and emotions are often involved.

Steps for Decision-making

Step 1: Decide: What is the issue to be solved?

Step 2: Brainstorm for alternatives (choices).

Step 3: Analyse the alternatives. List the consequences (results) of each. That is, list the pros and the cons.

Step 4: Decide what options are best. Try to select the alternative(s) with the most positive and the fewest negative results. Organize the alternatives in rank order, from the most desirable to the least desirable.

Step 5: What is your decision? Choose the "best" alternative.

Step 6: Evaluate your results. Ask yourself this:
• Was this a fair and effective decision? Why?
• What difficulties are expected from this decision?
• What benefits are expected from this decision?
• Faced with the same issue again, would I change my decision? Why?
• What changes or improvements might be made to this method of decision-making?

Decision-making Chart

Issue: _____ Step①_____		
Alternatives	Consequences	Priorities
1.	+	Step④
	−	
2. Step②	+ Step③	
	−	
3.	+	Decision Step⑤
	−	Evaluation Step⑥

Example

Issue: Should students be allowed to wear whatever they like to school?		
Alternatives	Consequences	Priorities
1. Wear whatever they like	+ kids have choices (happy) + no special school clothing; cheaper for parents	Most preferred #3
	− some wear inappropriate clothes, spoil it for others	#1
2. School dress code with restrictions	+ students learn how to be appropriate for future life	
	− kids have 2 sets of clothes— some kids better dressed than others − kids have no choices (unhappy)	#2 Least preferred
3. Moderate guidelines and casual Friday	+ kids able to express themselves sometimes + teachers and students feel they compromised and have choices	Decision #3 Compromise; less restricted but with guidelines
	− kids have 2 sets of clothes	Evaluation

Problem Solving

A problem is a difficult question that requires you to consider a number of possible solutions in order to choose the best. For certain kinds of problems (e.g., a math problem), there is one correct answer. However, there are many problems in life that have more than one solution.

Problems ask: Who? What? Where?
When? Why? How?

Steps for Problem Solving

Step 1: Define the problem. Decide what you want to find out.

Step 2: Come up with possible questions and a hypothesis to guide your research. (A hypothesis is a rough guess about the solution, based on what you know.)

Step 3: Do research to locate data (information) that relates to your hypothesis.

Step 4: Record the data (information) that relates to your hypothesis.

Step 5: Evaluate the information you have collected by thinking about whether it supports or disagrees with your hypothesis.

Step 6: Arrive at a conclusion by choosing what you think is the best solution—one that makes sense and solves the problem. Think about whether your conclusion agrees or disagrees with your hypothesis.

Step 7: Share your conclusion.

Problem Solving Retrieval Chart

Problem Step 1	
Hypothesis Step 2	
Research Solution	**Data**
1.	
2. Steps 3 4	
3.	
4.	

I think #_____ is the best solution because

Steps 5 6 7

Example

Problem: This year the school can't provide money for a class field trip.	
Hypothesis: If we want to go, we will need to get the money ourselves.	
Research Solution	**Data**
1. Earn it individually	— do chores — sell old toys — collect recyclables
2. Earn it as a class	— bottle drive — class garage sale — car wash
3. Get it from our parents	— some not able to go — it's for us and parents shouldn't have to pay for it
4. Not go on a trip	— saves on costs — miss out on interesting opportunity

I think #2 is the best solution because:
Everyone can help fundraise so we will earn more money and then everyone can go together.

Notebook Organization

Your notebook is your record of the material you have studied. It is intended to make your work easier to manage. Your notes need to be easy to use and study from. One method of organizing your notes in four sections is outlined on page 3: Activities, WordBook, History Journal, Learning How to Learn. Your teacher might tell you which categories to use, since she/he is familiar with what you will study. Often, one section for each chapter is used.

Suggestions for Organizing your Notes

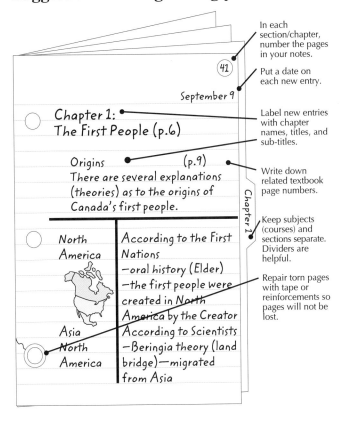

In each section/chapter, number the pages in your notes.

Put a date on each new entry.

Label new entries with chapter names, titles, and sub-titles.

Write down related textbook page numbers.

Keep subjects (courses) and sections separate. Dividers are helpful.

Repair torn pages with tape or reinforcements so pages will not be lost.

More Ideas

- Create a table of contents for each section and chapter.
- Keep the pages in order. Add new information to the back of your old notes.
- Compare your notebook with that of a partner to check for items that are missing or out of order.
- Use colours to underline, highlight, illustrate, and code your notes. Colours help us to learn material.
- Keep your notes neat and readable.

Note Making
T-Notes

T-Notes combine written notes and drawings. Use the format at the top of column two, or design your own.

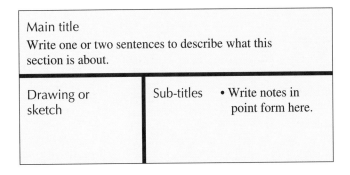

Main title Write one or two sentences to describe what this section is about.		
Drawing or sketch	Sub-titles	• Write notes in point form here.

Webs

A web is a graphic organizer that is used to generate ideas (brainstorming), illustrate ideas (using words and/or drawings), and link ideas. Coloured drawings may be added to webs to aid memory.

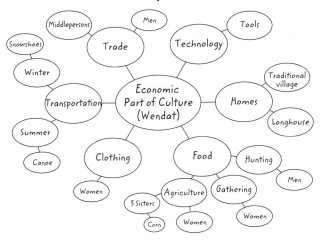

Mind Maps

Mind maps work much like webs. Each idea is placed on a separate line. Each word or idea must be joined by a line to at least one other word or idea. Coloured sketches and pictures are often used to represent words or ideas. They help us remember.

The mind map shown below is based upon ideas and concepts covered in Section I.

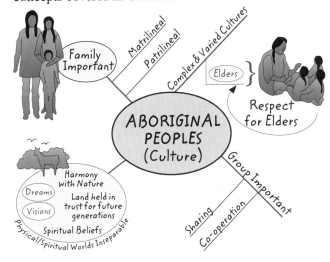

Presentations

In this book, presentation refers to communicating information in visual, oral, or written forms. To prepare and carry out a presentation, follow these steps:

Step 1: First, select one main topic or idea as a focus for your presentation. Everything you do must be related to or provide examples of this main idea.

Step 2: Select a method of presentation from the list that follows. Find out from your teacher or the library how you are to make or prepare it. For example, if you are making a diorama you first have to find out what it is and how to make it.

Step 3: Read about your topic or idea in the textbook. Review any information you have about it in your research notes.

Step 4: Plan on paper how you are going to prepare the presentation you selected. Establish criteria for how to assess your presentation.

Step 5: Prepare the presentation on the topic or idea you selected.

Step 6: Present your topic or idea to your classmates. Assess your presentation based on the criteria from Step 4.

Some Presentation Ideas

advertisement	cooking demonstration
banner	dance
booklet	debate
cartoon	demonstration
charades	diagram
chart	diorama
collage	display
collection	drawing
comic strip	exhibition
concept poster	fact file
construction	fairy tale

flow chart	play
game	poem
graph	poster
illustrated poem	project triangle
interview	puppet show
job description	puzzle
letter	questionnaire
magazine	radio show
map	rap
mask	riddles
mime	role-play/drama
mobile	scrapbook
model	scroll
mosaic	sculpture
multimedia presentation	skit
mural	slide/tape show
music	song
newspaper	speech
newspaper article	story
oral report	survey
painting	tableau
pamphlet	talk show
panel discussion	television show
papier-mâché	timeline (illustrated)
photo album	top 10 list
photographs	web page
picture	written report

Action Plan

1. Date of Presentation ....

2. Describe what you want your part of the presentation to look like and/or sound like.

   ....
   ....
   ....

3. Plan on paper what tasks have to be done. Assign a completion date for each task.

	Task	Completion Date	Done
1.	_____	_____	_____
2.	_____	_____	_____
3.	_____	_____	_____

(add to this list as needed)

Challenge yourself to complete a variety of presentations. Check the Arnold Publishing web site at **http://www.arnold.ca/** for information about completing presentations.

Vocabulary

Start a section in your notebook called WordBook. Record in it any new words you want to remember. Two strategies for recording vocabulary follow:

Spider Definition

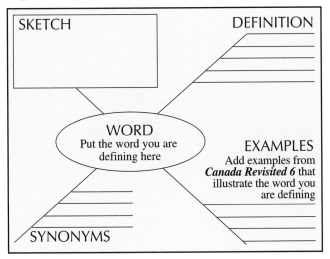

SKETCH

DEFINITION

WORD
Put the word you are defining here

EXAMPLES
Add examples from *Canada Revisited 6* that illustrate the word you are defining

SYNONYMS

Word Chart

Word Write the new vocabulary term here.		Picture Draw a simple sketch to help you remember the meaning. Colour this sketch. You are not expected to create something artistic and no one will see this drawing unless you want them to.
Meaning Write out the meaning in your own words. Use the information in the textbook, in the glossary, or from a dictionary to help you understand the meaning.	Example Write out examples from *Canada Revisited 6* to show how the word is used.	

Self-Assessment

When you evaluate your own work or performance to decide how well you have met the expectations of the activity, you do self-assessment. Check your own work against the ideas in Steps for Self-Assessment, at the top of the next column. Working with a partner, get him/her to also check your work, and you check his or her work. The goal is for both of you to improve the quality of your work.

Steps for Self-Assessment

1. Review the expectations for the assignment. Did you do what you were supposed to do?
2. List the criteria you will use to assess your assignment.
   Content Do you have a variety of ideas? Did you cover the topic? Did you support your ideas with details? Did you use examples, charts, drawings, and maps (if applicable)? Have you checked the facts in several sources?
   Structure Is your work presented in a way that is easy to follow? Did you use the correct form (e.g., survey, letter, biography, newspaper article)?
   Mechanics Are spelling, punctuation, capitalization, and grammar correct?
   Appearance Is your work neat? Can others read your writing? Does it have a title page?
3. Decide what you have to do to achieve Level 4 (highest rating) for each of the criteria. What would earn Level 3 (next highest rating) for each of the criteria? What would earn a Level 2? A Level 1?
4. Keep the criteria and rating descriptions in mind as you complete your assignment.
5. You may use the sample assessment format shown below. Change the criteria and descriptions to fit the assignment.

Self-Assessment

Criteria
(Expectations to be decided by the teacher, the student, or both.)
   1. _____
   2. _____
   3. _____
   4. _____
   5. _____

Personal Assessment   Level 1 2 3 4
(Circle one based on above criteria)

Reasons for circling the number I did:_____

Next time, I would _____

This is what I learned about the way I think and work: _____
_____
_____

Assessment by Teacher   Level 1 2 3 4
(Circle one based on above criteria)

Reasons for circling the number I did:_____
_____

Writing

There are many types of writing. The form in which you write could include any of those described briefly on these two pages, or others. Your purpose for writing might include telling, persuading, explaining, reporting, describing. Think about your purpose and your audience so you can choose the most effective form and words. Challenge yourself by writing in a variety of forms.

Storytelling

There are many ways to tell a story about an incident or series of events. Stories may include your personal thoughts, feelings, and ideas. They are often meant to entertain.

1. **Biography**
   - Written account of someone's life
   - Includes information and events from the person's life so the reader can "get to know that person"
   - Will require research
   - An autobiography is a biography told by the person him/herself

2. **Diary or Journal**
   - Personal account (description) of daily activities and experiences
   - Each entry begins with the date
   - Includes thoughts, ideas, feelings

3. **Friendly Letter**
   - Tells about events/information of interest to the person who will receive the letter
   - Can also ask questions, congratulate, comment on events, tell entertaining stories
   - Intended for someone you know (e.g., friend)
   - Format includes writer's return address, the date, a greeting, and a closing

4. **Hard News Story**
   - Describes a current event of importance to the reader
   - Answers who, what, where, when, why, and how
   - Factual but may include quotations that express opinions

5. **Historical Story**
   - Story based on historical fact (e.g., people, places, events) but may contain fictional parts (e.g., invented characters)
   - Requires research about people, events, and setting (description of place at the time)
   - See also Short Story (#7)

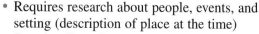

6. **Play**
   - A story presented as a dramatic performance
   - Includes title, character and setting description, lines to be spoken by actors, direction about costumes, set/stage design, actions and expressions of the actors

7. **Short Story**
   - Includes title, description of characters and setting, conflict (problem)
   - Series of incidents or events take place as characters try to resolve conflicts
   - Climax or point of highest interest comes when the problem is solved. (Note: Problem may be solved in a positive or negative way.)
   - Conclusion

Persuading

Persuasive writing is intended to convince your reader to accept your point of view. Take care to use appropriate language and visuals. Hurting or insulting people will not change their viewpoints.

8. **Advertisement**
   - Announcement or written notice for the public
   - Provides information that is meant to persuade people to act in a certain way (e.g., buy a product, vote for a candidate)
   - Words and pictures should catch people's attention

9. **Brochure/Pamphlet/Flyer**
   - Usually a small booklet or folded sheet providing details (written and visual) that highlight the most appealing features of a place, person, event, idea

10. **Editorial**
    - An article (short essay) found in most newspapers that expresses an opinion on behalf of the newspaper about a current event or issue in the news
    - Includes facts that support a point of view and strengthen an argument

11. **Letter to the Editor**
    - Written to a newspaper to express opinions about current events or issues
    - Includes facts that support a point of view and strengthen a position
    - May contain emotional and descriptive words

12. **Political Cartoon**
    - A drawing meant to express an opinion about political issues or people (e.g., politicians, public)
    - Many visual clues (e.g., symbols) work together with the words to give a message

13. **Review or Critique**
    - An evaluation or judgement of a product or performance (e.g., play, movie, artwork, CD, book)
    - Gives information that supports the writer's claims and opinions
    - Can include emotional and descriptive words

14. **Speech**
    - May serve many different purposes (e.g., entertaining, paying tribute, congratulating); often intended to persuade or convince (e.g., campaign speech)
    - Intended to be spoken to an audience
    - Words should be appropriate for the audience and the situation
    - Planning and practising out loud are needed. Volume, expression, pace, posture, and gestures give added meaning and impact to the words
    - Point-form notes (cue cards) may be used when presenting but should not be read

Explaining

This type of writing helps the reader understand how to do something and how/why something works as it does.

15. **Instructions/Manual/Directions**
    - Provide a step-by-step order
    - Use clear language that is easy to follow
    - Use special terms that relate to the topic and suit the audience (e.g., sifting is a suitable term in a recipe)

Reporting

Reports use knowledge gathered from a variety of sources and provide factual information.

16. **Census**
    - A specific count of the people living in an area
    - Might include information about ages, jobs, education, and religion

17. **News Report**
    - See Hard News Story (#4)

18. **Magazine/Newspaper Feature Article**
    - Provides information about people, places, and events that are of interest to the readers
    - Usually requires an interview or other research
    - Includes visuals

19. **Research Report**
    - Provides detailed information on a specific topic or issue (see Research Model on pages x–xi)
    - Can be presented in a number of ways (see Presentations on page 262)

20. **Survey/Poll/Questionnaire**
    - An investigation about a situation or issue
    - Includes clear, specific questions intended for a certain group
    - Poll should allow for responses that are easily recorded and counted (e.g., Yes/No responses)
    - Results may be presented in graphs, charts, tables, or paragraphs
    - Polls should avoid bias. Choose a large, random sample rather then just people you expect to answer a certain way.

21. **Interview**
    - Meant to gather information from a person
    - Questions should help to gather factual information and details about the person's ideas and opinions
    - May be a "live" interview or recorded and presented in written, taped/visual forms (with the person's permission)

Describing

Describing can be a part of almost any form of writing.
- Includes details that appeal to the senses (sight, hearing, smell, taste, touch, and balance). These help the reader become involved in the subject.
- Make careful word choices that are suitable to the form of writing (e.g., an instruction manual may need different descriptive detail than a brochure about a tropical resort).

Glossary

A

Adapt—to change in order to be able to meet basic needs better

Advertising—written or visual information used to persuade people to do something

Adze—a tool for shaping wood

Agility—the ability to move quickly and easily

Alliance—an agreement between nations or groups that benefits those in the union

Ancestor—a person from whom one is descended

Anishinabe—the name that the Ojibway people call themselves; also used in the Creation story to refer to the Original People of the Ojibway

Archaeology—the science of studying the history of people from ancient times through the remains they have left, including sites and artifacts

Artifact—an object or other evidence of human life in ancient times, such as a spearhead or a digging tool

Astrolabe—an instrument for calculating latitude position from the angle of the sun or stars

Authentic—genuine; proved to be what it seems to be

Awl—tool for punching holes in leather

B

Balance—having equal importance; for example, the relationship between humans and nature needs to remain in balance, with respect for all life

Band—an independent group of related families of First Nations people who lived and travelled together; a specific group identified under the Indian Act, usually on a reserve

Bay—a small body of water that extends into the land from a larger body like an ocean or sea

BCE—Before the Common Era; the same as BC (identifies dates after an agreed-on date)

Beliefs—what a person considers to be true. Spiritual beliefs may include a sense of the meaning of life, the sacredness of all things, belief in a Creator. Beliefs are part of psychological needs.

Beringia Theory—the belief that the First Peoples living in North, Central, and South America migrated from Asia over the Beringia land bridge during an Ice Age

Bias—showing a preference, making it difficult to judge something fairly

Big game—large animals such as moose, deer, caribou, or bear that are hunted

Breechcloth—pieces of material hanging from the waist in front and back

Brigade—a group of canoes carrying trade goods and supplies

British North America Act—1867 Act of the Parliament of Great Britain which created the nation of Canada

C

Caravel—a sea-going ship developed by Europeans that used the lateen sail and a moveable rudder to make the ship safer and easier to steer

Case study—a detailed example that shows how a theory applies to a real-life situation

CE—Common Era; the same as AD (identifies dates before an agreed-on date)

Ceremonial—formal, showing respect

Charter—written permission from a king or queen

Chronology—events related over time, when they happened and the order in which they happened

Civil—having to do with peace, order, and good government of citizens and their concerns

Clan—all of the people related by kinship or marriage to a common ancestor

Climate—the weather of a place, over a long period; includes temperature, precipitation, and seasonal changes

Colonization—one country bringing another region under its direct control; one method was through creating permanent settlements in the new region

Colonize—to create settlements in a new land in order to control the land and trade in the region

Common Era—CE, equivalent to AD; dates after an agreed-on date

Communal—activity done by a group and the products shared by everyone

Community circle—all of the members of a community have a place in the circle; children, women, men, Elders, sacred people, ceremony leaders

Competition—trying to do better than someone else

Conclusion—an answer or statement based on facts used as evidence

Confederacy—a union between groups, usually political; an alliance

Confiscate—to seize or take away; to claim in the name of the government

Coniferous—trees with cones and needles; most species are evergreen

Consensus—agreement; no decision is taken until all members of a group agree

Constitution Act—the Act (law) passed by the Canadian Parliament in 1982 that defined the country of Canada, the form of its governments, its official languages, and the rights of its citizens, including the Aboriginal peoples. The Act replaced the British North America (BNA) Act of 1867, which had created the nation of Canada

Contagious—easily spread from one person to another

Contemporary—the present time period

Controversy—a debate or disagreement

Convert—to change people's beliefs to one's own

Co-operative—working together as a group

Co-ordination—ability to do more than one thing at the same time

Council—representatives meeting to discuss problems and make decisions for a group

Counselling—when a person with wisdom or special training talks to someone to help with a problem

Coureur de bois—"runner of the woods"; French woodsman who travelled to the interior to trade for furs

Courting—getting to know someone with the intention of marrying

Cove—a small, sheltered bay

Creation Theory—the belief of many First Peoples and others that their ancestors were made by the Creator and placed on the Earth

Criteria—standards by which something is judged or put into categories

Critical thinking—examining several points of view about an idea or event

Cultural contact—the interaction between groups of people when they come into contact and exchange ideas and technology; conflict may arise when groups have different ideas and wish to change or control the other group

Culture—a learned way of life shared by a group of people, including their shared knowledge, beliefs, attitudes, customs, traditions, laws, and roles

Custom—the usual way of doing things

D

Data—facts that can be used for drawing a conclusion

Deciduous—broad-leafed trees that shed their leaves in autumn

Deforestation—cutting down or burning the natural forests of a place

Demand—want or need for goods or services

Descent—coming down through the generations from a certain ancestor

Dialect—a variation of a language, with some different vocabulary, which can be understood by people who speak other dialects of the same language

Diplomacy—skill in dealing with others; skill in managing negotiations between people or nations

Discover—to find or understand something for the first time

Discrimination—being rejected or mistreated because of belonging to a minority group; for example, racial discrimination

Displaced—moved from a place against one's will

E

Economic—having to do with meeting basic needs; earning or finding the necessities of life

Economic Part of Culture—the part of culture that deals with meeting people's physical needs and wants (for example, food, shelter)

Ecosystem— a community of living organisms, each one depending in some way on the others

Elder—an older person who is considered by an Aboriginal community to be wise and who is greatly respected

Entrepreneur—a business person who invests in a business, hoping for a profit but risking a loss

Environment—all the natural elements in one's surroundings: the landforms, water, air, vegetation, and animal life

Epidemic—disease quickly spreading among many people

Evaluate—to assess what something is worth; to decide what is best or important; to criticize, rate, defend, or grade

Excavate—to uncover by digging

Expedition—people sent on a journey for a special purpose

Exploration—when individuals or cultures seek new lands or new routes to lands they know; exploration may be for profit, adventure, control of territory, or scientific curiosity

Extended family—a family with three or more generations living together; includes cousins, uncles and aunts, grandparents, and great-grandparents, as well as parents and brothers and sisters

F

Fast—to not eat or drink

Fertile—rich soil, able to grow crops

First Nation—a group that identifies itself as having been a nation living in Canada at the time Europeans came; a nation is a group of people with a shared language, territory, way of life, and government.

Flint—a hard stone used to start fires by making a spark

Frontier—at the boundary of known or settled lands

G

Game—animals and birds that are hunted for food

Gatherers—a lifestyle based on collecting many natural resources from the environment for food, medicines, clothing, making tools, and building homes. All First Nations cultures gathered useful materials from the environment, as well as hunted and fished.

Generation—all the people born about the same time

Generalization—a statement that covers many specific examples

Geographer—someone who studies the earth and human beings' relationships with the earth

Geography—the study of the earth and the relationships between the earth and human beings

Grandmother (or Grandfather)—a term of respect for anyone of an older generation, whether or not related

Grassland—flat or rolling plains covered with grasses and small plants

Grid—lines across and lines up and down on a map or chart used to calculate the exact location of a place

Group (social) needs—the human need to live in groups, and the need of groups to sustain themselves; the need for group laws and security, leadership, and organization

H

Habitat—the environment where a plant or animal naturally lives

Habitation—a place to live

Harbour—a sheltered area of deep water where ships may dock to load and unload

Hearth—a firepit or fireplace

Hereditary—inherited; received from a relative

Historian—someone who studies the past through recorded sources; they may be printed, oral, or pictorial

History—the study of events from the past

Hypothesis—a rough guess about the solution to a problem based on what you know

I, J

Identity—a sense of who you are; a sense of self, often based partly on belonging to a group

Interaction—affecting each other

Interconnectedness—all things being related and dependent on each other; interdependent

Interpreter—someone who understands or explains the meaning of messages that are unclear or in a different language

Investor—someone who puts money into a company or project in return for a share of profits expected to be made

Isolated—separated or kept apart

Issue—a problem or question for debate; often written using the word "should." There is often no definite answer to an issue.

K

Kinship—having some of the same ancestors or being related by marriage

L

Land claim—negotiations between an Aboriginal group and a government to establish legal ownership of land, or payment for lands their ancestors once controlled

Landform—a natural feature of the earth, such as plains, hills, mountains

Language families—languages that are similar because they developed from the same original source

Lateen sail—a moveable triangular sail used on Arab sailing vessels that was adapted for use on European ships

Latitude—one's north–south position (distance north or south of the equator)

League—an old unit of measuring distance, about 5 km

Longitude—one's east–west position (distance east or west of 0°, which runs through Greenwich, England)

M

Majority—the largest group in a total population

Market—an environment or place where trade, buying, and selling take place

Mast—the long vertical wooden pole used to support a ship's sails

Matriarch—the oldest woman or the woman who is respected as the head of an extended family

Matrilineal—tracing descent through the mother's side of the family

Meditate—to think quietly and deeply, without interruption

Metis—persons with one First Nations parent and one (usually) European parent, or their descendants. The Metis way of life is a mixture of First Nations and European cultures.

Middleperson—a trader who acquires goods to trade them to a third party rather than to use

Migrating—moving from one place to another in search of a food supply or because of changing seasons; migratory

Millennium—one thousand years

Minority—smaller group, less than half of a total population

Missionaries—people who bring their religious beliefs to people who do not share them

Mixed forest—a forest with both deciduous and coniferous trees

Monopoly—a right granted for one person or group to control buying and selling

Mortar and pestle—a strong, cup-shaped container and a stone or post used to pound substances to powder

Muskeg—boggy land in a forested region; spongy, water-logged moss and other vegetation

N

Nation—people who live in a certain area, speak the same language, have the same way of life, have the same system of decision-making (government), and usually belong to the same group

Natural resources—(also called raw materials) materials found in the environment that are useful to people; for example, fish, animals, vegetation (trees, plants), and minerals (stone, metal ore)

Navigation—calculating the position of a ship and steering it along a route

Navigator—the person who navigates the ship, also called the pilot

Needs—basic human requirements for survival

Non-Status Indians—people who have First Nations ancestors but are not registered under the terms of the Indian Act

North Star—a bright star always found directly above the North Pole, used to determine direction; also called the Pole Star or Polaris.

Nuclear family—a wife and husband, or a single parent, and children

Nutrients—food in the soil to grow plants

O

Ojibway—one of the Algonquian-speaking peoples, also known as the Anishinabe; Ojibway can be spelled different ways, including Ojibwa, Ojibwe, and Chippewa

Oolichan—a small, very oily fish used for food and oil

Oral tradition—knowledge passed down from one generation to another through speaking and listening

Organism—a living body

Origin—beginning; where someone or something comes from

P, Q

Palisade—a wall or fence surrounding a group of buildings, often used for protection

Paraphrase—to express the meaning of a piece of writing in different words

Partnership—co-operating and working together for a shared goal

Patrilineal—tracing descent through the father's side of the family

Perspective—point of view; what one person thinks about something

Pestilence—plague; a serious disease that was usually fatal

Physical needs—needs that must be met to sustain life, including food, water, clothing, shelter, and physical activity

Plains—flat to rolling landform region, often at low levels

Plateau—a high but fairly level area found between or near mountain ranges

Policy—a chosen plan of action that guides future decisions

Political—having to do with government

Portage—to walk and carry the canoe past rapids or waterfalls in a river or from one lake to another

Potlatch—a large gathering to celebrate an event, at which the guests are given gifts; traditional among Northwest Coastal peoples

Post-secondary education—after high school; university, college, or technical school

Precipitation—moisture that falls in the form of rain, hail, sleet, or snow

Pre-Contact—usually refers to the period before Aboriginal people met any Europeans or used their technology; contact happened sooner for groups nearer to the oceans.

Prediction—a statement about what is expected to happen in the future

Preserve—to dry, smoke, or otherwise change something so it can be stored without rotting

Primary source—a written, visual, or audio account of an event by someone who saw or heard the event or lived during the time of the event; historical evidence from the time

Problem—a question or issue to be answered

Profit—when income is greater than expense in a business

Prospects—an advantage or market that is expected or hoped for

Prow—the front part of a boat

Psychological needs—needs related to the mind, including emotional, intellectual, and spiritual needs; needs for family, identity, support, comfort, love, acceptance, personal security, customs and traditions, communication, rest, leisure, challenges, and a sense of accomplishment

Puberty—the time when a child reaches the onset of sexual maturity, with the physical changes that accompany it

Purify—to make clean; to wash away dirt or evil

R

Raid—a sudden attack by a group for the purpose of stealing from another group

Rainforest—an ecosystem with huge trees and many species of plant life, produced by year-round rainfall and a mild climate

Raw material—a natural resource; something that is useful to people

Rawhide—animal hide that has been dried but not tanned

Recommendation—a suggestion that one favours

Re-enactment—to show a past event again, using actors

Region—a large area of the earth's surface with similar characteristics

Religious order—a group of people who live under a set of religious rules that govern their lives; members are usually either nuns or monks

Replica—an exact copy

Responsibility—something one is expected to do

Representative—a person chosen to act or speak for others

Reserves—lands set aside for the use and benefit of a First Nation

Role—a part played in life

Role model—an adult who sets an example for young people of how to behave

Rudder—a hinged, flat piece of wood used for steering a ship or boat

S

Sacred—holy; having high spiritual value and given great respect

Sacrifice—giving up something in order to accomplish something important

Sagas—long oral poems telling the stories of Viking history, which were passed down as oral tradition

Sapling—a young, flexible tree

Scurvy—a disease common among sailors who did not eat enough vitamin C, which is found in fruits and vegetables

Seasonal camp—a place where a group of people live together for a season, then move

Seasonal cycle—changes in weather and the environment or activities that occur every year at a certain time

Secondary source—information resources created after the time period being studied; often created using primary sources for research or reference

Self-reliance—the ability to look after oneself and make one's own decisions

Semi-permanent—lasting a long time but not forever

Sinew—tough, strong fibres that connect muscle to bone; bison sinew was used by people who lived on the Plains to make strong thread or cord

Site—a location; an archaeological site is a location where evidence of human activity in ancient times has been found, such as the remains of a village or a burial mound

Social—having to do with people's relationships with each other within a group or community

Social occasion—a time when people meet as a group to celebrate or visit

Spawning—fish laying eggs to reproduce

Specific—a single example with particular qualities

Spiritual beliefs—what is considered to be true about the spirit world; may include belief in a Creator

Spiritual practices—activities or ceremonies in which a person honours or addresses the spirit world

Sponsor—to support an activity with money or a guarantee of financial backing

Standard of living—amount of income available to pay for basic needs

Statistics—information in number form, often displayed in charts and graphs

Status—rank, social position

Status Indian—a person with First Nations ancestors who is legally registered under the Indian Act, and holds a registration number and card

Storyboard—a combination of image, text, and instructions (usually created as a series) to show and tell how a subject will be presented in some other medium such as video

Strait—a narrow waterway connecting two larger bodies of water

Supply—goods and services that are available for use

Support—to give strength or help to something or someone

Surplus—more than what is needed for existence

Sustain—to keep going, endure, support

Symbol—something that represents something else

Symbolize—to stand for, represent

T

Tableau—participants represent a scene by taking positions and not moving; tableaux can be based on a picture, story, or idea

Tactics—skills and ideas used in planning the fighting of wars or battles

Tan—to make animal hides soft and strong for making clothing

Technology—using science to change raw materials for practical purposes; includes new skills, ideas, and tools for making life easier and more comfortable

Teepee—moveable dwelling made of hides sewn together over a framework of poles

Theory—an idea about something; an explanation

Thunderbird—the Spirit of the Thunder

Timeline—a way of displaying events in the order they occurred

Trade—exchanging goods for other goods or money

Trading network—travel routes and contacts with many groups used to trade surplus resources and goods for others that are needed

Tradition—customs, beliefs, and stories handed down from one generation to the next

Traditional—believing in the old ways; following customs handed down for a long time

Travois—a wheel-less cart pulled by dogs or horses

Treaty—an official agreement between nations or groups

Treaty Indian—a First Nations person whose ancestors signed a treaty with the government of Canada and who is registered under the Indian Act

Treaty rights—what will be received by one group for giving up or sharing something else with another group, according to the terms of a treaty; for example, land, money, goods, mineral rights, hunting and fishing rights. Benefits could be in a single payment, over a certain period, or forever.

Trickster—a figure in stories that has the powers of both good and bad spirits. Tricksters have the power to change into any living or non-living thing. Different cultures have different names for the Trickster.

Tumpline—a broad leather strap worn across the forehead, with long lines to wrap around a bundle for carrying loads on the back

Tundra—the treeless cold desert; vegetation is low to the ground and not plentiful, mainly lichens, mosses, and low-growing plants and shrubs

U, V, W, X, Y, Z

Unique—the only one of something; not like others

Values—opinions about what is good or right or how things ought to be

Vegetation—the plants that grow naturally in a place

Vulnerable—sensitive, easily hurt or damaged

Wampum—white and purple shell beads woven into strings or belts and used as memory-aids by record-keepers

Weir—a fence built across a stream to trap fish

West Indies—the islands of the Caribbean Sea

Windigo—a frightening spirit in stories of the Algonquian-speaking peoples

Picture Credits

The publisher gratefully acknowledges the assistance of the various public institutions, private firms, and individuals who provided material for use in this book. Every effort has been made to identify and credit all sources. The publisher would appreciate notification of any omissions or errors so that they may be corrected.

CTC—Canadian Tourism Commission
DH—Darren Hanson
FC—Fred Cattroll
NAC—National Archives of Canada
NMM—NATIONAL MARITIME MUSEUM
PA—Phyllis A. Arnold
SVA—Shary von Arx

Legend

t	top
tl	top left
tc	top center
tr	top right
m	middle
ml	middle left
mc	middle center
mr	middle right
b	bottom
bl	bottom left
bc	bottom center
br	bottom right

9 Courtesy UBC Museum of Anthropology, Vancouver, Canada. Bill Reid/*Raven and the First Men*/#Nb1.481 **20** tl c PA; tr © CTC **21** tl tr © CTC; mr SVA **27** Courtesy of Provincial Museum of Alberta. © Photographer: PA **28** tl Carl Fontaine/© Arnold Publishing Ltd.; bc Neg./Transparency no. 5697(2) (Photo by Lynton Gardiner) Courtesy Department of Library Services, American Museum of Natural History **31** *The East Coast*, graphic design & illustration: Claire Tremblay (scientific design by J. Therrien & E. Lacoursiére) 1992 © SODART/CARfac © Collective **33** tl SVA; tr bl ml © CTC; mr br PA **38** tr SVA; mr mc ml PA; br bc © CTC **39** tr mr br PA; bc bl © CTC **40** tr DH; mr b PA; ml SVA **41** Illustrations by Jan Sovak, © Jan Sovak **42** Illustrations by Jan Sovak, © Jan Sovak **43** Illustrations and Drawings by Gordon Miller **45** tc PA; tr Corel Corporation, Ottawa, Ontario, Canada (This publication includes images from *Corel Gallery 2* which are protected by the copyright laws of the U.S., Canada, and elsewhere. Used under license.) **46** *Bella Coola Village*, painting by Gordon Miller; **47** tr ml Reproduced with permission of Lewis Parker and Gerald Lazare/National Wildlife Federation; bl Drawings by Gordon Miller; **48** br PA; bl *Potlatch*, painting by Gordon Miller; **52** © Lewis Parker **53** DH **55** Courtesy of J.C. Hill Elementary School **56** br Drawing by Gordon Miller; bl McCord Museum of Canadian History, Montreal **57 to 60** Provided by permission of Huronia Museum and Huron-Ouendat Village, 549 Little Lake Park, Midland, Ontario, L4R 4P4, (705)526-2844, www.georgianbaytourism.on.ca, e-mail:hmchin@bconnex.net (photography by PA) **64** br based on Charles William Jefferys/ NAC/C-070307 **66** tr based

on C-009892/ National Library of Canada/ Bibliothèque nationale du Canada; mr (detail) Thomas Wesley McLean/NAC/C-069766; bl Samuel de Champlain, from *Voyages et Descouvertes (1619)*, National Library of Canada; tl Drawing by Gordon Miller **68** tl (detail) #III-G-873, Reproduced by permission of the Canadian Museum of Civilization; tr Drawing by Gordon Miller; br Illustration by Gordon Miller **71** mr (detail) Charles William Jefferys/NAC/C-069786; ml Courtesy of Arnold Jacobs **74** Reproduced with permission of Lewis Parker and Gerald Lazare/ Sainte-Marie among the Hurons Historical Site **77** Reproduced with permission of Lewis Parker and Gerald Lazare/Sainte-Marie among the Hurons Historical Site **78** (detail) Charles William Jefferys/ NAC/C-069114 **84** tl Reproduced with permission of Lewis Parker and Gerald Lazare/National Wildlife Federation; bl Reproduced with permission of Lewis Parker and Gerald Lazare/Sainte-Marie among the Hurons Historical Site **85** PA **86** West Point Museum Collection, United States Military Academy **90** Illustration by Jan Sovak, © Jan Sovak **91** tr (detail) Thomas Wesley McLean/NAC/C-069766; br ml Drawing by Gordon Miller **92** Illustrations by Gordon Miller **93** *Woodland Indians in Camp*, Frederick Verner, Glenbow, Calgary, Canada (56.27.9) **94** Courtesy of Norval Morrisseau and Coghlan Art **95** mr © '99 Daniel Beatty Pawis; ml © Richard Masuskapoe **96** br Duval House Publishing; ml (detail) Charles William Jefferys/NAC/C-069786 **100** © FC **104** Paul Kane (Canadian 1810–1871), *Indian Encampment of Lake Huron* (c.1845–50), Art Gallery of Ontario, Toronto, Purchase, 1932 Acc. no. 2121 **105** (detail) Charles William Jefferys/NAC/C-073528 **107** br Illustration by Jan Sovak, © Jan Sovak; bl 970.1.S17. 4.Vol.3, pg 63. Toronto Reference Library; c PA **108** Courtesy of Norval Morrisseau and Coghlan Art **109** tr Courtesy of Norval Morrisseau and Coghlan Art; mr Blake Debassige, *Bear Feeding* 1975, acrylic on canvas, 76.5 x 76.5 cm, Purchase 1975, McMichael Canadian Art Collection, 1975.40.4; bl © Richard Masuskapoe **114** NAC/C-098232 **120** mr © NMM, London **122** tr Courtesy Hong Kong Tourist Association (HKTA); br Express Newspapers/Archive Photos; bl PA **125** AP/Wide World Photos **126** PETER BIANCHI/ NGS Image Collection **129** JORGEN MELDGAARD/NGS Image Collection **130** t Beinecke Rare Book and Manuscript Library, Yale University; m EMORY KRISTOF/NGS Image Collection **131** EMORY KRISTOF/NGS Image Collection **132** t Photo: Parks Canada/Shane Kelly/1996 **133** tl tr Photo: Parks Canada/ Shane Kelly/1996; br bl Photo: Parks Canada/Shane Kelly/1998 **134** tr bl ml Photo: Parks Canada/ Shane Kelly/1996; mr br Photo: Parks Canada/Shane Kelly/1998 **138** tr By Permission of the British Library, G8185/LVIII; mr *Unloading Oriental Wares at Venice*, Lewis Parker, from *Bold Ventures* **139** PA **140** br (detail) Thomas Wesley McLean/NAC/C-069711; bc © Nordbok International, Gothenburg, Sweden **141** tc © Nordbok International, Gothenburg, Sweden; br Ted Curtin for Plimoth Plantation, Box 1620, Plymouth, MA 02362 mc bc © NMM, London; **142** tc mr © NMM, London; ml Pierre Descellier/ NAC/NMC 40461 **143** Archive Photos **146** tl Carlo Carlevaro/ Archive Photos; tr Photograph by Charles Best from THE VOYAGES OF CHRISTOPHER COLUMBUS by John D. Clare, copyright © 1992 by Random Century Publishing Group Limited, reproduced by permission of Harcourt Inc. **147** Photograph by Charles Best from THE VOYAGES OF CHRISTOPHER COLUMBUS by John D. Clare, copyright © 1992 by Random Century Publishing Group Limited, reproduced by permission of Harcourt, Inc. **148** Judy Bauer/Arnold Publishing Ltd. **149** tl Photograph by Charles Best from THE VOYAGES OF CHRISTOPHER COLUMBUS by John D. Clare, copyright © 1992 by Random Century Publishing Group Limited, reproduced by permission of Harcourt, Inc.; tr Glenbow Archives, Calgary, Canada (NA-1700-149) **152** ml Metropolitan Toronto Reference Library, J. Ross Robertson Collection. MTL 1204; mr *First British Flag on North America*, by J.D. Kelly, by kind permission of Rogers Communications, Inc. **153** Photos: Tourism Newfoundland and Labrador **154** tr PA; br Illustration by Francis Back from *Canada Rediscovered*, pg 145. Reproduced by permission of the Canadian Museum of Civilization. **155** Herman Moll/NAC/C-003686 **162** Firenze, Biblioteca Medicea Laurenziana, Ms. Laur. Med. Palat. 249/Su concessione del Ministero per i Beni e le Attività Culturali. Duplication of this image is prohibited. **165** tr © NMM, London; ml *Using the Astrolabe and Cross-Staff*, Lewis Parker, from *Bold Ventures* **166** tl (detail) Théophile Hamel/NAC/C-041376; tr *The Discovery of Canada*, by J.D. Kelly, by kind permission of Rogers Communications, Inc. **170** Illustration by Francis Back from *Canada Rediscovered*, pg 119. Reproduced by permission of the Canadian Museum of Civilization. **172** (detail) Walter Baker/NAC/ C-011510 **173** mr (detail) Charles William Jefferys/NAC/C-070257; bl (detail) Giacomo Gastaldi/NAC /C-010489 **176** Hal Ross Perrigard/NAC/C-012235 **177** PA **178** (detail) Frank Craig/NAC/ C-010618 **189** mr Image: "The Trading Room" by C.W. Jefferys, Photo Parks Canada/Nathanial Tileston/1998; bl (detail) NAC/C-017338; ml PA **190** mr Courtesy Parks Canada East; br ml © Ragnar Treiberg; bl (detail) C.W. Jefferys/ NAC/C-106968 **191** tc Image: "Louis Hébert, The Apothecary" by C.W. Jefferys Photo Parks Canada/Nathanial Tileston/1998; tr Image: "The Governor's House" by C.W. Jefferys Photo Parks Canada/Nathanial Tileston/1998; mc Image: "Cook and Turnspit" by C.W. Jefferys Photo Parks Canada/ Nathanial Tileston/1998; bc Image: "Blacksmiths and Armourer" by C.W. Jefferys Photo Parks Canada/Nathanial Tileston/1998; bl Image: "Morning Toilet" by C.W. Jefferys Photo Parks Canada/ Nathanial Tileston/1998 **198** (detail) Samuel Champlain/NAC/ C-009711 **201** bc (detail) Samuel de Champlain/NAC/C-005750; ml (detail) National Library of Canada, C-005749 **204** *Champlain in Huronia*, by Rex Woods, by kind permission of Rogers Communications, Inc. **206** (detail) Louis-César-Joseph Ducornet/ NAC/C-006643 **207** t (detail) *The Voyages and Explorations of Samuel de Champlain (1604–1616)*. National Library of Canada; br (detail) C.W. Jefferys/NAC/C-073632 **208** *Madame de Champlain Arrives at Quebec*, Lewis Parker, from *Bold Ventures* **209** *The Founding of Montreal*, by Donald Anderson, by kind permission of Rogers Communications, Inc. **210** Northwind Picture Archives **211** tr Photo Courtesy of Lower Fort Garry National Historic Site (LFGtemp 1); bl Charles William Jefferys/NAC/C-103059 **212** (detail) Belier (ca. 1785)/NAC/C-015497 **213** *Radisson and Groseilliers in the Court of Charles II*, Lewis Parker, from *Bold Ventures* **214** Hudson's Bay Company Archives, Provincial Archives of Manitoba **218** 970.1.S17.4 Vol.2 pg 59, Toronto Reference Library **227** Sketch by Helmut Hirnschall from *My Heart Soars*, Hancock House, 19313 Zero Ave., Surrey, B.C., V4P 1M7, Reproduced with permission. **228** CP Picture Archive (Paul Latour) **231** © FC **232** br © FC; bc (detail) William Berczy, *Thayendanegea (Joseph Brant)*, Acc. #5777, National Gallery of Canada, Ottawa, Purchased 1951; bl (detail) NAC/C-018082 **233** tr #S99-1130, Reproduced by permission of the Canadian Museum of Civilization; br bl ml © FC **234** tr © FC; br © Ed Struzik; bl Canadian Sports Hall of Fame **235** mr © FC; b bc tc Courtesy The Aboriginal Multi-Media Society (AMMSA); mc Courtesy Aboriginal Peoples Television Network; **236** t tr mr ml c © FC; br Judy Bauer/Arnold Publishing Ltd. **237** © FC **238** © FC **239** © FC **240** © FC **241** tc tr c bl © FC; br Photo by David Young, Courtesy of the Centre for the Cross Cultural Study of Health and Healing, University of Alberta **242** John Lucas, *The Edmonton Journal* **243** © FC **244** tr Stamp reproduced courtesy of Canada Post Corporation; mr © FC; br AP/ Wide World Photos; ml © 1999 Time Inc. Reprinted by permission. **245** tr © FC; bl CP Picture Archive (Nick Procaylo) **248** © Craig Dickson, Woods Hole Oceanographic Institution **249** ml Popperfoto/Archive Photos; mr Archive Photos **250** tr, bl Courtesy NASA; br Sovfoto/Eastfoto **251** Courtesy NASA **252** mr mc ml Courtesy NASA; tr Russian Space Agency, Photo Courtesy NASA **253** Courtesy NASA

Index

A

Aboriginal organizations 235, 245
Aboriginal peoples, 2, 4, 31, 34, 120, 121, 123, 125, 126, 130, 146, 148, 226, 228–245, 247▲
Acadia 182, 188, 189, 192▲, 219. *See also* Atlantic Canada
adapt 15, 19, 46, 52, 69, 204
adulthood 75, 89, 94
advisor 28, 50, 93, 96, 145, 240
Age of Exploration 117, 136, 139, 183, 246, 247
agriculture 18. *See also* farming
Algonquian (speaking) peoples 69, 82, 84, 85●, 105, 107, 203, 231
Algonquian language family 18, 85, 104, 105
Algonquin 83, 85●, 186, 194, 198–201, 203, 208, 219▲
alliances 53, 77, 78, 194, 198–202, 199▲, 204, 206, 209, 219▲
animals 34, 41, 42, 84, 97, 107, 109, 125, 134, 142, 149, 177, 149
Anishinabe 13, 14, 18, 85, 104–109, 203, 212
Arab traders 136, 138, 143
archaeological dig 129, 130
archaeological site 14, 130–134
archaeologist 14, 44, 130–132, 149
Arctic 21, 33■, 249
artifact 14, 44, 74, 130–134
arts 48, 54, 71, 74, 97, 190, 231–234, 237. *See also* stories; musical instruments; dancing; decorating
Asia 121, 136, 138, 139, 145, 149–152, 156, 157, 160, 167, 172, 205, 206
astrolabe and compass 140, 141■, 145, 165, 207■
Atlantic Canada 33■, 85, 125, 136, 152, 153, 160, 167, 168, 171, 172, 182, 186, 206
autumn 54, 64, 66, 86, 106

B

Baffin, William (English explorer) 157
Baghdad 138, 139●, 143
balance 3, 24, 30, 45, 46, 48, 52, 54, 59, 64, 69, 71, 75, 79, 84, 85, 93, 94, 97, 100, 105, 109, 148, 224–226, 238, 239
balance of nature 28, 46, 48, 52, 84, 85, 91, 239
Band Councils 230, 243
bands 28, 93, 100, 106, 204, 236
basic needs 6, 19, 38, 39, 43

baskets 67. *See also* storage containers
Basque fishers and whalers 152, 155
BCE (BC). *See* Before the Common Era
beans 21, 59, 60, 64, 65, 67, 231
bear 42●■, 91, 105, 109
beaver 42●■, 86, 107■, 189, 202▲
beaver pelts 186, 187, 189, 204, 208, 211▲
Before the Common Era 117
beliefs 22, 24, 95, 108, 239, 240
Benton-Banai, Edward (Ojibway writer) 12, 14
Beothuk 18●, 125, 127, 128, 168
Beringia 4, 6, 9, 14, 122, 149, 224
boats 27, 122, 127, 134■. *See also* ships
Bonavista 153, 167
Boullé, Hélène (wife of Champlain) 208■
bows and arrows 26, 56, 62, 66, 75, 88, 97, 127
Brébeuf and Lalemant 209
Brûlé, Étienne (*coureur de bois*) 204■, 205●, 219▲
buffalo 21■, 26, 27, 41●■
business 237, 238, 243, 248, 251
Bylot, Robert (English explorer) 157

C

Caboto, Giovanni (explorer for England) 123▲ 131, 136, 147, 150–154, 192▲
Caboto, Sebastian 152
calendar 106
camp (summer/winter) 54, 86, 87
canoe 21, 46, 48, 60, 67, 68, 92, 93■, 105, 107, 129, 169, 190■, 199, 216, 231■, 237
caravel 140
caribou 16, 21■, 41●■, 84■, 91, 127
Cartier, Jacques (French explorer) 160, 166–179, 192▲, 198, 219▲
Cartier's voyages 166●, 167, 168●, 171–178
case study 25, 26–28, 45–48, 50–78, 82–100, 104–109
Catholic missions. *See* Roman Catholic; missionaries
cause and effect 140–142, 146–149, 201, 202
Cayuga 53▲●, 199. *See also* Iroquois Confederacy
CE (AD). *See* Common Era
celebrations and powwows 84, 86, 97, 241. *See also* ceremonies
ceremonies 24, 28, 48, 59, 60, 65, 67, 71, 84, 86, 93, 96, 97, 98, 108, 114, 239, 241, 242
challenges 204, 232, 234, 236–238, 242–246, 248–253

Champlain, Samuel de (explorer) 66■, 114, 188, 198–202, 204■, 205–208, 219▲
Charles II (King of England) 212–214
Charles VIII (King of France) 144
Charlesbourg-Royal 166●, 178
Chief Dan George 227■
Chief Donnacona 169, 172–174, 177, 178, 198
Chief Membertou 188
chiefs 28, 50, 77, 82, 100, 168, 188, 200, 243, 245
children 28, 50, 54, 74, 87, 94, 108, 126
China. *See* Asia
Christianity 138, 178, 185, 188, 195, 202, 208, 209, 219▲, 239. *See also* Roman Catholic Church
chronology 116, 117, 140, 192, 219▲, 247
circle 28, 94, 95. *See also* sacred circle; community circle
cities 229, 236–239
claiming lands 160, 166■, 169, 171, 178, 184–187, 192▲
Clan Mother 50, 61, 70, 75, 77
clans 50, 70, 77, 82, 90, 93, 100, 108
climate 20, 21, 30, 34, 39, 45, 46, 53, 84, 85, 105, 249, 251
climatic regions 35, 39●■
clothing 19–23, 27, 30, 43, 46, 54, 68, 75, 86, 91, 127, 168, 179, 191, 210, 216, 218, 231, 236, 241, 251, 253
coastal ecosystem 31, 33■, 46. *See also* Northwest Coast
colonies 121, 124, 125, 178, 182–185, 190–191, 194, 195, 206, 219. *See also* Acadia; Quebec Colony; Dutch colonization
colonists 178, 187, 208
colonization 178, 182, 184▲, 185▲, 192▲, 206, 251
Columbus, Christopher 123▲, 131, 136, 143–146, 186, 192▲
Common Era 113, 117
communal. *See* co-operation
communication 20, 24, 70, 93, 94, 204, 225, 240, 251. *See also* media
community 20, 70, 96, 100, 108, 207, 237, 239, 241
comparison 110, 257
competition 121, 140, 185, 199, 202, 215, 246, 250. *See also* power and wealth, gold and silver, territorial claims
conflict 53, 78, 100, 125, 126, 174, 178, 179, 199, 239. *See also* laws

```
┌──────────────── KEY ────────────────┐
│  ● map      ■ picture      ▲ chart   │
└──────────────────────────────────────┘
```

273

KEY
● map   ■ picture   ▲ chart

KEY
● map   ■ picture   ▲ chart

KEY		
● map	■ picture	▲ chart

X, Y, Z

U, V

W

┌─────────── KEY ───────────┐
│ ● map   ■ picture   ▲ chart │
└───────────────────────────────┘

Culture

Culture is a learned way of life shared by a group of people.

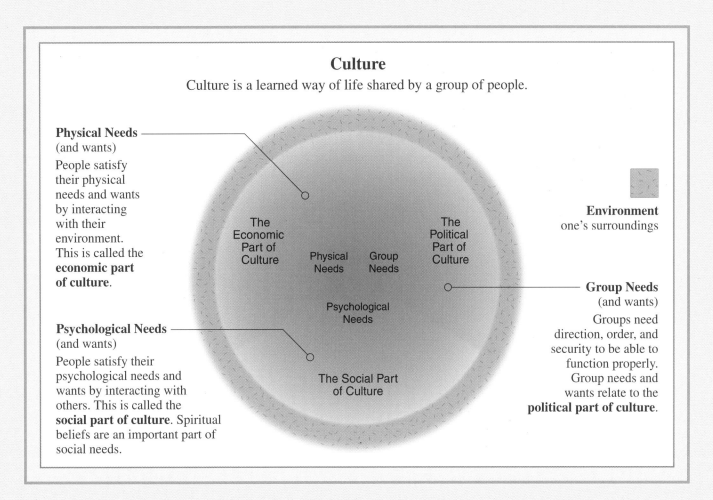

Physical Needs
(and wants)

People satisfy their physical needs and wants by interacting with their environment. This is called the **economic part of culture**.

Psychological Needs
(and wants)

People satisfy their psychological needs and wants by interacting with others. This is called the **social part of culture**. Spiritual beliefs are an important part of social needs.

The Economic Part of Culture

Physical Needs

Group Needs

The Political Part of Culture

Psychological Needs

The Social Part of Culture

Environment
one's surroundings

Group Needs
(and wants)

Groups need direction, order, and security to be able to function properly. Group needs and wants relate to the **political part of culture**.

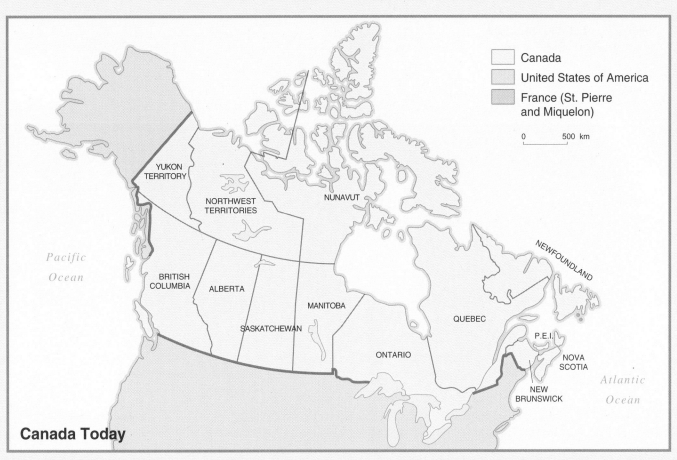

Canada

United States of America

France (St. Pierre and Miquelon)

0   500 km

Pacific Ocean

YUKON TERRITORY

NORTHWEST TERRITORIES

NUNAVUT

NEWFOUNDLAND

BRITISH COLUMBIA

ALBERTA

SASKATCHEWAN

MANITOBA

ONTARIO

QUEBEC

P.E.I.

NOVA SCOTIA

NEW BRUNSWICK

Atlantic Ocean

Canada Today

Climate Data Key

Temperature

very cold	under −20°C
cold	−20°C to −1°C
cool	0°C to 9°C
warm/mild	10°C to 19°C
hot	20°C to 29°C
very hot	30°C and over

Precipitation

sparse	(under 250 mm)	◌
light	(250 mm to 499 mm)	◌◌◌
moderate	(500 mm to 999 mm)	◌◌◌◌◌
heavy	(1000 mm to 1999 mm)	◌◌◌◌◌ ◌◌◌◌
very heavy	(2000 mm and over)	◌◌◌◌◌ ◌◌◌◌◌ ◌◌◌◌◌

Snowfall

light	❄
moderate	❄ ❄ ❄
heavy	❄ ❄ ❄ ❄ ❄

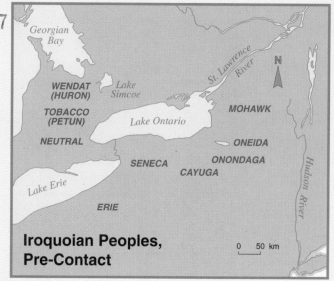

Iroquoian Peoples, Pre-Contact

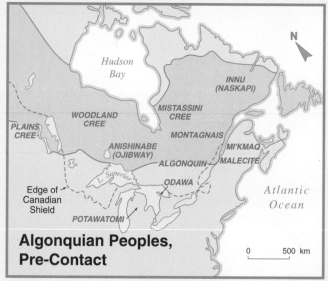

Algonquian Peoples, Pre-Contact

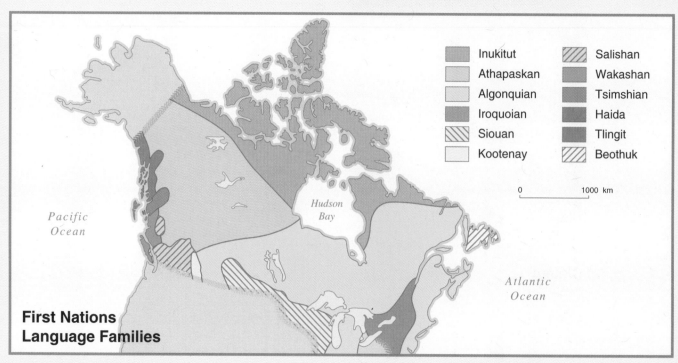

First Nations Language Families

Inukitut	Salishan
Athapaskan	Wakashan
Algonquian	Tsimshian
Iroquoian	Haida
Siouan	Tlingit
Kootenay	Beothuk